THE MEDORA, BY THE AUTHOR OF 'THE TWO CAPT. ARMSTRONG • F CLAUDIUS ARMSTRONG

Publisher's Note

The book descriptions we ask booksellers to display prominently warn that this is an historic book with numerous typos or missing text; it is not indexed or illustrated.

The book was created using optical character recognition software. The software is 99 percent accurate if the book is in good condition. However, we do understand that even one percent can be an annoying number of typos! And sometimes all or part of a page may be missing from our copy of the book. Or the paper may be so discolored from age that it is difficult to read. We apologize and gratefully acknowledge Google's assistance.

After we re-typeset and design a book, the page numbers change so the old index and table of contents no longer work. Therefore, we often remove them; otherwise, please ignore them.

Our books sell so few copies that you would have to pay hundreds of dollars to cover the cost of our proof reading and fixing the typos, missing text and index. Instead we let most customers download a free copy of the original typo-free scanned book. Simply enter the barcode number from the back cover of the paperback in the Free Book form at www.RareBooksClub.com. You may also qualify for a free trial membership in our book club to download up to four books for free. Simply enter the barcode number from the back cover onto the membership form on our home page. The book club entitles you to select from more than a million books at no additional charge. Simply enter the title or subject onto the search form to find the books.

If you have any questions, could you please be so kind as to consult our Frequently Asked Questions page at www. RareBooksClub.com/faqs.cfm? You are also welcome to contact us there.

General Books LLC™, Memphis, USA, 2012.

✂ ✂ ✂ ✂ ✂ ✂ ✂ ✂

THE MEDOKA, CHAPTER I. *Os* attaining his one and twentieth year, Henry Fitzharding, the hero of the following pages, succeeded to one of the largest private properties in England; a long minority greatly increasing the immense wealth bequeathed to him by his-father. Of his family it is requisite to give some few-particulars, that the reader may understand the situation of the different persons to whom he will be introduced,-and ' also to avoid interrupting the course of the narrative, as each makes his or her appearance, by explanations of who they are and why they come upon the *tapis.* But we will ascend the genealogical tree no further than the grandfather of our hero, who left two sons and two daughters to enjoy his property and honours. The elder son, Philip, inherited an estate in Dorsetshire, worth about three thousand a year, whilst to the younger was left the sum of twenty thousand pounds, and a share in a rich and very influential mercantile concern in which the testator had principally amassed his own fortune. The contrast in the character of the brothers was very great. The elder— gloomy, reserved, and cold in disposition,—soon after his father's death married a lady of similar tastes, and lived shut out from the world, wrapt in his own meditations; whilst the younger— handsome, generous, high-spirited, energetic, and of an ardent, aspiring mind,— plunged into commerce and its attendant speculations. He visited St. Petersburg, where his extraordinary abilities as an engineer attracted the notice of the Czar, who frequently conversed with him on the subject of his intention of settling in Odessa. Once, when on that favourite topic, Fitzbarding answered a question of the Emperor's in a manner that fully proved him master of his favourite science, and

from that moment his fame and fortune both rose. His plans and sketches of fortifications were adopted by the Czar, who was then looked upon by all Europe as a great and enlightened Sovereign, with a gigantic mind, eager to civilize and improve the subjects in his vast dominions.

Having received full power to follow up his plans and speculations, Fitzharding returned to England to complete his arrangements and resign his share in the firm of " Elder, Wilkins & Co." He visited his brother, who ridiculed his projects, regarded him as a wild enthusiast, and gave the enterprising man of the world so cool a reception that he soon bade him farewell, and prepared to return to Russia. But not alone did he set forth to form a home in a foreign land. A wife, the daughter of Sir Robert Manners, went with him to share his successes and participate in his anxieties. He had little to regret in quitting England, for his misanthropic brother could never be a friend, and the fate of both his sisters was overshadowed. The elder, Emily, was like all the Fitzhardings, very handsome, but gay, lively, and thoughtless, and threw herself and her fortune into the arms of a man whose sole recommendation was a showy person and manners, and a vast amount of assurance. He said he was an Irishman, called himself Captain Shaw, and certainly he frequented the highest society—talked well, and persuaded many besides his wife that he possessed considerable estates in Ireland—a little encumbered to be sure—but certain to turn up all clear in time. It was contrary to the wishes of all her friends that Emily became the wife of Captain Shaw, and went te Dublin accompanied by her s:ster Eleanor. More lovely than Mrs. Shaw, and six years her junior, Eleanor Fitzharding was wild, eccentric, and inconsiderate, and soon vanished from the circle in which she had shone. Her sister said she had eloped; with whom no one could conjecture; but it was quite evident that the absence of one brother and the selfish supineness of the other prevented any investigation as to her fate.

For five years Mr. and Mrs. Shaw kept their position. He became director to a company established for great things, and many were duped, by the inducements held out, to hazard their money; but suddenly the company dissolved, and Mr. Shaw was heard of no more; even Mr. Philip Fitzharding, who had now become nest heir to the title of the Earl of Courtland, forgot his sister's existence. The prospect of becoming a peer had no effect upon Philip. He did not care a fraction for titles, or wealth, and continued to live as usual, spending a few hundreds per annum, but doing good to no one. Meanwhile, under the protection of the Czar, his brother prospered, and when, after five years of married life, a son was born, he seemed perfectly happy. Four years after the birth of her brother the little Julia came to shed another joy upon the domestic hearth of the English merchant, whose position seemed so firmly placed that no storms could overthrow or shake its foundation. The year 1841 began with the cholera in Odessa, Mrs. Fitzharding was one of its first victims, and, ere many days, her distracted husband followed her to the grave, leaving his two children, of eleven and seven years of age, heirs to immense wealth, but orphans.

Some months before thtir melancholy death, the Fitzhardings had spent a short time in St. Petersburg with the Princess Warhendorff, whose husband, the General, was then with the army of the Czar in Circassia. The Princess was the daughter of an Englishwoman—one of the children of Lord Broughton, who resided in St. Petersburg—her father a ltussian Prince, highly esteemed by the Emperor Alexander, who, on the death of his favourite, conferred on his daughter, then a child, and her descendants, the title of Princess.

This Princess became the wife of General Warhendorff, who, a few years after his marriage, incurred the displeasure of the Czar Nicholas, and was sent into exile. His affairs became involved, and the first step of the Princess was to order the Palace at Odessa, with all its costly decorations, to be sold. Mr. Fitzharding became the purchaser; and when, three years afterwards, the General was pardoned and restored to his rank in the army, his mansion, furniture, and other costly articles were returned in the same state as when the Princess had ordered them to be sold. An amicable controversy took place, settled at length by Mr. Fitzharding consenting to take a yearly stipend till the debt was paid. A sincere friendship was formed between the families, and the Princess would often say, when gazing on the sporting children, and witnessing young Henry's affectionate kindness to his little playmates, that he should be her little Catherine's husband. Little Catherine idolized her companion, who responded to her affection by being her projector and playfellow, and was almost as sorry as his child-wife when the time approached for him to leave Ithe capital and return to Odessa with his parents. The little Julia was left behind, and thus escaped the danger of the cholera, and the sorrow of seeing those her young heart cherished become its victims. The sad loss of his brother caused no emotion in the breast of the future Earl of Courtland, he only grumbled at the will hastily drawn up and signed, and by which Sir Edgar Manners was left sole guardian to the children.

CHAPTER II.

At the period of Mr. and Mrs. Fitzharding's death, Sir Edgar Manners had retired from the navy with the rank of Commodore, a pension, and a wooden leg, and resided in a beautiful marine residence overlooking Babicombe bay, near the much-frequented watering place, Torquay.

No kinder hearted or higher principled man existed than the Baronet, the appointed guardian of the two orphans; but in his ways and habits of life he had become exceedingly eccentric..He was a bachelor, and at this period about fifty-eight, some ten or twelve years older than his sister, the late Mrs. Fitzharding. Passionately attached to his profession, his reluctance, when, with shattered health and the loss of a leg, he was compelled to quit the service, was great, and his residence, Wild Drake Lodge, betrayed how closely the feelings of the sailor clung around him in his retirement.

Visitors to the romantic village and bay of Babicombe gazed on the mizen mast of a sloop of war, with yards, rigging, &c., which rose majestically from the middle of the lawn. In front was a miniature battery of four 8-pounders and a brass swivel, which regularly every day announced the setting of the sun.

His chief attendant was his favourite coxswain, an Irishman, also with a timber leg. The Commodore's starboard, and the coxswain, Tom Delany's, larboard leg, were the lost members. Tom was quite as eccentric in his way as his master; but no one could manage the Baronet so well, especially when suffering under an attack of gout.

The black cook of his last ship also constituted a part of his household establishment, which consisted besides of five male domestics and one female; this last, a housekeeper of middle age, was the only female permitted to Bleep in the house; if one was found or seen on the premises after the evening gun, winter or summer, she was never employed again; and the Baronet stopped Tom's and the black cook's allowance of grog the next day.

Mrs. Davis, the housekeeper, was a highly respectable woman, and quite at liberty to employ as many female as she pleased to settle and keep the house in disorder, as the Commodore called it, provided they did not touch or move anything in his two particular rooms, which hia factotum, Tom Delany, had under his especial care, and whose duty it was to see that all the petticoata on the premises made sail as soon as the flag was lowered, and the gun told the set of sun.

Sir Edgar had, by the death of a relative, a very considerable addition to his father's property; and no person was more charitable, or kind, or more liberal in the vicinity of To. quay than the eccentric Sir Edgar Manners.

He kept a handsome carriage and pair of horses, but never used them except for attending Divine service, in which duty he was very regular. "When the news reached the Baronet of his brother-in-law's and sister's melancholy deaths he was shocked and grieved beyond, measure, for he had dearly loved his sister; and Mr. Eitzharding, in his last letter to him, solemnly promised that, as soon as his son reached his twelfth year, he wou'.d wind up his affairs in Russia and return to England for the finishing of the education of his two children.

The Commodore was suffering under a severe attack of gout, and what between grief, vexation, and torture, nobody save Tom dare approach him. It was of no use his getting into a rage with Tom, who was never in a passion, and would stump about the room as unconcernedly as if it did not blow great guns.

Once the Commodore was so furious at Tom's apathy, that, not having any missile at hand, and his gouty leg being incapable of supporting his huge frame—for he was a very tall, large man—he unscrewed his timber leg and hurled it at Tom's head, but missing the coxswain, who made a skilful dodge, it flew out through the window, smashing half a dozen panes of glass in its passage. Tom sat down very quietly, unscrewed his own wooden extremity, and threw it out of the window after his master's.

"You villain; what did you do that for?" roared the Commodore, red with rage.

"Be gor, your honour, it would not be becoming in me to see you dismasted and stranded like a huge porpoise on a sand bank, and I to remain with all sticks standing." "You precious rascal! I wish you had—oh, d it,

I wish you had this fellow that's sticking his claws in me, like grapnel irons, he'd teach you to pity another under suffering. Ring for Csesar!"

Tom hopped on his one leg to the bell, and Caemr made his appearance. He was a stout, well-put-together black,

not more than fifty, with a set of unrivalled teeth, which he displayed to advantage. When he beheld his master and Tom both without their wooden legs, and th© glass of the window scattered over the floor—

"Gor Almighty! what this for, massa?" said the black. "Hold your tongue, sir," growled the Baronet, " go down into the garden and bring up the two legs you'll find under the window."

The black withdrew, grinning siyly at the coxswain who, looking at his master, said:

"Those two legs, your honour, were cut out of the mizen topgallant cross trees of the old *Agamemnon;* they weathered many a breeze alongside one another, and, be gor, when the one went flying out of the window, the other nearly bursted my knee off, wanting to follow; so your honour must excuse my obeying the wishes of the old stick."

"If it had broken your figure head, you old rascal, you would have felt a twinge somewhere else than in your knee; you have smashed half a dozen panes of glass; I'll atop your grog for a week, to pay for them."

Tom only smiled, and Caesar returning with the timbers, the coxswain first screwed on his own and then his master's.

These kind of squabbles happened at odd times, but only when the gout rendered the good-hearted old Commodore irritable.

For two days after having the intelligence of his sister's death, and that he was constituted the guardian of the two orphans, the Baronet remained in a great state of agitation and vexation; the third morning, Tom was settling a cushion under his gouty leg, when the Commodore commenced a conversation with—

"What's to be done now, Tom?" feeling a twinge at the same time, " I am not fit for the guardianship of a young girl."

"Faix, that's true, you're not, your honour," returned Tom, quite coolly, skilfully adjusting the leg, which, rolled up and bandaged, looked like the limb of an elephant.

"What do you mean, you villain, by

saying I am not fit?"

"Be the pipers of war, you said so yourself, not me; I'm only an echo."

"You an echo," growled the Commodore, " you're a pretty specimen of an echo; what did you mean? I know you thought what you said."

"Well, by jabers, your honour, perhaps I did, and in reason; sure the dickens a woman you'll let sleep in the house, except old Mother Davis; if a petticoat is seen shaking in the wind after sunset, it puts you in irons; sure you can't take care of a young girl and an heiress without lots of women."

"Ha, you old vagabond, I see through your projects," growled the Commodore, making a hideous face from a severe twinge, "you want to turn my peaceful home inte a harem, and be at your old broils, stumping about with your timber leg, making an old fool of yourself; you are half the day, as it is, grinning and chattering like a lame magpie, with the women that old fool, Mrs. Davis, will bring into the house, to set things to rights, as she calls it. Set things to rights, indeed, it's turning the house upside down, she means; but hold your jaw, put that table near me, and my desk, I must write for my solicitor to come here; my poor nephew and niece must not be left with those Russian bears; mark me, if they don't show their claws some of these days."

"Be gor, if they does, ould John Bull has a fine pair of horns to toss them with," returned Tom.

"Not so sure of that, they are a long way off; the Czar is too wide awake for John Bull; he'll humbug him some of these days, and he'll have to pay the piper. I don't like em; never did. Can't think how my brother-in-law could like to live in that outlandish place, Odessa. "

"I thought I'd a never got out of it, when we went there in the P Frigate."

"It's always blowing great guns in that Black Sea. Don't you remember Odessa, Tom?"

"Oh, fair, I do, your honour, and a mighty fine place I thought it, and your honour's sister's house was like the palace of a king. Be gor, I had good right to remember it, though you used to say, when it was dry, you were smothered with dust, and when it was wet, you were up to your knees in mud; faix, there's fine brandy there!"

"Well, hold your tongue till I have written my letter."

Three days afterwards, Mr. Cathcart, the Baronet's solicitor, arrived at Wild Drake Lodge, and remained a couple of days; he then departed for London, to confer with the late Mr. Fitzharding's London solicitors, named in his will, and to commence at once settling the affairs, and securing the immense fortune left to the children.

By Mr. Cathcart's advice, a gentleman of high respectability, furnished with all necessary instructions and letters, was engaged to proceed to Odessa, to bring the orphan children to England.

Three months passed after the departure of Mr. Bowen, the gentleman recommended by Mr. Cathcart, before a letter from him reached Sir Edgar Manners, the contents of which perfectly astounded the Commodore and his coxswain; for Tom, as usual, was present at the perusal, and taken into confidence and counsel on the contents:—

"Odessa,

June the 4th, 1842. "My dear Sir,

"I arrived here from Constantinople, after a rather tedious and stormy passage in a Russian steamer. I should have experienced some little difficulty with respect 10 passports, had not the letter of the Russian Minister in London served me in my perplexity. I found young Master Fitzharding—who is one of the handsomest and noble looking boys I ever saw—in the mansion of one of the late Mr. Fitzharding's friends, Count Alexis Orloff, but I deeply regret to have to tell you, neither the Count or myself can gain any intelligence of the Princess "Warhendorff, or your niece, who was with the former at the time of her parent's death. All that is known of the Princess since her husband's disgrace aud death is, that she has left St. Petersburg, some say for Odessa, others for Taganrog, on the Sea of Azoff, but she has not been heard of, and it is dangerous to make enquiries after her, as

she, as well as her husband, incurred the anger of the Czar. From what I can learn, General Warhendorff was engaged in the merciless war now raging in the Caucasus; that his army was totally routed by the great Circassian leader, Prince Schamyl, and nearly all cut to pieces; that the rage of the Czar was excessive, and of the few officers that escaped the conflict, some were disgraced into the ranks, and others sent to Siberia, while General Warhendorff was either killed or made prisoner. The Emperor confiscated all his property, and it is said, even deprived his wife of her rank and her own personal estate. Be that as it may, I can gain no trace of her, or the little girl, your niece.

"Master Fitzharding is greatly and distressingly grieved at his father's and mother's death, the loss of his sister, and the Misfortunes of the Princess Warhendorff, to whom he seems greatly attached; he appears extremely precocious for his years, and vows, when a man—if he lives to be one—to return to Russia, and never stop till he finds his sister, if still in existence."

"Be gor, he's a fine little fellow," exclaimed Tom, with enthusiasm, giving such a thump with his wooden pin on the floor as startled the Commodore—adding, "and I'll go with him."

"You, you ungrateful rascal," exclaimed the Baronet, pausing and looking over his spectacles at the coxswain; '-So, you'll leave me, to go stumping over that barbarous country on a wild-goose cbase; what the deuce good could a one-legged, worn-out piece of old junk be to a young man? Why, you roving vagabond! by the time he's a man, you will be over sixty."

"Well, your honour, what's sixty? Be gor, if I'm not able to thrash a half-dozen of those Russians at sixty, it's not worth living till then. At sixty, my great grandfather—"

"Belay there," interrupted the Commodore, "and let me finish my letter. "You never had a grandfather. It's deuced lucky you had a father."

"Be the powers of Moll Kelly, your honour seems to think," grumbled Tom, "that it is only the harry stocracy that

have great grandfathers. My great grandmother—"

"If you don't put a stopper on that jaw tackle of yours, I'll stop your grog for a month."

"Go on, your honour, I'm all attention," quietly observed Tom.

The Baronet then resumed the letter, as follows:—

"I do not perceive that I can do any good by remaining longer here; indeed, Count Orloff strongly advises me to sail at once, as the Czar might take it into his head to prevent young Master Fitzharding's departure, he having been born in the Russian dominions.

"It is certainly a most strange circumstance, the disappearance of so many persons, without leaving some trace of their path.

"There is a very fine brig here belonging to Genoa. She sails in two days for Malta, where I can embark in the regular steamer for Eagland.

"I have been able, through the kindness of the late Mr. Fitzharding's friends and the interest of Count Orloff with the authorities, to ship for London, in the British barque, the Wave, all the pictures and costly effects belonging to Mr. Fitzharding's palace. There is a great deal of excitement in this country, owing to the defeat of the Russian armies by the great Circassian leader, Prince Schamyl. Prince Woranzw has left this for the Caucasus, and great preparations are making to totally crush that brave and gallant people.

"Hoping to have a speedy passage home, and trusting to find you, dear sir, in good health, I have the honour to remain,

"Yours, most obediently,

"james Bowen."

"Well, this is a confounded piece of business," exclaimed the Baronet, testily. "What is to be done? here's my niece either lost or hidden somewhere amongst a horde of barbarians."

"Be the immortals, it's too bad," said Tom, rubbing the back of his head; "faix, there's but two things to be done, your honour," and the coxswain looked-sagacious.

"Well, let us hear what you have

rubbed into your thick skull."

"Be jabers, we must either go ourselves to Russia, or—"

"Ha, ha, ha, we'd look well," interrupted the Baronet, "stumping through Russia on our wooden supporters. Come, that plan won't do. What's the other way of getting out of this difficulty?"

"Is'nt there a Russian Ambassador," said Tom, stoutly, "and 'can't he be made answerable for kidnapping a British subject?"

Sir Edgar looked thoughtful a moment, and then replied, "There's some sense in that; we have an Ambassador in St. Petersburg. I'll write to Lord L, and he will make enquiries in St. Petersburg after this Russian Princess and her daughter and my niece."

Two months after this Mr. Bowen arrived in England with his young charge safe and sound, and at once came to Wild Drake Lodge.

CHAPTER III. The Baronet received his orphan nephew with real and genuine affection. He was a remarkably handsome, fine boy, very tall for hia age, with beautiful features, and eyes black as a sloe. He appeared somewhat sad and depressed for his years, but not in the least timid or retiring in his manners. He embraced his uncle affectionately, saying—

"If I had been a man, sir, I would never have left Russia without my sister Julia. "

Several years passed, during which young Henry, under the care of Mr. Bowen, who was retained as tutor, progressed rapidly in his education, and became a general favourite.

Tom Dalany took a most prodigious liking to him; stumped after him everywhere; allowed him to climb the mizen mast on the lawn; fire the brass swivel at sunset; taught him to use a cutlass, steer the Commodore's pleasure barge, and told him every kind of yarn about pirates and slavers, till he embued the boy's mind with so ardent and strong a passion for the sea, that, when nearly thirteen years old, he said to his uncle, who gloried in his bold, high-spirited nephew—

"Uncle, I'm determined to be a sailor, and you must make me a midshipman."

Now a midshipman" was just the very thingthe Baronet was wishing him to be; he considered it required a few years at sea, passed amongst the true, hardy sons of Britain, to do away with the remains of hia Russian education.

But Henry was not likely to forget either Russia or her language; young as he was, his thoughts were often fixed upon his lost sister, and his beautiful playmate, the Princess Warhendorff's daughter. Still treasuring in his mind his determination, when a man, to go search for them.

In the meantime, intelligence reached Sir Edgar Manners, from the British residents in St. Petersburg, that all trace of the Princess Warhendorff was unaccountably lost; from what he could learn—for it was a subject dangerous to touch upon, lest the enquiries should come to the knowledge of the Czar Nicholas— General Warhendorff commanded the second army sent against the Caucasan leader, and was again defeated and cut to pieces. The General, it was said, was mortally wounded and carried off by the Prince, who was furious against his prisoner, from his terrible severity towards the Circassians, whilst the Emperor, frantic at the repeated losses he had sustained in his war with the brave Circassians, degraded and banished most of the officers who escaped from that terrible disaster, the whole of the Warhendorff estates were confiscated, and it was only by great intercession, and her own rank and connexion with the Imperial family that the Princess was allowed to retain her own family estate.

On hearing of her husbana's wounds and captivity, the Princess left St. Petersburg, to proceed, it was said, to Odessa. She travelled on loot, taking with her the two children and two female attendants; and, for protection, her head steward, Ivan Gortsare, a serf by birth, but a remarkable man, in many respects, for his situation. He had always been attentive to the person of the General, and had accompanied him t© the Circassian war. was near him when

wounded, and saw him taken prisoner. He then effected his escape from the country, and returned to St. Petersburg. Immediately alter which the Princess left the capital, and was traced to within a few leagues of Taganrog—not Odessa—where all tidings of her w ere lost.

"A pretty country that to live in," grumbled the Baronet, after reading the letter and stating the contents to his attentive hstener, Tom Delany, who was screwing on his false leg for the day. "No less, Tom, than six individuals swallowed up, as if by an earthquake; and to say no trace of them can be found—fiddlesticks. Do you think such a thing could happen in this country? HLa! there's a twitch! How's the wind, Tom f"

""Wind's east and by north, your honour; faix, it's very odd, but I thiuk this here timber leg of mine is growing, I feel as if I had a cramp in my toe."

"It's this infernal wind," growled the Baronet, "it has as many lives as a cat. I wonder what all the other points of the compass are at! But there, stir your stump, and order James to take the carriage to meet the London mail. I expect my old comrade, Captain Pack, to arrive by it.'

"With Captain P, young Henry Fitzharding was placed as a midshipman, to the great astonishment of all who knew of the immense fortune to which he would succeed; but our young hero was delighted; he seemed to have some plan or project in his young brain, which he was resolved hereafter to pursue; besides which, a natural love of the sea aided his inclination to become a sailor, and a sailor in right earnest he became. On board the frigate was a young gentleman named Edgar Erwin, a handsome, lively, high-spirited boy, to whom our hero became greatly attached, for, like himself, he was an orphan, and in many respects alike in disposition and temper, but widely different as to the smiles of fortune. Edgar Erwin was the adopted child of a highly respectable old naval officer in the service of his country, who had lost an arm, and though he served many years after, never rose higher than a lieutenant.

Just twelve months before his death, he contrived to get his adopted son appointed as a midshipman on board the frigate. This, with his blessing and about a thousand pounds, was all the worthy lieutenant was able to do for his *protege.*

The D frigate sailed nearly all round the world, and was six years absent from England. Several boat actions with piratical and slave schooners took place, in which Henry Fitzharding gained great credit for cool courage and gallant spirit. With a boat's crew and six marines he boarded a large piratical craft, on the coast of Mexico, under a terrible fire, and after a desperate resistance took her and carried her out from under a heavy battery. This was considered by Captain P as a most gallant and daring feat.

On his return to England he passed his examination ,with great credit, and shortly after was appointed first lieutenant of the *Grampus* brig, about to be sent to put a stop to the slave trade on the coast of Africa. There he also distinguished himself, and returning to England he resigned his commission, as he was now twenty-one, and the time had arrived to carry out his long contemplated expedition.

During the nine years he had served in the navy his education had been carefully attended to, having, fortunately, a highly-talented and worthy Chaplain on board the frigate. Henry Fitzharding read hard all the leisure hours he had; kept up a constant study ot the Russian language, which he spoke like a native; he also studied Italian and French, in which his natural talent enabled him to attain proficiency.

On returning to England his first care was to get his friend Edgar Erwin, who had also passed his examination, an appointment as third lieutenant on board the splendid screw frigate, the, commanded by old and gallant

Captain P, then fitting out as one of the Black Sea fleet—for war now seemed inevitable—all classes being justly and greatly exasperated by the atrocious act of the Russians destroying the Turkish fleet at Sinope. This appointment Henry had been able to effect through the interest of Lord Courtland, an eccentric nobleman, but kind, generous and affable, and who had taken an especial liking to the young man he considered as the heir to his title, and who was always cordially welcomed to his house and reluctantly parted from when his duties called him to his ship.

A short time before the war began, the two gentlemen were seated together in his lordship's library, and talking confidently and earnestly—the younger imparting wishes and designs, the elder listening with pleased interest, when, after a short pause, Lord Courtland, who was a hale, stout, fine-looking old man, observed, " Then, of course, you have abandoned all furthur intention of serving iu the navy?"

"For certain reasons I hare at present, my lord," returned our hero, " though, now there is every prospect of a fierce war, I should have wished to serve her Majesty; but I desire to remain unshackled, having, as I conceive, a sacred duty to perform; which is, if possible, to discover my long lost sister. I intend to purchase a large yacht, and join the fleet in the Black Sea, and hope to go into action as a volunteer on board the same ship as my friend, Edgar Erwin; but, at the same time, remain free, so as to be able to be guided by circumstances."

"Then you have an idea of penetrating into Russia?"

"I have, my lord."

"It's a dangerous experiment," said his lordship, thoughtfully, "I should not like this old title and place to fall to the next heir after you."

"And who is the next heir, may I ask, my lord?"

"The son of your father's eldest sister. She married, you know, of course, a Captain Shaw, an Irishman, a scheming adventurer, who, some time after, contrived to gull the public by some monstrous scheme of condensing sua beams, and thus being able to produce solar heat in the depth of winter; the company proposed to supply the" public with all kinds of tropical fruits, besides melons, cucumbers, Ac., at a price much less than a cabbage."

"By Jove," laughed Fitzharding, " he surely did not get fools to put down their names to so absurd and ridiculous a farce?"

"He did, though. The sun beams were not to be condensed—they dissolved, and so did the company, and your worthy uncle decamped, some say to Australia, with ten or fifteen thousand pounds."

"And has not been heard of since," remarked Henry, "for my uncle, Sir Edgar Manners, has exerted himself to trace him, as my poor father left a legacy of five thousand pounds to his children."

"Oh, depend on it," said his lordship, "either himself or his son will turn up one of these days. But you were talking of a yacht; I can recommend you one. I see you have enrolled yourself in the Royal Yacht Club. Well, Lord Broughtou built a magnificent ship yacht, over 300 tons, intended for a trip round the world, but it seems he has accepted a diplomatic mission to the

Court of, and I know he will be glad to get rid of the concern. If you like I will write to his lordship. Money is no object to you, the wealthiest commoner in England."

"I shall feel greatly obliged if you will, my lord. Whatever price Lord Broughton names, I am quite ready to give."

"Well, I will write to-night."

After spending a very pleasant week at Courtland Tower, and completing the purchase of the yacht, which was lying in dock in Portsmouth, Henry set out for "Wild Drake Lodge, to stay a short time with his worthy uncle, and to settle matters with his lawyers.

"Well, Harry, my boy," exclaimed the old Commodore, who was bale and hearty as ever, as they sat enjoying their wine and walnuts in the dining-room of Wild Drake Lodge, the windows overlooking the beautiful bay of Babicombe—"Well, Harry, how do you like his lordship? A straight-forward, honest old fellow, I'm told."

"He's just what a nobleman ought to be, sir, courteous, kind, and affable. I like him very much. He is rather disgusted at the delay there has been in declaring war, and he refuses to have anything to do with Government. They have been vacillating, and ruining, he says, our future prospects in this war, which is declared at last."

"He's quite right; it's a confounded shame. That massacre of Sinope might easily have been prevented—it's a foul disgrace to England. I suppose you will now abandon your project of going into the interior of Russia, it would be madness."

"No, indeed, my dear sir, I have not; but I will be cautious and guided by circumstances. I have purchased Lord Broughton's yacht, and by great good luck, stumbled upon a few old tars of the *Grampus,* who served with me on the African Coast last year, and now I'm looking out for a sailing master, who will have to take charge of her, should I be absent myself." "What's her rig and tonnage, Harry?" "She is rigged like a corvette, sir, carries eight Im-pounders, and has a crew of eighty men and officers."

"Ha, by Jove, you can stand a brush with a Russian sloop of war, should you meet one."

"Faith, I hope so, sir, and beat her too," replied Henry, with a merry laugh. "I should like that brush very well."

"You are sure to be in the thick of it, Harry," returned the Commodore, "especially as your old commander and old friend are both to be there."

"By the by, sir," said Fitzharding, "have you heard anything about my uncle and aunt, the Shaws? Your lawyers, I heard, put repeated advertisements in the papers about the legacy left them. Then there's my aunt Eleanor, who used to be such a beautiful girl. It appears so very extraordinary that, from the period of her elopement from her sister's house, she was never heard of, nor does it appear any one can say who she eloped with. If with an unworthy person, surely his first aim would be to demand her fortune: a sum of five thousand pounds would surely be an object to an adventurer."

"There is something very strange about the whole affair," said the Baronet, gravely; "the money still lies in the firm of Elder, Wilkins 'fc Co., bearing interest. Tour aunt Eleanor, I always heard, was of the most romantic, eccentric turn of mind, and adopted strange theories, detested the idea of marriage, said it was a chain that crushed young hearts, and other absurd and unworldly ideas. However, let her ideas be what they may, her disappearance for so may years is unaccountable, unless she is dead; even then, one would imagine, intelligence of the event would reach her relatives. But with respect to your aunt Shaw, and her dissipated, rascally husband, they must have gone to Australia or America with the money they swindled from others."

"Swindled, uncle! nay, not swindled," cried the young man, in a deprecating tone.

"What the deuce else can you call it, Harry," said the old Commodore; "all those kind of companies are a set of swindlers and robbers. But if they are dead, I wonder young Shaw does not claim his share of the legacy left them. He was a lieutenant in a regiment of infantry; but was allowed to sell out, instead of being turned out, for some gambling or swindling transaction. He also was a scamp; but a deuced handsome fellow, they-say. Maybe he also went off to America."

"Well, well," observed Henry, in a serious tone, "I regret all this; if I could find aunt Shaw I should be delighted to assist and relieve her from her difficulties, and pay any liabilities her husband may have incurred."

"What," sharply cried the Commodore, "pay fifteen or sixteen thousand pounds to encourage a rascal to swindle the public again; serve them all right; I won't leave one of the set a shilling; rather give it for the relief of our brave soldiers, should they want it, and they will, before this war ends, I prophesy. Your aunt Shaw was warned enough not to marry that fellow. By Jove! if you had told her to marry him, she would have protested she would die first."

"I perceive, sir," said his nephew, laughing, "you have not relented in your feelings for the fair sex; we should be miserable without them."

"The deuce we should," exclaimed the Baronet, "don't see that at all; I'm not miserable; never was miserable; but there's that rascal, Tom Delauy, going to make a fool of himself, with his grey hairs and wooden leg, he's actually going to marry that other old fool, Mrs. Davis, and all to make me comfortable, he says"—

Fitzharding laughed joyously.

"He says," continued the Commodore, "that I could not live without Mrs. Davis; that she made love to him, and if he did not return it, some one else would; and so, to save me, he sacrifices himself, the rascal."

"Well, upon my honour, uncle, I think Tom has done a very wise thing. Mrs. Davis is a very nice person, not more than seven or eight-and-forty, perhaps fifty, and Tom swears he is only fifty-eight; so they are not so badly matched after all, and Tom is a fine-looking fellow still. So, my dear uncle, you will be nothing the worse by the change."

"Oh, you don't know that rascal so well as I do. As soon as he is married he'll try and get some women into the house to help his wife; I shall have to shut myself up. The next thing that will happen is, Caesar will be wanting a wife; by the law, Harry, there will be a Turkish seraglio here by the time you come back." CHAPTER IV.

"Holks!" exclaimed our hero to a young naval officer he met at the hotel entrance, one evening, about a month before he left England, "what are you going to do this evening? Let us take a peep at the opera."

"Agreed," returned the gentleman addressed, "the Queen goes»to-night; I never saw her Majesty; and, as I sail for the Baltic in a few days, I should like to have a look at the Lady I am going to fight for."

"Very good," said Fitzgerald, "we will go to the pit; I do not wish to meet any town acquaintances; I am nearly knocked up with a round of balls, fetes, and concerts. I intend sailing myself next month."

"I wish it was to the Baltic you were going, Fitzharding; you would like the trip there better than to the Black Sea."

"Yes, if it was a mere trip of pleasure so I might; but such is not the case."

At an early hour they left for the opera, and found, as they expected, a crush; in fact, the house was crowded at a very early hour. As our hero had seen her Majesty several times, and under much more propitious circumstances, near the entrance of the pit he parted with his young friend, who was determined to push hia way down as near to the royal box as possible, while Fitzharding remained where he was, Jess inconvenienced, and where he could have a fair view of all the rank and fashion assembled in the boxes.

From his wealth and position as next heir to the Oourtland title, Fitzharding had the *entre* to the first society in the metropolis; his exceedingly handsome person, graceful manners and affability, with a natural frankness of disposition, made him a favourite everywhere, and many a bright eye, that night, rested upon the dark orbs of the handsome lieutenant with more than common interest.

But, strange to say, though extremely partial to female society, as most naval men are, and having passed many weeks exposed to the glances of some of the brightest eyes in Eaglaud, he escaped unscathed. A strong boyish attachment, strange and romantic as it may appear, influenced all his actions and swayed his feelings.

Though only eleven years old when he had last beheld the Princess Warhendorff in St. Petersburg, he remembered her parting words with a strange vividness. As she kissed her favourite—for she was exceedingly fond of the fine, high-spirited boy—the Princess said, as she saw her little daughter Catherine wind her arms round his neck— "Remember, Henry, and keep it in your little heart, that Catherine, if you both live, is to be your wife, whatever happens," and tears stood in the Princess's eyes; for, as she spoke, she had a foreboding of evil in her heart; she feared, dreaded, and trembled at the name of the Czar. "Eemember those words."

"I will never forget them," replied the boy, firmly, kissing the lovely child, who knew not what the words meant, only that Henry was always to love and take care Of her and be with her. And those words had remained engraven on his " heart of hearts." Often in the lonely hours of his watch, on far off seas, he repeated those words to himself, exclaiming—" Surely, surely, all cannot have died, or be totally lost, the Princess, Catherine, my sister Julia; I shall be a man by and by, and I swear I will devote my life to trace them."

Leaning against one of the pillars of the pit, Fitzharding stood listening to the bewitching tones of the enchantress Grisi, who was never in better voice, when the entrance of the Queen and Prince Albert created a momentary movement amongst the audience. "It does not require much penetration in a foreigner to judge how our fair Queen rules in the hearts of her subjects," thought our hero. As he looked along the line of boxes directly facing the royal box, suddenly his eyes were arrested by the face of a young girl seated in the front row, between two elderly ladies, evidently of rank. Was it the contrast, or what was it that struck Fitzharding with a strange feeling, as his eyes rested upon one of the loveliest faces imagination could picture or conjure up; but it was not the beauty of the £ce that so struck him, for startled he was. But as he gazed, some vision of the past floated in indistinctness before his sight, and left a confusion and bewilderment over hia mind and thoughts. The curtain fell, and in the momentary murmur of applause, fcc., the young girl he was gazing at got up and retired to the second row, seating herself by the side of another young girl, almost as beautiful as herself, though of a totally different stamp.

Urged by an irresistible curiosity, he gently and by degrees moved on to obtain a nearer view. After a time he gained a closer position; but, in doing so, brought his own very tall figure into more prominence. The curtain,drew up, and the audience again became absorbed in the scenes of the popular opera then performing.

"I certainly have seen features resembling both those young girls, somewhere," soliloquised our hero; but where, he could not determine. "She is wonderfully beautiful," he mentally exclaimed, referring to the one he had first noticed; "but I am not going to fall in love with those beautiful eyes—large, dark, and lustrous as they are."

At that moment the two girls—for neither could be more than seventeen or eighteen—happened to turn their eyes across the pit, and it chanced for a second, one—not the dark-eyed beauty—let her glance rest upon Fitzharding. As she did so, the colour forsook her cheek. Fitzharding did not imagine it, he was too near to mistake. She did change colour, and with a slight start, turned to her companion. She also instantly let. her gaze rest upon him—it was a look of not more than a second's duration. She did not turn pale, but her colour heightened as she changed her position, and both then gazed on the stage.

"This is very singular and very strange," thought Fitzharding. "I shall never get those dark and extraordinarily beautiful eyes out of my head; and that fair blond too, positively turned pale."

He was not a vain man; but it is useless to declare he was unmoved. He ws undoubtedly bewildered by the manner of the two girls, who were especially elegant in their attire.

They did not look towards him again; and, anxious to find out who the two elderly ladies were, and a stout, handsome, and stately-loo king old gentleman, who sat on the back seat of the private box—he moved on to where he saw a gentleman of his acquaintance sitting with a party of showily-dressed ladies; he was a regular townsman and knew everybody; so our hero thought that from him he could gain the information he required.

As he moved on by degrees, but keeping his attention on the box, the curtain fell amid a thunder of applause— the opera was finished; and looking back, to his infinite dismay, he beheld the whole party that Bo interested him leaving the theatre, and a whole bevy of fair faces taking possession of the vacant places.

"I will go out, and see if I can have a glance at them, and, perhaps, make out who they are," soliloquised Fitzharding; but to effect his exit speedily was out of the question. When he did get out and proceeded to the bux entrance, he could perceive numbers going in and out, but no trace of the party he was so anxious about could he discover. Passing the entrance, he proceeded to the circle where the private box was situated, and, finding the box-keeper, commenced enquiries; and, feeing the somewhat surprised box-keeper with a half-sovereign, requested to know who it was that had occupied the fourth box from the stage.

"It's a private box, sir," said the man, "belonging to the Countess of S. The first party that occupied it are strangers to me, quite strangers. The present occupiers—"

"It is the first party whose names I most wished to know," interrupted our hero, much chagrined.

"I regret, sir, I cannot inform you; they came with a private card, from the Countess herself. No doubt," insinuated the keeper, "by judicious enquiries at the Countess's mansion, in May-fair, you will gain the information you require."

Fitzharding smiled, thanked the man, and departed, returning to the pit to rejoin hia friend, with whom he promised to sup.

For several days, nay, weeks, Fitzharding could not banish the remembrance of the dark eyes of the fair incognito from his thoughts: a likeness to somebodv haunted him, whilst the young maiden with the blond hair and deep blue lovely eyes, also occupied a portion of his reflections. That she suddenly turned pale when her eyes met his, he could swear; he was quite close enough at the time to notice every feature aud change in those two beautiful faces that attracted more eyes than his. However, he became so occupied in fitting out his yacht, and settling his affairs, that in time the dark eyes of his unknown beauty began to fade from his thoughts.

Having completed all the necessary arrangements, on the thirteenth of August, 1854, the Medora weighed anchor, and, under a cloud of canvas, left the bay of Torquay, where she had remained for a few days, in order that the Commodore and his newly-married coxswain, who was in high glory, might visit and inspect Ler, and also bid farewell to the young officer, ere he departed from the Crimea.

Sir Edgar was delighted, and pronounced the Medora one of the handsomest ships of her size afloat, whilst Tom could almost have left his bride to accompany hia favourite; but then he reflected that his old master could not exist without him, whilst Cassar, the black cook, who had been transferred to the yacht, would diligently attend to the wants of the young one.

The master, who had sailed with our hero when a midshipman, was a married man, pleasing in manner and kind in disposition, and who gladly accepted the handsome income offered him by Henry in preference to a berth in a merchant vessel; besides which, as the service on which they were about to start was a dangerous one, the generous young sailor, in case of a misfortune to hia master, settled a liberal income upon the wife and children. Thus interest as well as friendship bound Mr. Bernard to the fortunes of the Medora and her owner, and no man was ever more fitted to fill the situation of adviser and friend.

The yacht had a fair time"going through the English Channel; but after running through the Bay of Biscay, the weather changed, and gave the crew an excellent opportunity of testing the sea,-going qualities of the Medora.

During forty-eight hours it blew a brisk gale against them, but the yacht bore it splendidly, working to windward slowly but steadily. On the cessation of the storm, a strong breeze from the opposite quarter, tested her powers of speed. Sailing at the rate of twelve knots an hour, and sometimes more, proved that she was a fast craft, as well as a noble sea boat.

"I think I can safely congratulate you, sir," said Mr. Bernard, as the vessel made the Straits of Gibraltar, and ran in, anchoring off the Mole, addressing Mr. Fitzharding—" in having as fast and as fine a vessel as ever carried canvas over blue water."

"I am of your opinion," answered our hero, highly delighted with the performance of the graceful Medora, "and I am also rejoiced to see our crew pull so well together."

The Medora was certainly a most dashing looking vessel, and, being full rigged and armed, had all the appearance of a corvette, whilst with her taut spars, square yards, and graceful hull, attracted unusual attention and admiration.

There were several vessels of war and some transports off Gibraltar, the commanders of which, though previously strangers, cordially welcomed the gallant owner of the yacht, who, on his part, resolved to remain amongst them a few days. By the Governor, to whom he presented a letter of introduction, he was received with kindness and attention.

After dinner, on the second day of their visit, Fitzharding and Mr. Bernard were sitting in the saloon of the Medora, when our hero's personal attendant entered the cabin, saying—

"There is a shore boat alongside with a foreign gentleman, who requests to see you, sir."

"Then show him up, "William. Bo not stir, Mr. Bernard; whoever he is, he need not disturb us."

In a few minutes the stranger was ushered in, Fitzharding very politely rose and requested him to take a seat, at the same time regarding him with some surprise.

He was a man rather above the middle height; in age apparently about forty-seven or fifty. His hair was abundant and jet black, as were his wiskers and mustaches. He was habited in the European costume, and appeared a person of great respectability; but of what country, Fitzharding could only conjecture; he fancied he might be a Pole or a Greek; the expression of his features was rather stern and sedate, but his dark eyes were penetrating to a degree. As he seated himself, Henry Fitzharding said—speaking in Italian—

"In what way can I serve you, Signor?"

"I am afraid," said the stranger in the same tongue, "that you will consider that I have not only intruded on you, but that what I am going to solicit will be considered out of all reason."

"At all events," remarked Fitzharding, good humouredly, "let me hear what it is you wish to solicit. At the same time allow me to offer you a glass of Madeira."

The stranger bowed, and after a moment's thought said, "Your listening to me thus far with patience and kindness emboldens me to state at once the object of my coming on board your yacht. You are proceeding to the Crimea, and, no doubt, will be induced to touch at Constantinople. Pardon me, if I appear to know so far of your intended voyage, but is not that the case, Signor?"

"Such is my intention," replied the astonished Fitzharding; "but, pray how came you to be aware of my intentions, for I have certainly not communicated them to any one here."

"I read the stars, sir," replied the stranger, seriously, "and they tell me you are undertaking an enterprise of peril, and one almost, if not quite insurmountable."

Henry looked at the stranger steadily, and with a slight tone of sarcasm observed, "Without the aid of the stars you may readily imagine that going to the Crimea, at this period, is a project attended with some risk."

"Ah," interrupted the stranger, with vivacity, stretching out his hand and helping himself to a glass of wine, which he put to his lips—" the imagination is a wonderful thing. Pardon me, but even at this moment you and your friend are labouring under the effects of imagination. Your servant brought you this wine when you ordered Madeira, and you are drinking it as Madeira, whereas, you are actually drinking sherry."

"Well, upon my honour," exclaimed Mr. Bernard, laughing, " you are now,

my good sir, trying to persuade us you are a conjuror."

"Pardon me," said the stranger, quite calmly, " what I say is fact. I am no conjuror, sir. Fill your glass and say if I am right."

"Stuff, Monsieur," returned the master, rather impatiently, whilst Fitzharding remained silent, deep in thought; he, however, filled his glass and put the wine to his lips, but the moment he did so he nearly let the glass fall, while he turned slightly pale. Fitzharding laughed, saying, "Well, my good friend, is it sherry or Madeira?"

"Sherry, by Jove," cried Mr. Bernard, quite astounded. "If I had not taken a glass or two before, I might say there was a mistake in the bottle, but if ever I drank Madeira, the first glasses I took from that decanter were real."

"Well, sir," observed Fitzharding, without at all heeding the mystification of his sailing master, and turning to the stranger—" as you read the stars, and are not a conjuror, pardon me if I doubt this latter assertion. If you will answer me one question, I will promise that if your request is not unreasonable, and I have the power to grant it, I will do so."

"Let me have your question in writing," said the stranger, " and I will answer it."

"Very good," and taking a tablet from his pocket, Fitzharding wrote on a blank leaf—" What do I seek and hope to find?"

The stranger immediately wrote underneath with the pencil handed him—" A sister."

"Very good," replied Henry, without evincing any very great surprise, and tearing the leaf to pieces, he added, " now, pray let me know what you solicit from me."

"A passage for myself and daughter, and a young Greek girl, her attendant, to Constantinople, and that no question will be asked where we come from or where we go."

Fitzharding did not hesitate a moment, but said, "Your request is granted. Your daughter and attendant shall have the state cabin off this saloon. You are welcome to such fare as myself and

friend partake of."

"Sir," said the stranger, with a flush upon his cheek, and a bright flash from his dark meaning eyes, "you are worthy of the wealth Providence has blessed you with. Before we part, I may be able to do you some service for your generosity and kindness. What time must we be on board to-morrow?"

"As early, Signor, as convenient to your daughter."

The stranger rose from his seat, and looking, with a smile, into the wondering face of the worthy Mr. Bernard, who understood Italian, said, " Pardon me, sir, for causing you to mistrust your sense of taste. You may now finish your wine, you will find it good Madeira; but, believe me, the imagination is all powerful."

With a bow, and the words good night, the stranger left the saloon—Fitzharding ordering his attendant to see him to his boat.

"You seem surprised and mystified, my good friend," observed Fitzharding, with a smile. "Have you tried the wine, whether it has come back to its original taste, for I can swear to it, that what I drank was Madeira, and first-rate Madeira too."

"Confound the fellow, he has staggered me," said the master, and taking up the decanter he poured out a fresh glass and drank it. "Well, I must be either a simpleton, or, as the strange fellow said, I have let my imagination overpower me. By Jove, the wine is Madeira, and no mistake."

"Depend on it he is a conjuror or a wizard, as they call themselves," laughingly observed our hero; "he may have dropped some subtle essence into the decanter in helping himself, which affected the wine, for a moment, without destroying it. He is a charlatan of some kind, I feel certain; though how the deuce he made out a project of mine, that even you, my good friend, knew nothing about, puzzles me."

"But, Mr. Fitzharding," said the master, anxiously, "is it not dangerous, or at least—pardon me—too generous of you to permit this stranger and a woman, who may or may not be his daughter, into your vessel?"

"Why, no," replied Fitzharding, still laughing, "he may be a first-rate wizard, and his daughter a witch, but I do not apprehend much mischief from them. I think he is a clever, intelligent, and probably a well-educated adventurer; but he is not an Italian, and certainly not a Frenchman."

"By Jove," cried the master, who had one or two weak points in his disposition, " perhaps he is a Russian."

"No, I should rather say he was a Greek."

"But those rascally Greeks are worse than Russians," rejoined Mr. Bernard; "I do not forget the desperate chase I once had, when a youngster, on board the Cambrian, after two Greek mistico-es, (pirates.) I hate a Greek worse than a Russian."

"Tou must spin me a yarn about that chase; I have heard you mention it before. It is early yet, so let us have it now, and another bottle of Madeira, that's not mystified."

"Very well, sir, here goes."

The master's yarn, however, we must give in our next chapter.

CHAPTER V.

"I Was quite a youngster when I served on board the Cambrian; not more than sixteen or seventeen. She was a fine flush-decked frigate, the Cambrian, and her commander, Captain Hamilton, as fine a looking man as you see in any country—a little eccentric, but a thorough seaman. He was the son of the celebrated Hamilton Eowan, who was so conspicuous in the Irish rebellion of '98, and who made so wonderful an escape from Ireland to France in a small boat not fifteen feet long.

"We were on the Mediterranean station, and had easy times of it enough. Now in Genoa; then at Villa Franca, close by Nice; at last we sailed for the East. It was the month of January, I remember it well, when we fell in with the Seringapatam, and shortly after both came to an anchor in Oreo's bay, on tho coast of the Island of Negropont. Here we had an idle life of it—all wishing for something to do. A brush with a pirate vessel would break the monotony of our lives, and was better than nothing.

"One evening a strange sail was seen running down the channel between the island and the main land.

"I was stretched on the deck, chatting with one of the master's mates, when a loud clear voice sang out, 'Shiver my timbers, if there aint two lattice-rigged craft after that one brig, and she's cracking on all the canvass she can.' Up started a whole lot of us, and gazed out over the bulwarks.

"Some of our officers were looking at the vessels with their telescopes, and could see the misticoes plying their long sweeps, as if in chase of the brig, when suddenly the order to 'out boats' startled us all from our idle employment into active life.

"The boats were down in a shake, and into them were tossed, in baste, provisions, ammunition, and a small cask of water. I was crazy for an expedition of some sort, and though a petty officer and might have avoided going, I easily got a berth in the boat, under the command of Lieutenant Marsham—as fine a fellow as ever lived. It was past three o'clock when wo were ready and shoved oft". There were seven boats, and about one hundred men in all.

"By this time the brig and the rascally pirates were a deuce of a way ahead of us, and could scarcely be discerned, except just.the tops of their lofty sails.

"Our lads bent to their oars with good will, and towards evening, after passing the brig, which was an Ionian vessel, we neared the misticoes.

"There was not a word to be heard on board the boats, unless a whisper or so when the men were relieved at the oar.

"We had then been more than six hours at the oar. The misticoes were making for the land, with their sails set, and pulling vigorously at the same time. Still, we came up with them hand over hand, when, suddenly, the largest of the two Greek misticoes let fly a volley of musketry over the boat I was in, which was the nearest.

Strange to say, I had only a moment before changed places with poor Bill Saunders, and the single shot that took effect killed him, the ball passing through his head. The next discharge wounded several men. A continued volley of firing was kept up against us and the next two boats, till we got furious, and some of our marines returned their fire; but the rascally pirates were like a swarm of bees in their crafts, and took deliberate aim at us as we came on. 'Now, my men,' said the lieutenant, 'bind your cutlasses round your wrists with a leather thong,' which we called a Becket, 'and strain every nerve to get on board those cursed pirate's vessels.'

"We flew through the water; the men could hardly keep their seats, with eager desire to get at the enemy, who, we saw, were armed with yataghans, which cut like a sickle. The next moment the boats were alongside, and a rush was made up the sides of the mistico. I fell back in my haste, and should have tumbled into the water, had not a tall, powerful seaman, Pat Collins, an Irishman, caught me by the waist and tossed me clean into the midst of a group of Greeks fighting like fiends. The next instant Pat was amongst them also, and, as I gained my feet, I saw him slashing away with his heavy cutlass, the whole time shouting, ' Hoorah, ye devil's darlings, ye shall sup with your daddy to-night.' Our men were actually half-choked with fury— their white trousers and check shirts forming a strange contrast with the coloured garments of the Greeks aud Albanians armed with musket, pistol, and yataghan.

"In a few minutes the decks were slippery with blood. Pat Collins cleared the way wherever he went, picked me up two or three times, and once actually drove me in the ftce of a large Albanian, knocking him clean overboard.

"Never was there a more terrible scene for the time. No quarter was given. The reports of the muskets, the quick crack of the pistols, the clash of steel, and the dull, heavy blows of handspikes and other weapons snatched up—as some lost their original weapons—formed an indescribable scene of confusion and uproar. Numbers of Greeks threw themselves from the yards into the sea, and swam towards the shore, distant about a mile.

Some were actually cut dwon in the act of leapin goverboard. I had several narrow escapes, and received several slight cutlass wounds.

"Christians! Christians!" shouted the pirates, imploring quarter; but no quarter could they obtain; the blood of the sailors was on fire, and they considered pirates not entitled to quarter; till at length Lieutenant Marsham put a stop to the slaughter and spared the few that remained. For the time it lasted this was the sharpest hand-to-hand encounter I ever witnessed, and many old sailors said so likewise, and that it was also the the bloodiest. The two misticoes were not gained without loss; though comparatively that loss was trifling considering the extraordinary ferocity with which the pirates fought. We did not regain the frigate till next day."

"The Cambrian was at Navarino afterwards, was she not?" questioned Fitzharding.

"Yes, sir, we were, and a desperate affair that was," returned Mr. Bernard, "though its utility was questioned. The poor Cambrian was lost afterwards—run down by the I sis—and I then shipped in the Csesar and returned to England."

"You have seen a good deal of service as well as a great portion of the globe, my worthy friend, and yet look as hearty as ever after it. So now let us to our couches. I am a little curious for to-morrow to come, to see what our fair guests will turn out."

"They will turn out a parcel of charlatans and conjurors," muttered Mr. Bernard to himself, as he turned in; "I don't like that business of the wine; I hate wizards, and their daughters too; I'll keep my weather eye open, I can tell them." And with this wise determination the old tar fell asleep.

The following morning, all were ready for sea on board the Medora, when Henry Fitzharding, standing near the wheel with a telescope m his hand, perceived a shore boat, pulled by two men, coming towards the yacht, and seated in the stem sheet was the stranger, and beside him two females, closely enveloped in mantillas and

veils—neither wore the European bonnet. In a few moments they were alongside, while the crew of the Medora regarded them with considerable surprise. Fitzharding, naturally kind and courteous to the opposite sex, had the accommodation ladder ready rigged, and he himself politely came forward to hand the females on board.

"I trust, Mr. Fitzharding," said the stranger, "we have not delayed your hour of sailing."

"Not at all," returned our hero. Struck with the tall graceful form of the stranger's daughter, he held out his hand to aid her, and for an instant the long veil fell back, and his gaze rested upon two sweet, dark, lustrous eyes, that, as they looked up at him, caused a singular sensation to steal over him. It was a soft, small hand that rested for a moment in his, which he fancied trembled in his grasp; the next moment, with a graceful inclination of the head, she took her father's arm,

The attendant threw back her veil without any appearance of timidity, aud looked earnestly into the very handsome, thoughtful features of Fitzharding, as she passed. Our hero regarded her with intense surprise. Was this, in reality, the stranger's Greek attendant? If so, she was as graceful and beautiful a girl as he had ever seen, and as she looked earnestly and strangely into Fitaharding's features, a singular expression—one of great thoughtfulness and tenderness—came over her features, and suddenly dropping the long veil over her face, she hastily went behind her mistress.

The portmanteau and other articles were handed up, the boatmen paid, and the orders given by the master to heave up, and prepare for getting under weigh at once,

"If you will follow me," said Henry to the stranger, recovering his usual calm, possessed manner, "I will show you to your cabins, and anything you may require, my attendant shall procure for you. By what name shall 1 address you during our voyage?"

"Paskovoi, if you please," answered the stranger, fol lowing Fitzharding into

the saloon of the yacht; "my daughter's name is Irene,"

"They are Greeks then, or Poles," thought our hero, as he threw open a side-door, saying, " Signor Paskovoi, you will find within two private cabins; our state rooms are on this side; pray order anything you may require for your daughter's convenience, and, if possible, it shall be procured."

"You are very kind, sir; our wants are few; we will give as little trouble as possible; neither my daughter nor her attendant suffer much from the sea in any of its moods."

Fitzharding bowed, and saying he would order their trunks to be placed in their cabins, left the saloon, and ascended to the deck, full of thought.

No sooner had the young man left the saloon than both females laid aside their mantles and thick veils.

Had our hero been there, he would have beheld in Irene Paskovoi one of the most fascinating and lovely faces the imagination of even a poet could fancy, or au artist put on canvass. She appeared not more than seventeen or eighteen years of age; she was exquisitely fair, with a rich bloom on a cheek eoft as a peach; large, dark, lustrous, hazel eyes, with brows so beautifully arched and regular that the beholder might almost fancy them painted; a high and noble forehead, and a profusion of jet black air, which hung in luxuriant curls over a neck unrivalled in *contour* and fairness; but her chief charm lay in the fascinating expression of her perfect features. Her figure was fully developed, and every movement graceful and dignified.

Her attendant was attired somewhat after the fashion of her mistress, in the Italian mode, except her boddice, which was like that of the better class of Greek females in the Morea. She appeared about the same age as her-mistress, equally fair, but her eyes were blue, and her liair a light auburn; not so tall as Irene Paskovoi, but light and graceful, with a sweet Hebe face, infinitely more resembling the countenance of a European than a Greek.

The Signor Paskovoi looked after the

retiring figure of Henry, as he left ttie cabin, and then closed the door, and turning round, looked almost sternly into the serious face of his daughter's attendant, saying, "Remember your oath, Ida, and take care; you know the penalty."

There came a flush over the beautiful girl's face, and a haughty expression for an instant curled her lips, and she was about to reply, when Irene Paskovoi, with an endearing look, and a voice sweet and musical, said— laying her hand on her attendant's, and pressing it—

"Dear friend, be not vexed at my father's reminding you of our vows: he means well."

"My own Irene," said the fair girl, throwing her arms round her neck, and kissing her, "there is no fear of my forgetting. Come, let us look at our sleeping cabins; this is a beautiful ship, and oh, what a graceful, noblelooking man is her owner!"

Irene made no remark, but rose, and taking their mantillas and veils, both passed into the state cabins of the yacht, which were beautifully fitted up.

The Siguor Paskovoi paced the saloon for a few moments, muttering some sentences to himself in the same language the two girls had conversed in, which was neither Italian, French, or English; he looked very serious, but suddenly taking up his hat, he proceeded on deck.

It was a splendid day; a fine breeze blew from the westward, the sea sparkling and rippling, and dancing in the glorious sunshine that was poured over its deep blue waters. The Medora was under a cloud of snow-white canvass, gliding out of the bay, at the rate of nine knots. The stern old rock rose like a mighty bulwark out of its ocean bed, frowning defiance, and casting its giant shadows far over the glistening waters.

The opposite coast of Africa was distinctly visible. Apes hill rising up directly opposite, like another Gibraltar, from the African shore.

The rock was soon left behind, for studding sails below and aloft were now added to the snow-white cloud the Medora carried. Fitzharding himself wassteering, for he loved the sea dearly, and his eye dwelt with pleasure on the lofty spars bending gracefully under the pressure of the breeze; the water sparkled and foamed under her hows, and seemed to fly by the sided of the vessel as she almost flew before the breeze.

"At this rate, Mr. Fitzharding," said the Signor Paskovoi, approaching our hero, and still speaking Italian *in* his peculiar accent, "you will reach Malta; in less than four days."

"Have you been studying the stars, Signor Paskovoi?" returned Henry, with a smile; "I do not remember mentioning to you my intention of visiting Malta."

"It would scarcely be worth while, sir," replied the stranger, without a change of feature, "to consult the stars on so easily imagined a conjecture. Mine was a very natural supposition: as Malta lies in your route, and few that never saw Malta would like to pass so remarkable a stronghold without visiting it."

"You are quite right," returned our hero, "it was a very natural supposition. Have you ever been in Malta?"

"Never landed there. Ha, here is my daughter," continued the stranger, "come up to have a look at your famous fortress. We are leaving it very fast."

Fitzharding called one of his crew to take the wheel, and turning to the Signor Paskovoi, he said,." Does your daughter speak English.

'-She speaks Italian or French, sir, sufficiently fluently to converse in either."

Irene Paskovoi, leaning on the arm of her Greek attendant, came upon deck. She had merely' the veil thrown over her head, and as Fitzharding drew forward one of the deck couches, he said, in Italian—

"I trust, Signora, you found in your cabin everything you require r"

Irene gently threw aside her veil, and in her sweet, musical voice replied—

'-Oh, in truth, Signor, they must be very hard to please, that could find fault with the arrangements of your beautiful yacht."

Fitzharding had a full view of her lovely features, and was struck forcibly with their exquisite beauty. He could not take his eyes off her, though her long, silken lashes fell beneath his gaze, and a flush came to her cheek; for his life Henry could not refrain from the long look he cast upon the blushing girl's face; a dream of the past came over him; he was bewildered, and in a hesitating voice said, seating himself on the other end of the couch—

"Your features sadly recall some dream of the past that bewilders me; pray pardon me, therefore, if my look was more earnest than it ought."

The fine, mellow tones of his voice were as pleasing as her own. Irene looked up.

"I am sure, Signor, you have been too kind and generous for me to feel offended at what was not meant as an offence.—We have a fair wind, have we not, Signor?" she added, as if wishing to change the subject.

"Very favourable indeed," returned the thoughtful Fitzharding, recollecting the words of the Signor Paskovi, that he was neither to ask where they came from or where they were going, and he thought how difficult it would be for him to converse with the fair girl beside him without infringing on this promise.

"How very grand and striking is the appearance of your gigantic fortress, Signor," observed the gentle voice of Irene, breaking the silence which had lasted several minutes.

The young man roused himself from his reverie, and replied, that it was the first time he himself had ever seen the rock; he had visited many other lands, but never beheld a finer or more striking object than Gibraltar presented, especially viewing it, as they then did, from the. eastward; for several hours it would be distinctly visible.

The Signor Paskovoi, who had stood some paces apart, gazing out on the blue waters, now joined them and entered into conversation, and for an hour Fitzharding was pleased and surprised by the varied matter of his discourse, and the quiet unobtrusive manner in which he brought forward his somewhat strange theories.

Shortly afterwards, the father and daughter retired to their private cabins, and the females did not appear again during the remainder of the evening, though the Signor joined our hero and Mr. Bernard at their wine, and, over a bottle of unmystified Madeira, won upon the good opinion of the worthy master, who began to look less suspiciously upon him.

CHAPTER.IV.

The commander of the Medoralay awake for many hours of the night. He satisfied himself in one thing—strange and mysterious as it certainly was—he firmly believed that in Irene Paskovoi and her attendant he beheld the two beautiful girls that had so attracted his attention at the opera, the night of the Queen's visit. The very first glance at Irene's eyes, as she stepped on board, electrified him; he did not at that moment recognize her, but he felt he had seen those eyes somewhere before; and even now, as he tossed and turned on his couch, he imagined that at the opera was not the first time that he had beheld them. Who could this Signor Paskovoi be? When he first consented to receive him and daughter on board his yacht, he considered him a clever, keen, quick-witted adventurer, whose knowledge of his destination, though it at first rather surprised him,did not, on reflection, create much wonder; but he felt interested in the Signor, his daughter, and her friend—attendant, he felt satisfied she could not be. The grace and beauty of Irene, coupled with her being the same lovely girl he had seen at the opera, strangely interested him—her presence, her features, her very voice seemed to recall a dim vision or recollection of the past—he was mystified, and vainly tried to convince himself that she bore an accidental resemblance to some face he had met with during his previous voyages

One thing he was resolved to do the next day—ask the Signor how he hecame acquainted with a project he had considered almost exclusively confined to his own breast —his intended search after his lost sister?

Our hero did not ask himself, was there no danger incurred in seeing and conversing with so lovely and fascinating a being as Irene Paskovoi, for days—perhaps weeks? No; he did not think upon that subject at all. He was a difficult man to please. Beauty had always charmed him; but he remained quite heart-whole, though for a year and a half he had mixed in the first circles of the metropolis.

The following day was again as fine as the preceding, but the wind extremely light, and the sea as smooth as a lake. Fitzharding was pleased to see Irene appear at the breakfast table; he held out his hand in the English fashion, and, with a gay smile, said he was happy to perceive that the sea had no power to banish the roses from her cheeks.

Irene, with an easy, graceful manner, placed her hand in the offered palm of our hero, and with a brighter colour said, "The motion of your yacht, Signor, was so easy and soothing, that I even slept sounder than I should ashore."

"I entreat," said Fitzharding, "that your fair countrywoman will take her meals with us. I think that arrangement will not be displeasing to you, for it strikes me that her attendance upon you is one of love, not service."

Irene coloured to the temples; but her glance, as her eyes met those of Fitzharding, was one of pleasure.

Before she could reply, the Signor Paskovoi observed—

"In truth, Mr. Fitzharding, you have hit upon a fact, and I pray you excuse my not stating that this was the case, at first. Ida Myreti is an orphan, but of as good blood as any Greek maiden in the Morea."

"Then pray,Signor Paskovoi," enquiredHenry,8eriously, ', why did you permit me to offer a slight to one so fair and well born i"

The Signor Paskovoi did not seem disturbed by the question; but his reply somewhat surprised our hero.

"Because, Mr. Fitzharding, there is so much mystery about us which cannot be explained, that I must beg of you to pass it over. Perhaps before we part I may be able to explain some things that now ap-

pear obscure to you."

"I shall be quite satisfied," replied Fitzharding, "if any endeavours of mine serve to render this voyage agreeable to your daughter and her fair friend."

Irene looked at her father, and then got up to retire to her cabin, and in a few minutes returned with Ida Myreti, attired precisely similar to herself, in the Italian mode. She was, in truth, though widely different from Irene, a very lovely girl, and with a graceful salutation to Fitzharding, she took her place at the breakfast table.

The Signor Paskovoi continued, with considerable tact, to get the conversation into a pleasing channel, so that any embarrassment that might be felt by the party quietly passed off, and an hour glided away agreeably and swiftly.

Ida Myreti spoke the.Italian full as well as Irene,but with a very different accent. Indeed, Fitzharding remarked that both her tone and accent resembled his own; nor could he for a moment fancy her a Greek maiden, so contrary did she appear to all his imagination led him to picture.

After breakfast, they all proceeded on deck. It was still remarkably fine and warm; but, to an experienced eye, there were signs in the heavens that betokened a change.

"As you are fond of the-study of the heavens, Signor Paskovoi," said Fitzharding, who had placed couches for the two fair girls, and then joined the Signor, "what signs do you read in yonder sky?"

"A heavy gale of wind from the 'south-east quarter, Mr. Fitzharding; and that, very shortly after sunset."

"Well, your idea corresponds with mine, " said our hero," only I do not think we shall have any wind of consequence till after the moon goes down."

"Gales in this sea are very sudden and very violent,'' said the Greek. "You see those long straight Hoes in the southeast extend rapidly and increasing in bulk without your perceiving where the clouds come from; the gale is not very far off, depend on it."

"I wish, Signor Paskovoi," said Henry, " to ask you a question which will not infringe upon the conditions agreed upon between us. May I inquire from what channel you gained your information respecting my present project in seeking my sister?"

"Well, in tiuth, sir, you will perhaps be surprised when I tell you my knowledge was gained by some trifling information obtained years ago, and with that information, combined with circumstances, I made a bold guess. Had you asked me auy other question," he added with a smile, " I must have assumed the wizard, and given a mystic answer. But I will acquaiut you how I first heard your name, and of some particulars relating to your family. Business, some years ago, required me to make a short residence in Odessa; it was at the period when the singular disappearance of the Princess Warhendorff caused so much talk and speculation in that place; the gentleman—I forget his name—who came from England for.the orphan children of the lamented Mr. Pitzharding, your father, exerted himself to the utmost to trace the Princess Warhendorff and the lost little English girl, but in vain. As I said, there was a great deal of talk about this matter, and of the immense wealth left by Mr. Pitzharding, to be inherited by his son.

"I heard the occurrence mentioned several times, and it was remarked, by many of the merchants in Odessa, that the orphan was a fine, noble boy, and that he resolved he would, when old enough, come back and seek after his lost sister. Of course, at that time, no one dreamt of a war with England, and, heaven knows, it would have been better that this terrible war of slaughter, of sickness, and of death, had never begun.

''Years passed, circumstances forced me to leave my native land, with my only child and the orphan daughter of a friend. I became an astrologer, foretold things to come, and revealed the past; but I have no wish to pass myself upon you, Mr. Pitzharding, as either a wizard or a conjuror. I worked upon the credulity of the human race, aided by science. I deceived, and gained a reputation in foreign lands for fortelling the future and divining the thoughts of those who consulted me. Of course this was a mere deception; but it was a harmless deception. Thus, in the course of time, I found myself in Gibraltar; extremely anxious, from intelligence I had received, to reach Constantinople; but there was not a single vessel there in which I could embark with my two girls. When your yacht came into port, I was visiting at the Turkish Consul's, and a gentleman comiug in, mentioned your name as the owner of the magnificent vessel just anchored. I immediately surmised that you were bound to the Crimea, and was struck at once by the name: and then the past remembrance of the Princess Warhendorff and your lost sister came over my mind, and I resolved to make a bold push for a passage to Constantinople; you know the result. As a feint, and, in fact, to gain an insight into your feelings and disposition, in stretching my hand across the wine decanter I dropped a subtle essence into it which gives any white wine, lor the moment, the taste and flavour of sherry. Had you been drinking port or claret, I could have changed them likewise. I saw at once, by your countenance and manner, you were not to be deceived, and that, if I attempted any of my sleights of hand, you would refrain from the intercourse I wished to establish between us."

Pitzharding remained thoughtfully gazing on the sea for a time after the Signor Paskovoi's explanation, then said—

"As you know my object in making this voyage, Signor, may I ask your opinion on the subject that occupies my mind and thoughts, to the; exclusion of eveiything else; you know more about those countries than I do; my boyish remembrances serve me but little."

"You, of course, speak the Russian language?" questioned the Signor Paskovoi, his eyes fixed upon the deck of the ship.

"I have made it my study, and I spake it like my native language, when a boy," returned Henry Fitzharding. "You, of course, understand it likewise; pray let us converse."

The dark cheek of the Greek showed an increase of colour, but he at once replied—

"My knowledge is very limited indeed; you are aware that Italian and French is universally spoken in Odessa; indeed, the inhabitants affect to scorn the Russian tongue; but I understand it perfectly, and shall know, when I hear you speak, what chance you have of passing for a Russian, provided you let your mustaches grow."

"That I intend to do after my arrival in Constantinople," replied Fitzharding, adopting the Russian language. "I do not dream of penetrating into Russia for a month or two, and by that time we shall have taken Sebastopol, which event will probably bring about a peace with the Czar.

"No," returned Signor Paskovoi, and with peculiar emphasis—" no, Nicholas, the Czar, will never live to hear of the fall of Sebastopol; for a reverse, or a symptom of failure in defending his favourite fortress would give his system such a shock that he would most likely die a sudden death. The family on the throne of Russia are a doomed race; none will ever reach the age of sixty."

Fitzharding looked fixedly into the face of the Greek, struck by his words, and the perfect ease with which he spoke the language of the Czar.

"Then you imagine, Signor Paskovoi, that we shall not be successful in this war."

"You may be, in the end; but you will be terrible sufferers, both in treasure and in men. The good and the brave will fall. As far as I have been able to judge, everything has gone wrong from the very beginning: promptitude, instead of vacillating and listening to the humbug of Austrian diplomacy, would have probably gained you your object in going to war before now."

"We have been extremely dilatory," returned our hero; "more firmness and decision might have shown the Czar that we were not to be trifled with; but now that war is declared, he will see we are in earnest."

"You are not, perhaps, aware," remarked the Signor Paskovoi, "that Sebastopol is one of the strongest fortresses, if not the strongest fortress in the world, and that to invest it will require an army nearly three times the amount England and France have sent against it. "

"But our magnificent fleet," observed Fitzharding, "Sebastopol will scarcely hold out against such an armament. The world has never seen a nobler sight than the allied fleet."

"I grant you the fact," replied the Signor; "but granite batteries of such enormous strength, and mounting so vast a number of guns, are fearful odds to contend against with wooden batteries."

"The wooden walls of old England," said Fitzharding, with a confident smile, "have laced granite walls, before now, 1 with success. If we fail, the failure will not be from the want of valour in the army and navy of England or of France. " CHAPTER VII.

Henry Fitzharding did not pursue the subject of the conversation related in the previous chapter, for a sudden shift of wind, and a violent squall at the same time, called his attention to the Medora, the ship being under a press of canvass. But Mr. Bernard was a skilful and careful navigator, and had been watching the weather, while our hero was engaged in earnest conversation with the Signor Paskovoi.

The lofty sails were soon brailed up and furled, and the top-gallant masts struck. There was no mistaking the weather.

The whole face of the heavens was changed; the temperature had decreased rapidly; the glass falling as quickly. In the Mediterranean, wind and sea rise rapidly, and before the setting of the first watch the yacht required double reefs in her top-sails.

Irene Paskovoi 'and Ida, after the evening meal, retired to their cabins for the night, leaving our hero and the Signor Paskovoi, who was not at all inconvenienced by the increased motion of the vessel, conversing.

"I commenced," said Fitzharding, addressing the Greek, "a short time since, by asking you what you thought cf my intended expedition. You did not give me a plain answer, for we got upon the subject of the war. We will, if you have no objection, return to the first subject of our discourse."

"I should feel very happy, Mr. Fitzharding," returned the Greek, "could I afford you any information; bat recollect, what chance of success have you in tracing the Princess Warhendorff and the two children, when the Czar's couriers failed?"

"A brother's love," replied Fitzharding, "is a widely different feeling from that of a paid messenger. My whole soul is wrapt up in the desire to recover my orphan sister. It has grown with my years, into a powerful and absorbing feeling. I would spend every fraction I possess, and glory in having done so, if I could recover my lost sister."

Had the speaker happened to let his eyes rest upon those of his companion, he would have wondered how his words could have caused those dark eyes to flash with such a strange expression of delight; it was but for an instant, and then his features resumed their calm, unconcerned expression, as he answered, after a moment's pause—

"Since I have had the pleasure of your acquaintance I have thought much about your project. As well as I recollect, there was the Princess Warhendorff, her daughter, and your sister, a male domestic, and two females, all trace of whom was lost at Taganrog. So I understood, whilst at Odessa."

"No," remarked Fitzharding, "they were not traced to Taganrog, but to a place called Slaviondrosk, fifty or sixty miles from Taganrog."

"When I think of this journey of the Princess," continued the Greek, "it strikes me as possible that she intended to ransom her husband from the Circassian Prince, Schamyl, and that perhaps she fell into the power cf those daring tribes that inhabit the Caucasus."

"Ha!" interrupted Fitzharding, with a start, "I never thought of that. Your idea, wild as it seems, is not improbable; but General Warhendorff was a prisoner. Would not the Czar take steps to liberate the General?"

"No, sir, he would not. So exasper-ated did he become against the officers employed against the Circassians, for permitting themselves to be defeated, that many were disgraced into the ranks, and some banished to Siberia."

"General Warhendorff was a marked man before his unfortunate defeat by the Circassians, and most likely his property became forfeited; but this is all surmise and conjecture. You, of course, will endeavour to reach Taganrog: suppose, instead of going there, you were to sail for one of the fortresses of the Circassians in the Black Sea. In the summer or spring, the singular beauty and grandeur of the scenery you would witness would repay you for the length of the voyage; and after all, you would not be more than three hundred miles from Sebastopol. You would be well treated by the Circassians, whose deadly enmity to the Russiaus renders them allies of your countrymen. You could there state your object to the highest in authority in the place you visit, and name your determination to ransom your sister, if she was alive and in their power. Depend on it, that with the Circassians, who even barter their own children with the Turks for arms to fight their battles with, your offer would fly through the length and breadth of their land like wildfire."

"But surely, if the Princess had fallen into the hands of the Circassians, she would have ransomed herself and the children," remarked Fitzharding.

"Supposing she had neither the means nor the power? If the Czar confiscated the General's property, as he did that of several other noblemen for very trifling offences; though in truth, after the passion or vexation has passed, he restores both the property and the offender to favour. But I will not speak against the Czar, who is a wonderful and a great man; he has done more for the Russian nation, during his reign, towards raising it into power, than any sovereign since Peter the Great."

Fitzharding, as he lay awake that night, thought over the conversation he had held with his guest. He considered it not at all improbable but that his conjecture concerning the Princess might, without any great stretch of the imagination, be correct; she might have been induced into a conference with one of the chiefs, and captured. Taganrog was not so very distant from the seat of war at that time. She might have embarked on the Sea of Azoff for one of the Caucasian fortresses on the Black Sea. He knew she was most devotedly attached to the General, whom he remembered as a remarkably handsome man, and equally devoted in his affection to the Princess.

From the Princess, Pitzharding's thoughts turned upon his somewhat mysterious guest and the two maidens. The Signor Paskovoi appeared to him, with all his care and solicitude, to be acting a part. Our hero did not give credit to the assertion of his being art astrologer. Neither did he believe him to be a Greek. He was quite as likely to be a Russian as anything else. He had closely watched his manner and tone in speaking to his daughter and Ida Myreti: there was no show or sign of atlection between them, as generally between child and parent. Irene's tone was mild and gentle when she addressed her father; but Ida seldom addressed him at all, and he sometimes caught her look fixed upon himself, with an expression of so much tenderness, if not affection, as quite puzzled him.

What could bring three such persons to Gibraltar? was a question he asked himself; and, who was it that Irene Paskovoi so much resembled?

It blew hard the whole of that night and the next day, with so heavy a sea, that the two females did not leave their cabins; but the following morning the vessel was in sight of Malta, the wind shifting a point or two in their favour; and before night they were at anchor in the harbour of Valetta. The weather had now completely changed into downright winter—cold, changeable winds, and boisterous.

As it blew a heavy gale from the east the day after his arrival, Fitzharding was forced to delay his departure; but it was impossible to find the time irksome or tedious with such beautiful and charming companions. The!:brary belonging to the yacht was both good and exten-

sive; there was music in abundance; there was a guitar; and he himself played the flute and the bugle—the latter exquisitely.

To his great surprise, he discovered that both maidens could read English with great facility, and converse in it also. This astonished him; for he remembered asking the Signor Paskovoi whether his daughter spoke English, and his answer was, that she spoke Italian fluently. He did not speak English to them himself; but he chanced to hear them while reading a book. The skylight being open, he heard Ida read out a sentence from one of James's novels as purely and with as perfect an accent as his own; and then, to his extreme surprise, he heard Irene say, in good English, but with a decidedly foreign accent, "How beautifufly he writes, when on his favourite subject!". Though extremely surprised, he made no remark, as they had never addressed him in English.

"There is a great deal of mystery about those two girls," said Fitzharding to himself; "but," he added, " it is no business of mine; I have no right to seek to penetrate into their private affairs or their reasons for preserving a complete silence with respect to where they come from—that they are going to Constantinople I am aware."

A week passed in Valetta harbour. Irene read, played the guitar, and sang with a voice and expression that sank into Fitzharding's heart far deeper than he was aware. The Signor Paskovoi passed most of his time in his cabin reading abstruse books and writing, leaving the fair girls to the society of our hero, who felt that there was an irresistible charm in their intercourse, which became like that of brother and sisters.

A change of wind on the eighth day enabled the Me- dora to get under weigh, and steer her course for the" Archipelago, within sight of whose numerous islands she soon came. The passage, owing to the variable winds, occupied several days, which enabled Fitzharding to enjoy the society of his fair guests. The Signor Paskovoi made

no furthur remarks on the subject of our hero's expedition, became more silent and reserved, and confined himself entirely to his cabin. Irene's graceful brauty; her refined mind and kind manner; her deep and witching tones of voice, struck a chord in our hero's heart hitherto untouched. For Ida Myreti he felt a brother's affection; and often in his own mind he thonght how happy ho should be if Providence permitted the restoration of his sister, and she should resemble her in mind and appearance.

Passing between Candia and Cerigo, the Medora, with a full sail, was threading her way through the glorious islands of the Archipelago; Fitzharding was leaning on the couch on which sat Irene and Ida, with his telescope, taking a survey of the islands, as they passed very close to the shores; there were several very large transports urging their way through the tranquil sea; and two majestic screw steamers, with the banners of old England, sailed within a league of them; yet, notwithstanding their steam and sail, they could with difficulty outsail the graceful Medora.

"That is the frigate, Captain," said Mr.

Bernard, who was standing near," I know her well; she is a beautiful craft."

"She is, indeed; an old and dear friend of mine, Lieutenant Erwin, is on board her. I dare say they will come-to off Stamboul."

"Is not this a glorious scene?" asked Irene, looking into the features of Fitzharding. "How lovely those islands look, and how placid the water sparkling on theic shores."

"They are lovely," replied Fitzharding, with a serious look and a sigh he could not repress; "but we are leaving them; and, lovely as they are, they will fade from our sight and be forgotten, like everything else in this world, when no longer before our eyes."

"I should never dream of your making such a speech," observed Irene, her large, lustrous eyes meeting those of Fitzharding; "you are not one, I should think, likely to support such a theory. I am sure I shall never forget the scenes I have witnessed lately; they will be as vivid iu mv mind's eye as when before my actual sight."

"Oh, Mr. Fitzharding did not mean what he said," cried Ida, looking affectionately into the serious features of our hero. "Now, tell the truth," she added archly and yet so innocently, "will you forget your grateful guests, who owe so much to your kindness, when you leave us in old Stamboul, and are gliding into that dreary, stormy sea, so well named? Surely it is a terrible risk, even for this beautiful and noble vessel, to go into such a stormy sea r"

"I must answer your former question first, fair Ida," replied Fitzharding with a smile. "Shall I forget you hoth, when you leave me to my own thoughts? I can safely answer—never. Your society has rendered this short voyage one of pleasure; and, I believe, it was the very thoughts of the sad desolation you would leave behind that caused the sentence to escape my lips, and which you so justly found fault with."

Irene's beautiful eyes rested upon the deck, and her features were thoughtful and serious; whilst Ida said, with a flush on her cheek, and, as Fitzharding thought, a tear in her bright eyes, forcing its way from beneath the lids that trembled over them—" If I thought you would forget us, 1 would have wished that we had never met; but, please God, we may meet again,"—and, taking Irene's arm, both quitted the deck.

Fitzharding was surprised—bewildered. He looked after their graceful forms as they disappeared down the companion stairs, and was only aroused from his reverie by the approach of the Signor Paskovoi.

"With this wind, Mr. Fitzharding, we shall soon run into the Bosphorus. In truth we have to thank you for a most agreeable voyage."

"Owing to baffling and contrary winds, it has been a somewhat slow one," returned Fitzharding; "but our distance is now short."

"I said," remarked the Signor Paskovoi, "that before we should part I would, if 1 could, render you some service. I have been thinking much and deeply over the many conversations we have had relative to your intended search after your sister. In this paper"—the Signor took a sealed letter from his pocket, and presenting it to Fitzharding, continucd—" in this paper I have set down my opinion and firm belief how you ought to act, and which, if you follow my advice, will, I sincerely believe, lead to success. There is one promise, however, you must make me, and that is, that you will not open this letter till within sight of Sebastopol."

Fitzharding, without thinking, or indeed without attaching much importance to the words or the letter of the Signor Paskovoi, very readily made the promise required, and shortly after, descending to his cabin, he locked the letter in his desk.

Early the following morning they made the Straits of Gallipoli, passed between Sestos and Abydos, and, with a strong breeze in their favour, steered up the waters of the Sea of Marmora. The following morning they were at anchor before the far-famed Stamboul.

CHAPTER VIII.

From the period of entering the Straits of Gallipoli, the two fair friends were almost constantly on deck. They were both extremely serious, and though the beauty of the scenery— as the yacht ran close along the varied lovely shores of the Dardanelles—elicited their admiration, and induced conversation, yet the spirit and liveliness that had hitherto constituted the charm of their intercourse was gone.

Henry Fitzharding was infected with the same kind of depression. In vain he argued that it was mere friendly, brotherly affection he experienced for these beautiful girls. Such was certainly the feeling towards Ida Myreti; but if he had taxed his heart more closely, he would have discerned that Irene Paskovoi had made an impression there not easily erased. His pride revolted at the very idea of being in love. "What!" he exclaimed, "in love with an astrologer's, or rather an adventurer's daughter! A man who acknowledges no country, and whose proceedings are shrouded in mystery!" He had yet to learn that love laughs at distinctions and classes, levels ranks, and elevates the peasant.

Thus, when the Medora let go her anchor in the Golden Horn, the rattle of the chain cable had a grating and disagreeable sound to more than one person on board.

The morning after their arrival at Stamboul the weather was stormy and gloomy; a heavy, drizzling mist hung over the famed towers, palaces and mosques of the oriental city, shutting out each object from the sight; but the roadstead and harbour were crowded with ships of all nations, from the noble three-decker to the graceful caique, whilst every moment the rear of caniaon proclaimed the arrival and departure of vessels of war, coming from and going to the seat of war. The Signor Paskovoi had all his luggage ready, the ladies were equipped, and every preparation for landing complete.

"I am sure, Mr. Fitzharding," said the Siguor Paskovoi, as they all arose from an almost silent breakfast, "we shall never forget all the kindness we have experienced from you. "We part now; and, for certain reasons, I am not at liberty to speak of my future proceedings or my further peregrinations, for I do not intend staying more than a few hours in this over-crowded city; still it is not impossible but that we may meet again, and under widely different circumstances; and, believe me, I am deeply grateful for the generosity of your conduct towards us."

"My only regret," replied Fitzharding, with some emotion, as his eyes met those of Irene, "is, that here ends our intercourse. Your charming daughter and her fair friend have rendered my otherwise solitary voyage one of exceeding pleasure. I sincerely trust that your future destination may be reached without difficulty or danger. I only wish," he added, with a smile, "that our route was still the same, you should be heartily welcome to the use of my vessel."

".Thanks," returned the Signor Paskovoi, bowing low; "I must hail one of the passing caiques," so saying he ascended upon deck, leaving Fitzharding with the two thoughtful maidens.

The singular emotion evinced by Ida

Myreti, as he insisted her in adjusting her mantilla and mufflings—for it was a rude and boisterous day to land, for the season of the year—surprised Fitzharding; she made no attempt to conceal her tears, as he took her hand and respectfully kissed it, bidding her farewell and wishing her every happiness. "Strange," thought Fitzharding, "that *she* should show so much feeling."

"You wonder, perhaps, Mr. Fitzharding," said Ida, with-a tremor in her voice, as if guessing her thoughts, "that I should show my grief at our separation so much; but I do feel it—bitterly feel it—and you—"

"Ida, dear Ida," exclaimed Irene, interrupting her friend, and with a peculiar expression of countenance, checking her speech, "my father is calling us; let us go on deck. "A thousand thanks," she added, turning to Fitzharding, "for your generous kindness and protection. These last weeks have passed like a dream; but, unlike a dream, my memory will retain for years the remembrance of this voyage. Farewell; may you be happy and successful in whatever you undertake."-Irene's voice trembled, but she held out her hand—a hand worth keeping, if Fitzharding had known all— it was a soft, fair, beautiful hand, though it was the hand of an astrologer's daughter. He did not kiss Irene's hand, as he had done that of Ida; neither did he utter a word, but his eyes met her's, and there was a world of meaning in that glance; it brought a flush to the maiden's cheek, and she felt the hand that held hers burn like fire, as, placing her arm in his, they ascended upon deck.

Alongside of the Medora was one of the graceful caiques, with its picturesque boatman. These oriental boats are from fifteen to twenty feet long, mounted on both ends with a kind of beak; the one in front, being much sharper than at the stern, is armed with a kind of spur, and both are carved and gilded. The costumes of the boatmen themselves are peculiarly striking; their heads shaved, immense loose trowsers, and their breasts merely covered with a sort of silken shirt. They row the boats with great dexterity, and, in descending

the Bosphorus, they can beat a horse trotting.

The Signor Paskovoi had all his effects in the boat, and nothing remained but for the females to descend. Fitzharding silently handed the fair girls down the side, and into the caiques, and again bade them farewell; the boat pushed off, and in five minutes more, they were lost to the sight of the abstracted commander of the Medora, in the dense mist that hung over every object enclosed in the still waters of the Golden Horn.

CHAPTER IX.

On the day following the departure of the Signor Paskovoi and his fair charges, the sun arose bright and clear, a strong breeze blowing from the northwest; lonely, depressed, and abstracted, Fitzharding was prepared to go on shore, when the gig of an English man-of-war dashed up alongside the Medora, and a young, handsome man, in a naval uniform, sprang up the side; and, with a pleased smile and a joyful exclamation, Henry held out his hand, which was heartily shaken by the stranger.

"I was in hopes your ship was here, Edgar," said our hero, speaking first, "and 1 intended looking for you, but you have been beforehand with me."

"By Jove, I am so glad to see you, Harry," said Lieutenant Erwin, "that I can hardly find words to tell you so. We heard of you at Malta, and I thought surely to overtake you somewhere. Our gallant captain is longing to see you; but, like every one else in this part of the world, he has a lot to do, and nothing of moment. "We saw you a league off, as we came past Candia, and, by Jove, with wind and steam, we could scarcely get away from you."

"Come down into the cabin, Edgar, we will have a glass of champagne, and then I will go on shore with you. I recognised your ship."

"Ah, we cracked on all the sail we could. Our captain was pressed to deliver some despatches at Gallipoli, *en passant,* but your yatcht sails like a witch, Harry."

"Yes, she sails well; but I am so glad to see you," and again the young men shook hands with all the affection of

brothers. A bottle of champagne was opened and drank, and then Fitzharding asked his friend if any news had reached him since the glorious battle of the Alma.

"No, I am sorry to say," replied Erwin. "It is said the Allies ought to have advanced at once after Alma, and then Sebastopol would have been won. Moreover, our fleet is prepared to attack it, I believe; but I fear it will, by all accounts, be a hard nut to crack. We sai after to-morrow, to join."

"Well, I intend leaving in a day or two myself, and will anchor with the fleet; I know Captain P will give me a volunteer's berth on board the frigate."

"That he will, Harry. We shall be rejoiced to have you. You know I alone knew the motive of your voyage here, and there has been many guesses at the reason why you did not accept the post as first lieutenant on board the T, the finest ship in the service; but all knew you were sure to be in the thick of it, if there was any fighting. By Jove, we ought, long since, to have had a slap at the Bussians, before they got under shelter of the batteries of Sebastopol."

"Ah, so it is thought at home, Edgar. We have had poor advisers; God send they do not make a mess of it again; there is grumbling enough at our minister as it is." . "Let us go on shore now, for I have some letters and papers to deliver, and to call at the custom-house."

"Faith, so have I, Harry."

"My sailing master went there two hours ago. You remember Mr. Bernard. "

"Right well; you could not have selected a more straight-forward, honest, and thorough seaman—-just the very sort of man for a craft of this kind; but let us be off"

In a few minutes they were seated in the gig and pulling away for the Topkhane, the well-known landing place at Stamboul.

"I suppose, Harry, you are picturing to yourself a mighty fine place in this Constantinople. Faith, its countless gardens, mosques, palaces, minarets, and towers, present a magnificent and glorious prospect, looking at them from the waters of the Bosphorus; but, by Jove, recommend me to the dirtiest town in Great Britain for cleanliness and convenience, compared to this oriental city."

"Oh, I am quite prepared, Edgar, for Jwhat I am to see; for though, when I left Odessa, nine or ten years ago, in a Russian steamer, we did not touch here, I heard quite enough from Mr. Bowen. No matter about the interior, the exterior is certainly like a fairy scene. Did you get a peep at the mosque of St. Sophia?"

",Yes, I did, yesterday, and was monstrously disappointed. I expected something magnificent, but I found all its ornaments gone; its beautiful marble pavements, that we read so much about, hidden by dirty carpets; its mosaics barbarously whitewashed; some of them broken, and others taken away; and scarcely a painting left that is not defaced and spoiled; in truth, there is but little remains of the famous Basilica of Justiniana. But give way, my men, give way; this is Friday, and this is just the hour when the Sultan goes in his state barge to the mosque. We may as well see all we can."

"You are right," remarked our hero, "I should like to have a glance at the Sultan."

The day was gloriouslyfine, and the scene, as they pulled out from the Golden Horn into the waters of the Bosphorus, wonderfully beautiful and picturesque.

The waters were rippling under a fine breeze, and a blaze of sunshine fell upon' every object with dazzling splendour.

Huge two-deckers, frigates, corvettes, brigs, schooners, and every diversity of vessels were working either up the Bosphorus, or coming to an anchor between the shores. Scutari, with its thick groves, and its beach covered with boats, full of military, landing and embarking, and the waters literally covered with all nations; but their attention was almost at once attracted by the approach of the Sultan's state barge.

This caique had, certainly, both young men confessed, a most gorgeous and graceful appearance, for the most brilliant colours and gilding were dis-

played in every part j there was a large figure of a peacock in the bows, and by it sat the sultan's sword bearer.

"There is the Sultan himself," said Lieutenant Erwin, and as the caique swept past, impelled by the six-andtwenty oarsmen, close by the English boat, in which all stood up and doffed their hats to certainly one of the most enlightened rulers Turkey ever had. The Sultan, recognising the naval uniform of Great Britain, returned a graceful bend of his head. Abdul Medjid was at this time about two-and-thirty; tall and slight, with a pale, delicate face, slightly marked with the small pox; the brilliancy of his eyes, however, gave a truly interesting expression to his features.

-' Not a bad-looking chap, for a Turk, Harry," said the lieutenant, "and a deuced sensible fellow, to boot."

"There is something in his features and look altogether," answered Fitzharding, "and I trust in God, his cause may prove successful."

"Faith so do I, Harry; but, by Jove, he must go about the business in another kind of way than we are going. Now, my lads," he added, " give way for the Topkhane."

The arsenal of Topkhane—a house of cannons, literally —is situated near the sea shore, just at the division of the Bosphorus into two arms; one of which flows into the sea of Marmora, and the other forms the Golden Horn.

The hundreds of caiques and boats of every description of rigging that were passing'to and fro before this well-known landing-place, rendered it a matter of some difficulty to thread their way through them. Fitzharding was much struck with the newly erected building and its splendid fountain. The arsenal itself of a quadrangular form; near which are the imperial mosque, with its cupola and Moorish minarets, and the sultan's kiosk.

The two friends soon finished their business at the custom-house; and Lieutenant Erwin having also executed some other commisions. they both agreed to proceed to a coffee-house, to refresh themselves, and have a look at the

strange characters to be seen there. As Lieutenant Erwin had told him, Fitzharding was astonished at the difference existing between the exterior of Constantinople and its interior.

Almost every Englishman nourishes in his own mind a poet's dream of oriental scenery, magnificence, or beauty; his fancy calls up pictures of bright skies, palm trees, soft climate, and, above all things, sweet perfumes; and this feeling is, to a certain degree, realised by the first view of Stamboul, and the really lovely shores of the Bosphorus. But, the moment you land, like a puff of smoke, your fairy visions vanish. The dingy, ricketty houses, the filthy black mud of those hilly, stony streets, with their squalid inhabitants, banish anything like fancy. No enthusiasm can stand the contact of such a reality.

At the custom-house, also, the friends were astounded at the bungling, clumsy, confused manner of transacting business; all their accounts kept on scraps of paper, and all huddled into a bag, and hung upon a nail. Fitzharding was informed that an officer would be sent aboard his yacht, to examine his books; and though this was very pohtely hinted, there was an annoyance in it.

"A couple of days will do for me here, Edgar," he said, as they pushed their way through a crowded bazaar; "it is a bad time for inspecting the curiosities of the place. Coming back, I will have a look at them; that is, if I get back. "

"Yes, by Jove, a man may say that, who comes out here. What with chnlera, fever, and the chances of war, I shall count him a lucky fellow that gets back to old England in a whole skin."

By this time they had reached the front of one of the most famous and most frequented coffee-houses in Stamboul. All classes in the city frequented these places of entertainment and amusement; though, in most of them, you get bad coftee, bad tobacco, and, in every respect, bad accommodation, yet there the Turks go, to smoke themselves into unconsciousness, and to dream they are wafted into the abodes of their

Houris. However, the house selected by Lieutenant Erwin was a first-rate place of resort. It stood facing the waters of the Bosphorus, and could boast all kinds of luxuries. Ordering some refreshments and cigars, the young men sat down, and with curiosity regarded the scene around. They were in an immense saloon, with divers recesses and private corners. Opening into other chambers, there was a group of dancing girls and a band of musicians. At one end, a famous story teller was holding forth to a party of long-bearded, grave-looking Turks, smoking their chibouks; Armenians, in their long robes; Europeans, in all manner of costumes; specimens of all kinds—army, navy, artillery and cavalry—each enjoying the luxury he most desired. It was a Babel of tongues, but all confounded in one continued buz.

The two young men sat at an open window, looking down upon the waters of the Bosphorus, which offered to the sight a much more elevating and inspiring scene.

"What a paradise this might be made," exclaimed Fitzharding. "Nature has been lavish in her bounties; but the creed of the Prophet mars all; it will take centuries to root out old customs and prejudices amongst the Turks."

"This war," replied Edgar, " will do a great deal in that way. They say the creed of Mahomet is doomed. We come to save the Turk; but, conquer or fall, the Turk is fated to become extinct. But tell me—for we shall have little time to ourselves in this meeting—how do you intend to proceed in your project? I almost regret that I am not at liberty to share your perils, if there are such in your path?"

"I have thought of that, Edgar; but I would not bar your path to promotion: I trust you will have a fair field to gam laurels in. Of course, the war has changed my plans altogether; there is some difficulty now; but still I am resolved even to risk life in discovering my sister."

"There is another thing strikes me, Harry," said Lieutenant Erwin, laying his hand on his friend's arm, "you who

used to be the life and soul of our mess, whose spirits never flagged under peril or difficulty—how is it I see you so depressed? You cannot hide your feelings from your old friend and companion."

"Well, I admit it, Edgar; I am somewhat low, but shall I make you my father xxmfessor," he added, with a smile.

"Oh, by Jupiter! now I see through the matter. In love at last, I'll stake my existence—you, who always laughed at a midshipman being in love."

"Faith, Edgar," returned Henry, with one of his old laughs, "do not you talk to me of love; every petticoat you saw, whether it covered the ankle of a mulatto or one of the copper-coloured damsels of Cape Coast, became an object of attraction for the time."

"Well, upon my honour, Harry, you must admit that the flutter of a petticoat in the wind is always a signal for a mid's heart to get a palpitation. We could not live without a little love now and then. It is the salt junk and tough dough we eat, causes this curious kind of indigestion; but now I see it's a complaint of that kind that affects you. I'm quite easy. So you are caught at last. What is she? A woman, of course; but, as our long-bearded allies say: 'Bishmilla'—may your shadow never be less. Tell me Eh, who the deuce have we now'?" suddenly exclaimed Edgar Erwin, interrupting his discourse, and looking up.

His companion turned also, and, as he did so, he beheld a tall man, habited in the long flowing robes of an Armenian, with a high, conical cap. His immense beard, whiskers, and mustaches, concealed every part of his face, except his long hooked nose and a pair of piercing grey eyes, darting eager and enquiring glances at the two young men.

"Signors," said the man, in good Italian, "I am an astrologer and fortune-teller; for ten copecks I will disclose to you the past and the present, and for ten more, the future."

"What the deuce is the fellow saying," cried Lieutenant Erwin, "I can manage enough French to keep me from starving; but of Italian, not a word."

"He says he is a conjuror or fortune-teller, and will tell you the past and the present."

"Confound his impudence," said the sailor, laughing. "I can do that myself. Can't he do anything better than that?"

"If you give him twenty copecks he will give you a peep into the future."

"Now, that's just what I do not want to know. I hate forestalling things. If am to be shot in this war, it would not serve me a jot to be told so."

"Well, friend," said Fitzharding, facing the silent and motionless figure of the Armenian, "neither my friend nor myself are at all fond of astrologers or fortune-tellers; but here are a few copecks for your trouble, and loss of time in accosting us."

"And yet, signor," returned the Armenian, in a calm, steady voice, "though you are not an admirer of astrologers, you have lately felt a deep interest in an astrologer's fair daughter."

Pitzharding gave a start, quite observable to his friend, and his cheek flushed, as he fixed his eyes, with an enquiring glance, upon the Armenian.

"What the deuce has he said to make you flush in the face so, Pitzharding?" demanded Lieutenant Erwin.

Before our hero could muster his thoughts or reply, four or five English naval officers came laughing and chatting across the room; and, seeing Lieutenant Erwin, they advanced towards him.

The Armenian, in a low voice, said, bending his head towards our hero, "I shall be here, signor, this same hour tomorrow; if you will believe in the stars, I may give you intelligence worth more than four hundred copecks; and, turning rapidly round, he mixed with the crowd that bustled and moved through the wide saloon of the coffeehouse.

Pitzharding was introduced, by Lieutenant Erwin, to his brother officers; and a couple of bottles of champagne having been discussed, they all returned to their boats. Our hero changed his attire, and then proceeded to dine on board the frigate, commanded by his old friend and former commander, Captain P.

CHAPTER X.

A Night of anxious thought followed the dinner on board the frigate, where Pitzharding had been received with all the genuine kindness and hospitality for which English sailors are famed; and to the exhihrating effects of which, he, for a few hours, had yielded. But again alone in his yacht all his uncertainties returned, and sleep was long banished by the conflict. The resolve to seek his sistea was as strong as ever; but his hitherto determined devotion to the young princess had vanished before the captivating influence of Irene. In vain fie considered it impossible for him to wed the daughter of a man who acknowledged himself to be a charlatan, and *to* whose mysterious conduct he could obtain no clue. Even whilst he made the resolution to think of his late companions no more, the vision of Irene rose to his view, and his heart told him he loved her. Nor was the remembrance of Ida without its effect; her affection, never sought to be concealed, soothed his agitation, and, in spite of the suggestions of pride, he treasured the memory of their few short weeks of intercourse.

The words he heard from the Armenian in the coffeehouse were strange, but he wondered more at the man's motive for seeking him than at the knowledge he possessed concerning his affairs. He would not become the dupe of a mere juggler; but he would see him again, and for that purpose his previous intention of leading in com pany with the frigate should'be abandoned.

The next morning, as he sat at breakfast with Mr. Bernard, the latter said—

"There is a fine leading wind through the Bosphorus, sir, into the Black Sea, and it's a rare wind here; do you think you will sail to-night?"

"Yes," returned Fitzharding, "perhaps before sunset. I am anxious to reach the fleet; so you may be ready the moment I return on board. I have an appointment at a cofiee-bouse to-day, at two o'clock, which will delay me an hour; so that we shall have daylight to make a start with. "

Making a hasty meal, Fitzharding proceeded in his gig to Topkhane, and thence to the coffee-house, which contained its usual'amount of visitors. Seeking out as private a recess as possible, he waited patiently the arrival of the Armenian. Amused for a time by the singular spectacle the saloon exhibited—so many and so varied were the costumes; at length he beheld the Armenian making his way through the crowd, his keen, grey eyes roaming all round the various recesses of the saloon, till his glance settled upon our hero, to whom he at once advanced, and making a very humble salutation, stood silently, with his eyes bent upon the floor. Fitzharding did not utter a word, but scrutinized the man from head to foot, and from present, combined with yesterday's observation, felt satisfied that he was not an Armenian.

The man at length lifted up his eyes, saying, in a low voice—

"Signor, I have been consulting the stars, and"—

"Stop there," replied Fitzharding, in a firm and rather commanding tone; "I do not want to have any more of such cant and hypocrisy. I have seen quite enough of astrologers, conjurors, and charlatans; therefore I will now speak plainly," and, taking from his purse, as he spoke, some pieces of gold, he laid them on the table, adding, "that money shall be yours on certain conditions."

The man's eyes glistened as they rested on the coin; but he bowed his head, and crossing his arms, said meekly—

"Let the Signor speak his will."

Fitzharding had selected a lonely recess, and ordered a few rather expensive luxuries, requesting the attendant not to place any one in the same recess with him; he was therefore quite out of hearing.

"You have," he began, addressing the Armenian, "obtained certain information, (how, it matters not to me) of persons with whom I am acquainted; now, if you can give me any important information respecting those persons, I will double that sum. Pray, are you aware of whom I am speaking?"

"Perfectly, Signor;" returned the Armenian, "you are speaking of a person, calling himself Paskovoi, whom you met in Gibraltar, and whom you brought here in your yacht. He had two young and very handsome females with him; one he represented as being his daughter—the other as a Greek maiden. Am I correct, Signor?"

"You are," observed Fitzharding, in an agitated voice and flushing cheek, wishing, yet dreading, to hear more; but, looking the Armenian steadily in the face—" now answer me a few questions. In the first place, was the Signor's name Paskovoi? and, was one of the females his daughter?"

"No, Signor, his name is not Paskovoi; neither is either of the females his daughter."

"Then, who are they?"

"Signor, I will even answer you. As your offer of payment is liberal, I would serve you fairly. I shall neither injure you or this Paskovoi, as he calls himself; but, Signor, I must have your sacred word, that what I confide to you goes no further. It is a somewhat dangerous revelation; but I want gold, and for gold I would do much. Have I your word, Signor, neither to question me concerning myself or my proceedings, and that, when we both leave this coffee-house, you seek no further to trace me?"

"You have my solemn word, that in no way shall 1 seek to injure you, or, in fact, make the slightest inquiry after you. In an hour from the time we separate I shall be under weigh for Sebastopol."

Our hero felt singularly excited as he thought of the beautiful, the fascinating Irene proving to be a different person than what his mind and thoughts pictured her. He burned with curiosity, and yet almost wished to refrain from further questioning; but, making an effort, he conquered his feelings, and said—

"Now then, say, who is this Paskovoi? and who are the females with him? There is a sum," putting down a few more coins," that may tempt you to speak the truth.'

"I shall speak the truth, Signor, and state only what I know to be truths, and which I heard myself from this Paskovoi." As he spoke those words, the Armenian closed the glass doors of the recess, and pulled the curtains across the glass, so as to prevent any one even, seeing them discoursing. He then continued—"Signor, the man you knew as Paskovoi is a Eussian."

"A Russian!" exclaimed Fitzharding, though not much surprised. "And the young female calling him father r"

"All I know of her, Signor, *is,* that she also is Russian; that she was taken to England seven years ago, by that man calling himself Paskovoi, to be educated and trained, so as to follow the same occupation as her supposed father."

Fitzharding started.

"What! her father professes to be an astrologer; surely, surely, he does not mean to make "—

"Nay, Signor," interrupted the Armenian, calmly, "you are in error; Paskovoi, though quite capable of being an astrologer or-wizard, is not such in reality. He is a paid spy or agent of Russia, and it was intended that his supposed daughter should ha;e become one also."

Confounded and dismayed, a feeling of infinite disgust came over our hero. So abhorrent is the character of a spy.

Then the thought struck him—could this information be depended upon; and yet, what object could this man, who was, no doubt, a Russian himself, have in deceiving him?

After a few minutes, looking up into the face of the Armenian, he demanded—

"What proof can you give me that what you assert is fact?"

The Armenian put his hand within his vest, and drew forth a parchment, folded into several parts, like the leaves of a book. Opening this, be selected a page, and then, turning to our hero, said—

"Can you read writing in the Russian language?"

"As well as my own," returned Fitzharding.

The man seemed surprised; but, holding the side of the parchment, which had an official seal of some kind attached to it, towards Fitzharding, he said—

"In this document the names of eight individuals employed by the Russian government are set down, the country they are resident in, and the signs and tokens by which they may be known to other agents of the government. Here, you see, is the name of Paskovoi—real name Ivan Gortsure."

"Ivan Gortsare, did you sav?" exclaimed Fitzharding, springing from his seat as if electrified. "Good God! that is the man that the Princess Warhendorff"-

The Armenian fell back a pace or two, evidently startled; for he thrust the parchment into his breast, saying—

"How is this, Signor? Do you know Ivan Gortsare, and yet did not recognize him as Paskovoi?"

By this time Fitzharding had recovered his presence of mind. He easily conjectured that this man was also a paid spy of Russia, and that whatever he knew of Ivan Gortsare, he could know nothing of his connexion with the Princess Warhendorff, and he determined he should remain ignorant; but bitterly he regretted that the knowledge he had now gained was not learned while he was yet. a guest on board his yacht.

Suddenly a fresh idea entered his brain, which drove all the blood in his body to his head. Was it possible that the likeness he had always seen in Irene to somebody he had once seen, was a strong resemblance to the Princess Warhendorff. And Ida—"Heavens!" he mentally exclaimed, "Ida is as surely my lost sister, Julia!"

Long as it takes to describe the thoughts and reflections of our hero, they consumed but a few seconds of time. Turning to the Armenian, he said—

"You have fairly earned the gold, take it, and there are a couple of pieces more. Your information is to me valuable. Render it more so, by answering me another question:

"Who is the Greek maiden that accompanies Ivan Gortsare's supposed daughter?"

"That, Signor, I really cannot do. He told me himself that she was an orphan English girl, who attended upon his supposed daughter, and who had accompa-

nied her into other lands. You have all the information I can give you, Signor. Are you satisfied?"

"1 would, if I knew where to find this Ivan Gortsare, willingly pay twenty gold pieces."

"Signor," replied the man, speaking firmly, "that I dare not tell you. Ou that point I am sworn—sworn on the cross. No gold shall make me break that oath. "

"God forbid I should tempt you," said Fitzharding, seriously. " Tou may now go. But stay; may I ask you, what induced you to accost me? and how you knew that I was owner of the yacht that brought Ivan Gortsare here?"

"Those questions are easily answered," returned the man, carefully stowing away his gold, " and you will be surprised by their simplicity. I was crossing the Golden Horn, from Galata. When Ivan Gortsare was leaving your ship, I passed within a few yards, and recollected him at once. I told the man to pause who was rowing the caique I was in, for I was struck by the circumstance of Ivan Gortsare being on board an Ealish yacht, with two females in his company. My profession calls for a keen and watchful eye. I observed j'Ou, Signor, and I recognised you again, when I observed you here, yesterday. It occurred to me to try if a gold piece or two was to be made in my character of an Armenian fortune-teller. The start you gave, and your change of colour when I hazarded a few sentences, proved to me you were somehow interested in Ivan Gortsare or the females under his charge; and as I wanted money for a certain purpose, I hit upon the scheme by w'hich I gained it. I have told you the truth. My intention has not been to injure any one, and I do not think I have. You may, and, of course, do detest the character of a tpy; but did you live under the iron rule of a Russian Czar, you would think twice before you refused an office, hateful and degrading as it is."

With a quiet salutation, the pretended Armenian turned, and opening the glass door, silently glided out amidst the noisy and bustling throng without, and was lost to Fitzharding's sight, who, with his mind and thoughts fully occupied with what he had heard, left the coffee-house, hastened to the landing-place, and, entering his gig, pushed off for the Medora.

CHAPTER XL

In less than an hour after the return of our hero, the Medora was under full sail. The Golden Horn was left, and, with, a strong wiud, the yacht was cleaving the narrow waters of the Bosphorus, on her pasaage to the Black Sea. Disturbed and perplexed in mind, as he undoubtedly was, Fitzharding could not but gaze with admiration—that for the time absorbed all other feelings —on the shores between which his vossel glided on those bright, sparkling, quiet waters, forming such a contrast to the turbid waves of the sea he was approaching. On one side was Constantinople with itfs thousand domes, minarets, and mosques, with the suburbs of Galata, Pera, and Tophana; on the other, Scutari and its adjacent villages; whilst towering over all, in the distance, rose Mount Olympus. Each instant presenting fresh objects of beauty, the Bosphorus stretches its silvery length, uniting two seas and separating two worlds.

"How extraordinarily lovely"—observed our hero to Mr. Bernard, who was near him—" are both sides of this beautiful water! You know these Straits. What place is this before us?"

"You should see it, sir," said the master, "in all its glory, when the vineyards are green, and flowers of every hue are mingled, with fig, plantain, and orange trees peeping out from amidst the luxuriant foliage of those valleys, shining domes, gilded minarets, and glittering kiosks. As you proceed, you will nevertheless, see, amid all this beauty, some grim old ruins, scathed and blackened by time."

"No doubt," observed Fitzharding, "those ruins could tell strange tales and tragedies of the olden time."

"No doubt of that, sir. I don't like the Turks, never did; but, beg your pardon, you asked what those buildings are. They are the European chateaux. There

is Eoumeli Hissar. I was told by a very intelligent Greek, who sailed with us through this strait, that Mahomet II. built it, as far back as the fifteenth century. There is the Valley of Sweet of Waters."

"This sail," observed our hero, who continued gazingupon the scene with intense pleasure, "repays the traveller for much of previous toil. Look there! those kiosks and magnificent gardens; terraces actually overhanging the waters; imperial palaces, in every shape and style of architecture; frowning castles, no doubt built by that once powerful people, the Genoese. Altogether, it is truly imposing"

"You will see a strange contrast, sir, when you open the waters of that dreary sea before us. We are now running through the Narrows; and, even with this strongbreeze and press of canvass, we make but little way, the current is so very strong. It's called the 'Devil'sCurrent.'"

"I should like," observed Fitzharding, as they attained a more open spread, "to spend a day or two in the proper season, at anchor off Bebek, so as to visit the Valley of Sweet Waters. It is described as well worthy of inspection, for there meet all the youth and beauty of Turkey; crowds of Greeks, Armenians and Turks, without number; storytellers, Arabian musicians, and Circassian dancers; even the ladies of the Sultan and their children use the fountains, and repose beneath the shade of those great plantains."

"I do not wonder at their being glad to get under the shade of those fine trees," observed Mr. Bernard, "for it is confoundedly hot in this part of the world, duriug the summer months—quite an oven."

It was quite dark before they made the waters of the Black Sea, when, shaping their course for Sebastopol, their canvass reduced and all snug, the watch set, and the weather looking moderate, Fitzharding retired to his berth, not to sleep, but to ponder over the events of the last twenty-four hours.

The intelligence he had received from the false Ar iaenian was perplex-

ing, and, in many respects, painful. Notwithstanding his assertion that Irene was a Russian, and had been educated to act the part of a spy, he had no belief in it whatever. In his own mind he felt satisfied she was the Princess WarhendorfPs daughter, and that Ida was his lost sister, Julia; but to attempt to unravel the strange mystery of their being with Ivan Gortsare, and submitting to such deception—for he felt assured-both maidens were quite aware who they were, and consequently who he was. Some strange and incomprehensible cause must exist to prevent Ida, knowing their relationship, from declaring herself." His next wonder was, where could they be going to. They had left Constantinople almost immediately; so, at least, he surmised, from what the Russian agent said. Ponder over each circumstance which way he would, he was singularly puzzled how to proceed. The only consolation he had, was in the perfect conviction of his sister and Catherine being in existence.

In the midst of his troubled reflections, our hero recollected the letter left with him by Ivan G-ortsare— not to be opened till within sight of Sebastopol—perhaps that might throw some light upon this, to him, incomprehensible affair. The distance from the Bosphorus to Sebastopol is about three hundred and fifty miles. With the breeze as it then was, in their favour, the Medora would run that space in less than forty-eight hours.

On ascending to the deck next morning, Fitzharding perceived they were out of sight of land, the sea was considerably agitated, and the weather looked stormy and wild; dense masses of cloud came up from-the southwest quarter, though the wind had shiftad more into the southward, blowing off the coast of Asia Minor. He inquired of his first mate if the wind had been steady during the night.

"Off and on, sir," replied the mate. "Squally; but we tried the log several times: we never made less than nine knots, and sometimes over ten; but we shall have some rough weather, sir, before niht."

"So I think," observed Fitzharding.

"I would rather not make the coast of the Crimea during the night. It's a wild shore with this wind, and there must be a vast number of transports and shipa-of-war either at anchor or cruising off the coast, and these nights, though short, are intensely dark."

"You can shorten sail, sir, at sun-down, or lie-to," answered the mate, "till day-light. Mr. Bernard has just turned in; and he was thinking the same, sir."

"I see half-a-dozen vessels in our wake; what are thay? I suppose you passed them."

"Oh yes, sir; went by them as if they were at anchor. Two of them were large, heavily-laden transports; the rest were private merchant vessels, I should sup-pose. 'We passed a frigate working to windward, sir, just about dawn, and Mr. Bernard showed British colours and the royal yacht flag."

Mr. Bernard appeared at breakfast, and Fitzharding stated to him his opin-ion respecting approaching the Crimean coast during the night.

"I perfectly agree with you, sir. I see every probability of this wind increas-ing, and it sends a very heavy sea, in-deed, in upon the coast of the Crimea; it's an ironbound shore. I do not know how our ships can ride out the heavy gales so common in this stormy sea."

During the day the wind and sea in-creased, and before sunset the Medora was under double-reefed top-sails, and her top-gallant masts struck. After set-ting the watch she was hove-to, and making excellent weather of it, Fitzharding left the deck about twelve o'clock, and shortly after retired to rest.

Towards morning the gale increased; but as soon as it became light, Fitzhard-ing and the master came upon deck to relieve the two mates. The Medora bore away for Sebastopol. The waves were not near so mountainous ast in the At-lantic or the Mediterranean; but a bro-ken, dangerous kind of sea, much more unmanageable than the long swell of the Atlantic.

As the day advanced they passed sev-eral vessels—some lying-to; others labouring heavily in the broken seas.

Two or three large steamers were making head against the gale; plunging, at times, their entire bows under the wa-ter, sending vast clouds of foam and spray over their decks, hiding them from view.

It was the first of October, and the weather was even then giving symp-toms of what it would do in the dreary winter months, Before twelve o'clock, the high land of the Crimea—the unfor-tunate land of the Crim-Tartars, wrested from them by cruel deceit and the over-whelming power of grasping Russia—was visible.

Fitzharding could not but gaze upon that land, then the scene of a momen-tous conflict, without a strange feeling pervading his mind.

British blood, as well as that of France, had already watered that land; and no man could tell how much more was destined to flow! He knew not that even at that moment our brave army was beginning to feel the bad policy that led to sending so small a body of men, at so late a season of the year, and so ill provided, to battle against the might of Russia. He was not then aware that Bala Clava was in possession of the British; or, indeed, any harbour on that inhos-pitable shore; but he expected to see the fleet riding at anchor before Sebastopol.

As they ran in with the coast the gale began to abate; for the changes in the Black Sea are rapid and strange— from summer to winter, and *vice versa,* is on-ly the work of a few hours.

The dark, lowering sky began to open, and the thick atmosphere over the shore to lift, and the view to become ex-tended.

Two hours after mid-day, they could make out their situation and the land be-fore them, and every eye on board was directed towards the shore they were ap-proaching, expecting to make out Se-bastopol and the allied fleet. The fleet they discovered stretching in one vast line along the shore. Hundreds of ves-sels, of all sizes, were lying at anchor, riding with top-masts struck, pitching heavily in the swells.

, ""We are several leagues to the east-ward of Sebastopol," observed Mr.

Bernard to our hero, who was exam-ining a recent chart of the Black Sea. "That must be the harbour of Bala Clava the fleet are lying off. They have taken possession of it, no doubt."

"Yes," exclaimed Fitzharding, "that must be Bala Clava, by the look of the hills and the stupendous cliffs bodering the shore;" and taking up his telescope, he directed it towards the coast. After a minute's survey, he handed the glass to the master, saying, "You can make out the old ruined castle, perched upon a high cliff, forming one of the entrances to the harbour. Bala Clava is celebrated in Genoese story."

In another hour they could discern the different ships. Amongst them the huge Agamemnon and the Britannia, Vice-Admiral Dundas.

Looking along the line as they ap-proached, Fitzharding ceuld see Captain P.'s ship, on board which was his friend Edgar Erwin. She was riding at anchor, very close to the Vengeance, Lord E. Russell, and the Arethusa, Captain Sy-monds.

"Where would you like to come-to, sir," enquired Mr. Bernard, having shortened sail. "I suppose it will be nec-essary to ask permission to enter Bala Clava, which I would now advise you to do, sooner than remain in this exposed situation."

"I will do so, to-morrow," said Fitzharding. "At present, stand in and pass under the stern of the frigate, and anchor between her and the Arethusa; there is abundance of sea room."

As they neared the frigate, Fitzhard-ing beheld most of her officers on the quarter-deck. Amongst them

Captain P and Lieutenant Erwin. As they rounded her stern, Captain P raised his hat, and Edgar Erwin and the other officers waved theirs.

"Come-to, Fitzharding, as close as you can," cried

Captain P, through a speaking trum-pet. "We have taken possession of Bala Clava, and the army has driven the Bus-sians before them."

"Hurrah!" pealed through the air from the delighted crew of the Medora, who, as she passed the several vessels of war, was gazed at with surprise aud admiration, so graceful was her build and rig, and so man-of-war shape was everything about her. In a few minutes, the sound of the chain rushing through the hawse-hole was heard, and the yacht swung easily and gracefully to her anchor. In as short a time as any man-of-war's men could do it, her sails were furled, her yards squared, and with her stern to the iron-bound shores of the Crimea, the Medora rode at anchor.

CHAPTER XII.

In this chapter we must request our readers to return with us across the waters of the inhospitable sea, as the early navigators styled the Euxine, to Stamboul, to follow, for a while, the footsteps of the false Paskovoi, and the two fair girls under his protection.

As the caique receded from the side of the Medora, in the Golden Jforn, Ida Myreti felt her heart sink within her, and she burst into tears. Irene, who held her hand in hers, and though Ida's face was concealed by the hood of her mantle, knew she was weeping. She knew too well the cause; and, though her own heart was sad enough, she pressed the hand of her friend, and whispered words of comfort and hope in her ear, as her head rested on her shoulder.

Paskovoi himself remained in great abstraction till th; boat touched the landing-place, and then he roused himself from his fit of reflection.

There are abundance of portera always at hand in Stamboul, watching the landing of Europeans; and telling two of these men to take charge of his luggage, the Signor turned to the two maidens, and telling them to keep their hoods well over their faces, he assisted them up the long flight of stairs, and then desiring the porters to proceed t J a street he named, they all moved on, traversing the crowded and bustling narrow streets of the city, till %ey reached that named by the Signor Paskovoi; then the porters paused, demanding which house.

Paskovoi pointed out in this quarter—almost entirely inhabited by Greeks—a house of rather better appearance than the rest, and there, on the door being opened by a woman of the lower order of Greeks, they deposited their load. Just as the Signor Paskovoi was about to follow the two maidens into the house, he felt his arm grasped by some one from behind, and turning with a start, he beheld a tall man in the Armenian dress and conical cap, with long flowing beard and mustaches.

He stared at the stranger uneasily for a moment, till he whispered a few words in his ear. Paskovoi looked round with a start, and then said—

"You here, since when?"

"Since Gottzen died of the cholera," returned the stranger.

"Well, come back in an hour," remarked Paskovoi, seemingly much chagrined, " and we will have a talk over our affairs."

"Very good," returned the Armenian in Russ. "How luckily I caught a glimpse of you coming up from the landing-place."

Paskovoi cast a look of vexation after the tall form of the Armenian, muttering—

"Lucky, you call it. My evil star sent you in my path."

He then entered the house, and found the two girls sitting in a large and well-furnished chamber, and the Greek domestic very busy in putting aside their mufflings, and seemingly anxious to make them comfortable.

"Who are your inmates now?" demanded Paskovoi of the woman.

"Not a soul these last three days," she replied.

"So much the better; however, you must go out and purchase some necessaries; we shall remain a day or two, perhaps it may be more, though I think the steamer sails to-morrow; however, I will go and enquire. Is there. anything, Irene, you would wish me to purchase for your comfort, previous to sailing?" he demanded of his supposed daughter.

"I require nothing," said Irene, with a sigh, "except to return, as soon as possible, to my beloved mother."

"Your wish will soon be gratified," returned Paskovoi, "for I trust the steamer for Trebizond sails in the morning. I will go this moment and enquire; the office is close by." So saying, he left the chamber, the woman going out after him, and locking the door, put the key in her girdle. The girls, thus left alone, sat for an instant silent and motionless, till Irene, putting her arm round Ida's neck, drew her towards her, and kissing her pal© cheek, said—

"You must not give way to despondency, beloved Julia, at this parting from your brother; it will only be for a time. Surely it was a great and unexpected blessing for you to see him, to know him, and to be able to say he is all a fond sister could wish."

"Yes, it was a blessing, dear Catherine," returned Julia Fitzharding, for such was the real name of the fair Ida Myreti. "A noble, generous, true-hearted being is my dear Henry. I glory in him. Ah, Catherine, how often have you and I talked of him, and pictured him to ourselves. You loved him as a boy, Catherine. Now, confess, does he not only realise our imaginary portraits, but infinitely surpass them?"

There was a flush on Catherine's cheek as she replied: "He is, in truth, all you could wish him to be. At times you frightened me, on board the yacht. Your feelings, oftentimes, were near betraying you."

"Yes," said Julia, " they frequently overpowered me; he must have thought my conduct very strange, if not unfeminine. Do you remember how positive I was it was he? He saw me at the opera. But I tell you what makes me more depressed than I otherwise should be now that I knew my dear brother has not forgotten his lost sister, but is actually proceeding to risk his life in searching for her."

"Then what is it so particularly depresses you, Julia, knowing that Ivan Gortsare has left a letter that will be the means of guiding him to you, and that a few thousands will restore you to his protection and to your country? Alas! Julia, it is I that feel the depression you speak of acutely. You, whom I love with, if possible, more than a sister's tenderness, will be separated from me, for, perhaps years may not liberate my beloved mother or myself."

"And do you think, my own Catherine," said Julia, in a tone of gentle reproach, "that I will leave you in captivity? No, no. I have read both your heart and Henry's. You love him, Catherine. You always loved him, even as a child; but now, your love equals his own; and I know he will never be happy till he finds you, and throws himself at your feet, and devotes himself to you for ever."

"And yet," answered the young Princess, for our readers, of course, are, long before this, aware that Irene Paskovoi is no other than Catherine, daughter of the Princess Aarhendorfi—the title being hereditary in the female line. "And yet," added the young Princess, in a touching and mournful tone, "he parted with me, thinking we should never meet again."

"Yes, dear Catherine; but did you observe the terrible struggle that was taking place within his breast—the real anguish he showed—how his hand burned, and no words could pass his lips. I saw his look, it was one of deep love and devotion; but, recollect, what could he do or say. Coming, as we did, in a manner so suspicious and mysterious, on board his yacht, looking upon you as the daughter of a man he must suppose either a charlatan or adventurer, what could he say or do."

"You forget, dear Julia," replied Catherine, "that I am a Russian, and that a deadly war now rages between our two countries."

""What cares love for those obstacles," returned Julia, with a faint smile. "As to this war, it cannot last. Old England will gain the day, and your mighty Czar will be glad to make peace. You must not be angry with me, dear Catherine, for giving victory to my gallant countrymen. You know you are nearly half English yourself."

"Yes," answered Catherine, with a serious smile, "my mother's English blood caused the Czar's resentment and cruelty to my beloved father. But we have wandered, Julia, from our subject. You said you had other causes for depression, what are they?"

"I will tell you, Catherine, though you may think them unfounded, or, at best chimerical. I fear Ivan Gortsare. He has some strange projects in his head. He was always a moody man, and you know his mother was a Circassian, nobly descended, he says, and torn from her family, in one of the frightful massacres of those noble and high-spirited people, and brought into Russia by General Warhendorff's father,"

"Well, there is no mistrust to be entertained of Ivan Gortsare, dear Julia, because his mother was a Circassian. There are many hundreds of Circassian women who, during the late and present wars, were carried off and afterwards married to Russian serfs."

"Ah," remarked Julia, " yours is a cruel and degrading custom; and, one day or other, these wretched serfs, or rather slaves, will overpower their masters, and take terrible vengeance upon their oppressors."

"You know, dear Julia, I do not deny the justice of your remark; but it is in vain for us to talk of these things. Go on with the cause of your suspicions against Ivan Gortsare. I acknowledge I never liked him; still, he has hitherto acted with strict fidelity to my family. But for him my beloved mother would never have seen my poor dear father before he died; and it was through his intercession we were permitted to be brought up in dear England, which I shall always love and remember. So far, Ivan Gortsare has been our friend."

"All this I acknowledge, Catherine; but I think he had hidden motives in being so," Then, looking steadily into the beautiful eyes of the Russian maiden, and drawing quite close to her, she whispered—" Are you aware that Ivan Gortsare is a, paid spy of the Russian government?"

"Good Heavens, what is that you say!" exclaimed Catherine Warhendorff, with a start and a pale cheek.

"Hush, the key turns in the lock," said Julia; "she or he is coming back; and, though the woman is kind, she is a Greek, and not to be trusted. We will resume this conversation when we go to bed."

Ivan Gortsare and the woman, Alexina, entered the room together; the latter carrying a basket full of provisions.

"I am happy to tell you," remarked Ivan Gortsare, '' that the steamer for Trebizond sails to-morrow, as early as eight in the morning. She sails but once a fortnight; therefore, we were lucky to arrive as we did in time, and not be delayed here. Alexina will prepare whatever refreshment you may wish. I shall not see you any more to-night."

The young girls quietly bade him good night, and he retired to another, but remote, chamber in the house, where there was wine and refreshment brought vhim. In half an hour, the Armenian made his appearance, and was at once introduced into his chamber by the Greek woman.

As soon as she had retired, the Armenian sat down, and helped himself to wine, saying—

"Here's your health, Ivan Gortsare, and success to our missions. How have you sped in England; are the Islanders as easy to gull as the followers of the Prophet?"

"It requires but little art to deceive that nation of shopkeepers," returned Ivan Gortsare; "pay them for what you get, and they won't trouble you with questions; besides, the country is overrun with mustached Poles, Germans, and foreigners of all kinds, in the shape of artists, players, singers, and foreign quacks, who all humbug John Bull out of his cash, that a regiment of Rus-. sians might live dispersed over the country, and do and see what they like. All they seem to think or care for, is making and spending money, and seeing sights, no matter of what kind. They have crystal palaces turned into huge taverns, where they gorge, and drink, and amuse themselves; for nothing is to he done in England without drinking. As to the war they are disgusted ahout it; furious with their ministers, and advisers, and generals; and yet, with singular apathy, make no attempt to get rid of them. J often thought, while in England, to turn quack doctor; there is nothing pays like it. You can't take up a paper, but it teems with wonderful cures, pills, wafers, elixirs, and works upon the million and one diseases these Islanders seem to en dure: coughs of nine years' standing cured in ten minutes; cancers, incurable ones, cured by pea meal, under a splendid name; and all the inventors make their bread by them, and spend thousands, besides, in advertisements."

"Bishmilla," said the Armenian, with a laugh, "it's a fine country, it's wonderful! Here, it's all bosch; there's no money to be had; your quacks would have to eat each other. But, Ivan Gortsare, tell me, did you get many plans of their dock-yards and defences? Did they admit you P"

"Nothing easier than to get to see them. I have not been idle: I have forwarded much information to St. Petersburgh."

"And who are the females you have with you?" asked the Armenian, with a keen inquiring look. "I caught a glimpse of their faces as they came out of the caique—they are lovely!"

Ivan Gortsare tried to look composed and unconcerned, but he was evidently uneasy; he, however, replied— "One of them is a native of St. Petersburgh, who went to England, before the breaking out of the war, to learn the language and manners of the people, she will be employed by the government; the other is a poor English girl that attended on her, and goes with her; she is an orphan, and will be made useful."

"But how did you procure a passage in that magnificent yacht belonging to that English milor? did you run no risk from such intimate intercourse, and with two such handsome girls in your company?"

"Curse your inquisitiveness," mentally ejaculated Ivan Gortsare; but he still replied patiently, "I only came from Gibraltar in the yacht; the vessel I left England in sprung a leak off Cadiz, and with great difficulty we reached the Rock, and. then, as it was blowing hard, she ran aground near a place called Europa Point, and was so damaged as to require unlading. The yacht belonging to the English gentleman came into Gibralter the next day, and hearing she was bound to the Crimea, I made a bold move and requested a passage for my-

self and daughter, and her Greek attendant; I passed myself off for a Greek, and as we kept to our cabins the voyage was easy to get over."

"And what is taking this English milor to the Crimea? He must be immensely rich to have such a yacht, and manned by eighty men, and armed, too! Were you able to make out his design for such a trip at this season of the year?"

"Curiosity; what else?" returned Ivan Gortsare, a little impatiently, " he has been in the English navy, and was a lieutenant in a ship of war. But," he continued, l, how came you to replace Gottzen? I thought you were destined for Sebastopol, and to penertate into the English and French camps; so it was, settled when I saw you last."

"Ah! I contrived to get out of that situation; it was not to be trifled with; if caught, it is certain death. Gottzen happening to die at the nick of time, and fortunately, knowing the Turkish language, I got his berth. Where do you go next, Ivan?"

"For the present, I proceed to Sinope, by the Trebizond steamer."

"Well, I wish I could get a mission to England," said the pretended Armenian, " I should do very well in that country; here I try my hand at fortune telling, and at times pick up a trifle from foreigners; the Turks are too poor. I should like to try my luck with that English milor, I suppose he is as easily gulled as the rest of his countrymen."

Ivan looked at his companion for a moment, and then laughed, as he replied—

"You had better let fortune-telling alone, my friend; and, above all things, avoid that Englishman, he has no faith in the stars, and would laugh at you; he sails, however, in a day or two."

"By St. Nicholas," said the Armenian, "I wonder he did not try and coax one of your pretty companions from you! Ah, you look serious at that; perhaps you intend to take one of them for your own wife, eh?"

Gortsare looked daggers; but, for some reason or other, he did not appear to wish to quarrel with his companion,

for he merely again laughed, saying—

"It's a dangerous thing for a man of fifty to take a wife of eighteen. However, it's getting late; I have some letters to write, and one or two in cipher, so I must waste no more time."

"Well," observed the Armenian, rising, "I will see you in the morning, or some time in the day. I have a little project in my head that might suit you to join in. You know our salary is not so large that an addition to it would be inconvenient." He then took up his conical cap and departed. Gortsare saw him to the door, and there bade him good night. When he returned to his room, he locked the door, and threw himself into a chair, with a look of intense vexation, muttering to himself sundry sentences, such as—

"That fellow would sell us both, if he could pocket twenty copecks and keep his head on his shoulders. I'm not safe an hour where he is; but I will get rid of him before I quit this. I'll hand him over to the tender mercies of the Turks."

Having made this resolve, he filled himself a goblet of wine, and then took his desk and passed two hours in writing letters in ciphers, before he retired to rest.

CHAPTER XIII.

The steamer to Trebizond was a Turkish boat, of some one hundred and fifty horse power, neither remarkable for its beauty or its cleanliness. The saloon was small and inconvenient, possessed neither state cabins or private berths, and was crowded with an extraordinary mixture of passengers of all kinds.

Ivan Gorteare, and our fair heroines, on getting on the deck of the Trebizond, were confounded by the confusion and noise, the Babel of tongues, and the extraordinary diversity of dress and costume. There did not appear, however, to be either a French, English, Italian, or German passenger; but there were Turks and Jews, Armenians and Circassians, Persians and several other strangely-attired Asiatic tribes, the entire deck was scattered over with piles of luggage and cargo; the funnel was throw ing out volumes of black smoke, and there being little wind at the time and a hazy atmospere, everything was covered with black smut; what with the roar of the steam, and the shouting of the sailors, who appeared to be mostly Greeks, and the gabble of the numerous passengers trying to get their luggage and goods into a safe place, the two girls became confounded; they saw that the cabin was even in a worse state; so wrapping themselves in their fur mantles, Ivan Gortsare placed them for the time near the wheel, seating them upon a couple of boxes, being part of their own luggage. In such a state of confusion the steamer weighed anchor, the captain telling the angry passengers they would have time enough to settle themselves and their luggage before they opened the rough waters of the Black Sea. ""We shall have a miserable time of it, Catherine," observed Julia, "if rough weather sets in. What a contrast to the elegant and orderly deck of the Medora!"

"It will only last two or three days;" returned Catherine "Warnendorff, in a resigned tone, "and if it does not rain I would rather remain here, wrapt in our fur mantles, than go below in that crowded cabin. What a strange contrast to the English steamers!"

"Ah!" said Julia, with a sigh, " dear England! when shall we see your shores again?"

"And yet, after all, Julia," said her friend, in a gentle tone of reproach, " you are a Russian by birth, and so is your brother; you must not despise the land where you first drew breath." -"I would never despise the land that calls my own Catherine its child," replied Julia, pressing the Bussian maiden's hand, " let it be as wild as the summits of the Caucasus, on which we have so often gazed in our childhood with so much awe.—Look at those Circassian women crossing the deck, how graceful and fine their figures appear, in their pretty costume, to those clumsily attired Armenian women they are speaking to."

"The Circassians are a fine people; as generous as. brave. Alas! my dear father went, with reluctance, to fight against them; but he censidered he was doing his duty in obeying the cruel mandates of the Czar. What a punishment we have all suffered in consequence! My beloved mother confined for years within the limits of a Caucasian fortress! And but for the noble generosity of Prince Schamyl how miserably hard might all our fates have been. The clouds have dispersed a little, owing to this terrible war; and, perhaps, we may look forward with hope."

"Yes," said Julia, thoughtfully; "if once we get back safe to the fortress of Prince Schamyl." They ceased conversing, for several of the Armenian and Circassian women came up and settled themselves near them. The steamer, in the meantime, ploughed its way through the Bosphorus, and then into the open waters of the Black Sea, when it became exceedingly stormy; and Gortsare having secured two berths for the two half-perished maidens, they proceeded to take possession of them, and partaking of some slight refreshment they carried in their little baskets, they laid down in their berths dressed as they were, drew the curtains, and strove to forget the disagreeable noises that proceeded from the machinery and the gabble of some thirty or forty passengers, who not only eat and drank in the saloon, but smoked their pipes and chibouks till the two girls were nearly suffocated with smoke. The distance from Constantinople to Trebizond is above seven hundred miles; but the steamer had to call at Sinope, a place that will be long remembered as the first port where the cruel massacre was permitted to be enacted by the Russians upon the unfortunate Turks. With the memory of that savage and cowardly outrage ringing in the ears of all Europe, why was Odessa spared?

At this period there was entertained no fear or apprehension of.Russian vessels of war in the Black Sea, as the English fleet blockaded Sebastopol, and the Southern Coast was supposed to be quite clear of the enemy, as the Russian forts on the East Coasts were.without shipping. It blew a heavy gale during the night; but, nevertheless, the steamer—though neither a fast or a very seaworthy boat—as she kept near the coast, and the wind blew off it, held her way, and on the evening of the second day they opened the fine bay of Sinope, and, running in, came to an anchor.

The weather was considerably milder at Sinope, and as a great number of the passengers left the steamer, our fair heroines gladly came on deck, anxious to behold a place rendered so remarkable by Russian barbarity.

Seen from Bos-Jepe (Bull's-head), Sinope has a picturesque and singular appearance. No matter from what quarter the wind blows, ships ride at anchor with safety between its two roadsteads. The girls gazed with a melancholy interest upon the ruined walls and shattered defences—upon its wilderness of cypress, and laurels, and olives, and pomgranates; the tin cupolas, tiled roofs, and minarets, peeping up here and there. Towards the cape they perceived it was flanked by huge Byzantine walls and towers, mostly, however, in ruins. The town they saw was also surrounded with walls and extensive fortifications. While they were gazing at the scene around them, Gortsare approached, and addressing Catherine Warhendorff, said, that as the steamer would stay two days at Sinope, they might land, as he could procure good accommodation in a Greek house, and, perhaps, be able to hire a Greek girl to accompany them the rest of the way, as an attendant.

They were rejoiced to leave the steamer, if only for a couple of days; the variety of passengers, and their strange manners, and more than disagreeable customs, making their stay on board anything but agreeable. Accordingly a boat, manned by Greek boatmen, was soon procured, and they were pulled ashore. Having landed in the vicinity of the ship-yard, they followed Ivan Gortsare through the few regular streets Sinope possesses, and stopped at a Greek coffee-bouse, a species of hotel.

The number of coffee-houses in Sinope is prodigious; and both Greeks and Turks have a great reputation for idleness and drunkenness: it is said, between them, they consume nearly sixty-four thousand quarts of brandy yearly.

Having procured a private room,

Catherine and Julia enjoyed the quiet and repose the place afforded, besides a most magnificent view over the western roadstead. An aged Greek, his wife, and three daughters, kept the house j two of the girls were pretty, good-natured maidens, and did everything they could to make the young ladies happy and comfortable.

Ivan Gortsare, in-the evening, had their luggage brought them, and very kindly inquired if there was anything he could get them to make them more comfortable.

"No, thank you," returned Catherine Warhendorff, "we are well attended here."

"It will be well worth your while," continued Gortsare, "if to-morrow is fine, to ascend the hill above this Greek quarter; there is an old Roman aqueduct in ruins, and near it a small mosque and the tomb of a Khan of the Crimea. This place is of great antiquity. You can have the two Greek girls to attend you.

"If, as you say, the day is fine, we shall do so," quietly replied Catherine.

Wishing them good night, the Russian left them to themselves.

The next day they were greatly gratified rambling up the hill above the town, obtaining magnificent views over both the adjacent country and the broad waters of the Black Sea.

This two days' respite from the discomfort of the steamer refreshed our travellers exceedingly. The third day, the steamer sailed, and, without accident or encountering any very severe weather, reached Trebizond in fifty hours, thus ending, as they supposed, their sea voyage.

Ivan Gortsare was not acquainted with Trebizond, he therefore was forced to depend on the services of a Greek to take them to a mansion where they could be accommodated with rooms to themselves. Everything else they had to procure, for Gortsare would, on no account, take up his abode in a Turkish house of entertainment.

It was night before they were enabled to procure all the articles necessary to their comfort. Ivan Gortsare spared neither trouble or expense, and the two

maidens felt grateful for his attention. Indeed, latterly, Julia began to think she had judged him rather severely. 'A paid agent of the Russian government, she was satisfied he was; but she was well aware, that, if the arbitrary nature of the Russian government willed him to be an agent, there was no resisting the mandate.

"Perhaps he will explain matters to-morrow," said Julia," you know he promised to do so when we reached Trebizond. We are to have a week's rest, and it will be very acceptable. I wonder what my dear brother Henry is about. I am sure he will never be satisfied at being a mere spectator of the proceedings at Sebastopol. It makes me feel very miserable and uneasy about him: that terrible war has cut off so many of our gallant and devoted army."

Catherine Warhendorff sighed and looked very serious, saying—

"War is a fearful thing to think of. I somehow think kings and potentates must have a terrible responsibility on their heads, when it's either their head-strong passions, ambition, or love of sway, that plunges thousands of their ill-starred subjects into misery and mourning. But it is late, dear Julia, let us to rest, and trust to the mercy of Providence to free us and my beloved mother from the cruel thraldom we shall have to endure, perhaps for years yet to come."

'CHAPTER XIV.

The following morning, immediately after breakfast, Gortsare visited his fair charges, who were much refreshed, and appeared more cheerful and resigned.

"I am come," said he, seating himself, " to give you the explanation I promised, and to consult with you, at the same time, on the best means of reaching the fortress of Prince Schamyl; for I am a little puzzled myself, from the news I have heard, how we shall contrive to get there. I will first explain the past to you; for, in many respects, you are both quite ignorant of how you came to be placed in the strange situation you are in; and, to do this fully, I must go back to the period"—addressing Catherine particularly—" when your lamented father, General Warhendorff, became

detested by the haughty and implacable Circassian Chief, Kasi Mollah."

We must, however, dear reader, pursue the narrative after our own fashion; for there are some that require explanation, and which would not be touched upon by Ivan Gortsare.

It is unnecessary to dwell upon the intense desire of the Czar Nicholas to crush the brave and gallant Circassians. His orders to his generals were, "not to spare them, man, woman, or child."

Now, General Warhendorff, though a kind and humane man in private life, a doating husband, a fond father, General Warhendorff is, of course, as far as *name* goes, a fictitious personage. was a most unsparing general. He falsely considered it his duty to obey the Czar's mandates to the letter; and thus he incurred the hatred of the Circassians and their chiefs.

The Tcherkissians were at that time under the command of Prince Schamyl, who survived, in a most extraordinary manner, the terrible massacre of the " Murids," in the sacking of the Fortress of Hunri. This escape was considered by his religious followers to be miraculous, and, in proportion to the intense devotion felt for him by his followers, so he became hated and feared by the Russians.

Kasi Mollah, the leader of the Tcherkissians, was mortally wounded at the sacking of Hunri—which cost the. Russians twenty-five days' siege, and a terrible loss in men—and just before he breathed his last, called his favourite disciple, Schamyl, to his side, and appointing him his successor, made him swear a sacred oath, never, with life, to surrender to Russia; and that should General "Warhendorff fall into his hands, to put him to as cruel a death as the General had inflicted on thousands of hia brave followers: and should any of this noted General's kith or kin fall into his hands, never to release them, unless they paid a ransom that would beggar them.

This oath Schamyl took according to the most sacred form of their faith. How he escaped the massacre is unknown to us, but escape from Hunri he did, and became the leader of the Circassians.

Prince Schamyl then retired to his famous fortress of Alkucho, General Warhendorff followed him, and, after four months' warfare, and losing a vast number of men, he gained possession of the fortress, and again were all the inhabitants massacred, hoping to slay the Prince, but again he escaped—this time through the devotion of his followers. The effect of this escape was paralyzing to the Russians, who began to look upon the deeds of this brave man with awe and fear.

After the massacre at Alkucho, Schamyl retired to the almost impregnable fortress of Dargo, and there also the

General, Warhendorff, followed him. Dargo is one of most remarkable strongholds in Georgia; built on the summit of a mountain, in the midst of steep rocks, there is no approaching it except through immense forests and tortuous and barren denies.

Schamyl, bent upon revenge, permitted the approach of G-eneral Warhendorff, till he became shut up iu a narrow gorge, and then pouring down his troops upon the appalled Rusisans, like a mighty avalanche, who, hemmed in before and behind, became an easy conquest, nearly all were slain. General Warhendorff, covered with wounds, fell into the hands of Prince Schamyl. The Prince ordered him and his follower, Ivan Gortsare, to be carried to the fortress of Dargo, and then he first recollected, with pain, his oath to Kasi Mollah; for Schamyl was a noble, generous warrior, far from being either cruel, sanguinary, or despotic, though when he recollected that the four-and-twenty Murids massacred at Hunri were slain by General Warhendorff's troops, and by his orders, his heart became in some degree steeled against his prisoner. But General Warhendorff was insensible from his wounds, and the surgeon who dressed them declared that he could not long survive.

When Gortsare was brought before the Circassian chief, the Prince demanded " Who are you; you are not a soldier?"

"No," returned Ivan, calmly, "I am not; I am the personal attendant of General Warhendorff. My father was a Russian, but my mother was a Circassian."

"Ha!" exclaimed the Prince, "a Circassian — her name?"

"She was your father's sister, O Prince; her name was Alexina Anapoli. "

Schamyl gave a start of surprise, and said, " What proof have you of this unlooked for assertion?"

"I have heard my father say," replied Ivan Gortsare, "that my mother was carried off from the fortress of Soucha, after its defenders were slain, and taken to Russia. She married my father, and this"—taking from. Lis neck where it was fastened by a silk cord, a curious purple stone, on which was carved some curious hieroglyphics—" this was round her neck at the time of her captivity."

Prince Schamyl looked grave; he took the amulet from the hands of Ivan, and examined it most carefully. "Yes," he exclaimed, "this is the stone I have heard so much of, he or she who wears it cannot perish by the sword. I remember hearing of my aunt's being carried as a slave into Russia, and that she alone, of all the garrison, escaped being slain by the sword, as she wore this charmed amulet."

"Then keep it, my Lord Prince," replied Gortsare, earnestly; "my heart was always in my mother's land, and from childhood I have panted for freedom; the degradation of a serf has cut into my very suol. Nought but the kindness I experienced from the General Warhendorff and the Princess, his wife, restrained me seeking to raise the serfs on her domains, and endeavour to regain, our freedom or die. When the General was ordered into this country, I implored to follow him, hoping to regain the land of my mother's birth, and obtain my freedom."

"Prom this hour you are free; but a Russian name will not do to dwell with us. You must drop your father's and take your mother's. You are welcome to share my fortunes from this day, and, if willing, you may do us good service."

Ivan Gortsare, as we shall still, to avoid confusion, call him, willingly agreed to the Prince's proposition, but begged permission, while the general lived1, to remain as his attendant, saying, "he is wounded to the death, Prince, and will not long trouble you."

"So much the better," replied Prince Schamyl. "otherwise I must keep my oath, and put him to death."

Ivan Gortsare, who was a man of deep thought and reflection, was imbued with an intense love of freedom; he had always abhorred the state of serfdom in which he lived, and the degradation the serfs are always subject to. A serf may arrive at a state of affluence; he may even become so opulent as to reside in St. Petersburgh, keep his servants and carriage, and frequent the best society; but, at any moment, he is liable, at a word from the lord whose serf he originally was, to be pushed from his position, and to become the meanest drudge of his master. To escape such a liability was Ivan's greatest anxiety, and he formed a plan, which his frequent conversations with Schamyl upon the subject of the war, seemed to render easy of accomplishment. The grand want of the Circassians was the sinews of war. Money was their aim, for without it they were unable to procure arms and ammunition. So eager were they to maintain their freedom, that they frequently bartered their daughters with the Turks of Stamboul for arms.

"I will put you in a way, Prince" said Ivan Gortsare, "of procuring a vast sum of money."

"How?" cried the Prince, eagerly.

"Your prisoner, the general, is dying; but it is by slow degrees. He burns with a deep anxiety to behold the Princess (his wife) and his child. The Princess adores him: she would sacrifice life—if such was to be the penalty—in order to see him again. I will return to St. Petersburgh, and engage to bring her and her child here. She would pay an immense ransom for her release, after her husband's death."

"No," said the Prince, "that would be acting with treachery. Besides, were the Princess once in my power, I have sworn never to release one connected by ties of blood with General "Warhendorff, except by extorting a ransom that would beggar them."

The Prince was generous and bold in his nature; but the Circassians wanted arms and ammunition, and the other chiefs were not so scrupulous. Ivan Gortsare's project found favour with them; and, while Schamyl proceeded into Albania to carry on the war, Gortsare set out for St. Peterburgh as an escaped prisoner, with the full intention of bringing the Princess to her husband, who still survived, and who earnestly implored him to do so, not being aware of the fate that awaited her, if she followed the dictates of her heart, but firmly believing that a moderate ransom would release her.

Ivan, without being a very bad man or a very good one, was yet playing a deceptive part with all parties. He loved freedom; but it was not the species of freedom to be enjoyed in Circassia that he admired. Every man among the Tcherkissians, 'capable of bearing arms, went to the wars. Ivan was not a warrior, he was not a coward, but he was no soldier; he would not injure the Princess Warhendorff personally, but he had no scruples in making use of her to further his own views; his project was to gain a handsome independence for himself, and then retire to some European state, out of the reach of the Russian power—he fancied England—and towards England his thoughts were turned. On reaching St. Petersburgh, he found the Princess Warhendorff in deep affliction and despair; the Czar, exasperated at the loss of his army, had confiscated the property of General 'Warhendorff, and sent the few officers who escaped from the battle to Siberia.

The Princess feared her husband was dead, and her joy was excessive when Ivan Gortsare secretly informed her that he was still alive, though a prisoner, and that he ardently desired to see her and his child, and had hopes of gaining his pardon by ransom, should he recover from his wounds.

The princess immediately and eagerly proposed setting out for Odessa, and

there leaving the young daughter of Mrs. Fitzharding, proceed by sea to Trebizond, and thus gain the Portress of Dargo. But this mode of proceeding did not suit the views of Ivan Gortsare, and before he had quite settled his plans, news reached the Princess of the death of Mr. and Mrs. Fitzharding.

She was shocked and horrified; Ivan Gortsare persuaded her to proceed at once to Taganrog, keeping the two children with her. The English child, who had now no parents to protect and watch over her, would be happier to remain with her beloved companion than living with strangers.

Anxious to reach her husband, the Princess made no objection to the proposal, but left St. Petersburgh and proceeded on the journey to Taganrog; and, so cleverly and well did Ivan Gortsare manage the route, that he baffled all attempts to trace the Princess further than G-olagouzki.

After a long and difficult journey, they at length reached the Circassian Portress of Dargo, and, to her infinite joy and delight, the Princess found her husband still alive, and, as she considered, with every prospect of recovery; but in this she was deceived, for, after lingering for four months without suffering much pain, he died.

Prince Schamyl, on his return to Dargo, was grieved to find the Princess Warhendorff an inmate of the fortress. According to his oath he could not release her without demanding the entire fortune she possessed., That question was soon settled; for the Czar, exasperated at the flight of the Princess, seized her estates and mansion, and, having a strong suspicion that General Warhendorff was not dead, and that the Princess had gone to join her husband in his captivity, to punish her for disobedience to his orders—for he had forbidden her leaving Saint Petersburgh—confiscated her property.

This Ivan Gortsare did not expect; but it was not upon her fortune that he built his future hopes of independence—he actually conceived the idea of being able to secure the wealth that would, without doubt, be left to the young Julia

Fitzharding.

CHAPTER XV.

Time rolled on. The Princess and the two children, shut up in the Portress of Dargo, till Prince Schamyl, too generous and lofty in his ideas and projects to render the afflicted Princess more miserable than she need be, removed her and the children to another fortress, beautifully situated in one of the valleys of the Caucasus.It was not an important place, and not likely to be attacked, by Russia, as it was more a rural retreat than a fortified castle, but the country around it was beautiful and peaceful, and the air mild andsalubrious.

Gortsare had arranged with some of the Circassian leaders that he should play the part of a spy upon Russia, and return, as if escaped a second time, to St. Petersburgh, and discover what the Czar's designs were; for there was even at that time symptoms of his attack upon Turkey.

His return, after an absence of two years, created considerable surprise to the friends of the Princess Warhendorff, who now expected to gain intelligence of her whereabouts; but, in twenty-four hours after his arrival, he was seized and imprisoned by order of the Czar; and when this became known, the name of Ivan Gortsare or the Princess "Warhendorff were no longer mentioned.

We must not, however, weary our readers with minute details of Ivan Gortsare's proceedings. In two months he was visited in prison by the chief of the police. After a lengthened conference he was released, along with two other Russian serfs, like him, men of great intelligence and education; for being a serf does not force a man to be either ignorant or deprived of resources; the better informed they become, and the higher the branch of trade or employment they enter into, the larger the sum they can afford to pay their lord and master for their liberty; but the rod is for ever over their heads.

Gortsare was appointed a government agent or spy, along with Gottzen and another, named Perkoff. This man was also a serf of the Princess Warhendorff, and had formerly much intercourse with Ivan, and he it was who personated the Armenian fortune-teller in Constantinople, to which place he was removed after the death of Gottzen.

Gortsare's destination was Stamboul. There he passed for a Greek, under the name of Paskovoi; but he had no intention whatever keeping faith with Russia. So, as soon as he could do so with safety, he was preparing to escape to Circassia, when he received a mandate to proceed to England, containing instructions how to act, and how to correspond in cipher.

In some respects this suited his views. Quitting Constantinople, as if for England, he made his way to the fortress of Dargo. Conveying intelligence of movements in Russia and Turkey, of infinite importance to the Circassian chiefs.

G-ortsare then proceeded to see the Princess Warhendorft", who always considering him a faithful follower, and devoted to her family, beheld him with great pleasure. The difficulty the Princess laboured under was, how to get the two beautiful girls, whom she loved with equal kindness, to England. Prince Schamyl consented to their,going for a few years, but a meeting of chiefs deliberated, and finally insisted that they should, after the lapse of a certain period, return to the care of the Princess, and then, if the sum agreed upon was paid, in either money or arms and ammunition, they should all be restored to liberty.

Anxious in her heart that the children should receive a European education, she removed from the secluded fortress they inhabited, and where they were unavoidably exposed to much peril, in many ways. The Princess, though it grieved her heart to part with them, agreed to the terms proposed. The Princess's family was one of rank and station in England. Lord B was the head of the family, and resided at the family mansion in Dorsetshire. The PrincesS was permitted to confide the children to his care during their stay in England, both being represented as the Princess's daughters. The letters they were to take

with them were to represent the Princess in,banishment, and that on no account whatever was it t o be known that she was even in existence; as the future fate of her children depended on her strictly obeying the Czar's orders. When leaving St. Petersburgh she had carried money and jewels with her to a large amount— and these she had still at command—so that Ivan Gortisare was fully provided with funds to bear all expenses during their absence. The Princess then undertook to prepare the two girls to take the solemn oath, to keep what they knew to themselves secret, and to implicitly,obey Ivan Gortsare.

This parting from their mother, for the Princess had' conscientiously performed a parent's duty to the little Julia, caused the poor children much sorrow, and many hitter tears.

They were both, for their age, singularly well instructed; they could speak the English and Russian equally fluently; could read French and Italian, but of music they knew nothing whatever; for no musical instrument found its way to the Fortress of Nachltz, if we except the species of guitar, used by the Circassian women.

Gortsare was intrusted with the two children, who were of an age perfectly capable of understanding the consequences of breaking the sacred pledge exacted from them. There was no difficulty in reaching England at that period; all the countries they passed through were at peace, and modes of travelling easy and commodious; steamers plied to all parts, so that starting at a favourable period of the year, their apparently long voyage was accomplished without risk, or much fatigue.

Lord and Lady B received their relations with intense surprise, but exceeding cordiality and hospitality; they read the Princess's letter, and did not feel much surprised at the mystery that was thrown over her fate, knowing right well the terrible despotism that reigned throughout the Russian dominions. Charmed, with the two graceful and beautiful children, pitying their situation, and their future uncertain fate, and

that of their mother, Lord B resolved to be a father to them.

If happiness was to be enjoyed, away from their beloved mother, the two maidens would have been most happy under the hospitable roof of Lord B——
.

Masters of all kinds were procured, and a governess of high respectability; they were introduced to his lordship's circle of acquaintances, as the orphan daughters of an old and esteemed, but distant relative, of the name of Fortescue.

Gortsare having performed hia part to the satisfaction ,of the two young girls—to whom he had showed every attention during the journey—took his leave, impressing on their minds to be cautious and silent for the Princess's sake. From Lord B he received a very handsome donation; and remained in England, transmitting to Russia various letters in cypher, but of little consequence to the interests of the country he was in, till rumours of the approaching war induced him to make a journey to Circassia.

Embarking in the regular steamer to Constantinople, he crossed the Black Sea in another steamer to Soucha, and thence to the fortress.

He found the Princess—still remarkable for her beauty —contented, now that her child and her *protegee* were in a country she dearly loved, and with relations who were able and willing to protect them.

Everything was done by the noble Prince Schamyl to render the Princess's abode in the lovely, but secluded Fortress of Nachtlz, as desirable as possible; her two female jattendants were persons of a highly respectable grade, and greatly attached to their mistress. Another year, and her beloved children would be restored to her.

After exhausting every question fond affection could devise, concerning her children, of Ivan Gortsare, the Princess began requesting information respecting Henry Fitzharding.

Ivan Gortsare had been most particular in his enquiries concerning our hero, and he informed the Princess that he had been placed in the navy by his uncle and guardian, and, just before! he had left England, he learned that he become, by the death of his father's brother, the nest heir to the ancient title of Courtland, and that every one in the vicinity of his uncle's residence talked of the enormous wealth he would succeed to.

The sum expected by the Circassian chiefs for the release of the Princess, her daughter, and *protegee,* amounted in English money to the really enormous sum of one hundred thousand pounds; a sum that would have absorbed the entire of the Princess's property and estates, had they not been confiscated by the Czar.

"And how," said the Princess to Ivan Gortsare, "is this immense sum to be paid?" She spoke in an exceedingly depressed tone. "For I see no chance of the Czar's relenting. With the permission of Prince Schamyl, I forwarded, many months ago, a humble petition to the Emperor, beseeching his forgiveness for seeking my husband's death bed, contrary to his orders. After a time, I received the Emperor's reply; gracious and kind enough, but still leaving me hopeless. He even condescended to answer the letter himself, and sent it by a special courier from Taganrog, who delivered it at one of the advanced posts in the Caucasus.

The Czar declared he regretted my captivity, but that it was my own seeking; that if free, he was quite willing to restore my rank and estates, having suffered enough from my disobedience; but to restore them, so that the enormous sum of one hundred thousand pounds British, should be paid for my daughter's ransom, was out of the question, as it would be the means of supplying an enemy he was resolved to crush with the means of resisting him; it was not to be thought of; but,' before another year should expire, the whole Circassia, Georgia, and all the rebellious Provinces, should either submit to his rule or be exterminated by fire and sword.

"But, Madam," said Ivan Gortsare, after a moment's thought, "Mr. Fitzharding, when of age, will eagerly

pay that sum to release you. He will have over sixty thousand pounds a year. What if he does sacrifice ten thousand pounds a year of that income to raise the one hundred thousand pounds; he will still possess a fortune beyond the wants of any individual."

"True," returned the Princess, with a sigh; "but who can tell how that young man's mind may be biassed. The love of gold is very powerful in the human heart. Possessing thousands, we crave millions. He may not be willing to sacrifice so large a sum; though, in truth, he was a noble, high-hearted, generous boy, and vowed he would love and protect my Catherine through life."

The tears ran down the cheeks of the Princess, and her beauty at that moment looked so touching—she was but four-and-thirty—that Ivan Gortsare, whose heart was not naturally bad, was overcome. At first he turned very pale and looked agitated, then cast one look at the sorrowing Princess, whose kindness and generosity had always been extended towards him—whose father had released him from a life of drudgery, educated him, and placed him in a situation far beyond his hopes—and yet he was about to betray ber and deceive her.

That cold, iron heart gave way, and, throwing himself at the astonished Princess's feet, he exclaimed—

"Forgive me for what I have done, and by this sacred symbol"—taking a cross from bis breast, "I swear to you, that all my future efforts shall be to restore you and your child to liberty."

"Oh, Ivan, Ivan, what is this you say?" exclaimed the Princess, pale as death, and clasping her hands. "You deceived me! Ah, my God! is there no faith on earth?"

Ivan Gortsare rose to his feet, pale and dejected in look, but perfectly calm and collected. After a moment, he said, looking steadily into the features of the Princess, who was weeping, "I have sinned, madame, but my repentance is sincere; it was not my iutention, believe me, to injure either you or your daughter; I sought my own aggrandisement, and my own freedom from the degradation of serfdom, which galled me to

the soul, and made every hour of my life one of torture."

"Still," said the Princess, "I do not understand how you have deceived me; I came here at my own discretion, I was aware I should have to pay a large sum for my release, and to a certain extent I was aware that the Emperor would resent my disobedience."

"Ask me not, madam, what my projects were, I have abandoned them, they were chiefly directed against the wealth of the English maiden. I intended to secure an independence in other lands, by appropriating a portion of her future' fortune—but the idea that I was a eerf galled me. From the period when I first conceived this project, I have known no peace, for it was to be carried out by deceiving you, and retarding your emancipation. Prince Schamyl dare not break his oath, and the other chiefs of the Tcherkissians are all of one mind, in demanding the sum of one hundred thousand pounds for your release.

"Till Mr. Henry Fitzharding is of age, it would be useless negociating; neither will the chiefs permit my attempting to do so, unless they hold in their power the two young ladies; they say that if anything of the kind was attempted, and it was known they were in England, their friends would not permit their departure. They therefore bound me, by the most sacred oaths, not to reveal their names while in foreign lands, but to bring them back here, and then communicate with Mr. Fitzharding."

"But if this war actually takes place—and Prince Schamyl declared that either Turkey must be assisted by England and foreign powers, or else she will fall a victim to Russia's desire of aggrandisement—if this war then breaks out, how will you be able to reach this Fortress with my daughter and Miss Fitzharding? Russian men of war will scour the Black Sea; if you fell into the hands of Russia, I might never see my child again; for the-Czar would claim my daughter as a Russian subject, and Miss Fitzharding would remain in captivity."

"But the was with England is not declared yet," said Ivan Gortsare, "even if it was, we can reach Constantinople at any time; and then, if necessity required it, procure a passage in a Greek vessel to Trebizond, and thus avoid all Russian vessels and ports."

After some further explanation, Ivan Gortsare left the Princess to ponder over what he proposed, while he himself sought an interview with Alanza Gour.

CHAPTER XVI.

It was finally settled that Ivan Gortsare should depart at once for England, and return, without delay, with the two girls. The Princess, who had suffered much grief at the confession of his duplicity, saw him depart, with full confidence in his sincerity. At parting she said—

"If ever it is in my power, I will not only restore you to liberty, but render you independent for life."

Gortsare kissed the Princess's extended hand, and swore to be faithful and true to her, and to bring both children back to her arms, safe and uninjured.

Ivan Gortsare carried with him letters to Lord B from the Princess, in which she stated she had every reason to hope she should soon be reinstated in her rank, and her estates restored. She expressed her deep gratitude for his lordship's paternal care of her daughters, and trusted that no war would break out, to interrupt the friendly intercourse of the two nations, as it was the dearest wish of her heart to visit England, and return thanks in person.

She also wrote to her daughter, and to Julia, telling them to confide in Ivan Gortsare, and obey his instructions, as she now felt perfectly satisfied he would faithfully perform his duty.

In the lapse of years—for nearly seven had passed from the period of their quitting Circassia—the two fair girls had grown up into womanhood, the admiration of all who beheld and associated with them. 'In manner and appearance, Catherine Warhendorfi' had become quite as English as her friend; each treasured in her heart a vivid memory of the past. Nothing from their earliest childhood was forgotten; and for hours they would sit and converse over the scenes and adventures of their girlhood in Russia and Circassia.

Henry Fitzharding was the constant subject of their conversation. Catherine Warhendorfi" cherished the memory of her early playmate with a singular and fervent tenacity; it was a feeling grafted in her heart, that neither time nor absence effaced or weakened.

Lord B knowing the connection that had formerly existed between the Warhendorff family and the Fitzhardings, often talked about the large fortune inherited by Henry Fitzharding, and the untimely death of his sister; for his lordship had heard the same version of the story as the Czar, from Ivan Gortsare, that Miss Fitzharding was carried off by the cholera on the journey into Circassia.

The girls, therefore, without exciting any surprise, were enabled to ask many questions concerning their early playmate. They heard he had entered the navy as a midshipman, and become a Lieutenant, and had, as far as lay in his power—considering times of peace—distinguished himself.

Time rolled on, till the rumours of war became reality; they heard of Henry Fitzharding's return, from the coast of Africa, and of his quitting the navy on coming of age.

Every day they expected the arrival of Ivan Gortsare, and as the time for their departure arrived, Lod and

Lady B began to feel that losing them would be a severe blow to their domestic happiness; for the two girls had won not only their esteem, but the sincere love of their generous host and hostess.

Just at this period an event occurred that had an influence on the after fate of Julia Fitzharding. Lord B 'a estate was on the estate of the sea coast of Dorsetshire, within half a mile of the harbour of. During a sudden gale, and dense fog, the S sloop-of-war went on shore, and was only got off by throwing most of her guns and heavy metal overboard, and loss of her false keel and foremast. She wass with some difficulty, got into the harbour of, and then her officers and men commenced recovering their guns, &c.

Her commander, Captain the Honourable George

D, was a distant relative of Lord B 's, and was at once invited to the hospitable house of his lordship during the time employed raising the guns and repairing damages; his officers were also' often invited. Lieutenant Edgar Erwin was one, and during a dinner party given by his lordship, chanced to sit next Julia Fitzharding.

Julia was pleased at meeting a naval officer, particularly when that officer was a tall, and very handsome young man, full of life and vivacity, and as chatty and agreeable as young naval officers generally are. Every opportunity to hear of her brother was eagerly sought by Julia, who ventured a question she heard with delight answered by the young officer—

"Oh, dear, yes; I served six years in the ship you have just named."

"It must be very distressing," again remarked Juliav "after living so many years in companionship with your brother officers, to be suddenly and unceremoniously separated from them."

"That, Miss Fortescue, is one of the miseries of ar sailor's life. In the same ship, I had a comrade I loved as a brother; no finer fellow ever walked a deck than Henry Fitzharding."

A slight exclamation escaped the lips of the delighted girl, the rich colour in her cheek rivalled the peony, and as the sailor looked into her features, he muttered to himself "by Jove, she is too lovely; those blue eyes of hers would breed a mutiny in a three-decker."

Two or three times Lieutenant Erwin visited Lord

B 's, who took an especial liking to him. His frank and pleasing manner, high spirits, and graceful person won upon them all, and it was with great regret that they beheld the departure of the sloop-of-war.

It cost Lieutenant Erwin a struggle, also, to say good bye. He reasoned with himself and laboured to convince himself he was under a delusion, as it was quite impossible that he could fall in love with a ward of Lord

B 's. He, a poor lieutenant in the navy, with scarcely enough pay to find himself in uniforms and cigars.

It was no use, his arguments. Lieutenants in the navy are quite as liable to fall in love as any one else. So poor Edgar Erwin took his leave, vowing, if fighting could make him an admiral, he'd give the Kussians enough of it. He forgot, as he made this vow, that we never make admirals or generals in the English service till nearly too old to be of use, and certainly too old to think of love.

Julia did not bid the handsome sailor farewell without feeling something more than common regret in losing an agreeable acquaintance; but, situated as she was, she strove to steel her heart against the shafts of Cupid.

Ivan Gortsare arrived in England, but he did not immediately proceed to Lord B 's mansion, as he first was anxious to discover what our hero was about. It is remarkably easy to obtain intelligence of the movements of a man in the position and possessing the wealth of Henry Fitzharding. His having purchased one the finest and largest yachts in England, and his intended,voyage to the Black Sea, and the seat of war, convinced him that Fitzharding must have some intention of tracing his lost sister. By patient and cautious enquiries, and being perpetually on the alert, he knew pretty accurately, his time of departure for the Crimea, and then concocted his own plans.

On reaching Lord B 's mansion, he found that the family were in London. One evening, at the opera, as Julia happened to look across the pit, her eyes for an instant rested on the features and tall form of Henry Fitzharding; was it nature that spoke to that fair girl's heart, or was it memory wakened up after a lapse of years? The moment their eyes met she felt a tremor over her frame, her heart beat wildly, and pressing Catherine's arm, she whispered "Good heavens! see, there is my brother Henry, looking intently at us."

Catherine felt her cheek blanch, as, turning round, her dark and brilliant eyes met those of Fitzharding.

"It is he, as surely as I live! oh, Julia; there is no alteration in his expressive features, except that he has grown *jaore* manly; I dare not look at him any longer."

Turning to the Hon. Mrs. Grenfell, under whose care they had visited the opera, she whispered in an agitated voice—

"Pray, madam, do you happen to know who is that tall gentleman in the pit, leaning against the fourth column from the entrance?"

Mrs. Grenfell, who knew every body in the fashionable world, looked carelessly round, and then said, with some animation—

"Oh, dear, yes; that is the handsome Fitzharding, as the ladies call him—the man with the iron heart; he isa millionaire, has mixed in the first circles, seen the most beautiful women in England, and is actually going out to the Crimea to be shot or die of the plague, and he the next heir to a fine old title, and who might aspire to the hand of the proudest beauty in England."

We pass over the parting with Lord and Lady B.

who were, in truth, greatly grieved to lose their children, as they had often called them, and who now sent them forth laden with valuable presents and letters to their mother.

Ivan had arranged his departure from England so as to reach Constantinople before the Medora, little foreseeing the storm which disabled his vessel and compelled him to take refuge in Gibraltar.

As soon as he beheld the Medora in the bay, he resolved to make the attempt to gain a passage on board her for himself and his two charges. He should thus, if he succeeded, bring Henry Fitzharding intimately acquainted with the beautiful Catherine "Warhendorff, which, he made no doubt, would hereafter facilitate the negotiations for their release. Extorting a sacred promise from the two overjoyed girls, that they would neither by word, deed, or in any way betray their individuality to Henry Fitzhardiug, he proceeded on board his vessel. *"We* have seen how he succeeded.

These details are much more explicit than Ivan Gortsare chose to give in his explanation to the two girls, as we thus avoid useless mystery and windings up in the sequel, when the interest of the story ia over.

He was listened to with surprised attention by the two girls; for though aware that the Princess Warhendorff was a captive to the Circassians, they did not know know that there existed so much difficulty in restoring them all to liberty; or that so enormous a sum was required for their ransom; but, after a moment's thought, Julia said, emphatically, that her brother, she felt confident, would, if it deprived him of three parts of his fortune, cheerfully, resign it, so that he could release them all from thraldom. "Besides," she added, "I understand my own fortune, left me by my dear lamented father, is forty thousand pounds; that will go a long way-towards it."

"I am in great hopes," observed Gortsare, touched by the generosity and nobleness of the English girl, "that the Circassian chiefs, under the present circumstances, will considerably abate their demands, now that England-is fighting their battles with the Czar; for every victory gained by England is a victory to them also. The grand difficulty now is to get to the Fortress. It would be ruinous to fall into the hands of Rusaia in the present state of affairs. Prince Schamyl is marching upon Tiflis, and the Russians have advanced posts all over the Caucasus; every one coming from the Turkish frontier will he seized and examined with a terrible scrutiny. It strikes me that the only way to reach the Fortress will be to proceed to Batoum, the best Turkish harbour on the frontier; for as the Eussian forts along the coast are destroyed, we could run along the Bhore in a Greek fishing boat, and make a landing on the Circassian coast, near to Holetra; thence we might readily gain the-fortress, going only through the Circassian territory."

His companions replied, that, as they could know but little of the localities, they would abide by his judgnjent; indeed, they preferred the last-named mode of proceeding better than the long land journey, with its risks and inconveniences.

Accordingly, they embarked in a trading brig for Batoum, and there engaging a large Greek zetee, used for trading with the ports in the Sea of Azoff.they embarked, with a calm sea and a land breeze, for the coast of Circassia, keeping within gun-shot of the land. Here we must leave them, and return to the allied fleet lying before Bala Clava.

CHAPTER XVII.

It was the month of October; the allied army had began to invest Sebastopol on the south side, and the fleet to reconnoitre the forts at a respectful distance. Our hero, after spending a few days off Bala Clava, and dining on board several of the ships, sailed in company with the vessel? of war destined to make the attack upon Sebastopol.

The next day was bright and clear; after leaving Balaclava, and rounding Cape Khersonese, and standing away to the north north-west, they came in sight of the farfamed Sebastopol.

It was with an indescribable feeling of intense interest that Henry Fitzharding gazed out over the bulwarks of the Medora upon that gigantic fortress we were led to believe, by several writers, to be so ill constructed, and its batteries so rotten, that on the first discharge they would crumble to pieces, or so ill ventilated were the casemates that the gunners themselves would be smothered.

Viewed from the sea, Fitzharding thought its batteries presented a most formidable appearance. Whilst the ships of war were taking up their positions, one or two of the steam frigates, with the Medora, stood nearer in, to have a better view. It was a beautiful day; the wind blew right out of the harbour of Sebastopol; the sight was altogether most imposing and magnificent. The allied fleet, under easy sail, were spread across the bay, at a distance of three miles from the shore. Steam frigates, and screw line of-battle-ships were clewing up their canvass and anchoring. Signals were flying from the City of Paris, Admiral Hamelin's ship, and the Britannia, Admiral Dundas, with the

Vengeance and the Arethusa, came-to with beautiful regularity, furling their sails and squaring their yards like magic.

"With his glass, Fitzharding had a splendid view of every battery and fort; even the great line-of-battle ships of the Czar were distinctly visible.

Having brought the Medora to anchor clear of the fleet, Fitzharding retired to his cabin, and unlocking his desk, took out the letter Gortsare had given bim, and which he now considered himself fully justified in perusing He was fairly in sight of Sebastopol.

At the first glance, he perceived the letter was in the Russian language, and was a long one.

"You will be surprised, Mr. Fitzharding," it began, "when you learn that the two young females you so hospitably received on board your yacht are the young Princess Catherine Warhendorff and your own sister. It is quite impossible to enter into details here; neither is it necessary. My object now will be to explain to you how you may restore your sister, the Princess Warhendorff and her daughter, to liberty. They are the prisoners of Prince Schamyl, the Circassian leader and prophet, who swore a sacred oath, by the side of the dying Kasi Mollah, that he would never release General Warendorff, if he took him prisoner, but put him to a cruel death; and should any of the blood or connexions of that hated General fall into his power never to release them, unless they paid a ransom that would beggar them. The ransom, therefore, of the Princess Warhendorff, her daughter, and your sister, is fixed at the sum of one hundred thousand pounds British money, as that sum, if raised from the Princess's estates, would deprive her of everything she possessed; but, as the Czar confiscated the Princess's entire property, they will be likely to remain prisoners for life, if you do not come forward to their rescue."

Good God! exclaimed Fitzharding to himself, pausing in the reading of the letter, why did he not state this to me when together? "What care I for a hundred thousand pounds, when put in the

scale with the liberty of those Bo dear to ine? I would, at Constantinople, have negociated, and paved the way for raising the money. Now there will be a tedious delay; but let me read to the end.

"You will wonder," continued the writer, "that I did not communicate with you when in your company; but I was bound by oath not to do so. Your best plan of proceeding will be to sail in your yacht for Batoum, the frontier town of Turkey. At Batoum you must enquire for an Armenian merchant, by name Abdalla Merzon; for a certain sum he will furnish you with an Armenian passport and dress. The Armenians are the principal traders with the Circassians and the Russians, and pass unmolested through the Russian and Caucasian provinces. Your object will be to reach the army of Prince Schamyl, and.negociate with him for the release of his prisoners. He will have you conducted to his Fortress of Nachltz, where the Princess and her daughter and Miss Fitzharding are or will be residing by the time you reach the place. It is now quite possible, owing to the breaking out of the war, that Prince Schamyl, looking upon the English as allies of Circassia against Russian aggression may reduce the Princess's ransom to a more moderate sum. Of this I feel satisfied, that Miss Fitzharding will be released at once, on your demanding her restoration from the Circassian chiefs; they dare not retain a British subject. Trusting you will not delay sailing for Batoum as soon after the reading the of this letter as possible, "I remain,

Your obedient servant,

Ivan Goktsaee."

"Well, thank God! all this is satisfactory, though somewhat mysterious," thought our hero. "Ah, here are a few lines on the other side."

"In the fourth drawer of your Chinese cabinet, in your private cabin, you will find two miniatures, portraits of the young Princess Catherine Warhendorff and Miss Fitzharding; they were taken in England, previous to their leaving London; with their consent, I leave them with you; they will be a proof, if one be necessary, with Prince Schamyl, that you are Henry Fitzharding."

Springing from his seat, with a rush of blood to his face and temples, Fitzharding ran to his private cabin. The Chinese cabinet stood inserted in the panels; it was a curiosity of workmanship, and had belonged to his lamented mother; it contained numerous drawers and recesses, each containing some cherished memento.

Opening the drawer indicated, which contained many beautiful trinkets, and a portrait of his mother, exquisitely painted, he pulled forth from beneath the trinkets two miniature-cases. Opening one, he actually started —so good, so real, was the beautifully executed likeness of Catherine Warhendorff. Laid on the miniature was a slip of paper, and in a beautiful female hand was written: "In the Palace of the Princess Warhendorff, in St. Petersburgh, in the year 1844, Henry Fitzharding vowed 'he would love and protect Catherine "Warhendorff through life.'"

"And so with the blessing of God I will," exclaimed Fitzharding, with enthusiasm, as he gazed, enraptured, on the lovely features before him. Those large, lustrous, searching eyes seemed to speak and sink into his heart.

His sister and all the world were forgotten, as he gazed, wrapped up in his own thoughts, upon the features of the young Princess—when he was roused by the cheerful voice of his friend, Edgar Erwin, calling out from the saloon—

"Hello Harry! where the deuce have you stowed yourself?"

Placing the portraits back in the drawer, which closed with a spring, it first struck him to marvel how Ivan Gortsare got the miniatures into the drawer; but, wishing to join his friend Edgar, he deferred looking at his sister's portrait to another time.

"Well Harry," said Edgar, "here we are before the stronghold of the Czar, and a very pretty looking mass of granite and iron his forts appear; we are going to hammer the fortifications to-morrow, Harry; and so as my luck may be to fall in this glorious contest, for glorious I trust it will be, I have come to spend a few hours with you."

"I shall be alongside of you, Edgar. Captain P has accepted my services, and the services of forty of my brave fellows who have volunteered to go into action— they would all go if they could."

Well, Harry, it may appear strange to some that you should seek to go into action; but, knowing you as I do, I feel no surprise at all; it will be a desperate conflict, depend upon it!"

"I agree with you," replied Fitzharding; "I am glad you are come, Edgar; if you had not, I was going this evening on board your ship. I must draw up a will for fear of accidents; I have found my sister."

Erwin sunk back in his seat, with a look of the most unmistakeable amazement. "Found your sister!" he repeated—" well, by Jove! and you here before Sebastopol!"

"We have never had a solitary hour to ourselves," eaid Fitzharding, "since we parted in Stamboul; and when there our time was limited and intruded upon. Now, after dinner, I will give you a full account of my adventures since I left England, and you will then understand fully my sister's position, and how necessary, if we go into action to-morrow, that I should make arrangments for her and others' benefit should a stray shot shorten, my log. You know my property is my own to will or do as I like with; it's no hereditary estate, to go to next heir; and I should not like it to fall into the hands of a worthy cousin of mine, in default of a will."

"Ah, I understand," said Edgar; "but you'll not get a scratch; you never did, though you have stood exposed to a shower of grape and canister within pistol range, and thrown yourself, single-handed, into a score of bloodthirsty pirates. You are one of Dame Fortune's especial favourites; while I come in always for a share of her frowns, the jade. " CHAPTER XVIII.

Duhixg dinner, Fitzharding gave his friend a full account of Iris meeting with the false Paskovoi and the two ladies, and candidly confessed the deep feeling of love he imbibed for the supposed Irene Paskovoi, and his vexation in hav-

ing allowed himself to be so fascinated. Situated as he was with respect to the Princess Warhendorff, had partly caused the great depression Erwin had observed when they met in Stamboul.

"My interview with the Armenian at the coffee-house in Constantinople opened my eyes," concluded Fitzharding, "for there it was I became convinced that in Irene Paskovoi I had beheld the young Princess, and in Ida Myreti, my sister."

"By Jove, she must have been singularly lovely," said Erwin, seriously, "to have cause you—who, for years, talked and thought of no other than Catherine Warhendorff—such feelings. You must have felt that it was the young Princess. An unknown feeling must have prompted you in the love you felt for the supposed Irene. The Princess must be very beautiful."

"You shall judge," observed Fitzharding, rising. "A likeness to some one perpetually haunted me. While in her presence, her very voice struck some chord of the past; but yet, the wildest dream of my imagination could not bring forth the thought, that, in Irene Paskovoi, I beheld Catherine "Warhendorff. But stay, I will show you her portrait; you will then be able to judge how such beauty acted upon me, excited by an unknown feeling besides."

Fitzharding retired to his cabin, and, opening the drawer, took out both miniatures and returned to the saloon. Opening the case that contained Julia Fitzharding's portrait by mistake—for the cases were the samehe handed the miniature to his friend. No sooner did Lieutenaut Erwin cast his eyes upon the features so minutely portrayed, than he started to his feet, his cheeks deadly pale, exclaiming— "Good God! This, this Catherine Warhendorff!" Though astounded at the paleness and the agitatated expression and manner of his friend, Titzharding hastened to open the other case, saying—

"No, that is my sister; here is Catherine Warhendorff."

Erwin fell into his seat, all the blood rushing back to his face and temples, while he uttered, in a low, agitated voice— "Thank God, I'm spared that blow," and bending his head upon his hands, he remained silent some minutes.

"Edgar, dear friend," cried Pitzharding, laying his hand upon his shoulder, "what is the meaning of this— what has moved and agitated you?"

Edgar looked up, letting his hand rest on that of his friend, while his handsome features glowed with excitement, as he replied—

"Had all the batteries of Sebastopol exploded at my feet, they would not have caused the intense anguish I experienced when you handed me the portrait. And so that is your sister. Good Heaven! how mysterious; but show me Catherine Warhendorff. I will explain by and by. Ah, here is a fold of paper; it must have fallen from your sister's miniature."

Our hero opened the missive. It was in the same hand-writing as the paper in the other miniature; both written, as it appeared, by Julia Mtzharding—

"Dear, dear Henry," began the fair writer, "how in my heart I have yearned to throw myself into your arms; but I restrained myself, for, ah, I trembled often, for I remembered my solemn vow, not, till permitted, to betray my secret. How often my oath was near being forfeited; but for dear Catherine my heart would have betrayed me. Oh, Henry, you love our Catherine, and she loves you. Ivan tells us that he has arranged iu his letter how you are to trace us, and permits me to write these few lines I have put in these cases. God bless you, dear, dear Henry, and remember, go not needlessly into peril, for there are three hearts that beat with love and affection for you, and who look to you as their deliverer.

Your sister,
Julta."

Fitzharding turned, much moved, to his friend, whowas sitting gazing at the two portraits, buried in profound abstraction.

"Well, Edgar what think you? and now, pray explain to me your strange expressions; for I see, like myself, you are a man of mystery."

"Faith, Harry, a few moments ago I felt as miserable as any poor devil condemned to the knout, and am still very far from being comfortable. I have been trying for many months to disguise my feelings and sensations, by an apparent exuberance of spirits, which had you not been under a depression of mind yourself, you would have noticed."

"I certainly have been so wrapt up lately in my own thoughts," said Fitzharding, "that anything unusual in your conduct has quite escaped my observation; but how, in the name of wonder, could the portrait of my sister Julia have so strange an effect upon you?"

"That is very easily accounted for, Harry," replied his companion. "When I beheld the portrait you presented, and which you stated to be the likeness of your beautiful Princess, I felt as if a hot iron was thrust through my brain; for, astounding as it appeared to me, the portrait was that of one I most passionately love—mad and absurd as such a feeling may appear. In truth, I am. insane to nourish such a passion."

Though Henry Fitzharding was amazingly surprised,, he laid his hand upon that of his dearly loved friend,, saving—

"Why such words to me, Edgar? Why should it be madness in Edgar Erwin to love the sister f Henrv Fitzharding? And where, in the name of wonder, ould you have met Julia Fitzharding?"

Erwin was much affected. He pressed his friend's hand warmly, as he replied—

"I "will soon explain that mystery; and afterwards I must let you into some other secrets you are yet ignorant of."

He then made our hero acquainted with the manner in which he got introduced to Julia Fitzharding and the young Princess Warhendorff, at Lord B 's.

"Feeling, as I do," continued Edgar, "a passionate attachment to your beautiful sister, I consider myself bound not to take advantage of your disinterested friendship and noble generosity, without making you entirely acquainted with every circumstance of my life."

"If it will please you, dear friend, to

do so, and relieve your mind of any impression it may have conjured up, as offering a hindrance to a union with Julia, I will listen to you; but I who have associated with you day by day, for seven long years—who stood by your side when balls fell thick as hail around us— back to back, we have stood the brunt of death from overpowering numbers, and when I fell, who carried me on his back, under a scorching sun, till help was gained—I, who knew every action and thought of your heart during those long years—do you think that anything you can say can alter my opinion, or my resolve? because, whatever you have-to say, I know has no reference to your conduct or your principles. Now, aay on; you cannot change my resolution."

CHAPTER XIX.

"My first recollections, carry me back," began the narrator, "to about my sixth year. This period of my life is most painfully impressed upon my memory, by an event that occurred when about that age; and most singular, it appears to me, as if my life began at that period, for I have no recollection of any event before it, or of persons, or things, or of my having had any other name than Edgar.

"I remember being in a small boat, with a boy of some ten or twelve years, and that we were drifting out to sea, and both of us crying bitterly, for it was blowing fresh. I remember that, for the water splashed over the side of the boat. The boy's name was Will. As we drifted away from the land, he tried to pull with an oar; but it fell into the water, and the ill-fated boy, in stretching over to get it, must have overbalanced himself, for he fell into the sea. It must have been his terrible scream, as he sank, that made so deep an impression upon me; the horror of his dying look, as I screamed in terror, did not leave me for years. After this catastrophe, I must have cried or frightened myself into insensibility, for all I know of the matter afterwards, was, that I was on board a large barque, and that I must have been picked up, the following morning; or perhaps I was two days, for we were out of sight of land, and I was reduced to great weakness. I recovered in a few days, for every kindness was shown me; but my memory and ideas seemed knocked of a heap. Still I recollect all that occurred on board that ill-fated ship, with a wonderful distinctness. It was bound for China, and was called the Ocean Queen, and was commanded *by* Captain John Randal. I almost fancy I can see, at this moment, his fine, open, and kind-hearted features. He was an elderly man, and as kind to me as to a child of his own. There were twenty-four men and three mates in this vessel. I was able to tell Captain Randal a great deal more about myself, at that time, than I remembered afterwards— very probably the name I bore, and who had the care of me, and how I came to be ia the boat; but the lapse of years, and the fearful fate of poor Randal, obliterated all trace of the previous years of my life from my mind. However, the long voyage to China, and the scenes I beheld, began to banish my grief, for I became a prodigious favourite with the crew and their excellent commander. How long we were getting to Canton I cannot say; but we did arrive, unloaded and reloaded, I suppose, for we got again under weigb and dropped down the river, and then got into the open sea. I suppose our captain had been warned to keep a sharp look-out for the proas of Malay pirates, who swarmed about the Java Sea, into which we were to go. So, as soon as we got well to sea, I observed the crew of the barque getting up all kinds of rusty fire-arms and pikes. There was one eight-pounder on board which attracted my attention greatly. I was by this time quite at home in the ship; could run up the rigging and out on the yards, to the infinite delight of the men, who, poor fellows, studied to please me in everything. Captain Randal had garments made for me at Canton; in fact, I wanted for nothing, and got quite reconciled to my position.

"One morning—it was a very calm day, not a breath of air—I had climbed up the rigging with one of the men, and was getting out on the yard, when, as the sailor was reeving the studding-sail gear, he called out that he saw the mast of a proa, dead ahead, and immediately after, when hailed from the deck, he sung out that he could make out several more, but only the masts, and he was sure they were Malay proas. He ascended to the main royal, and could then make out their peculiar kind of masts, which generally do not exceed forty feet in height, so that they could not be more than twelve or fourteen miles off. All now became bustle and activity on board the barque. I came down from my station to watch the loading of the eight pounder with childish glee, little imagining the frightful scene that was to take place on the deck of that doomed ship.

"Two men were sent up to remain aloft to watch the proas, while Captain Randal made his appearance upon deck in a pair of Chinese slippers, a cotton shirt, and a spy-glass. A short time served to convince the captain that they were proas, and that they were coming towards us very quickly. Before ten, we could see them very distinctly from deck, for they were propelled by long, heavy sweeps—each proa rowing twenty-four oars a side. There were three of these large proas; and just visible above the horizon were the masts of two more.

"The boats pulled on till they came within a mile, and they lay upon their oars. I was looking at them eagerly over the bulwarks, climbing up on the carriage of the gun, that was brought to bear upon them—

"' Now, my little pet,' said Captain Randal kissiugme, 'you must go down in the cabin, for fear you get hurt, while we beat those bad men away.' But no persuasions could get me off the deck. One of the men tucked me up under his arm and was walking off with me'; but I roared, screamed, and kicked so, that the captain said, 'Let him be, he is too little to be hit behind the bulwarks. If they do—which God forbid—get on board, carry him down then; but it will be all up with us, my men, if we let the villains board us.'

"Everything was done by the captain and crew to give the Malay pirates a warm reception. The cook had his coppers full of boiling water, to throw in the face of any who might attempt to board; and the cannon, loaded to the muzzle, was so placed that it might pepper them, on whichever side they attempted to board.

"I am telling you my story, Harry, in the words and thoughts of mature years. I was but just seven years old at the time this occurred; still, I retain a distinct recollection of all the events. My sea phrases, 'fcc., 1 borrow for the occasion; for, of course, I knew but few at that early period.

"During these' operations I was in a state of great excitement, but far from frightened; for I knew nothing of the terrible consequences of Malay pirates boarding a ship. I only longed to see the great gun fired.

"Our ship's company consisted of the captain; first,, second, and third mates; seventeen men before the mast; a supercargo, who was a terrible coward and tried to hide himself; a gigantic black cook, who had for-a weapon a huge harpoon; and a steward, who kept the supercargo in countenance, being quite as great a coward, but a desperate boaster.

"Ten men were stationed with the captain on the quarter-deck, the same number on the forecastle to work the gun, and four in the fore and main tops, to act as sharpshooters.

"While we were making those preparations the distant proas had joined the others. So anxiously were we watching the pirates and they us, that neither perceived the royal masts of a ship coming up from the eastward, with a light breeze, while we were in a dead calm. The live poas were huddled close together, consulting, no doubt, which way to attack us. After a while they separated, one of the large proas making for our bows, the other coming up so as to take us two on each side.

"I had contrived to climb up unseen, and got upon the main top, with an Irishman named Bill Houlaghan, to whom I was very partial. He put me alongside of him; so I had a clear view of all that occurred.

"The proa that approached the bow was a very large one, crowded with a ferocious-looking set of half-naked men, armed with all sorts, as Bill said, 'of outlandish weapons,' and also, he added, with a very blank look, 'some muskets.'

"'Be jabers, if they get aboard,' said Bill to me, 'don't you show yourself; hide under this tarpawling, for they will surely murder us all; there are a hundred of them altogether.' This rather startled me. I said,' sure you won't leave me here, Bill, and go down and be killed.' Bill put a plug of tobacco in his cheek, shook his head, and looked to the priming of his rusty musket, saying, 'Be gor, I'll pepper some of their hides first, anyhow, th& devil's children.'

"As they came in range of our great gun, the mate became anxious to try to disable the boat; but the captain had not much faith in the mate's skill as a gunner, and thought it better not; but at last the mate gained his end and applied his match; but the captain was right, the aim was defective, for I could see the shots tearing up the water a long way beyond them. "With frightful yells, the pirates, like evil spirits, urged on their boats. The mate, however, humbled by the failure of his first shot, now loaded the gun to the muzzle with grape and canister, and swore he would not fire till they were close under the bows.

"In the bow of the advancing boat was a colossal monster of a Malay, who appeared the leader; he was quite naked, only wearing some ornaments on his head and round his neck. 'I'll have that chap down,' said Bill, resting his musket and taking deliberate aim, and firing; but he stood untouched, though the ball killed or tumbled over the man behind him. Bill loaded again, with an oath. As the proa reached the martingale, a,dozen men sprang into the rigging, followed by half a hundred more, the huge Malay at their head, whom, straDge to say, Bill missed again, but still knocking over one of the wretches. Just then the mate applied his match. The great charge put in the gun did horrible execution at that distance. I then, for the first time, saw what a cannon could do. The shrieks and yells of the mangled pirates appalled me; but my eyes were fascinated by the gigantic Malay—who, with a frightful yell,

brandished a ponderous kind of hatchet, and escaped again, as if by a miracle, the grape from the cannon— leaped on to the forecastle, amid the discharge of the muskets, and, with a blow of his hatchet, he brained the ill-fated mate. The other boats reached the side, and a swarm of swarthy, naked monsters clambered over, our men cutting them down and blowing many of their brains out; but still, on they came, yelling and screaming like fiends.

"' God bless you, my boy,' said Bill Houlaghan, with a, fierce execration at the pirates, 'I have no, more powder; I must go down and die by the side of my,comrades; take this, and if ever you hear tell of my poor wife, as lives in Plymouth, Kate Houlaghan, give her that, and God send you reach old England. Don't you get out from under this; they won't come here.'

"' Oh, Bill, Bill,' I cried, the tears in my eyes— 'they will kill you!' The poor fellow kissed me, thrust a greasy pocket-hook into my breast, under my garments, and then slid down on the bloody deck. On tLtat sc.ne of horror I must not dwell. I saw our dear old captain backed to pieces, and every man slain brutally, except Bill, and him 1 saw knocked overboard by a blow from the butt of a musket. The deck was literally swimming in blood. The unfortunate supercargo was the last murdered. They tied the wretched man to the mizen mast, and each, with a frightful yell, plunged their knife in him. His cries were horrible, and while bleeding to death, they threw him overboard. The deck was covered with their own dead. Hardly had this frightful act been committed, when the loud boom of a cannon startled the pirates from their work of plunder. I felt ready to faint, for I was quite sick; but the sound of the gun roused me, and imprudently, I stood up to look towards the sound. The pirates, with yells and curses, beheld a sloop of war coming towards them with a fine breeze, and the smoke of the gun was curling up from her bows. Instant confusion and panic took place. What plunder they had collected was tossed into the boats. Just then, one or two wretches

saw my head above the coil of tarpauling, and, with a yell, they snatched up their muskets and fired. I gave a shriek of pain. I was hit in the side, and fell across the tarpauling;.but'I was not insensible. Another gun from the armed sloop caused the monsters to tumble headlong into their boats; but first they set fire to the ship in three places; two took effect, and the flames burst up from the forecastle and main cabin at the same time. "With sail and oar—for the breeze had sprung up—the wretches pulled from the ship, their proas sailing marvellously; but the increasing breeze drove on the good sloop-of-war as an avenger. Two of her boats were lowered and pulled towards the burning ship, while she pursued, firing round shot after the accursed Malays, and, as I afterwards learned, sinking four of them, with all their crew, one alone of the five escaping, by her extraordinary speed. In the mean time the ship was in flames from stem to stern, increased in fury by the strong wind. I could not move a limb though the flames came rapidly towards me; but I screamed with all my might for the boats. So terrible had become the flames, they were keeping to windward. Luckily, or rather by Ood's mercy, I was perceived in the main top by a Lieutenant Erwin, commanding one of the boats. In an instant the boat pulled round, arid after a time this brave and noble-hearted man got a footing on the ship, and, despite the terrible risk, he pushed up the rigging, with the flames hissing and raging as they rushed on from the flaming ship towards the only spot unscathed, the main top.

"' My poor boy,' said the kind-hearted sailor, seeing my clothes covered with blood, and my pale haggard face—' only you alive on board this ill-starred ship, and wounded, perhaps to the death.' I could not reply. He caught me in his arms and descended; but the fire crossed his path, and his men shouted—'the stirboard side, sir, the starboard side is freer of flames.' The vessel had shifted her position. Retracing his steps, he descended the other side, and finally was forced to throw himself, with me in his armes, into the sea, a sheet of flame suddenly interrupting our path. I was then insensible, and, indeed, for many days after, knew nothing of what was going on or where I was..

"From that time, Harry, I became the son of that noble, generous man, Lieutenant Erwin. I have little more, dear friend, to record. 1 have shown how I came under the care of Lieutenant Erwin, who vowed to protect me through life. The ball was extracted from my side by the surgeon of the sloop-of-war, the *Vengeance,* and we returned to England. Lieutenant Erwin was one of those brave, generous hearts one often sees neglected and unthought of in the army and navy. Without patronage or influential friends, he served his country as long as he could, and then, invalided from, «limate and reduced health, retired on the miserable half-pay of a lieutenant."

Erwin remained for more than an hour conversing with his friend, and then, in rather a serious mood, returned to his ship. Fitzharding, in bidding him farewell, said he would join with his volunteers at daybreak.

CHAPTER XX.

It was on the 28th of September, that a large ship, extremely leaky, with the los of her mainmast and mizen, approached the west coast of Ireland. This ship was the "Lord of the Isles," from Australia to Liverpool. She had encountered tremendous gales some days before, sprung a leak, and lost, as stated, her main and mizen mast in the hurricane. The gale had gone down, though the sea continued to roll in on the coast in mountainous swells. The breeze, however, blew steadily towards the iron-bound coast before them, about south-west and by south. The ship was under her foretopsail and topgallautsail, and the crew were actively engaged in getting up a jury mizen mast, so as to be able to set some after sail, to enable them to weather Three-Castle Head, and thus gain either Cork Harbour, or even Milford Haven, so as to be able to repair damages.

"The Lord of-the Isles," however with the heavy swells propelling her towards the land, made great leeway, owing to the want of after sail; for the wind was scant to weather the headlands, so she kept drifting rapidly in with the coast, accelerated by the send in of the south-west sea.

There were about fourteen or fifteen steerage and half a dozen state cabin passengers, but all were on deck, looking anxiously upon the high rocky mounts forming the Mizen and Three-Castle Heads, and against which the huge surges as they rolled in broke with tremendous violence, casting their white foam, like a snow drift, high up on their precipitous sides. They were not more than three miles from the shore; it was three o'clock in the day, and the dark lowering sky showed that the coming night would probably be another stormy one.

The captain, an Englishman, a stout, weather-beaten looking veteran, stood eyeing the land with his glass, and then looking at the leeway the " Lord of the Isles" made, the three mates were actively engaged hurrying the men in their labours with the mizen jury masts.

Amongst the steerage passengers were two connected with our tale. The elder was Mr. Shaw, once known as Captain Shaw, and Director of the Condensed Sunbeam Company; the other was his son. They were both, shabbily dressed, their garments threadbare, and of the very commonest kind worn by the hard working men seeking for gold in Australia, and finding none. The father looked old and careworn; in figure, spare and emaciated, with hair and whiskers thin, and almost white. His son, though equally badly dressed, was a tall, strongbuilt, handsome young man, with dark hair and sunburnt complexion; his features very good, and his eyes keen and penetrating; but there was a reckless, almost savage expression resting upon his face, extremely unpleasant to the beholder, which completely marred nature's work. Their story during the period of eight or nine years is soon told. Mr. Shaw, with his wife and daughter, sailed for Australia, after the bankruptcy of the Sunbeam Company, carrying with him £10,000, gained by trickery and deceit. With this sum Mr. Shaw might have been a very wealthy man in Melbourne, but the money gained by deception and fraud was not likely to be judiciously employed.

The same propensity to villany urged its possessor into schemes and projects, that in less than four years stripped him of every fraction of his ill-gotten plunder. Poverty and misery followed. To add to his degradation, Mr. Shaw became a drunkard, and in six months broke his poor wife's heart. His daughter's fate was more fortunate; she was a good kind of girl, married a respectable man who was clever and enterprising, and who, shortly after his marriage, left Melbourne and went to settle in New Zealand.

Just after this event, Mr. Shaw's son arrived from England, having had just enough money left from the sale of his commission to pay his passage to Australia, where he expected to find his father in affluence; instead of which he found him a pauper, carrying loads as a porter, and actually earning his bread by loading and unloading ships.

George Shaw was shocked, not exactly at the degradation his parent was suffering; but at his poverty; he could give him no help. They then agreed to go gold hunting, but after suffering incredible hardships, they returned to Melbourne with just sufficient money to pay their passage home; they were induced to return to England, having by a singular chance stumbled upon an old newspaper, in which they saw an advertisement concerning themselves; it was one of those inserted by order of Sir Edgar Manners, concerning the legacy left by Henry Fitzharding's father. "We had better," said Mr. Shaw to his son, "Take over certificates of your mother's and sister's death, as this advertisement hints at the legacy being to you and your sister. She is provided for, so you had better secure the whole, whatever it may be."

George Shaw thought so also, and having got a certificate duly prepared and witnessed, attesting his mother's death he immediately forged a similar one for his his sister, imputing her death to the fever. They had embarked in the "Lord of the Isles," for Liverpool, extremely anxious to know the amount of legacy left them; at the same time, it required great caution, for the father incurred danger in visiting England, but he knew himself to be so strangely altered in personal appearance, that he scarcely felt any apprehension. Father and son were gazing out upon tbe high rocky coast before them, which the ship was approaching much too rapidly for the safety of the passengers and cargo, when the first mate hastened to the Captain, saying—

"It's impossible, sir, to weather Three-Castle Head, you had better run into Dunmanus Bay, which we can do safely."

The Captain looked attentively, first at the head, then over the side, and then at the crew working to get up the jury mast, ere he answered—very fortunately for the passengers he was a seaman, and one open to reason— "You are quite right, Mr. Jones. Let the jury mast alone, for the present; square away the yards, and get everything ready for anchoring; there is very good anchorage in KUlmore Bay, to the eastward of Three-Castle Head."

The various passengess felt considerable relief, when the good ship, gliding safely by the bold head, over which the surf flew in snow-white wreaths, ran steadily up the bay, and gaining the safe anchorage of Killmore Cove, dropped her anchor.

"I tell you what we will do, George," said Mr. Shaw to his son, "now that we are on this coast; we are not laden with luggage," he added, with a facetious grin, "and it's not twenty miles from this place to Bantry."

"Bantry—and what's to be done at Banlry?" demanded George Shaw, " we have not a shilling to spare, so I think the sooner we get this legacy the better, for tear of accidents."

"Ah, you don't see before you! who knows what the lapse of years may have done; you must know, George, my Killcranky Estate is not altogether an imaginary one."

"The deuce it isn't," returned the son,

with a sneer; "I always consider it to be in the moon."

"Why, certainly," said Mr. Shaw with a sigh, and helping himself to some very bad salt pork and biscuit, the last of their stock of provisions," if you have to look for the estate of Killcranky, you would not And it; but, nevertheless, we will land here, it's worth the walk of twenty miles. This ship can't leave this place, I heard the mate say, under a week."

"But what is to be seen at Bantry."

"Why, I will show you the mansion that was built by your great-grandfather, llobert Coleman Shaw, Esq.— and the estate is called Killgerran."

George Shaw looked at his father, who was making 'very long faces while masticating the hard pork, and washing it down with indifferent water from a rusty can.

"Well, upon my honour, sir, I never dreamed that I had a paternal great-grandfather—I suppose I had a.great-grandmother also?"

"It would have been well for you," returned the father, "that you had never had a great grand-mother, "for she it was who persuaded my father's younger brother to turn Protestant and claim the estate; and my,father—disgusted and indignant—quitted Ireland, and enlisted; being a man of education he rose to be an officer, but he unfortunately married a—a—woman—"

"Oh, I see—a woman!" interrupted the son with a rude laugh, "a woman not quite so respectable as my great grandmother, he?"

"Why, not exactly," returned Mr. Shaw, sighing as he handed the can of water to his son. "This is horrid stuff, George—horrid!"

"It's not good, father; but we had worse in the pit; we'll make up for it when we finger the legacy; but let me know about this Killcranky Estate."

"Killgerran, George, that's the name; you see, my father's brother married and had three sons—so there was no fear of the estate wanting an heir. My father, though he became a Protestant in after years, and reared me one, never even talked of the property—he was killed in battle—I was then an ensign;

and after his death, my mother married a corporal, and I never heard what became of her, as she went out to India. Now I should like to have a look at the old place, which I never saw, and learn who it is that possesses it.',

Accordingly father and son landed the following morning on the beach, near Killmore, the captain telling them if they were left behind it would be their own fault, as he would rig jury masts in 48 hours and sail.

"Faith, you are welcome to what we leave behind us,"-said George Shaw, with a reckless laugh; "we shall be none the poorer."

On reaching Killmore, they inquired of a countryman in a long frieze coat down to bis heels, but hitched up on his back like the hump of a dromedary; he was digging up the staple commodity of the country, potatoes, "how far it was.to Bantry."

"Be me soul, that depinds which way yew goes to it; bedad, ye don't look as if you came from the gould regions, as they say yere ship comes from them."

"Which is the shortest way to Bantry, my man?" again demanded George Shaw

"Be dad, right over the mountain, if ye knew it; when ye 're at the top, be gor, ye '11 see Bantry right before ye, and thin ye can take the shortest way to it; you dom't want a lad to carry the gould for ye," he added, with a broad grin on his great potatoe face.

"If we did," said Mr. Shaw, we would not pick up such an owmadaun as you."

"Wow, it would break my back," shouted the countryman, as they commenced ascending the steep hill, or-rather mountain, before them, and over which ran a very indifferent stony road.

It took them five good hours to reach Bantry, George grumbling the whole way at the folly of taking such a useless tramp, but old Shaw was determined to get there, and he promised his son a good meal and a tumbler of whisky punch to refresh him, saying, " I have a couple of sovereigns left."

On reaching Bantry they proceeded to the best inn, and ordering a dinner, Mr. Shaw commenced proceedings by asking the woman who attended if there was not a place called Killgerran in the vicinity.

"Bedad there is, and a very dacent place it was when I was a little girl, but it's gone to the bad since it fell into the hands of the present proprietor; and he won't hould it long; they say he's the last of the Shaws, of Killgerran."

Both father and son pricked up their ears at these words, but as there were several of the people of the place taking their evening drink of neat whisky, Mr. Shaw did not pursue his inquiries concerning the house -of Killgerran, but asked the woman if there was an attorney in the place.

There was a loud laugh from all present as Mr. Shaw asked this, to them, astounding question.

"Oh, by the immortals!" said a man, dressed like a small farmer, and who was just tossing down a stiff glass of whisky, and making such curious contortions of features as would lead an observer to imagine it was a nauseous draught.

"Do you suppose, honest man, that we could live without an attorney?"

"Oh, be Gor, it would be a kind of Paradise if we had not half-a-dozen of them. Do you want one, neighbour?" and the fellow looked with a wink at his comrades; "for faix, if you do, I'll recommend you to one of the right sort, a raal broth of a boy; won't charge ye more than six-and-eightpence, and never goes beyond the eighteenth tumbler when you ax him to dinner."

"Oh,-Jim Bullfinch is just the boy to shute ye, Sir!"-exclaimed another; "he's 'customed to take stray jobs, all kinds of dirty work, and never burns his fingers. "

Mr. Shaw very well knew it was quite useless getting on a high horse with his countrymen; the only way to, disarm them was to take them in their own way. Though he saw his son's face flush, he merely said, laughing:; "Faith, boys, that's just the chap on a pinch. But I only asked from curiosity."

"From what part of Ireland do you come, neighbour?" said a pedlar, sitting in a chimney corner; "I heard you ax,

was there such a place as Killgerran in this vicinity, which shews you never were here before."

"I do not see that that follows," retorted George sharply; "we might have been here, but did not require to be informed were Killgerran was."

"No offence, neighbour, no offence," replied the pedlar: I judged by your looks ye were from foreign:parts, and mayhap wished to hear news of relations or driends."

The attendant telling them their dinner was ready in a little back room, put an end to the conversation, and1 father and son proceeded to make a better meal than they had had for months.'

"Well, here's a bit of news, George," said Mr. Shaw. "Who knows what may turn up; the heirs of the Protestant Shaw are, it seems, extinct, except the one in possession, and he is the last of them; and the landlady said he would not hold out long."

"But it does not follow," said George Shaw, "that we can come in for anything; the present possessor, no doubt, will will it to some one, for it seems either you are nobody, or they consider you dead."

"It's worth inquiring about, at all events. As soon as I have had a tumbler of punch, I will go and look for that attorney, Bullfinch, and make some inquiries about the present possessor; there can be no risk in letting him know who I am, in this remote district."

"Well, perhaps not; but this attorney will not give you his advice for nothing. "

"I will manage so that he does; he is not the first in the profession I have had to deal with."

"No, faith," returned the son, mixing himself a very stiff tumbler of whiskey, his worthy parent commencing a second, "but I think you had better go after that tumbler, for fear this Bullfinch should ask you to take a glass with him—by all accounts he likes the liquor— lest you both get muddled, and then you will make a mess of it."

George knew his father's failing, and that once he got beyond a certain quantity, he disclosed everything, no matter

who it was that was with him at the time. Mr. Shaw muttered something or other, and then got up, finished his glass, and sallied out into the street, leaving his son quietly seated at the table with his punch; whatever his failings and errors—and they were many— *be did not indulge in drink of any kind, beyond what he considered sufficient, and that was a very moderate quantity.*

CHAPTER XXI.

Me. Shaw walked up the principal street of the "town" Bantry; indeed, when we say principal street, we mean the only street, which constituted the "town"— the bylanes certainly not coming under the denomination of streets. Accosting the first woman he met, he enquired for Mr. Bullfinch, the attorney's house.

"Just five doors further up," answered the dame, "that house with the green railing in front."

Mr. Shaw reached the house indicated, and saw a tolerahly good cottage, with about two yards of garden in front, and a large brass plate on the door, with Mr. Bullfinch's name and profession in large letters on it.

Notwithstanding his remarkably shabby dress, and hat which had long since parted with its nap, he gave a good sound double rap at the door, which caused the head and face of a man to appear over the green Venetian blinds of the parlonr, and two female heads over the dimity blinds of one of the upper rooms. A servant girl, with an apron up to her mouth, opened the door, and gazed at Mr. Shaw with great surprise, dropped her apron, saying:

"Arrah, what did you give such a rap for?" Mr. Shaw drew himself up and said very haughtily, "For you to open the door, of course; tell your master a gentleman wishes to see him."

"Paix, that's goo8! a gintleman!" said the girl, laughing; "and what's your name, Mr. Gintleman?"

"Tell your master Mr. Shaw of Killgerran, wishes to see him."

"Musha, man, do you want to make fools of us?" enquired the girl, inclined to slam the door in his face; "do you think I never saw Mr. Shaw?" but just then the parlour door opened, and a short, dapper little man made his appearance, and very politely saying: "pray Sir, what can I do for you?" Now, Mr. Shaw was a gentleman by birth and education—had mixed in society—and, at one time, was a handsome, dashing-looking individual; time, misery, and drink had changed bis looks, but he could still be a gentleman in manner when he pleased.

"Sir, I presume you are Mr. Bullfinch," he observed, "I wish to have half an hour's conversation with you; my name is Shaw—one of the Shaws of Killgerran."

The attorney gave a start, looked up into the face of the speaker, and then replied—', Walk this way, sir." He led the way into a very neat, well-furnished parlour, fitted up as a private office, with a neat book case, various tin cases labelled, pigeon holes full of papers, parchments, &c. In the middle of the room a table scattered over with papers, &c.

"Pray take a chair," said the attorney, and Mr. Shaw sat down; the girl took a good stare at the shabby visitor, and then retired, closing the door.

"I beg your pardon," said the attorney, breaking the silence, "but I think you said your name was Shaw?"

"That is my name, sir; I have called upon you wishing to ask a few questions; but as it is not just to employ your time without remuneration, I merely state, that if I can put anything in your way, in consequence of the information I may receive, I shall be most happy."

Mr. Bullfinch cast a look at the speaker, whose exterior so ill corresponded with his manner and language, and replied very cautiously, that any information he had it in his power to give, he would be happy to impart.

"As a resident of this place,"«observed Mr. Shaw, "you are probably acquainted with the family of the Shaws of Killgerran?"

"I was most intimately acquainted with the late Mr. Robert Shaw of Killgerran," replied Mr. Bullfinch; "was his agent, and transacted all his law business."

"The present possessor is his son, then, I suppose?" questioned Mr: Shaw.

"No," said the attorney, "there were three brothers —the present owner of Killgerran is the youngest—not one of them having married."

"Then who succeeds to the estate after the present possessor, should he die without heirs?"

"The next of kin, if he dies without a will, of course," answered the attorney; "though where he may be found no one knows. I always understood,— be looked very keenly into Mr. Shaw's face—'I always understoood that their father's brother enlisted as a soldier, and was killed in India."

"Such was the case," observed Mr. Shaw, "but he was a married man, and left one son: I am that son."

"God bless my soul!" exclaimed the attorney, starting to his feet, and gazing at Mr. Shaw with evident amazement, "you are the son of the elder brother."

"Certainly," said Mr. Shaw, "my father's brother became a Protestant, and thereby gained the Killgerran property. I understand he left three sons, who are, by your account, all dead, except the one in possession, and none of them married. Now, the question is, has the present possessor the power to will away the Killgerran estate."

"He has," returned the attorney, "ofthatIcan give you positive proof; but the present possessor of Killgerran will never make a will."

"How so," asked Mr. Shaw, rather staggered, and looking eagerly at Mr. Bullfinch, "the possessor of Killgerran could will it away;" and yet in some degree consoled, by hearing that he never would.

"Did you never anything of your three cousins?" demanded Mr. Bullfinch.

"Never, always considering that with three male heirs between me and the property, there was not the most remote chance of succeeding, aa it was most probable all three might marry."

"Excuse my asking you a few more questions,'! observed the attorney thoughtfully. "Have you proofsCan you clearly establish your father's birth, and your own.

"Most circumstantially—his birth, he was born, of course at Killgerran. I have his marriage certificate, my own, and every requisite paper, to prove my own and my only son's rights to any property that might hereafterdescend to us. My wife was sister to the millionaire,. Mr. Pitzharding. You may have heard that name."

"Now," said the attorney, with a very meaning look,. "I understand who you are; you will excuse me if I err; you were director in the great Sunbeam Condensing Company."

Mr. Shaw coughed, coloured a good deal, and then answered, "Unfortunately I was, that was the cause of my ruin. I lost a very large sum of money, became responsible for large amounts, and was forced to fly to Australia, where my son and myself underwent great privations, as you may perceive. But how came you to know anything of me or the company you allude to."

"I will shew you," said Mr. Bullfinch, getting up and proceeding to one of the pigeon holes full of papers, and over which was the year and month printed. Looking over several papers, he selected a letter, and opening it held it in his hand, and then looked steadily into Mr. Shaw's face, "I will read you this, but I must beg you not to be offended or disconcerted at what you may hear j this is from my London correspondent, an attorney concerned for the great house of Perdoe and Pipkin— "Mt Deab Sib,

"Will you make enquiries in your county, and find out if there is an estate called Killeranky, belonging to one Robert Shaw, late a director in a company which has turned out a complete swindle. This Eobert Shaw has got off with above £10,000 of ours, and no doubt by this time is on his way to Australia. He stated he possessed a valuable property in Kerry, called Killeranky, but that there were some mortgages on it. Set enquiries on foot, and let me know as soon as possible." Mr. Bullfinch paused, saying' "the rest of the letter refers to a law cause we were both engaged in at the time."

Mr. Shaw fidgetted in his chair, with a very uneasy look—he was rather puzzled what to say; at last, finding Mr. Bullfinch remained silent, he remarked, "They accused me very unjustly of having secured the sum of money mentioned in that letter; I am aware that Perdoe and Pipkin held shares to that amount, hut—"

"Now, my dear sir, the less we eay about that business at present the better. I am satisfied you are the Shaw, next of kin to the present possessor of Kilgerran. Now, the thing is, to secure you the succession."

"Precisely," cried Mr. Shaw eagerly, "but the present possessor may live many years."

"It's impossible he can live many days," returned the attorney quietly.

"Good God, how is that?" asked Mr. Shaw, with intense eagerness.

"Simply that he is committing suicide in a legal way; he is starving himself to death with above £20,000 in hard cash, and in various securities he has much more."

"Starving himself to death," repeated Mr. Shaw with amazement, and astounded at the mention of £20,000 in. possession of the owner of Killegerran.

The attorney remained in a thoughtful attitude for several minutes, and then looking up, said with much animation, "Now Mr. Shaw, we may as well understand each other, and come to a perfect and clear settlement as. to how we shall proceed. I think, indeed, I am positive if you possess the proofs you say of your identity, that before a month is out, you will succeed to the Killgerran estate, and all the money hoarded up by your extraordinary cousin, Timothy Shaw, of Killgerran; the moment you do so, it becomes my duty to assert the claims of Pardoe and Pipkin against you; and there are others, I suppose, who have claims also; very probably the entire property would be swallowed up in litigation."

Mr. Shaw looked aghast, the attorney continued: "If you will sign a paper, placing yourself in my hands, and agree to give me £5000 for my services, I will undertake to settle all the claims against you for half the amount; and, having important papers in my hands as agent

of the late Robert Shaw, the present possessor's brother, absolutely necessary to support your claims, I will put you,, in possession of the property, and allow you a certain amount now, if you require it, till the death of Timothy Shaw enables us to proceed; but it is necessary that you should keep quiet, and not let your return from Australia become public."

To this proposal Mr. Shaw most eagerly consented, without the slightest hesitation—merely asking: "But how is it that my cousin, Timothy Shaw, starves himself, to death—this appears a strange circumstances?"

"Three words will do that," replied Mr. Bullfinch; "Timothy Shaw is a miser, but one of a most extraordinary kind; you are aware that there were three brothers— the eldest, George Coleman Shaw, possessed the property only four years: Robert Steadman Shaw succeeded, lie was of a most strange, eccentric turn of mind, and only returned to Killgerran on the death of his brother. He was a remarkably handsome man, and strange stories were afloat about his previous life—but that has nothing to do with our intentions and your rights.

"He made me his agent, permitted his brother Timothy to occupy the house, and farm the land. Again, he absented himself for five years, returned much altered in manner and disposition—took the agency from me, and deputing his strange brother to manage matters for him, again went away. Five more years passed, and he returned and shut himself up in Killgerran, saw no human being save his brother. Between them they did not spend one hundred a year, and he finally died of a fever and want of medical advice.

"After his death Timothy Shaw,— there being no will —succeeded, though it was reported Robert had had some connexion with a lady of great respectability, and deserted her and her children; but it was hard to believe those stories at that time: at all events, he died without leaving any provision for her or her children,

"Now it was, that the extraordinary disposition of Timothy Shaw, shewed

itself—every soul of the establishment of Killgerran was dismissed. I must tell you that Timothy Shaw was born a deformed dwarf, and is scarcely four feet high, and hideously distorted—but, nevertheless, of a singularly gifted mind. In his latter years, he has become a miser, and shuts himself up, seeing only the tenants who go to pay rents. Once or twice I havehad interviews with him on business. He completely dismantled the house, sold every article even to the glass of the windows, the gates, and timber of the outoffices; stripped the roof of the lead and sold it, and finally confined himself to one single room, living only on bread and water-cresses.

"About this time he wrote me a note, desiring me to furnish a cottage on the estate for a widow of the name ofKavanagh; and, to my surprise, he desired me to do it handsomely. I did so, and the widow arrived and took possession. Now, it is my firm belief this widow was his brother's mistress. Here she has lived in total seclusion two years. During the last twelve months, her daughter has arrived from some remote part, and now lives with her. Strange to say this daughter, a young girl of some 16 or 17 years, is allowed admission, to the miser's room, and supplies him with food. I had one interview with this Mrs. Kavanagh; but it was in thedusk of the evening, and the room of the cottage was gloomy from the evergreens growing over it. She stated to me that Timothy Shaw could not live a week, he was so emaciated and feeble he could scarcely rise from his bed. I saw him three months ago, for he employed me to renew the lease of a farm; but he never paid my ex pences, saying he could not afford it; he did not even let me into his room. The interview took place in what was once the drawing-room of Killgerran. It was melancholy to behold this fine room, the windows devoid of glass, and the walls teeming with damp. I thought then he was dying, and said he ought to make a will. 'A will,' he almost screamed, looking me savagely in the face. 'A will! for what? I have nothing to leave — doyou think I am going to die at fifty?—go away man—I do not want your advice. When I am going to die it will be time enough to leave this old ruin to somebody.

You shall have it for your costs,' he added, with a frightful grin, and then left me."

"What a character," observed Mr. Shaw, thinking of the gold the miser must have hoarded up. He then put his hand into the breast pocket of his coat, and pulled out a large and somewhat dilapidated book, which opening, he took out several papers, and laid them before Mr. Bullfinch, " those certificates will convince you," he remarked, " that I am Robert Shaw, son of George Shaw, of Killgerran, and that the said George held a Captain's commission in the infantry regiment, and that I formerly held a Captain's commission in the foot.

My son has other papers in his possession, which you can see tomorrow, for I shall not return to the ship now lying in Dunmanus Bay."

"Then you only landed this day?" asked the attorney, eagerly, "you have not been in England."

"No, only came from Killmore here; we put in there with loss of main and mizen masts.""

"Then take a lodging here," said the attorney, " under another name, till we see what will turn up. I am satisfied Mr. Timothy Shaw will not live a week. I suppose," he added, "you are not burthened with cash, if I may judge by your account of yourself."

"Not at this moment," said Mr. Shaw, but taking an old newspaper from his pocket, he looked over it, and then handing it to Mr. Bullfinch, said, "you see there, our presence is required in England. My son is entitled to a large legacy, left by the late millionare, Mr. Fitzbarding, the great Odessa merchant. "

Mr. Bullfinch read the paragraph: it appeared to make a great impression upon him, and his manner changed wonderfully; he started up, and ringing the bell, observed, " We have been talking a long time, which is dry work, allow me to offer you some refreshments."

When the girl entered, he said, "Tell your mistress to send in some port and sherry; but, perhaps, Mr. Shaw, you would like so try our native production—whiskey. Judy, bring also hot water and whiskey. Come," he added, rubbing his hands, " we will have a cosy chat for an hour or so."

Leaving them to enjoy what they both were rather addicted to, we will return to the sou.

CHAPTER XXII.

Having finished his tumbler of punch, Mr. George Shaw rose up, and thought as there were still two or three more hours of daylight, he would have a walk; he had a fancy to see this Killgerran House his father talked so much about. Accosting a respectable person in the street, he enquired which was the way to Killgerran House.

"Killgerran House!" repeated the person addressed, and looking very hard into the face of the enquirer. "Yes," said George Shaw, "is there such a place?" "Oh, faith, there is; it's there still, all that's left of it," replied the man, "go straight up the street till you come to the turnpike, then take the road to the right, and in half-an-hour's walk, faix, you'll see Killgerran House; and when once you see it, be dad, ye won't forget it."

""Well," thought George Shaw, "there's something singular about this Killgerran;" and he walked on to the turnpike, took the road to the right, and continued on through a very pretty and picturesque country, ascending. a slight hill crowded with wood, and commanding a fine view over Whiddy Island and the wide expanse of Bantry Bay, with the long tongue of lofty land, called Bear Island, on its western shores.

For a quarter of an hour he walked on without seeing any house or mansion, save a dozen or so small cabins, but just as he turned an angle of the road, after descending the hill on the other side, he saw a large building before him that he at once set down as Killgerran. He wallen on till he gained a clear view of it, and then he paused" perfectly astounding. As he halted, a young woman wrapt in her grey cloak, with the hood off her bare hear, and her feet and leg as

Nature made them— uncovered—was passing.

He called to her, demanding " if that was Killgerran."

"Be dad it is, Vick," said the girl, "it's a quare place, ain't it?" and without waiting for a reply, she walked on rapidly.

"Faith, it's a queer place, sure enough," muttered Shaw, passing between two massive and once handsome pillars, adjoining the entrance gateway, but gate there was none; the house at one time had been evidently surrounded on three sides by fine old trees, for innumerable stumps remained above ground; there were ornamental shrubs and evergreens also, all gone to decay, or grown into a wild and shaggy state; there had once been a lawn of some four or five acres, but it was then devoted to the culture of potatoes. A road to the house and gravel walks once existed, but they were now covered wivh grass and weeds.

He stood within twenty yards of the mansion, which he considered uninhabited and in ruins. It must formerly have been a large and very handsome building, of a square form, with an almost flat roof, with a kind of battlement round it. There was a lofty flight of steps to the hall door, which was black with dirt, age, and decay. All the lower windows of the house were rudely filled up with boards aud rough stones; the upper had neither frames, glass, nor sashes. At the back appeared extensive outhouses, all in ruins, and to the left was what he supposed to be a high walled garden. Such an air of desolation and misery did the place bear in the dusk of the evening, that George Shaw felt a strange sensation creeping over him, as he stood with his eyes resting upon the building where his great grand-father had lived, and which was built by him. There was no habitation in its immediate vicinity, that he could see. Suddenly, a loud strangely unnatural scream came from the interior, and then, distinctly on the still air, rose the appalling cry of "murder.

Shaw, with all his faults, was a brave and stout-hearted man. Without hesitation, he sprang upon the steps, the hall door gave way, the rotten lock flying off at the vigorous push he gave it. Another scream, the cry of a female in great agony and fear, rung through the house. The young man shouted at the top of his voice, and then rushed up the stone stairs; he heard a door slam with violence. Lying on the floor of the lobby, was a small crow bar, and snatching this up, he rushed on till a door barred his progress. He heard voices within, and curses loud and deep. The next moment he dashed in the door; as he did so, two men in long frieze coats, without hats, and with short-stout sticks in their hands, made a furious rush at him, exclaiming in Irish, "D'iowl take you," at the same time aiming a blow at his head. Shaw had fought his way through the rough gold seekers of Australia, and was not easily frightened. Springing on one side, he avoided the blows, and with the crow bar felled the nearest ruffian to the floor with a terrible blow, when the other, with a fearful curse, dashed through the door, and disappeared. George Shaw was bent on pursuit, when a female voice cried out in agony—

"Stay! in God's name stay! he may not be dead!"

He paused, bewildered, and then gazed amazed around him.

He was in a large room, scrupulously neat and clean; there was a bed at one end, and near it an immense chest bound all over with iron; but what attracted his attention and excited his astonishment, was a young girl, in a peasant's dress; her dark and glossy hair thrown wildly into disorder, disclosed a face pale, it is true, but still interesting, if not beautiful. She was kneeling on the floor, supporting on-her lap the head of a man—but what a head; it was not only in its huge size, but the distortion of its shape and the ugliness of the features rendered it hideous. There was a cut on the forehead, deep and ghastly to look at, and the blood ran down the face, which the young girl strove to staunch.

"Give me the water from that jug," said the girl, in a trembling voice, "it may revive him.". Dropping the bar, Shaw seized the jug, and kneeling down beside the girl, he bathed the face of the singularly deformed being, whose heard rested on the young girl's lap.

While he was doing so, he did not perceive that the ruffian he had struck down was cautiously dragging himself towards the door, which he reached, and then suddenly rising stealthily disappeared.

"Oh, my God!" exclaimed the young girl, "I fear he is dead!"

As she spoke the deformed opened his eyes, and they rested on her anxious face; a shudder shook his frame, and then in a low voice he said, in broken accents:

"'Tis no use, Nelly, 'tis no use, 'tis a judgment against me; I murdered your father—yes, yes, 'tis true; if I had sent for a doctor, but I would not. I saw him die by inches, but I wished him dead to have his gold."

"Oh, God! hush, uncle, you are raving. Oh, sir, go for a doctor, he might save him."

A violent shudder shook the dying man's frame, and lifting his hand he pointed to the great chest, saying in scarcely articulate words;

"The will and all the papers are there."

The next moment he was dead, and a loud cry escaped the girls lips.

Shaw was perfectly bewildered; he looked round him— the man he had knocked down was gone. It was getting rapidly dark, and there he was in that ruined, desolate house, with the young girl, and the corpse of the last of the three Shaws of Killgerran.

Both remained for a moment speechless, then Nelly burst into a flood of tears, burying her head in her hands. The sound of that young girl's sobs in the stillness of that desolate house, affected the heart of George in a new and strange way. Though his thoughts were confused and bewildered, he felt for her sorrow, and laying his hand on her arm, he said, in a low, kind tone: -"Do not grieve so, I pray you; tell me what I can do to serve you, where to go for assistance. If it will give you confidence, I now tell you I am a Shaw, and spring from the same stock as he who lies there at your feet. Allow me to lift him on the bed."

The girl rose to her feet, and in the faint light looked up into the face of the speaker; we have said he was a tall, and when unmoved by passion, a very handsome man.

"I do," she replied, "feel confidence in you, whether you are a Shaw or not, for you saved my life at the risk of your own, for those men would assuredly have killed me. If you are not afraid—but I am wrong to say afraid —I mean, if you will do so much for me and the dead as to watch here till my return, I will bring those who will care for my poor, ill-fated, miserable uncle; the brutal wretches struck him down before I could rush in between them."

"I will stay," said George, "till you return. Can you get me a candle?"

"Oh! yes," she answered; and opening a cupboard she took out a candlestick with a candle in it, and with a lucifer lighted it. She shuddered as she saw the young man lift the body on the bed, exclaiming," Oh! my God, this is a terrible scene!" and then wrapping her grey cloak round her, and covering her head with the hood, she was leaving the room, when she paused, saying, "but good God! if those men should return?"

"Never fear," said George, taking down from a nail in the wall an old dragoon sabre in a steel sheath, kept brilliantly bright, "with this I am quite safe."

She then departed, closing the door after her.

"Well," soliloquised Shaw to himself, and sitting down and recovering his usual manner and thoughts, "this is a strange adventure; how will it end? There, lies the last of the Shaws, of Killgerran, heirs of the younger brother, and yet," he started, as the words of the murdered man recurred to him, "the will is there, and the other papers," and then he recollected that the *youaj* .girl he called Nelly was his niece.

' Ha," he continued, starting to his feet, and gazingon the uncovered face of the dead, "we may not be theheirs after all. That will," he stepped close to the bed, and then gazed earnestly round the apartment; everything was scrupulously neat, there was only the bed, the chest, a table, and two chairs in the room, but against the wall was a bookcase, containing about fifty or sixty volumes. The gazer's eyes rested on the steel plated chest, and suddenly recollecting that the hand of the dead man grasped something like steel rings or keys; he paused—listened—not a sound disturbed the silence of that lonely, ruined house.

Evil thoughts and evil resolves again entered Shaw's brain. Approaching the bed, he threw back the quilt that partly covered that strange deformed body, and there he beheld, grasped in the bony emaciated fingers, two singular-shaped keys, united by a steel ring.

Without hesitation he took the keys from the firm grasp of the dead man's hand, and then again he listened. All was still, but the night air rising came with a moaning sound against the window, and the low howl of a dog at some distance were the only sounds heard. Taking thekeys and the candle, he proceeded to the chest; one glance satisfied him that the keys fitted the lock and the padlock that fastened the chest. With a desperate determination he unlocked both, threw up the lid of the chest, and held the candle so as to look into the interior. It was full of small bags, ticketed and sealed, and on the top was a folded parchment. This he took up, and on it he read with astonishment the words, "The last will and testament of Robert Steadman Shaw, Esq., of Killgerran." Thrusting this document and the other small ones into the breast of his coat, and buttoning it, he shut the chest, re-locked it, and replaced the keys again in the hands of the dead.

As he threw the quilt over the body there came a sound of voices up from the exterior of the house, and then the tread of several feet was heard in the corridor, the door was pushed open, and, to George Shaw's extreme -surprise, his father, Mr. Bullfinch, the attorney, whom of course he did not know, and two policemen entered the room.

The amazement of Mr. Shaw on be-holding his son in a chamber of Killgerran House was equally great.

"God bless me," he exclaimed, "how is this, George? You here? Are you the person, then, that put the murderers to flight?"

"Yes, but unfortunately I did not, as you may perceive, arrive in time; but perhaps I prevented a double murder."

"This is your son, then, Mr. Shaw?" asked Mr. Bullfinch very thoughtfully, while the two policemen were carefully examining the room, and two others in the front keeping out stragglers, who kept arriving every moment.

Just then was heard the sound of horses' feet, and Mr. Bullfinch exclaimed, "Here is the magistrate, Mr. Daunt."

In a few minutes a very gentlemanly looking personage entered the room. Mr. Bullfinch received him with a low salutation, saying—

"This is a sad affair, Mr. Daunt; there might have been two murders but for this gentleman's interference," directing his attention to Mr. Shaw, jun.

At the word gentleman, Mr. Daunt looked hard at-George Shaw, but notwithstanding his somewhat strange and shabby attire, there was an air and manner in the young man that denied his dress as befitting him.

The attorney tben introduced father and son as the nearest relations to the deceased. Mr. Daunt looked surprised, bowed, and then asked, " Where is the young girl or woman who was here at the time, and who gave intimation of this crime being committed?"

One of the policemen replied, "Her name is Elinor Kavanagh, sir. She is the daughter of Widow Kavanagh, as the people call her. She is a stranger to this place,,and lives in a cottage a quarter of a mile from here. When she met me just by the turnpike, she told me, in a hurried, confused manner, tr go to Mr. Bullfinch, the attorney, and tell him Mr. Shaw, of Killgerran, was-murdered; and that, only for a gentleman, she would also have been killed. Before I could get a word morefrom her, she fell down in a faint."

"And where is she now?" said Mr. Daunt.

"I carried her into the turnpike house, sir, and left her under the care of the wAman who keeps it, and then ran down to Mr. Bullfinch. He ordered me to send a policeman for you, sir, and then we came on here with more men."

"Do you know this Mrs. Xavanagh, Mr. Bullfinch?'" questioned Mr. Daunt.

"Yes, sir," returned the attorney, with a little hesitation in his manner; and then, taking the magistrateaside, he conversed for a moment in a low tone. During this conversation, the elder Shaw was questioning his son eagerly, as to how he came there, and who was the young girl he had found with the murdered owner of Killgerran. Having explained all to his father, he added—

"With respect to the young girl, I can only tell you that the old man who lies there dead, called her Nelly, and she ad dressed him as uncle; for he had sufficient power to say so much before he expired."

"Uncle!" exclaimed Mr. Shaw with a start, and turning pale, "impossible!"

Before the son could reply, the magistrates' clerk entered the room, and Mr. Daunt at once commenced his investigation and examination of George Shaw, who gave a plaia statement of facts as they occurred. The clerk wrote down his account, and then other investigations took place. The body was examined, and the keys taken possession of, Mr. Bullfinch claiming them in the name of Mr. Shaw, as the next heir of the deceased, until a will was found, or any other claimant tothe property sppeared.

Two or three policemen were now despatched to endeavour to track the murderers. George Shaw described them as tall men, in long grey frieze coats, one strongly pock-marked, and both about thirty-eight to forty years of age.

"There is a man named Timmins, Joe Timmins," said the sergeant of police, addressing the magistrate, "he is a returned convict, and lives near this place who answers to that description; he is pock-marked and about thirtyeight or forty."

"Then send immediately and see if that man is in his cabin. You would be able to identify him, Mr. George Shaw, would you not?" enquired the magistrate.

"I could swear to him positively," returned the person addressed, "for he looked me steadily in the face, as he aimed a blow of his loaded bludgeon at me. No doubt the young girl will be able to swear to either of them, should you be able to secure them."

"Ah, very true," observed Mr Daunt.

Further arrangements were then made, a sergeant and four policemen were left in charge, the locks of the chest sealed by the magistrate, and then Mr. Daunt, Mr. Bullfinch, and the two Shaws proceeded towards Bantry, intending to stop at the turngike gate to see and question the young girl.

"You say, Mr. Bullfinch," enquired the magistrate as they walked on, one of the policemen having the care of his horse, "that you do not know this Elinor Kavanagh, though you know so much of her mother."

"The mother has been here three years, and the daughter only the last year. Till her arrival, I did not know Mrs. Kavanagh had a daughter."

"Do you think a will was made by that unfortunate man, whose life must have been a perfect torment. Was he aware of this Mr. Shaw's being in existence?"

"I should say not. As to a will, I should say there was none, he could not have made one without assistance and witnesses; besides, his right hand was so deformed that he always wrote his name with his left; the mention of a will drove him furious."

"Then you have no idea of who this Mrs. Kavanagh was, before she became connected with the late Eobert Steadman Shaw."

"No idea whatever, sir; I was ordered by the late Timothy Shaw to turn out Collins, who then inhabited the cottage Mrs. Kavanagh now lives in, and to get it ready for the present occupier. I was surprised at the widow's appearance when I saw her, though she evidently wished to hun observation. She was

very handsome, and in manner far above the class I supposed she belonged to."

"I had several interviews with Mr. Timothy Shaw some months afterwards, and, to my surprise, he told me that Mrs. Eavanagh was connected with his brother Robert, and lived in England with him, previous to his becoming owner of Eillgerran, and that he intended to provide for her, but he never said a word about her having a daughter."

"Ah! here we are," said Mr. Daunt, stopping before the Turnpike House.

For what passed there, we refer our readers to our next chapter.

CHAPTER XXIII.

On entering the little room of the Turnpike-gate House, they found the woman who had charge of the gate Mrs. Eisby by name, in a considerable state of agitation.

Only the magistrate and the attorney, and Mr. Shaw entered, the two policemen remained outside, for what purpose was not very apparent, unless indeed to attend on Mr. Haunt.

George Shaw walked on towards the inn where he had dined, rather anxious to get rid of the documents he had so nefariously become possessed of.

"Well, Mrs. Risby," said Mr. Daunt, addressing the woman, who hastily dusted a chair, and huddled other articles out of the way, "where is the young girl, Elinor Kavanagh, who you so kindly gave shelter to; is she here still?"

"She is, your honor," answered Mrs. Risby, "and, poor thing, she's been desperate bad since she come, but her mother is with her now, and she's coming round nicely —Lord save us!" and Mrs. Risby crossed herself very devoutly; "they wanted to murder the poor thing as well as Mr. Shaw.

"So it seems," uttered Mr. Daunt, sitting down: "is there any chance of her being able to answer one or two questions to-night; if not, we will postpone any further enquiry until to-morrow."

As the magistrate spoke, the door between the two rooms opened, and a female entered the chamber. There was only a small candle burning on the

table, but as the light, indifferent as it was, fell upon the features of Mrs. Kavanagh, Mr. Daunt involuntarily rose from his chair, struck with the extremely handsome features and easy graceful manner of the lady. She was very simply attired in a plain cotton dress, but it was neat and genteelly made. She wore no cap and though forty, or perhaps more, her hair was jet black and beautifully glossy.

"You are Mrs. Kavanagh, I presume," said Mr. Daunt, politely offering a chair.

"Such was the name I was obliged to assume, sir," replied Mrs. Kavanagh, in a calm, serious tone, sitting down at the same time; circumstances now permit me to resume the name I am entitled to. I am the widow of the late Mr. Robert Steadman Shaw of Killgerran."

Mr. Shaw sprung from his chair with a startled, bewildered look, and an exclamation of intense astonishment, and became very pale as he exclaimed in an agitated voice:

"Good God! I thought I knew you. " "Yes, you ought to know me, Mr. Shaw," interrupted Mrs. Steadman Shaw, as we shall now call her, in a very bitter tone, and then turning to the surprised magistrate and the confounded Mrs. Risby, she added, "my maiden name, Sir, was Elinor Fitzharding."

Mr. Shaw sunk back in his chair, confused and overpowered, while Mr. Bullfinch, the attorney looked, staggered and confounded.

"That I should feel puzzled and amazed, Mrs. Shaw;" said Mr. Daunt, recovering his usual manner and tone, "will not surprise you, as I never knew that the late Mr. Steadman Shaw was married; but as that is not an affair for me to inquire into or investigate, I will not intrude at present any further on you than to inquire whether the young girl, whom, I presume, is your daughter, will be able to answer a few more questions to-night, if not we will postpone it till to-morrow."

"I shall feel greatly obliged, Sir, if you will postpone your questions till to-morrow; she is now much more overcome than at the time the crime was committed; the energy she then called up has abandoned her—she is quite exhausted."

"Very good," said Mr. Daunt, rising, "we will say no more now; pray can I be of any assistance to you—had you not better send for a doctor?"

"1 do not think it will be necessary," returned Mrs. Shaw; "in an hour or two I will get her carried home. Pray, Sir," she added, with a slight hesitation of manner "is the chest in the chamber where the crime was committed left in safe charge; I do not feel any apprehension for the gold it may contain, but I am aware it encloses papers most valuable to me and my child."

"It has not been opened, Madam," said Mr. Daunt, "I saw the keys taken from the lifeless hands of the unfortunate Mr. Timothy Shaw, and I put my own seal upon the locks before 1 left; there are also two policemen and a sergeant remaining in the house, so that you may rest quite easy with respect to whatever remains in the place. Tomorrow then, Madam I will take your daughter's desposition—say ten o'clock."

"Certainly, Sir; she will no doubt be able to state all she heard or saw, till Mr. George Shaw, jun., came to her rescue. I owe him, at all events, deep gratitude for the preservation of my daughter's life."

"There is a good deal of mystery and perplexity about the affair at present," observed Mr. Daunt, taking up his hat, "which I hope will be in a measure cleared away tomorrow, and perhaps the villains may be captured by that time."

Mrs. Shaw returned the salution of the magistrate, and at once, without waiting for his departure, retired into the adjoining chamber.

Mr. Daunt seemed thoughtful as he paused outside the cottage, till joined by the crestfallen Mr. Shaw and the astounded attorney.

"This is a monstrous singular affair, Mr, Bullfinch," said the magistrate. "I suppose you were not aware that the late Steadman Shaw left a widow? No one here, I believe, ever dreamt he was a married man; and his wife turns out to be the beautiful Miss Fitzharding, whose disappearance some twenty or twenty-two years ago, made such a stir in Dublin. You, Mr. Shaw, must know something more of this affair than we do, if you are the Captain Shaw from whose house the young lady eloped. If she proves her marriage, she and her daughter will succeed to the Killgerran Estate, and the money saved up by the murdered Timothy Shaw, who, by the bye, could have had no right to the property at all."

Captain Shaw, as the light from the lamp by the turnpike gate fell on his face, looked very ghastly; he, however, answered:

"I know very little about the elopement of Miss Fitzharding. I was astounded when I saw her, though the lapse of years confused my memory for a moment, but that she became the wife of Steadman Shaw I had not the slightest idea. / She had a fine fortune of her own, which, most strange to say, has never been claimed;, in fact, she has been considered dead. Her nephew, Mr. Henry Edgar Fitzharding, is one of the wealthiest men in England, and next heir to the title of Lord Courtland."

"Lord who did you say P" interrupted the magistrate,, looking into the pale features of Mr. Shaw.

"Lord Courtland, of Courtland Tower, Dorsetshire," repeated Mr. Shaw.

"By Jupiter!" said Mr. Dauut, "then the Mr.!Fitzharding is Lord Courtland now. I saw his Lordship's death in yesterday's *Herald*—died suddenly of disease of the heart. However," continued the worthy magistrate, "there's no use standing talking here; I shall bid you good night, and to-morrow, at ten o'clock, I shall expect to see you and your son at the Rose and Crown, when this shocking affair will be fully investigated."

"So saying, Mr. Daunt, after giving some private directions to the two policemen, mounted his horse and rode off. He lived about a mile from the town, in the direction of Glengarriff.

Mr. Shaw and the attorney walked slowly down the street.

"This is an astounding blow to you, Mr. Shaw," observed the attorney, seriously; "if Mrs. Steadman Shaw proves her marriage and the birth of her child you lose the property; it's most extraordinary. You can't oppose her; I know how the Killgerran property goes; that miserable miser, who now lies stark and stiff in his den, had no right to it, as sure as fate. That man who committed the murder, and described by your son as pockmarked, and in years about forty-five, is that fellow, wellknown here as a most abandoned and desperate ruffian, James Hillas by name; he only returned to this his native place about six months ago; he was caught and convicted of smuggling and running cargoes, and nearly killed one of the coast guard, for which he was sentenced to seven years' transportation, and now he's come back."

"I am quite bewildered," returned Mr. Shaw, in a low tone, " I can scarcely believe she" was married; and was a most extraordinary girl."

"Stay," interrupted tht attorney, "what's this crowd about our lock-up house, they have captured one or both of the ruffians no doubt."

On approaching the crowd', which several policemen were keeping back, Mr. Bullfinch enquired what was the matter.

"Two of the men, sir, have just apprended James Hillas on suspicion," returned the policeman; "he takes it quite coolly, however, and laughs at us; he says he will clearly prove to-morrow that it was quite impossible he could be one of the two men, as he was talking to the gentleman who rescued the young girl from being murdered just a minute or two before; he says he thought he heard a shriek himself as he walked towards the town. However, he is locked up till to-morrow morning; we shall have Mr. Daunt and a couple more magistrates here early."

"If your son, Mr. Shaw," said the attorney, "affirms that statement, it 'will prove his innocence altogether. I will now wish you good night; we shall meet at the Rose and Crown to-morrow, at ten o'clock—good night."

Mr. Shaw said good night in a very disconsolate tone, and walked on to the inn, where he anxiously expected to see his son.

We must first, however, follow the footsteps of George Shaw as he proceeded to the inn to deposit the documents he had concealed «bout him.

There was perhaps half a mile from the turnpike-gate to the entrance of the town, and it was at this time quite dark. Just as he approached a narrow lane, leading between the thick hedges that opened out on the main road, a man rushed out from the deep gloom and caught George Shaw by the arm; his first impulse was to wrest his arm from the grasp of the man, and then to seize him, saying, " villain, you are the man, I know you."

"Arrah, hould me fast now you have me," said the man, with a curse and a hoarse laugh, " but if ye want to keep what ye tuck from the chist, come into the lane till we talk a bit."

George Shaw felt all the blood in his body rushing to

'his head; he felt as if annihilated, and without opposition allowed himself to be led by the man deep into the shade.

Having got to the back of the hedge, the ruffian, who was no other than James Hillas, and the very villian who struck the blow that killed the miser, said to George Shaw, "80 you know I was the man you saw in the miser's room at Killgerran."

Shaw rapidly guessed he had heen watched. He rapidly regained his presence of mind, and resolved to see how far he was in the ruffian's power. He therefore Teplied—

"Yes, I can swear to your being one of the men I saw at Killgerran."

"And by I can swear you are the man I seed take the keys from the ould miser's hands, and open the chist, and tuck from it a big parcel of papers, and put them under your great coat, and be the token you have them about ye now. "

This was just what Shaw expected, but he coolly observed, "Tou are not aware that I am the nearest relation of the man you killed, and that I only took

those papers for fear of accidents."

"Oh, be gor," returned the man, with a fierce curse, and a sentence in Irish, which his companion did not, understand, but which implied that he was as great a villian as himself. "I'm wide awake; ye knew ye were committing a robbery, for ye tried to make the dead man's fingers grasp the keys back again, but they wouldn't. I saw you. When you knocked over my comrade, I thought you had kilt him, and I bolted, but I went round, for I knows every inch of the ould house, and got into a room that has a small window in it, and looks down into the miser's chamber, and I seed you and the girl, and then how my comrade stole out made and ,off. I could not hear what the ould miser said, but when the girl left I seed you look cautiously round, and then take the keys, and, as I said, open the chist, and take the papers. Ye did not touch the gould; the papers were more value; aren't I right master?"

""Well," observed Shaw, quite calmly, " I admit this— I want those papers; they may be important, or they may not, but I took them for fear they should. Now, isell me what you expect of me, for money I have none as yet."

"I don't want money, now," said the man, "hut I.on't want to quit the country; and faix, I don't want be hanged, it ain't pleasant. You must swear, when I'm taken, for taken I will be, and brought before you. You must swear I'm not the man you seed, and that just a minute or two before you heard the girl's cry, you met me in the road, and axed me if yonder house was Killgerran, and I tould you it was, and that then I went on towards Bantry."

George Shaw was staggered and startled, but after a moment's thought, he said, "You forget that the young girl must have seen, and will remember your face, as well as I do. She will swear you are the man."

"Bother," returned James Hillas, "her testimony after yours, won't be worth that," and he snapped his fingers.

"Then your comrade may be taken, and turn informer' and ruin us both."

"Oh be gor, if ye wait till Darby

Mulline turns in-' former you'll live to a fine ould age be jabers; you made A hole in his head you could put a turnip in; faix he's as dead as a herring."

"Dead!" exclaimed George Shaw, astonished, "why he bolted, you told me, from the room."

"Faix, so he did, but he had only strength enough to crawl to a secret hiding place of ours, and there I found him dead, so I took and carried him into the next field; they will find him when daylight comes. So you see you need not heed him."

Shaw shuddered; he felt humiliated—worse than degraded; he had, in Ffact, by the commission of a foul crime, placed himself in communion with a murderer, become an accomplice. Bad as he was, this climax he had never contemplated, and yet he saw no other way to extricate himself from his horrible companion. By the act he had committed, he had, if betrayed, incurred the penalty of transportation. Still it was not compunction for his own act, he felt, hut fear of the discovery of the crime by the villain beside him.

"Well," enquired James Hillas, "what be ye thinking of. Faix, there's no time or need of thinking, for," and he swore a fearful oath; "if you will not save me I'll inform on you the moment I'm taken; and from this I won't fly, for I should be pursued and taken, after your description of my person.".

"Well, be it so," replied George Shaw, "I may not be put on oath; at all events, I will say sufficient to clear you; take care what you say, if yon are taken and examined."

"Tare an' nouns, do you take me for an omadaun.

Here's my hand; by I will never betray you, if you don't me."

"Agreed," said Shaw, turning away with disgust. As he did so, a coarse, brutal laugh saluted his ears, as the man sprang over the hedge and disappeared in the lane on the other sibe.

Terribly depressed and annoyed, Shaw got into the lane, and turned into the town. There were groups here and there in the streets conversing about the murder of Timothy. Shaw, of Killgerran, but he passed on rapidly, and entering the inn, found the kitchen full of people, all eagerly uttering their comments on the event.

The tale of a murder spreads with lightning speed. Everyone has his own version of the crime, and to listen to each would puzzle the best jury that ever sat to find the true version of the affair.

Luckily for the yonng man, he was not known by those present as the principal person who figured in the tragedy enacted in Killgerran honse, so he passed quickly on, and meeting the girl of the house, he procured a candle, and retired to the bed-room prepared for them, telling the girl to tell his father when he came in that he was gone to bed: it was a double-bedded room allotted to them.

Locking the door, George Shaw shut the window shutter, and then having examined the room, he sat down by the small table the room contained, and drew the bulky packet from the breast of his great coat.

"I shall henceforth know no more peace," he exclaimed almost aloud, a habit he had when excited, "as long as that ruffian lives. He will haunt me; I feel satisfied he will seek to extort gold next, and after all, this will may be only a copy."

Untying the red tape, he perceived that the packet contained five other documents, all neatly folded and tied with tape. On one he read, "Marriage Certificate and Certificate of Birth of Elinor Fitzharding."

George Shaw paused in intense surprise, repeating to himself, "Elinor Fitzharding! how is this possible?"

A loud noise beneath the room which was over the kitchen made him pause, and the sound of footsteps ascending the stairs caused him to bundle up the papers, wrap them in his great coat, and thrust both under the bolster of the bed. The next moment the handle of the door was turned, but those without finding it locked, knocked, and then he heard his father's voice requesting him to open the door; he also heard a strange voice talking to his father outside, so throwing

off his under coat, waistcoat, and stock, he approached the door, and unlocking it, admitted his father and a policeman.

The first glance he cast at the former's countenance convinced George that something had occurred, for he looked greatly depressed, and very pale, but the policeman came briskly into the room, and looking up into George Shaw's face, said:

"I am happy to tell you, Sir, that we have taken one of the murderers."

George started, and for an instant looked confounded, but the next instant said, a little sharply:

"How do you know that, policeman?"

"Why, Sir, he tallies so exactly with your description, there can be scarcely a doubt, though he takes his capture very easy—faith, he even laughed at us, saying he had evidence to prove that he could not have been at Killgerran at the time of the murder."

"Do you require my presence to-night?" demanded George, taking up his coat.

"Oh, no, Sir, you need not trouble to-night, I only came to let you know, thinking it must be a satisfaction to you to hear that one of the villians is taken—at all events, we shall soon have the other, probably before morning.

"When did you take him?" demanded Shaw; "I should fancy this must not be the man to be so easily and soon detected; being a pock-marked man, and about the age I mentioned, will not identify him as the murderer; but I would know him at once. By the way, now I think of it, just a minute or two before I heard the cry from Killgerran House, I stopped a man passing me, and who was dressed in a long frieze coat; he was marked with the small-pock, and had a cut over his left eye, ugly to look at."

"Be dad," said the policeman, quite crest-fallen, "that's the man we nabbed going quite coolly into his cwn cabin—James Hillas is his name, a rum cove he is; we keep our eyes open upon him; he is a returned convict—faith, I was sure we had him this time."

"It may be him still," replied George in his usual manner, "though I certainly

saw no scar on the face of the man I attacked in Killgerran House."

"Well, Sir, I won't keep you any longer," said the policeman; "to-morrow at ten o'clock the magistrates will meet at the Rose and Crown; you will please to be there;" so wishing them both good night, the policeman retired, leaving father and son alone.

CHAPTER XXIV.

After the departure of the policeman the young mau locked the door, and then approaching his father, who was sitting with his hand supporting his head in a most disconsolate attitude, and his features wearing a most troubled expression, he said, sitting down near him, "you seem most seriously depressed."

"Can you wonder at it," replied his father sharply; "just as I considered this rich inheritance ours, it is snatched out of our hands; and that's not the worst of it, this affair will get into all the papers, our return will be made public, and I shall be forced to fly and hide myself from the crew of sharks that will be ready to snap at me. You will be safe enough; you have luckily no liabilities."

"But perhaps," said the son, "this wife of the late Steadinan Shaw may not be able to prove her rights to the Killgerran estates and property left by the murdered miser."

"Ha! you did not hear what occurred at the Turnpike-gate House; do you know who the wife of Steadman Shaw turns out to be?"

"Elinor Fitzharding," returned the son quietly.

The elder Shaw started, and roused himself from his apathetic manner, looking at his son in great surprise.

"How did you hear that, George?"

Now George Shaw had at first hesitated whether he should make his father acquainted with the act he had committed or not, but reflection convinced him of the necessity of doing so.

Therefore, in answer to his father's last question, he said, "listen to me now, sir, attentively, and make no exclamation of wonder that may be heard." He then distinctly, in a low voice, made his fathsr acquainted with the act he had committed, and the consequences as regarded his situation with the murderer, James Hillas.

Mr. Shaw caught his son's hand with an expression of extreme joy and triumph on his wasted features, instead of compunction and regret at his steeping himself in crime.

It is the first step that costs, and that had been taken long before, father and son being equal to commit almost any crime short of murder, to raise themselves to opulence.

"You have saved us George," he exclaimed, "we shall now triumph over this proud woman; it will be no loss to her, she has a noble fortune when she claims it; the mystery is why she never did claim it; through the passage of so many years its very interest is a small fortune. But where are the documents? Let me examine them, and then the safest plan will be to burn them, and scatter the ashes from the window, it blows fresh."

"The safest way, certainly," replied the son, proceeding towards the bed. He drew back the curtains, and turning up the the bolster, pulled out his coat, but with an exclamation of horror and terror, he let it fall, and staggered back into the room.

"Good heavens, what's the matter?" exclaimed Mr. Shaw, catching his son by the arm, and gazing at the coat.

"Ruined, destroyed," returned bis son, striking his hand passionately against his forehead. "Here is some terrible mystery; the papers are all gone."

"Gone," repeated Mr. Shaw, turning pale as death. "How, impossible; you never stirred from the rooms did you?"

Snatching the candle from the table, George Shaw, as pale and agitated as his father, approached the bed, and drawing back the faded chintz at the back of the bed, perceived a narrow door, leading into another room or closet.

George Shaw was so agitated that for some moments, ho found himself unable to try whether the door was locked or not, for the terrible consequences that would follow the loss of the papers to him appalled him. As to Mr. Shaw, he appeared stupefied.

"Some one must have opened that door," said George Shaw, recovering himself, "and, concealed by the curtains, have taken the papers from my coat while we were conversing with the policeman. But why such an act should be committed amazes me. They must have watched my putting them there."

He tried the door; it was fast, though a weak, frail door.

"I must force it open."

"Good God, take care," said Mr. Shaw, extremely agitated and quite unnerved.

"I can incur no greater penalty than I now lie under," observed his son, in a determined manner; "I must see the other side of this door, or to-morrow I may be the inmate of a felon's cell."

So saying, he took his strong clasp knife, and easily pushed back the weak bolt that held the door, having first pushed away the bed.

"Be cautious George, be cautious," cried Mr. Shaw, as he beheld his son stoop and pass through the open space, with the candle in his hand.

"Hush! stay where you are," said the son, in a low voice.

Entering the room, George Shaw held up the light and paused to examine it. It was a tolerably large apartment, and contained a large bed and a small one, and both were occupied, but the occupiers were eound asleep.

On the floor and on the large table, were scattered various toys, and dolls of all sizes, and looking towards the window; he perceived it was crossed with iron bars, and that the fire which burned in the grate was protected by a strong and lofty wire fence.

The sleeper in the large bed breathed heavily. Shading his candle, the intruder approached, and perceived it was occupied by the servant girl of the inn; ho recollected her face; looking into the bed alongside, he discovered a young girl's face, covered with a profusion of light glossy ringlets; she appeared not more than twelve or thirteen; she was in an uneasy sleep, and tossed her thin, but very white arms about, as if troubled in her dreams.

Stepping cautiously back, still shad-

ing the light, he carefully examined the room, there were no traces of the the papers to be seen; he opened two cupboards without success, and still the sleepers did not wake.

Perplexed and bewildered, and no little startled at the posit on he was placed in, he returned into his own room, closing the door, but unable to push back the bolt.

Mr. Shaw looked into his son's serious disturbed features, anxiously demanding what he intended to do and who were those in the room.

Putting down the nearly expiring candle, for it was by this time nearly one o'clock in the morning, George Shaw said, " This is a most serious and distracting affair, and I am puzzled what to do. Some one has evidently taken those fatal papers; there is no sign of them in that room, as far as I dare examine, for if I awoke the servant girl and the child sleeping there, the house would be roused, and that would make things worse."

"George, George, this is terrible," cried the father,-deprived of all power of thought and energy; "How will you save yourself? Whoever took those papers, must know something concerning them."

"That does not follow," said George Shaw, " there is but one person can prove I took them from Killgerran, and he will not inform. Neither the servant in that room nor the child could have taken them; but they may, and indeed must kuow who did. By cautious inquiries tomorrow, I may learn something. At present nothing can be done and the candle is out. Try and rest, father, if you can, nothing is to be gained by repining over what cannot now be avoided. Your sudden and unexpected summons at the door, and your having a stranger with you, startled me, and I thus incautiously thrust the coat and papers behind the bolster without sufficient reflection; and yet even then I must have been watched, but how seen I cannot fancy, for the chintz curtains hang over the door, blocking even the keyhole."

"-It's a strange affair," said Mr.

Shaw, with a sigh; "I thought I had suffered misery and privation enough, but this blow annihilates me."

Thus didthis man, without heart, feeling, or rectitude of principle, argue; he thought he had suffered misery enough, but he never admitted that all the misery and privations he had complained of, were solely the fruit of his own deceitful plotting and scheming life.

It may be imagined that neither father nor son enjoyed repose during the remainder of the hours of darkness; it was a miserable period to both. George Shaw, however was young, and naturally of a courageous, energetic disposition; he thought over all the circumstances of his case, and resolved to meet whatever might occur on the morrow, with firmness and boldness. Had his courage and energy been exerted in a good cause, it would have been praiseworthy, but no thought of repairing the evil he had committed entered his brain; he only planned to avert the evil consequences of his villany, even if his schemes required further crime. He slept towards morning, but was roused by hearing the key turned in the lock of the door behind his head; he listened but could only hear the murmur of a child's voice, and the tender tones of the girl.

"Indeed, dear," the latter said, "you are a great deal better than yesterday."

"But I was not ill yesterday, Betty," returned'the child, "I don't remember anything about yesterday. Where was I yesterday?"

"There, lie still acushla, it's too early for you to get up. I must go call the mistress."

There was then silence, and George Shaw heard a door close, and he determined to follow and question the servant girl, as to who had access to the room besides the child he had seen, and the girl herself before the the inmates of the house were up. He sprang out of bed, and began his toilet. His father, worn out, had just fallen asleep. It was about six o'clock, and barely light, but having dressed himself, he proceeded down stairs, and hearing a noise of scrubbing on the right of the passage, he entered the room, which was a neatly

furnished parlour; the servant girl was raking out the grate preparatory to lighting a fire.

"Faix, Sir, ye're up early," cried the young girl staring at him, "but I'll get you your shoes, they're ready."

"Thank you, my girl," said George Shaw, "I'm an early riser, but pray tell me who slept in the room behind my bed; I felt a draught, and putting out my hand, found there was a door open at the back."

"Faix, sir, it must have been Miss Lizzy as got at the kay and opened it; sure enough I found it open this morning. I am sorry, sir, you were kept awake, but there was only the child and myself slept there."

"It was lucky I was not aware I had so pretty a neighbour," returned George Shaw, with a gay laugh, which brought a bright colour into the girl's cheeks; "but who is Miss Lizzy," continued Sbaw; "I had dangerous neighbours, it seems."

"Indeed to goodness, sir, I would not have slept so well as I did had I a knowed the door was open. Mips Lizzy, you asked who she is, sure she's Mr. Bullfinch's the attorney's, youngest daughter."

"Mr. Bullfinch," repeated George Shaw, with a start; "how is that, what brings a daughter of the attorney's here?" and slipping into the girl's hand a half-crown, he had but three in his possession, he went on, "just answer me a few questions, like a good girl, for I am likely to come and live near here."

"Oh, faix? we knows who you are now, sir," observed the girl, quite pleased at being questioned by so handsome a young man, and equally pleased with the halfcrown; "you are the gentleman that saved poor Widow Kavanagh's daughter from being murdered."

"Why, sir, Missus is Mr. Bullfinch's wife's sister, and his daughter Miss L'zzy, poor thing, is subject to fits, and they lasts four or five days, and then she getsquite well again; her mother takes on so-when Miss Lizzy has the fits, that she goes distracted-like, so Mr. Bullfinch has her brought here a day or

so before the fits comes Od, for Missus doats on Miss Lizzy, and I sleeps at nights in the same room to watch her; last night was the last of the fit; and her father couldn't come'to see her till very late, 'cause of the murder of Mr. Shaw. "

"Good God!" involuntarily exclaimed George Shaw, "then he was here last night!"

A loud ringing of a bell caused the girl to jump up, saying, " Laws, "Missus's bell, and I talking and doing nothing all this while," she was hastily leaving.the room, when Shaw repeated his question.

"Yes, sure he was, and sat a few minutes with his daughter, till she fell asleep."

The girl then ran up stairs, and one or two other female servants came down from another part of the house. Asking for his shoes, George Shaw, completely,bewildered and startled, opened the front door and walked out into the street; " as sure as fate," he muttered to himself, " Bullfinch, the attorney, took the papers! how it was done, or why— Ah, he must have been in the next room when I was talking half aloud to myself; a cursed habit; my voice or my words must have attracted him; it was easy to take them; the curtains of the bed concealed his movements, and while I talked to the policeman, he managed to steal them; we are ruined, and yet he may be bought."

This time he was correct in his surmises; the papers were actually in the possession of Mr. Bullfinch; and we will briefly explain how this strange event took place. Mr. Bullfinch; was an attorney, but this by no means insinuates that he therefore must be a dishonest man; there are, we dare say, many very honest, worthy men in that profession, though it is our misfortune to nave never employed one. Mr. Bullfinch was a clever, sharp, intelligent man, sprung from the ranks of the people. With but a very indifferent education, he had pushed hisway on till he had attained a respectable position. He was by no means a rich man, but he was a good husband, and a very affectionate father to his two children, who were girls; the youngest, unhappily, became affected with periodical fits, during which she suffered so terribly that it affected her mother's health to witness her in them; her sister, who kept the Mariner's Inn, and who was a widow and childless took the child to her house, and fitted up a room for her, for she was greatly attached to the poor little sufferer, who, when well, was an extremely pretty, engaging child, and the father's favourite.

An eminent physician gave it as his opinion that the fits would leave the child as she advanced in life, and latterly they had become less severe. Mr. Bullfinch, by his profession, maintained, as we said, a respectable situation in his native town, but still it was by hard work, and some difficulties at times, according to the litigious dispositions of his neighbours; he was anxious to make a fortune, but a fortune was not to be made in the town of Bantry, even by an attorney, and we must confess it, not by any means a scrupulous one. The introduction of Mr. Shaw on the eventful evening of Mr. Timothy Shaw's murder, roused the energies of Mr. Bullfinch into action; here was a prospect of making a considerable sum without employing any very disreputable means; he felt satisfied he could settle with Mr. Shaw's principal creditors provided they remained ignorant of his accession to considerable property. This was all in the way of business; he had a right to make the best bargain for his client that he could, and he had also a right to secure as large a sum for himself as he was able.

So far all went well, but the death of Mr. Timothy Shaw, and the discovery that there was a widow of Mr. Steadman Shaw, and also a child living, and that there were important papers proving her rights, and her child's rights to the Killgerran estate and money accumulated, completely upset his sanguine dreams of sudden prosperity.

It was late that night ere he proceeded to the Mariuera' Inn to see how his little Lizzy was. On reaching the child's room, he put down the candle, and sat by her bedside; she was asleep; he fell into a reverie, from which he was roused by hearing a voice he recognized in the next room; he knew George Shaw was there, for his sister-in-law mentioned it to him. So, prompted by curiosity, be approached the door of communication, and listened; it was a thin, ill-fitting door, and the sound came distinctly enough through the crevices, but knowing the rooms well, he gently turned the key and let the door fall back, for the first words he caught startled him, and created intense curiosity. Our readers may remember that George Shaw, being exceedingly excited when he opened the papers, exclaimed, "Henceforth, I shall know no peace, while that ruffian lives."

These words astonished Mr. Bullfinch; he knew the bed stood with its back against the door, and that it had chintz curtains. Cautiously and carefully drawing these back, he succeeded in gaining a view of George Shaw, as he sat at the table, with his back to the bed. An attorney's eyes are extremely sharp in detecting law papers and documents; his glance alighted upon those upon the table' and he heard the young man mutter, "This, after all, may be only a copy; the old miser may have lodged the will elsewhere."

Just then came the knock to the door, and Mr. Bullfinch had scarcely time to drop the chintz, and partly close the door, when he heard George pull up the bed, thrust something under, and then unlock the door, and admit his father and the policeman. An overpowering anxiety to obtain those papers, which the attorney at once conjectured Shaw had by some means secured while in Killgerran, took possession of Mr. Bullfinch's mind; he could not resist the temptation; he locked the room door; his child slept soundly; so putting the candle inside the cupboard, he again cautiously opened the door of communication; he heard the three persons within conversing; kneeling down, he passed his hands under the chintz and under the bolster of the bed, and then felt the coat, and in a minute extracted from its folds all the papers; *he felt* he was very pale, and his hand shook, though he did not consider he was acting wrong in outwitting one who evidently had committed a rohbery, but, at the same time, he could not blind himself to the fact that he had no right to take the law into his own hands; however, he possessed the papers, and thrusting them, without bestowing upon them a look (when he took up the candle), into the breast of his coat, and buttoning it over them, he greased the key and bolt, and relocked the door; he was descending the stairs, when he met the girl coming up to bed.

"Miss Lizzy is asleep, and much better," said Mr. Bullfinch, "and will be able to come home to-morrow; here is a half-crown, Betty, to buy you a new ribbon for our fair."

Betty dropped a curtsy, said she was very glad the dear child was better, went on to her room, and was soon in bed; and like all those who work hard, and have a clear conscience, fell asleep in a minute.

Mr. Bullfinch reached home, answered his wife and daughter's anxious enquiries about Lizzy, and making some excuse at its being so late, and about having a paper to prepare for the next morning, proceeded to shut himself up in his office parlour; he laid the papers down upon the table; and before he looked at one of them, he paused to recover his nerve, and to think over what might be the consequences of the act he had committed; he thus communed with himself.

"He will, of course, miss the papers; and knowing he never left the room, he will seek to find out how they disappeared; the door will be discovered behind the bed; he may, probably, search the room or make cautious inquiries; ne will learn, probably, that I was in the house, and in the room next his at the time; and he may even be positive I took them. Still, whatever his thoughts are, he dare not make them public, for these papers he himself evidently stole from Killgerran. I am quite safe," and the attorney rubbed his hands, recovered his nerves, and drawing his chair to the table, took up what he knew to be a will.

"Ah!" he continued, " this is strange indeed, incomprehensible; this is the will of Robert Steadman Shaw, Esq., of Killgerran;" he laid it down, and taking up an another paper, saw it was the marriage certificate of Robert Steadman Shaw and Elinor Jane Fitzharding; "and these," looking at the other papers, " are certificates of birth of two children, and a boy and a girl. Humph! where is the boy? let me see, looking at the date, 1833; he would, if alive, be now of age; the girl five or six years younger. All this is very mysterious."

Taking up tbe will, the attorney snuffed the candles, and commenced reading. This did not occupy him hal-fan-hour, but it made him very thoughtful; taking all the papers and tying them together, he locked them up in an iron safe; he stood for a moment thinking, and then muttered to himself, "Yes, it must be, Mr. Shaw and his son shall succeed to the Killgerran estates; but I must secure to myself ten thousand pounds out of the property they will possess. I would rather the widow and child had it, but there are two reasons why that cannot be. I must betray myself, and let the world look at my act; state it how I may, they will say I committed a crime; in the next place, I should not gain £10,000, and £10,000 is a fortune I can never otherwise expect to gain—*Ce que premiere pas qui coute.* " The attorney took that first step and retired to bed, determined to wrong the widow and orphan, and, "henceforth, he was to know no more peace, for this was his first step in crime." CHAPTER XXV.

Leatino the shores of the Emerald Isle and the Shaws of Killgerran to fight their battle of right against treachery and wrong, we again turn our steps to the troubled and death-strewn land of the Crimea.

. On the seventeenth October the siege of the stronghold of the Czar began in down-right earnest. By land and by sea Sebastopol was attacked at once. Very early on that memorable morning, Henry Pitzharding and his forty volunteers proceeded on board the frigate. commanded by Captain P, where he was received by his friend, the commander, and all the officers, with great kindness and marked attention.

"Come down into the cabin with me, Henry, said

Captain P, who, having known him from childhood, always addressed him by his Christian name. "There is something concerns you in these letters and papers received from England this morning; the Reindeer gunboat has just come to an anchor, she brought the mails from Varna."

"Nothing of serious import, I hope," remarked Fitzharding, entering the cabin with Captain P

"No, faith, returned the Commander. "Some people would call the news glorious, but I know you better."

Taking up the *Morning Post* of the nineteenth of September, he handed it to our hero, saying, "at all events, let me be the first to wish that you may live many years to enjoy the title that is now yours; you are now Lord Courtland."

"What!" exclained our hero, in a tone of regret. "Is his Lordship indeed dead? Though a distant relation, and only seeing him once, I sincerely regret such an event."

"I know you do, Henry," said Captain P.

"Those are not mere words with you. But read the article, and then come on deck; we are getting down all our top hamper, and shall presently take down our cabins, so as to have a clear deck for action."

"Thus speaking, Captain P returned on deck.

Our hero let his eyes rest on the article in the *Post,* which ran thus—

"We greatly regret to announce the sudden death, from disease of the heart, of the Right Honourable Lord Court-land, of Courtland Tower—a nobleman of highest descent, and of a most kind and liberal disposition, and greatly loved and regretted by his numerous dependants. His Lordship never married. His title, and the estate of Courtland Tower therefore descend to the next heir, Henry Edgar Fit zharding, lately a Lieutenant in the R.N..already one of the wealthiest private individuals in England. Lieutenant Fitzharding highly distinguished himself on several occasions while serving her Majesty, but left the service on attaining his twenty-first year. Some mnoths ago he purchased the magnificent yacht built for Lord

B, and, by this time, is with the fleet in the Crimea.

Those who know the present Lord Courtland declare that he is sure to be wherever hard fighting and hard knocks are to be found. We are rejoiced to hear of an old title falling to the lot of one who is worthy of the highest station."

"Upon my word, Mr. Editor," exclaimed our hero, laying down the paper, "one would think you aud I were either very great friends, or you"

"You, what, Harry?" enquired his friend, Edgar Erwin, entering the cabin. "I still call you Harry, though you have become a great lord. I wish you joy— we all knew it; but Captain P would be the first to announce the event, and he now sends me to be the second on the list of well-wishers."

"If ever you call me anything else than Harry, my dear Edgar, we shall have a fight. I regret Lord Courtland's death; I would rather, if it were God's will, he had lived for years—I had no wish for a title. But I was saying, when you came in, that the Editor of the *Post* was very profuse and polite."

"Oh! he's a decent fellow, is the Editor of the *Post,* by far the best paper we get. But come on deck, it is a glorious day, and a noble, inspiring sight; wo shall be playing bowls in two hours more."

The next moment the friends were ou deck. It was at this time near ten o'clock in the morning. There had been a fresh breeze blowing into the harbour in the morning early, but it was dying away fast; it was a clear, bright day, and the rays of an unclouded sun fell upon the hundreds of ships forming the allied fleet. All had their top gear down, whilst the Turkish and French ships were getting under weigh, and the Eoglish Admirats signal was flying, and all the British ships were obeying the signal.

Nothing could be more inspiring or animating than the scene; the roar of guns from the distant shore could be disiinotly heard; volumes of white smoke rose gracefully into the air, and ever and anon a noble war steamer shot past, and proceeded to take some ship in tow.

In a few minutes all were under weigh to take up their positions before Sebastopol.

Those ships without screw power were towed by steamers lashed to the port side.

Henry Fitzharding, or rather, Lord Courtland, was standing a short distance from the wheel, with a telessscope in his hand, intently regarding the movements of the French and Turkish ships, who were the first, as Lieutenant Erwin said, to open the ball. Each ship, as she bore down, poured in her broadside, and then took up her position, as easily and gracefully as if manoevring at Spithead; while, at the same time, the huge batteries on the shore opened fire, with a tremendous uproar, and at the earns moment, there rose in the air the din and roar of the assault on the land side.

Next to Captain P 's frigate, was the Trafalgar, towed by the Retribution, lashed to her port side.

Lord Courtland observed that Captain P kept away towards Fort Constantine, and so did the Trafalgar, both coming to an anchor nearly at the same time. This movement had scarcely been effected, when a shell struck the mast of the Retribution, and burst immediately over tho vessel, the broken mast dropping through the deck.

It was a grand and magnificent sight when, the smoke clearing for a few minutes, the gazer could turn from the frowning batteries of the invested city to the forest of masts before it, each vessel shewing busy sailors who inspired by the scene, and resolved not to be eclipsed by those on shore, worked resolutely at their duty, regardless of the showers of red hot shot and rockets falling like hail around them. Many fell, never to rise again; many were badly wounded; but the attack went on with vigour. Many there had never before had the opportunity of braving death in the service of their country, and with them the resolve was strong to prove

their devotion, and gain a name in the annals of England.

In the midst of the confusion, Lieutenant Erwin exclaimed, as he was passing our hero, who was then with his own ship's crew, desperately busy running in and loading the guns.

A very nice place, Harry, for a nervous old gentleman, in quest of quiet lodgings."

"Give him a headache, Edgar, I think," replied our hero, laughing; but he had hardly spoken the words, when a 68-pounder shot struck the bulwarks, about ten yards a-head of where he stood, scattering and shattering it to atoms, and ripping up a large portion of the deck in its passage, killing three men and wounding several. Before they could collect themselves after this unwelcome visitor, a huge shell fell with a thundering noise on the deck, where it burst with a frightful explosion. Lord Courtland felt dizzy and, for an instant, bewildered, though he was not wounded, and had remained standing; recovering, he looked round him, and beheld his friend, Edgar Erwin, lying motionless. He was the first to reach him, though Captain P and the first lieutenant, also hastened to the spot. Nine of the men were wounded, but Only one of those belonging to the Medora.

"You are not hurt, Lord Courtland, I trust," cried

Captain P. "Ah! Erwin is," he added, as our hero stooped down, with a feeling of intense sorrow, and lifted his friend in his arms, who was insensible, and bleeding from a cut in the head.

"I think he is only stunned," observed Lord Courtland, pushing back the hair, and looking at the wound.

The surgeon was soon by his side, and some men assisted him in carrying Erwin below.

During this short interval the firing never ceased, the Albion, beyond them, was, by this time, completely disabled, but the Trafalgar appeared almost untouched; although the nearest to Fort Constantine, and most exposed, the balls seemed, magically, to fly over her.

As Lord Courtland stood conversing with Captain

P, a midshipman came running across the deck to him, saying hastily, "The surgeon desires me to say, my lord, that Lieutenant Erwin is not dangerously wounded; his left arm is a little shattered, and a fragment of the shell struck him in the head, but he has recovered his senses, and desired me to tell you not to trouble about him, but fire away till all is blue."

"Well, that we are doing," said Captain P f smiling at the boy's ardour and coolness; for, while delivering the message, a red-hot shot tore through the mizen rigging, and knocking a huge piece out of the mast as it whirled on, a splinter passing within a few inches of the youngster's head.

"A miss is as good as a mile," cried the mid, with a laugh, as he walked off quite unconcernedly.

"I am rejoiced," said Lord Courtland, "to hear it's noworse with my old friend. I felt a sad shock when I saw him down."

"God knows, so did I," replied Captain P, looking anxiously at the shattered condition of the Albion. "We are making no impression on those granite walls," he continued; "too long a range. We ought, between ourselves, to have made a run in of it. We shall do nothing here, we are too far off, I fear."

At this instant a powder magazine exploded.in the fortress, amid the continued roar of artillery; and then a dense mass of smoke settled over the shore, the batteries, and the shipping—shutting out the horrors of the scene. What the effect of their tremendous firing was, could not be seen; for the day came to a close, and orders and signals went through the fleet, and then each noble ship weighed her anchors, and stood off, and took her previous station. But still the thunder of artillery roared over the Crimean shores, mighty rockets shot up into the sky; while the shells, many bursting in mid air, offered a strange spectacle. The demon of destruction still hovered over the camp of the Allies, and over the stem stronghold of the Czar—that mighty mass of stone and granite—that undauntedly defied the proud armament of Britain and of

France united.

'Twas night, and Lord Courtland sat by the couch of Edgar Erwin; by his own wish and the permission of

Captain P, he had been removed on board the

Medora, quietness being the chief thing required for his severe wound in the head; he was not allowed to speak, but he listened to his friend's account of the termination of the day's cannonading, evidently with intense interest; he had every comfort, if not luxury, on board the Medora; a roomy and ventilated cabin, and the constant presence and conversation of his friend; therefore though his sufferings were intense, they weregreatly alleviated.

The following day was fine and clear, though very cold, with the wind blowing out from the land; several steamers stood in to have a view of the damages done to the batteries by the cannons of the fleet. As the sea was perfectly smooth, and the motion could not inconvenience the invalid, Lord Courtland, to the great delight of Mr. Bernard and the crew of the Medora, ordered the yacht to be got under weigh, and stand in; it was a fine working breeze, and in a few minutes the graceful Medora was under weigh, with her top gallant sails and royals set; standing in amongst the steamers, she attracted universal admiration from her symmetry, and the velocity of her motion through the water; as her young commander stood on towards Fort Constantine, he rapidly overhauled the D sloop of war, one of the fastest vessels in the fleet; in half-an-hour he was close up with her, and could have passed to windward, but from courtesy dropped under her leeward quarter, close, enough to speak with her commander, Captain 8 with whom he had been acquainted in England, and on board whose ship he had dined with Captain P.

"We have no chance with you, my lord," said Captain

S, leaning over the side; "you can spare us your topgallant sail, and beat us; how is Lieut. Erwin; I heard this morning he was severely wounded yesterday."

"The injury is chiefly in the head," returned his Lordship, "but he improves hourly. Had you mauy hurt? 1 heard you had none killed."

"We had sixteen hit by splinters, but only two severely. The Albion is awfully mauled, and her crew suffered severely. She will have to go to Malta to repair."

The Medora shooting ahead, the conversation ceased; a perfect silence reigned over the fortress and in the camp of the allies. Not a gun was fired

The Medora ran close in shore, so much nearer than any of the war steamers, that she obtained a magnificent view of the fortifications, where the people were too intently occupied repairing damages to heed the vessels cruizing, though they were within gun-shot

"We have a fine view of the place," observed Mr Barnard to Lord Courtland, as the Medora's topsails were backed, and she lay almost motionless within a mile or so of Sebastopol.

Built upon a gentle slope, they could see from the deck of the Medora into the interior of the town, and with a glass could perceive immense masses of soldiers busily removing and repairing the damages; the town itself did not appear to be injured; a few houses appeared to have been struck by round shot and shell, and one or two looked as if they had been on fire, but the face of the forts appeared pitted with shot, and the edges of the stone work knocked away, though the solidity of the forts remained uninjured.

Having anchored close to the frigate commanded by

Captain P, the surgeon and one or two of the officers came aboard to visit Lord Courtland, and see how Lieut. Erwin was progressing.

"I bring you an invitation, my Lord," said the second Lieutenant of the frigate, with a smile; "one that might not be thought very agreeable by most people. Captain

Turner, of the, an old acquaintance of yours, is very anxious to see you; he can't come off himself, but he sent a message by one of the officers of the,

screw line of battle ship, who passed a night on shore, and was engaged in a night attack; he invites you to his tent; he says he cannot promise you champagne or venison pasties, but the food you will get will be quite a treat to you, and give you some idea of camp life before Sebastopol."

"I shall certainly go," replied Lord Courtland, "I have have had a most polite invitation from Lord, and intend proceeding to Balaclava to-morrow; Captain Turner is just the man I should like to pass a night or two with, if there should be anything going on. 1 shall be sure to be in the thick of it if he is concerned."

The surgeon said he considered Lieut. Erwin going on very favourably, but some time must elapse before he would become fit for active service again; but as it appeared most probable the fleet would remain inactive during the winter months, he need not feel impatient.

In the evening he was able to converse a little with our hero, and as the pain in the head abated, his spirits became better also.

The following day the Medora joined that portion of the fleet anchored off Balaclava.

It was on the third of November that the Medora took up her berth in Balaclava bay.

On his first arrival her commander had landed and walked through this singular and romantic town, so extraordinary in its situation, and its land-locked harbour. A few weeks had strangely altered the little town and its then busy port; it was busy still, but busy with misery, disease, and death; a scene of astounding confusion. But all this has been quite sufficiently described by graphic and able writers therefore we shall say nothing more than that Lord Courtland was amazed at the scenes he beheld.

Spending the day with Lord and some of the most distinguished officers in command, he proceeded to take up his quarters with Captain Turner, who, by good luck, possessed a tolerable tent. Our hero did not come on shore single handed. By considerable exertion and personal labour, he had contrived to get a couple of huge hampers, packed with all kinds of creature comforts, conveyed to Captain Turner's quarters, which so delighted and rejoiced the worthy Captain, that he invited several brother officers to the banquet. But this feast was doomed to be broken up; fortunately, as Captain Turner observed, towards the close, when the body was well fortified and able to endure what it had to go through.

The early morning of the fifth of November was dark and drizzly; a heavy grey mist hung over the camp. Captain Turner belonged to the light division of General Codrington.

It was almost daylight before the party broke up, when just as some of the officers were about to return to their own quarters, a sharp rattle of musketry was heard down the hill on the left of the picquets of the light division.

It was Major-General Codrington's custom to visit the out-lying posts of his own division; he first heard the firing, and galloped back to turn out his division; the alarm spread like lightning that the Russians were down on them in great force.

"By Jove, my Lord," said Captain Turner, as he hurriedly threw on his accoutrements, "you had better fall back; this is unhealthy."

"Not at all," replied our hero, quietly arming himself from some of his friend's stores of weapons; "I came to visit, and to share whatever should turn up. "I must borrow this grey coat of yours for the occasion."

So saying, he put on a coat, tightened a belt round hia waist, and with a couple of Colt's revolvers, and a good, heavy sabre, followed his stout friend into the busy and stormy scene without. This was the first warning of the celebrated fight of Inkerman—one of the most gallant and chivalrous actions, that will probably ever be recorded in the historic page.

The dawn was breaking; a gray, dull, lowering day, with a soaking, drizzling rain.

The picquets of the second division were retreating up the hill, hotly contesting every inch of ground. Lord Courtland looked around him with intense interest, but the eye could not travel far through the drizzly rain and foggy atmosphere. By this time the alarm was general all over the camp. Brigadier General Pennefather at once got under arms, and also Generals Sir George Cathcart, Goldie, Torrens, and Sir George Brown. Dim and obscure as every object was, the scene was magnificent, as the great masses of men moving rapidly forward, the sounds of the bugles, the rattle of musketry, and the loud roaring of the cannon in the direction of Balaclava, was exciting and inspiring to a degree to a disposition such as Lord Courtland's. He had long wished to see a battle-field, so widely, so essentially different from all naval engagements; and now he stoodnot merely as a looker on, but sharing in one of the bloodiest and fiercest contested actions ever fought on the Crimean shores. The battle was a series of desperate deeds of individual valour, for so dense became the vapours, that it was impossible to tell what was taking place only a few yards from the spot on which each party fought.

As the contest proceeded, the incessant thunder of the guns, the rattle of the muskets, and the rifles was deafening.

Lord Courtland followed by the side of Captain Turner, and in a very few minutes they were hotly engaged in a hand-to-hand encounter with a strong party of Russian infantry. They could only see the persom with whom they were engaged, but they knew that all that was to be done was to conquer or be conquered.

Gallantly and fiercely the Russians contested the ground, but British valour and indomitable perseverance drove them back. Twice Lord Courtland saved the life of his friend, who fought with a gallantry not to be surpassed. On that day every soldier was a hero. Bayonet to bayonet, with their muskets like clubs, did the battle rage, till with a cheer Lord Courtland inspired the men around him, and broke the Russian wall-like front. They gave way, and in rushed the gallant soldiers, with an ardour still undamped.

"By Jupiter, you're a trump!" exclaimed Captain Turner to our hero, as they plunged through the mist and rain, driving their foes before them; now and then a shell falling amongst them, dealing death to many a brave heart. Yet on the survivors went; they knew not where; they could not tell even where the enemy were. In darkness and gloom, and rain, the officers had to lead on their men, through thick, scrubby bushes, and thorny brakes, that broke the ranks, and greatly annoyed the men; while the perpetual volleys of musketry, fired by unseen enemies, each moment thinned their ranks.

Suddenly the company led by Captain Turner came upon a column of Russian infantry, who were pouring a deadly and destructive fire upon the division led by General Cathcart. A perfect shower of bullets fell around1 the spot where the gallant but doomed Sir George rode.

"That is General Cathcart," exclaimed Captain Turner, as his men formed, and then charged with the bayonent into the middle of the column. At that moment, as Lord Courtland cut down a Russian soldier, with his bayonet within an inch of his breast, a balP struck the General, and he fell from his horse, close tothe Russian column.

"Good God! he is slain," was our hero's reply, cutting his way, with a dozen or more of men, to rescue the body. But the fight had become a terrible hand-tohand conflict. Nearly five hundred men were scattered dead about that fatal spot, where lay the body of their gallant leader, stark and stiff.

But help was at hand: the Connaught rangers, the 88th, and the 47th came up, and with a hearty cheer swept the Russian Column before them.

A few moments after this, during a dense mist, *a* body of Russian horse artillery opened fire upon them. At the same time, entangled in a thick brake, the men, scattered and and disunited, were charged by a formidable body of. Russian infantry, of the regiments of Yladimar. In the *melee,* the friends, whose footsteps o'er that bloody-field we have followed, were separated. The young sailor;was assailed by Russians with their bayonets in hand. With his revolver, he shot the foremost, but whilst warding off the bayonet of the second, he received a blow from the butt of a musket, that stretched him stunned, but not insensible, into the middle of a thick brake.

There was a deadly contest for a moment, and then an overpowering Russian force drove the English back.

CHAPTER XXVI.

I,OBD Cotjrtland rose to his feet a little dizzy; the rain was still falling, and he could not see ten yards before him. The roar of artillery, the rattle of musketry, and the shouts of furious combatants came distinctly upon the ear from all sides, and balls dropped here and there around him; but the press of the combat was some hundred yards in advance. He was surrounded by dying and dead, both English and Russian. As he extricated himself from the brake, the uniform of an English officer caught his eye, and, with a start, and a feeling of horror and grief, he recognised his friend, Captain Turner. He had fought his last fight, and there he lay— one (hand grasping his broken sword, the other fast clutched on the collar of a Russian officer, also quite dead.

As he stooped, grieved and shocked, beside the body of his friend, he heard a voice near say, "For the love of the Virgin, take these three bastes of Eoosians off my chist, your honour."

Leaving the dead in order to help the living, Lord Courtland approached the spot whence the voice came, and beheld a soldier in the uniform of the Connaught rangers, lying on his back, under several bodies of dead Russians.

"My poor fellow, are you much hurt?" he cried, dragging off the bodies.

The man sat up, rubbed the heat drops of agony from his brow, and then, looking Lord Courtland in the face, he said—

"Long life to your honour, I've a leg shattered, and one or two balls that have took lodgings in my ould carcase, bad cess to them, but that's all."

God knows, bad enough, thought our hero.

"Jist put your hand,; your honour," the man continued, "into one of those Roosian's pockets, and you'll surely find a drop of something. My lips is parched entirely."

Lord Courtland complied with his request, and pulled out a canteen, with which the Irishman commenced an acquaintance; muttering, "Arrah, bad luck to them, they've sucked it pretty dry, the bastes. But load your pistols, your honour," he added, "and look out; the firing is coming nearer, and if some of those bloody Eoosians come this way they'll murder us."

Lord Courtland reloaded his revolver and a couple of muskets, which latter he placed by the side of the Irishman. Just then a tremendous shout and a rapid and repeated volley of musketry sounded close to them; the next instant they perceived a large body of Russians in full retreat, and who would evidently pass right over them.

The Connaught ranger, as he spoke, with a desperate effort, turned himself over, and lay upon his face. Lord Courtland, with his revolver in one hand, and his sabre in the other, stood his ground. The next moment he would have been slain without a doubt, had not a body of French infantry broken through the mist, and with a loud shout turned the course of the retreating Russians. Still a few rushed over the brake, and several shots were levelled at Lord Courtland, who seemed to have a charmed life, for they missed him; but the Russian officer who was on horseback rode right at him. Seeing him cut down a man who struck at him, with a bayonet, a shot from his revolver jbrought down the horse, and the officer rolled over in the sod. The next moment Lord Courtland was by his side, and despite his desperate struggles, secured him and held him fast. As he did so a French officer of rank rode up, and looking at our khero with great surprise and ardent admiration, enquired,

"Who are you, Monsieur; you do not appear to be in any kind of uniform, and yet I have just seen you fight most gal-

lantly, and also secure this Russian officer."

"I am merely a volunteer, Monsieur, and this morning accompanied my friend, an English officer, into action, who unfortunately lies here, slain in a severe hand-to-hand contest."

This French officer was the gallant General Bosquet.

"Well, sir, you are a brave gentleman; the fight is now over, the Russians are in full retreat over the bridge of Inkerman; you can safely rejoin your countrymen. We will take charge of your prisoner till you send for him." So saying the general saluted his lordship very courteously and rode on, the Russian officer following in charge of a French detachment.

By this time it was past one o'clock; the day had cleared a little; the Russians were in rapid retreat over the bridge of Inkerman and into Sebastopol, leaving above 9,000 of their countrymen dead upon this hardfought field. Sad and grieved at the fate of his friend Captain Turner, Lord Courtland turned to the spot where bis body lay, and spoke kindly to the poor patient Irishman who was then sitting up, looking very pale and much exhausted from loss of blood.

"My poor fellow," said our hero, " if you could get on my back I would carry you to the tents. If the mist comes on again you may be left here all day, and perhaps all night."

"Thank your honour, and God bless you," said the man, "but faix, my left leg is only hanging on by the skin, so I'd better stay till your honour send some of my comrades, the 88th, your honour. Be gor, your'e a fine brave man whoever you are."

It had now cleared so much that Lord Courtland, could perceive the whole field of Inkermann before him. He was then on rising ground; below him were to be seen vast masses of troops moving in all directions. Horsemen galloping across the plain. Numerous tents were pitched here and there, and in the distance was a windmill.

As he was debating which way he should direct his course, he beheld a body of English infantry, with an officer on horseback, approaching the very ground on which he stood, and whom, on a nearer approach, he gladly recognized as Lieutenant-Colonel W, to whom he had been introduced the preceding day by Lord.

As he reached the spot where our hero stood, the Colonel recognized him.

"I am rejoiced to see you alive and well, my lord, after this bloody but glorious day," he exclaimed. "Major Armstrong told me, you had accompanied Captain Turner's division into action, and I fear the gallant captain has fallen."

"Such, alas! Colonel, is the case. His body is here."

Colonel W dismounted, and his men dispersed, seeking for the wounded. Lord Courtland acquainted

Colonel W with the events of the morning, and how terribly Captain Turner's company were over matched in the combat in which he so gallantiy lost his life.

His body was carried to the camp, and the poor Irishman, also, was taken to his regiments quarters.

The field of battle, even after the most glorious victory, is a sad and terrible sight, and struck Lord Courtland forcibly. It was, in truth, a melancholy picture of the horrors created by ruthless war. That day he passed in the camp with the officers of Captain Turner's regiment, and in the following morning attended the last sad rites paid to those who had fallen in the struggle. His friend was buried on a hill called Cathcart Hill.

Before he left the camp, where lay the soldier of the 88th; his leg had been amputated, and the poor follow was doing well, and was quite pleased and gratified at our hero's visit, and the handsome present he left with him; for he considered he owed his life to the man's advice to reload his pistols.

"What is your name my man?" said Lord Courtland; "I-should like to remember it."

"Darby Houlaghan, your honour, and long life to you; they tell me you belongs to the fleet, and sure I have a brother as is a sailor aboard the S frigate."

His lordship repeated the name, as he inserted it in a tablet. "Houlaghan. And you have a brother in the fleet you say. What's his christian name?"

"Bill, your honour," replied the soldier, looking surprised.

"Is he older or younger than you, my man?" asked our hero.

"He's seven years older, your honour. He was many years prisoner to the Malays, but escaped, and got home in a merchant ship. But when poor Bill got home, your honour, he found that his wife had gone oil' to the Crimea with a sodger, thinking him dead; so Bill entered aboard the S frigate, thinking as how he might find his wife out here, your honour."

"Well, this is singular," said our hero to himself. "This must be the same Bill Houlaghan that Erwin was so fond of on board the Ocean Queen, when she was attacked by the Malay pirates."

Turning to the wounded soldier, he said—"Tour brother shall know how you are getting on, when I return tomorrow to the fleet; for the S frigate is lying off Balaclava." Then rapidly writing a few lines on a strip of paper, he folded it up and gave it to Darby Houlaghan, saying, "Take care of that. When you are sent to England invalided, if you reach that country alive, follow the directions in that paper, and you will be provided for comfortably for life." Then shaking the astonished soldier by the hand, he left the tent, and before evening was in Balaclava, and late that night was once more on the deck of the Medora.

His return created a universal feeling of joy on board the yacht. The master and crew had been extremely uneasy, for the cannonading and firing at Inkermann had been distinctly heard, and continuing for so many hours caused much anxiety.

Lieutenant Erwin was slowly mending. His arm was doing well, but his head prevented his leaving his couch, though in a reclining position. He suffered no pain whatever, and was able to converse cheerfully.

"You are determined, Harry, to get shot, if shot and shell will touch you,"

he said, as he listened to his friend's narrative.

"But now, Edgar, I come to a part that has something to do with you."

"With me," cried the Lieutenant, rather astonished.

"Yes, with you. Did you not tell me that there was a seaman on board the Ocean Queen to whom you were very partial, and whose name was Bill Houlaghan?"

"Yes, poor fellow, he was knocked on the head and fell overboard. Where did you hear anything about him? Not on the bloody field of Inkermann, surely."

"It led to my hearing of him, nevertheless," said our hero, "and instead of being knocked on the head and drowned, he is most likely alive and hearty. At all events, I have heard he is actually a seaman belonging to the S frigate, lying off Balaclava Bay."

"You amaze me," exclaimed the young man. "If it is the same man, and it certainly appears probable, he must have fallen into one of the pirate's boats, and they unaccountably spared his life."

"I will go to the frigate to-morrow," said Lord Courtland, "and get leave to bring the man here. Very few questions will decide as to his identity. The name of" Houlaghan struck me at once. Now this man may be a great help to you in trying to trace your parents, relations, or friends; for he must know off what part of the coast of England you were picked up, and very probably there was some name on the boat you were found in that may lead to further enquiry."

"Well, by Jove, I am astounded! Who would have dreamt that your madly risking your life at Inkermann would lead to such strange results. This man's evidence may hereafter be very important indeed."

"Do you know," demanded Lord Courtland of Captain P, " the commander of the S frigate?"

"Most intimately; the frigate is not a mile from us."

Our hero then briefly stated that he wished to see and speak to a seaman on board, of the name of William

Houlaghan, who formerly sailed in the same ship with Lieut. Erwin, who was extremely anxious to see him, he being possessed of important information which would be useful to Lieut. Erwin.

"I will write a note to Captain Gobalt, and state your wish; he will send him back in your gig."

"You will oblige me greatly if you do so," said Lord Courtland; "another time I will give you my reasons for requesting this favor."

"It's a mere trifle," said Captain P, descending to his cabin.

In a few minutes he returned with a note, and Lord Courtland's coxswain was despatched to the frigate with it.

In less than an hour he returned with Bill Houlaghan, and a polite note from Captain Gobalt, stating that he felt most happy to oblige Lord Courtland.

Bill Houlaghan was a fine, hale, able-looking seaman, about five or six and forty, and looked every inch a manof-war's man. He appeared very much surprised at being told that a lord wanted to speak to him, but hitchingup the waistband of his trousers, declared "it was all the same to him if the Czar Nicholas wanted to speak to him, he was quite welcome."

"I saw your brother, Darby Houlaghan, yesterday," said,Lord Courtland, entering his gig, and addressing Bill, "and I am sorry to say, poor fellow, he lost a leg in yesterday's hard fought field."

"He has lost it in her Majesty's service, God bless her," observed Bill, respectfully touching his hat "and he musn't grumble, though it is a bad job. He bears his lot well, sir, I hope?"

"He bears it like a man," answered Lord Courtland, pleased with the man's manner and mode of expression. He had much the advantage of his brother, and with scarcely a remnant of his country about him.

"I think," continued his lordship, "some fourteen years ago you served as third mate in the Ocean Queen, commanded by Captain Kandal."

Bill Houlaghan started, and looked into his questioner's face with marked surprise, at he replied in a serious, if not

sad tone:

"I did, sir; she was a doomed ship."

Just then the gig shot up alongside the Medora, and ascending upon deck, to the greater surprise of Bill Houlaghan, Lord Courtland requested him to follow him down into the cabin.

There he ordered the steward to place a glass of grog before him, which Bill, notwithstanding his amazement, drank off to his lordship's good health.

"When on board the ' Ocean Queen,'" said our hero, "on your voyage from England to China, did you not pick up a boat adrift, and in it a young child?"

Yes, sir," returned the seaman, astonished more and more, and looking very serious; "I remember the circumstance as if it was yesterday, and a fine, handsome child it was; he came to a miserable end in that doomed ship, sir. She was burned to the water's edge and every soul murdered by those bloody villains, the Malays. I loved that boy dearly, sir," and Bill rubbed his hand across his eyes, "and he loved me, too, poor boy."

"I am happy to tell you that the boy not only escaped the dreadful fate of those on board the Ocean Queen, but lived to become an officer in her Majesty's service, and is now in this ship; he was wounded in the storming of Sebastopol."

The astonishment and real unaffected joy of the seaman was great, there was no end to his expressions of surprise and satisfaction.

"Now follow me," continued Lord Courtland, "and you shall see him; he is getting every day stronger, but unable to leave his bed."

Lieutenant Erwin was as pleased and delighted as his former kind protector, who swore he would have known him anywhere, and tucking up the sleeve of his shirt, Bill smiled as he beheld the confused and indistinct remains of the anchor he had punctured on the arm.

"Well, Bill," observed Lieutenant Erwin, "your preservation, after I beheld you knocked on the head and thrown overboard amazes me."

"Faith, Sir, I was knocked on the

head sure enough, to say nothing of a half a dozen gashes the villains gave me with their knives, but you see, when knocked over-' board, I pitched into one of the proas alongside; there were half a dozen dead bodies there already, and they broke my fall. I suppose I was insensible, and did not recover till the villains were pulling off from the doomed ship. They were pitching the dead bodies overboard, and I was dragged up by the leg, and was on the point of following the others, when I recovered sufficiently to catch the pirate by the throat, with such force —the clutch of death— that they could not separate us for a moment, and then came a round shot from the pursuing frigate, dashing the water right over the stern of the proas. Why they spared me I don't know, but they did, and having a wonderful fast boat, we only out of the fire escaped. I saw the poor Ocean Queen blazing away in the distance, but did not know that the ship pursuing us had sent her boats to her. For seven long: years I remained a slave to these pirates, the Malays; but at last an opportunity of escape presented itself. An American gun-brig gave chase to a proa; I was aboard, but the proa ran away from her. Watching my opportunity, I jumped overboard, and escaped the three musket shots and arrows the villains fired at me. It was a wild chance of liberty or death, but I swam on towards the brig, raising my arm and shouting, and when at the last gasp, I was seen and rescued.

"I served two years in this brig, and was very well treated. At last we returned to New York, and having received some money for my services, I shipped for England, but misfortunes still pursued me—we were wrecked on the west coast of Newfoundland in a dense fog.

"The second mate, myself, and four others only, reached the land, out of a crew of sixteen, and fifty-four ill-fated passengers, and we only owed our lives to being washed overboard on the foremast."

"We made our way to Halifax, and there I entered as a seaman aboard the Lord Melville, Falmouth packet, she having lost several of her seaman in her passage out. In her I arrived at Falmouth, thence went to Plymouth to look after my wife, whom I left there very well and comfortable when I shipped in the Ocean Queen, but she, thinking me dead, had either married or gone off" with a soldier to the Crimea. I shipped, shortly after this, in the S frigate, Captain Gobalt, and since we came here I tried to gain some tidings of my wife, but without success. So, sir, you see misfortune still attends me, but thank God, you are alive and well, and I hope we shall take this here place; it's costing our brave fellows ashore misery and hardship enough, while we're lying idle with as fine a fleet as ever sailed upon the ocean."

"Patience, Bill," said Erwin, with a smile, "when they come to loggerheads at home, they will let us. ike this stronghold; at present they are wasting their breath in useless negociations at Vienna, and Austria is feeding our ministers with lollypops—they are fond of sweets; but John Bull will get very angry by-and-bye, and then he will show his horns in right earnest. Now, I want to ask you if you remember off what part of the coast of England you picked me up in the boat."

"It wasn't off the English coast, sir, we picked you up; 'twas off Bantry Bay, in Ireland. The boat was a fishing punt, and had the name of Thomas Dermot—I remember it well—roughly painted on its stern, and hailed from Castle Town. We had thoughts of running into Bantry Bay, having sprung our main boom, and stood close in for the land, but the weather getting thick we hauled our wind, and in the fog came against the boat you were in. The captain, poor Captain Sandal—you remember him, sir, I daresay, kind-hearted man as ever lived—he took the greatest care of you, wrote down in his book all the particulars of the finding you, for he said you were some gentleman's child, your garments were so neat and fine, and when he got you other clothes in Canton, he locked the others carefully up, but God help us, he and my poor messmates met a miserable death, and I

suppose the old ship after burning went to the bottom. I remember when you first recovered after coming amongst us, you did nothing but cry after your mother, and you called yourself Eddy Shaw. "

"Shaw!" exclaimed both his listeners with great surprise.

"I have no remembrance of that name, Bill," said Lieutenant Erwin. "My christian name, Edgar, seemed to stick to my memory, but of the name of Shaw I have no remembrance."

'-I remember it well, sir," said Bill Houlaghan, "because I come from Bantry myself. My family hailed from there, and when you said your name was Shaw, I was struck with it, for theres an old and wealthy family called Shaws, that live near Bantry, the Shaws, of Killgerran. When I first left home I was about seventeen or eighteen, so I remember well all about Bantry; and I know when you were picked up, and said your name was Eddy Shaw, I thought of the Shaws of Killgerran, and fancied you might be one of them, and told Captain Randal what I thought, so he put it down in his book, and he intended when he got home to make enquiries, but all was lost in the Ocean Queen."

After some further questions and conversation, very satisfactory to Lieutenant Erwin, Bill Houlaghan was rowed back to his ship, his pocket book restored, and a munificent present from Lord Courtland, who expressed a wish to have him in his yacht, but under the then existing circumstances that could not be; still, considering how very important Bill Houlaghan's statement of the picking up at sea of the child, the date and year, &c. would be, he proposed seeing Captain Gobalt, and obtaining his permission that Bill Houlaghan's account of the event should be made before proper witnesses, so that, should any accident occur to Bill, his statement would still be of service to Lieutenant Erwin.

At the same time Lord Courtland declared he would write to his solicitor, to make enquiries in Bantry about the Shaws of Killgerran.

CHAPTER XXVII.

During the period that the events recorded in the last chapter were taking place, our fair heroines were waiting at Batoum till they could procure a vessel to take and land them on the coast of Circassia. At length they found a Greek Zetee, of some eighty or ninety tons, manned by a padrone and eight Greek sailors. The accommodation on board the Zetee, considering the kind of vessel, was tolerably good. She was of a light draught of water, usually plying in the sea of Azof, from Taganrog to Kertch. She was then bound to the last-mentioned place, but the commander agreed to land his passengers on the coast of Circassia, near some port.

It was at this period, early in November, usually a stormy and wild season in the Black Sea, though so far south and east as Batoum and the coast of Circasaia, the weather is much less severe than at Sebastopol, or on the coast of the Crimea.

The little cabin of the Zetee was given up entirely to the two maidens and a young Greek girl Ivan Gortsare had hired to attend on them, and who was quite willing to go into any part of the world with them. With a fair wind, such as was then blowing, their voyage was not expected to exceed three days.

The morning they left Batoum was fine and clear, the wind off shore, and the waters consequently smooth. The two girls kept on deck, regarding the singularly wild but picturesque shore along which they sailed.

"How very fortunate," said Julia Ktzharding to her beloved companion, "that the forts along this coast were destroyed, or we should never have been able to effect a landing. If we fall into the power of your countrymen, Catherine, it will be terrible. We should be separated from your mother, and Heaven only knows when we should see her again. She must be in great anxiety about us, now this terrible war has broken out."

"I fear, indeed, she is doubly anxious on that account," Catherine Warhendorff replied. "How I long to throw myself into her arms after these long years of absence. The sight of those lofty mountains with their snowcapped summits, reminds me so forcibly of our childhood. These are the same mighty mountains that we used, Julia, to gaze upon so much awe and reverence from our early home."

"I can never look upon mountains," remarked Julia, "without a feeling of reverence and awe; they always strike me powerfully."

Towards evening the breeze 'freshened, and the sky became overcast. Ivan had been very serious during the day, and observing that the Greek padrone kept further off the land as the night came on, he demanded the reason.

"Why," said the captain, " you said you did not wish to meet any Russian vessels of war. Soukum Kaleh is still in their hands, and I know they have a war steamer and two brigs cruising off the coast, and they would overhaul me if seen. 1 fear nothing, if you don't."

Ivan Gortsare made no answer, but he did not like the man's manner; it was'not so humble and obsequious as before leaving Batoum. He knew well the Greeks are never to be trusted. He was also surprised to hear that Soukum Kaleh was still in the possession of Russia; for he believed that the three fortresses of Soukum Kaleh, Sotcha, and Touaps, were either destroyed or abandoned, and that Anapa alone remained capable of defence. He did not retire to his couch till very late, and was awoke early in the morning by a considerable bustle on deck.

The two girls were also roused, and almost immediately afterwards the loud boom of a cannon caused them to spring from their berths, and hastily attire themselves.

Gortsare was on deck first. It was daylight and quite calm.

!Not three miles from them lay two vessels, distant from each other about a mile or so. The Zetee was lying motionless upon the water, and all her crew were congregated in her bows, anxiously observing the two vessels.

"What is the matter?" demanded Gortsare. "Why do you regard those two vessels so, and what was the gun fired for?"

"Don't you see that ship on the starboard bow? She is an English corvette," said the Greek padrone, "and the other is a llussian man-of-war brig. I know her; she belongs to Sotcha, and carries eighteen guns, and is full of men. She fired the gun, and hoisted Russian colours. I hope she will take that English corvette."

"Why do you hope that?" asked his companion.

"Well," returned the padrone, " I may venture to tell you now. After I land you, I am bound to Anapa, with articles that are contraband of war, for the Russians. If that English corvette were to overhaul us, he would seize vessel and cargo as a prize."

Ivan had suspected something of the sort, but as long.is they landed him and his fair charges, he could not be injured by their nefarious traffic.

The men were now very busy getting out huge sweeps to urge the Zetee onward, and in the direction of the shore, which was about three leagues distant.

Just then the young ladies came upon deck, and looked anxiously around them. But the moment the princess's eyes rested upon the English cervette, she caught Julia by the arm, exclaiming—

"Oh! Julia, that is the Medora. My heart tells me it is."

Julia turned round with a start and an exclamation of intense joy, and looking eagerly at the ship, which was lying with her broadside towards them, repeated—" The Medora; yes, thauk God that he is here."

Ivan Gortsare was standing near, and on hearing the name of the Medora remained rooted to the deck. He was rather near-sighted, and did not make out the vessel as distinctly as the sharp, keen sight of the girls; but there she undoubtedly was, lying gracefully upon the slumbering ocean, under topgallant sails; and only a mile or so from her lay her formidable antagonist—the Russian brig, Idisoovor, mounting eighteen eight pounders, and one hundred and ten men.

With the padrone's glass, Ivan Gort-

sare readily recognised the Medora.

"She will surely," he exclaimed, "never attempt a-contest with the Russian."

Catherine heard those words, and for the first time looked at the Russian brig, turning pale as she did so. It was not a larger vessel to look at than the Medora, and both girls turned to Gortsare, anxiously asking him why he seemed to fear that the Russian brig would be too much for the yacht, if they did engage.

He was evidently uneasy, but merely replied, "In the first place she is a vessel of war, heavily armed, and full of men. "The Medora is only a yacht, certainly well armed, and no doubt with a gallant crew; but the odds are too great. One thing is certain, the yacht can run from her antagonist when she likes."

"Ah," said the princess emphatically, "that Henry Ktzharding will never do."

"No," responded Julia with a flushed cheek and a flashing eye," the Medora will never owe her safety to flight. My brother will fight her to the last."

"You are Fitzharding's sister, no doubt of that," said Gortsare, looking at the high-spirited girl with a serious expression of countenance.

During this short dialogue the Zetee, under four heavy sweeps, was beginning to gather way, and the Greek padrone called their attention to the Russian brig by observing, "She has caught a breeze, and is closing fast upon the English corvette."

As he spoke a wreath of smoke burst out from the side of the brig, and the roar of her cannon pealed over the deep. All eyes became fixed upon the Medora, whose guns as yet breathed no defiance to her foe. Catherine Warhendorff hardly breathed, so intensely did she feel, but watched the Medora with a beating heart.

The graceful yacht caught the breeze—her yards were braced sharp up, and crossing the bows of the Russian brig, she poured a well-directed broadside into her, bringing down her foretopmast with all its hamper upon her deck.

She appeared to create a slight confusion amongst the crew of the Russian vessel, though she returned the fire, as the Medora stood on the same tack— the breeze freshening. As she sailed on she passed within a quarter of a mile of the Zetee, only then just catching the breeze. At that instant some of the crew of the Zetee caught sight of the smoke of a steamer coming out from the land. The padrone declared it was the war vessel belonging to Soukum Kaleh.

"This is a small steamer," he remarked, "but she carries four heavy guns."

"Good Heavens!" exclaimed Julia in a low voice to Catherine, "this will be fearful odds against the Medora; she may now fairly withdraw from the contest."

But the Medora seemed to have no such intention, for having repaired some damage to her rigging, she tacked, and this time passed so close to the Zetee, who had caught the wind, and payed off to the westward, that those on board must evidently have recognised the ladies, for a loud cheer saluted their ears, and the agitated girls beheld a man spring upon the bulwarks and wave his hat in the air.

The padrone of the Zetee then said: "That vessel is not a man of war; what can she be?" addressing Ivan Gortsare.

"She is an English yacht," answered the Russian, "but it seems she is quite enough for the brig."

Both vessels again crossed each other, at five hundred yards, and both poured in a broadside. What effect the Bussian discharge had upon the Medora, those in the Zetee could not see, but none of her sails or masts appeared injured, while the broadside of the Medora completely crippled her antagonist, bringing down her foremast altogether.

But the Zetee was rapidly widening her distance, setting all the sail she had to a strong westerly breeze.

The girls, with eager and anxious hearts, kept their eyes on the Medora, who, leaving her crippled but still formidable antagonist lying, clearing away the wreck of of her mast and yards, was evidently preparing to receive the steamer, which was rapidly closing with her, coming out from the shore between the Zetee and the yacht.

Deeply as they deplored the course taken by the Zetee, neither they nor Ivan Gortsare could alter it. The padrone was anxious to get away, and Gortsare himself felt rather desirous of leaving both the yacht and the Bussian war vessels. They were now nearly four miles away, when a fresh cannonade between the Medora and the steamer took place. This continued nearly as long as they kept in sight, but the breeze became very fresh, and a thick mist came suddenly on, which hid the vessels from all on board the Zetee.

"Oh! this is dreadful," observed Catherine to Julia in a desponding tone, "we are left in a fearful uncertainty as to the fate of the Medora. What can she do against a war steamer?"

"Oh, much may be done, dear Catherine, with the courage and energy Henry possesses; a steamer may be crippled, you know. My brother came out into this sea well prepared for anything that might occur, and I feel satisfied he would not wait for this steamer to come up with him if he had, not good hopes and expectations of disabling her."

"You are a dear, good soul, Julia; you always keep up my flagging spirits. I never knew your courage fail, under all our trials, but once."

"Ah," said Julia, " I was overpowered then, I confess, whilst on the voyage from Gibraltar to Constantinople. I always expected—at all events, I hope— that some event, some unlooked-for cause, would lead to a discovery of who we were; that Ivan Gortsare might relent or alter his views, and permit this ardently-wished-for discovery to take place; but no such event happened; so that, when we parted at Constantinople without scarcely a shadow of hope remained, my heart sank, I confess, and despair seized me for the moment. But listen; I do not hear any more firing," continued Julia, "God send Henry may disable the steamer; if so, he will follow us."

"Ah! and if she disable him," said the princess, in a despairing tone, "what will become of him and us? Alas! misfortune seems to pursue us still."

"Say not so, dear Catherine," answered Julia, throwing her arms round her friend's neck; "I have every hope and confidence in the bravery and skill of Henry. Recollect, if the Medora is only a yacht, Henry is a thorough seaman, accustomed to peril, and has faced worse odds and overcome them. Mr. Bernard, also, is an old and tried seaman, and almost all the men on board are old men-of-war's men, and would fight to the last, both for the honour and glory of their flag, as well as from love to their commander. Ah! Catherine, always hope. Does not Kozlay say—' We are born in hope, we pass our childhood in hope, hope governs our whole existence, and not till the beating of the heart shall cease, will its benign influence leave us.'"

Catherine smiled sadly as Gortsare joined them, saying—" How very singular this strange meeting with the Medora; I trust she may get away from her antagonist. She completely crippled the brig; her metal is evidently heavier. She may do so to the steamer; our padrone says she is but a poor sailor, though her guns are heavy."

"Would it not," asked the young Princess, " have been practicable to have remained, and witnessed how the contest ended. We are in a dreadful state of uncertainty! Mr. Fitzharding evidently recognized us with his glasses, attracted no doubt by seeing females on board this Zetee."

"That he recognized you, I have no doubt," answered Ivan thoughtfully, "and that he would have boarded us had we remained, and succeeded in beating off his antagonists; but the padrone, I am sorry to say, is not to be depended on. He is a kind 'of contrabandist— carrying to Anapa goods which, if found in the Zetee by English or French cruisers, would lose him his craft and his cargo. I did not know this when I engaged him, but I suspected it yesterday, hearing some words between him and one of his crew."

"But are you sure," enquired Catherine Warhendorff, "that he will fulfil his contract, and land us where he agreed?"

"I trust he will," said Gortsare

thoughtfully; "if he refuses, I regret to say we are in his power."

The girls looked very serious, but, like their companion, they saw no way of compelling the Greek to fulfil his contract.

Towards sunset the mist cleared off, and all looked back in the direction where they supposed the contest to have taken place. One vessel only was to be seen—a lofty rigged ship, carrying royals. Catherine Warhendorff's and Julia Fitzharding's hearts beat with increased hope. This vessel was following in their wake: it must be the Medora. It was certainly not a steamer, and the Russian vessel could not carry royals after the damage she had received.

The Greek Zetee, like almost all those vessels, was an extraordinary fast craft, and the padrone, who suspected the vessel following was the English yacht, carried every stitch of canvass he could, With anxious hearts, as the gloom of night came on, and the mist again spread at times over the deep, the maidens retired to their berths, not to sleep, in truth, for their thoughts were too busy, and their minds too anxious concerning the morrow.

As the dawn made, Gortsare hurried on deck—the horizon was clear, and he saw at a glance that the Greek padrone intended to betray him, for right before them was Anapa, and right astern was the Medora, then within two miles of them.

Ivan Gortsare was now exceedingly perplexed. He discovered, when too late, that a crooked policy will not always succeed. His wavering between right and wrong had now, he feared, brought trouble on them all, and, in the end, most probably defeat all his projects. He looked at the Medora, which, under a cloud of canvass, was tearing through the water. He looked at the Zetee; she was flying through the white crested waves, carrying more canvass than she evidently well could bear; for at times she buried her shaip bows in the seas, and trembled under the pressure of her canvass.

The Greek captain and his crew were most anxiously watching the coming up of the English yacht; and certainly, if they had had six or seven more miles to run, they must be overtaken; but Ivan Gortsare saw the port, ramparts, and forts of Anapa, much nearer than that, and he felt convinced the port would be gained long before the Medora could come up. As he watched the yacht, a wreath of smoke curled out from her hows, aud then the loud boom of her shotless gun pealed over the deep.

"Ha!" said Ivan Gortsare", "they despair of overtaking us; so much the better. At present it would not do."

He then walked over to the Greek, who seemed pleased and said—" She cannot overtake us now, signor."

"You have broken your contract, and will put me to inconvenience," said Ivan, angrily, to the Greek captain;

"you are running into Anapa."

"I am," replied the Greek; "what else could I do? You don't know your own mind; you said last nigbt that you did not wish that English yacht to overtake us. Had I attempted to make a landing on the coast with this wind and sea it would be dangerous, in fact scarcely possible, and I should have been overtaken by that yacht, who must have some government officers in her, or why pursue me? You can probably tell me the reason."

Gortsare certainly could; he did not wish to be overtaken by the Medora, for that would defeat the plans agreed on by the Circassian chiefs—not that he entertained the slightest doubts about our hero not fulfilling the conditions required for the liberation of the princess and the two girls, but it would prove to the chiefs that he himself had outstepped the limits of his instructions, and that, in his anxiety to undo the mischief he had formerly intended, he had, in fact, partly broken his oath and faith to the chiefs; he therefore did not wish to be overtaken by the Medora. The delay at Batoum, and the Medora's being forced so much to the eastward by the terrible storm that raged after-her departure from Balaclava, had led to their strange meeting.

Catherine and Julia were both roused by the young Greek attendant, with the intelligence that the English ship was following them.

"Oh, thank God!" exclaimed both, starting up with their hearts beating with joy and renewed hope.

"Then the Medora," continued Julia, "has beaten off her foe, and Harry, dear Harry, is safe and well, or she would not be following us."

In less than ten minutes they were on deck, and their gaze instantly rested on the1 Medora, which, under every stitch of canvass available, was overhauling them fast; she was not two miles astern, but the port of Anapa, was within a mile of them, its forts bristling with guns.

"Good God;" exclaimed Catherine, "we are running into a harbour with the Russian flag flying over the forts. Oh, Julia! this is Anapa; do you not remember it? Look, there is the very mole from whence we stepped onboard the steamer when we left Circassia."

Gortsare now approached them—he looked very anxious and uneasy.

. "I suppose," he remarked, "you both remember this place, but no one here will recognise either of you; this rascally Greek has betrayed his trust, but I pray you have no fear, for I have the means of defeating this unexpected event. Ha! by St. Ivan, the Lower Fort has opened fire upon the Medora," and, as he spoke the words, the loud roar of the canon from the outer fort, echoed from the lofty cliffs along the rocky shore.

All eyes were upon the Medora, which gracefully bore up in the wind; as a second and third gun was fired, they could see the main-royal and its mast knocked into the air, and fall; but still the yacht payed away on the other tack without firing a shot—which would, indeed, have been a useless bravado, the English ensign floated out boldly from her peak, as gun after gun was fired without etiect. The Mole and quays were crowded with eager gazers, wondering at the single English ship approaching so daringly near the forts: for, as far as the eye could distinguish, not another sail was in sight. There was not a single armed at that time in port—two large steamers having sailed three days previously for Kertch and Taganrog.

There was no time for conversation or reflection upon their situation, for the Zetee ran in and anchored within the piers.

CHAPTER XXVIII.

The Zetee had scarcely swung to her anchors when a custom-house boat, with two officers of the Customs and an individual in military attire, pulled up alongside.

The officers and the Greek padroue immediately entered into an animated conversation, while the military individual walked up to Ivan Gortsare, who was alone upon deck. After looking at him from head to foot, he said in rather an imperious tone—" A passenger I suppose!"

"My daughters, an attendant, and myself, are passengers in this vessel," returned Ivan Gortsare.

"You are Russians—where are your passports and what is your business in this place?"

Gortsare had expected these questions; so taking a large, clasped pocketbook from his vest, he opened it, and selected a fojded piece of vellum, and without a word handed it to the government officer; who, reading the first few lines, turned the page, looked at the signature, and then littered an exclamation of surprise; but he gave back the document, saying—" When you and your family are settled on shore, you will have to attend at the Commandant's. Where are you ordered to in this quarter?"

"It was not my intention to land here," said Gortsare. "My mission is amongst the Circassians; I intended to penetrate into the war district, under the guise of an Armenian merchant."

"What vessel was that pursued you to the entrance of the harbour, and so audaciously braved the guns of our forts. It is not a vessel of war, for we could see with our glasses that her complement of men is small, and she does not carry a pennant."

"I fancy she is an English yacht."

"A yacht!" exclaimed the Russian officer in exceeding. surprise, and curling his long, bushy, grizzly moustachios.

"St. Ivan! a yacht in the Black Sea in winter, and in time of war; these islanders are lunatics in some things. But why did she pursue this Zetee?"

"I do not know that she pursued the Zetee," said Ivan Gortsare.

Just then the two custom-house officers came up, and addressing the government official, said, "Only think, Captain Kickemoff, that English vessel is a pleasure yacht, and had actually the audacity, the hardihood, to attack the Czar's 18-gun brig, and, this Greek padrone says, completely crippled her; he says too that the steamer from Soukum Kaleh must have engaged her, for he saw her coming out, but a mist prevented his witnessing the result."

"The result!" repeated Captain Kickemoff, in a vexed and passionate tone, "did we not see the yacht uninjured. Here is some deception; she must be a sloop of war, and have her men concealed, and is reconnoitering this port. Those cursed islanders will get a hot reception if they come here."

""Where do you intend to put up?" enquired the captain, turning to Ivan Gortsare, "are you acquainted with the town.

The person addressed hesitated a moment, and then said, "I have been here before. I shall put up at the Hotel of the Grand Duke Constantine."

"Very well," remarked Captain Kickemoff, and entering the boat with the custom-house officers, pulled away from the Zetee.

"So far," cried Gortsare, "we are safe. "

In less than an hour, he and his two supposed daughters were comfortably established in the hotel, which, standing on a rising ground, overlooked the harbour, the two forts, and the wide expanse of water beyond.

"It seems, dear Catherine," observed Julia Fitzharding as they sat in the well-stoved chamber of the hotel, gazing over the dark watera of the Euxine, " that we are likely to escape the danger apprehended from our being obliged to enter a Russian garrison town."

"The document, constituting him a secret agent," replied Catherine, " has

saved us from suspicion at present; but, still, he has only been questioned by a subordinate officer—suppose the Governor or Commandant of this place should take it into his head, before we are able to leave, to examine Ivan more strictly, and request to see his letter of instruction, appointing him a mission amongst the Circassians, he would be puzzled what to say; awaken only a suspicion, and we should surely be discovered not to be his daughters. Our situation, I think, is perilous."

Ivan Gortsare, when he returned from a visit to the Commandant's, a messsenger having been sent, ordering him to go there, looked pale, and his manner was agitated.

"Yon look vexed, Ivan," remarked Catherine kindly; "has anything unpleasant occurred at the Commandant's?"

"I cannot conceal it from you, Princess," said the Russian, very seriously; who always, when by themselves, styled Catherine Warheudorff—Princess.

"What has occurred, then—does the Commandant suspect anything wrong?"

"No, Madam, no; but, though you were too young to remember him, this Governor of Anapa remembered me instantly. I confess I was confounded when I beheld him; he constantly visited at the General's palace at St. Petersburg, and was one of the General's aide-de-camps in his last campaign in Circassia. "

"Who is he, then?" asked Catherine Warhendorff, rather startled.

"The Count Alexander Zouboski."

"Ha!" exclaimed Catherine, colouring and looking really alarmed; "I have a strong recollection of that name; I have heard my dear mother mention it, and heard her say he was a wild, dissipated man."

"You are right, Princess—too right," said Ivan; " this nobleman has been disgraced, and sent by the Emperor to this distant and remote post for five years. This man once aspired to be betrothed to you, Princess, while you were yet a mere child."

"Heavens! is that possible?—I have

no recollection of that, or of him personally."

"Such, however, was the fact," said Gortsare; "but your mother spurned his offers and proposals, and I believe from that time, he became a bitter enemy, and secretly was a spy upon all your lamented father's transactions in the Caucasus."

"But tell us," interrupted Julia Fitzharding, who had listened anxiously, " what passed in your interview with Count Alexander Zouboski."

"I will do so," answered Ivan. ""When I received the summons, I proceeded to the Commandant's house, unfortunately without asking who he was—if I had, I should not have been taken so much by surprise. I was shown into a saloon; where sitting at a table, with wine and refreshments on it, was a tall, powerful looking man. He lifted up his head; and with a start and no doubt a change of colour, I beheld Count Alexander Zouboski."

"'Ha!'" exclaimed the Count, looking at me evidently as surprised as myself, what, is it you, Ivan Gortsare? how is this. I understand from some one I saw lately,, that you were employed in England, and here you are, and I understand with two charming, beautiful daughters. You are a widower, I suppose, as I have not heard that you brought a wife with you.'"

Both Catherine and Jidia coloured to the temples.

"The Count looked at me keenly as he spoke.

"' I was in England, Count,' I replied; 'but it was thought, with my knowledge of Circassia, I could be of more service there.'

"Pray, who do you communicate with f" he demanded, observing me very steadily.

"I was prepared for a question like this, and answered withovit hesitation, 'With his highness Prince Woronzow inTiflis.'"

"' Humph! I'm told that he is there now, and that Schamyl is advancing upon that place. But kow came you so much out of your course? I hear you came from Batoum. What part of the Caucasus or Georgia are you going to?'

" I intended, count, landing somewhere between Soukum Kaleh and the fortress of Touaps, but my rascally Greek padrone had a concealed cargo for this place, and refused to land me.'

"' And what are you going to do with your handsome daughters, Ivan,' asked the count. 'It's a dangeroua place to take handsome girls to; those Circassian rebels will rob you of them. Better leave them under my charge.'

"' I thank you, Count Zouboski, but they are necessary to my projects in the country I am going into,'

"' There are rumours afloat,' remarked the count,' that the Princess Warhendorff is held a captive by Prince Schamyl; do you know anything concerning the princes3 and her daughter? who, if she is in any respect like her mother, must be a very handsome girl. I remember her when a child; she promised well.'"

There was a shade over Catherine "Warhendorff's fair and expressive countenance as Gortsare proceeded in his account of his interview with Count Alexander Zouboski, that proved her heart was ill at ease; while Julia Fitzharding's short upper lip curled with a contemptuous, proud expression; but Ivan, though he caught the expression of their features, continued without any remark.

"' How do you intend to proceed from this place?' asked Count Zouboski, not repeating his previous question.

"' With the first party of Armenian merchants, count, that pass through from Kertch and Kaffa. I hear the monthly steamer is due.'

"'Yes,' replied the count,'but they suspect some of the English or French ships are cruising in these waters; but the season is getting late, and the enemy will not attempt operations against our forts during the winter months, and before the spring we shall be too strong for them. You may retire,' he added,'I shall see you again; and as I have heard so much said about the beauty of your daughters, I shall pay them a visit tomorrow or next day.""

"Oh, heavens," cried Catherine in a vexed tone, 'cannot this most unwished-for honour be prevented?"

"It is that very visit troubles me," said Ivan Gortsare. "I know this Count Zouboski to be a mostunscrupulous, unprincipled man, capable of anything. In this remote district, with nearly eight thousand men under his command, he is a person whose will is law, at such a period as this; besides, I dare not attempt to leave without his permission."

"Suppose we feign illness and refuse to see this abominable Count Alexander Zouboski," said Julia Fitzharding; "at all events, you, Catherine, can keep out of the way, for fear your singular and remarkable likeness to your mother might strike him. I do not fear to see him— he can see nothing in me."

"Except a very lovely, captivating maiden," observed Catherine with a smile, putting her arm round Julia's neck affectionately: "and that man is not to be trusted with such a sight, if we can avoid it."

"Ob, I am not at all afraid about myself, for Ivan's document is a strong safeguard, provided you are not recognised; then, indeed, it would be impossible to avoid discovery. The Count would, no doubt, send us to St. Petersburgh, and imprison Ivan."

While they were thus conversing with Ivan Gortsare, the Commandant of Anapa, Count Alexander Zouboski, was pacing the saloon where the latter had left him. He was a tall and very powerful man, and had formerly been one of the Czar's guards. He stood full six-feet-four, and was accounted a remarkably handsome man; at this time, he was not more than four or five-and-thirty. Some act he committed, displeased the Czar; who removed him from the Guards, though he continued in some degree the favorite of the Emperor—for he was a brave and unflinch ing soldier, but totally unprincipled and unscrupulous. He therefore made him Commandant of Anapa, and banished him from St. Petersburgh for five years.

The Count Zouboski, after the departure of Ivan Gortsare, rose from the table and commenced pacing the room, and then rung his bell—" Send Captain

Kickemoff here," he said to the attendant who entered.

Captain Kickemoff soon made his appearance—he was the Count's right-hand man—what we in England would call a ' toady,' a kind of spy upon all the other officers; and, in fact, upon all within the forts and town of Anapa.

"Well, Kickemoff," said the Commandant, " have you pumped the Creek rascal, who commands that Zetee quite dry—have you gained any further intelligence. I have had an interview with Ivan Gortsare, and I feel satisfied there is some mystery with respect to the two girls he calls his daughters—no more his children than you or I. I shall not let him out of this place till I can get information from Prince Woronzow,whether he employed him or not; for, I suspect not."

"I have learned quite enough, Count," answered Captain Kickemoff, "to satisfy me that those beautiful girla — and they are exquisitely beautiful — are not his daughters. That Greek padrone would sell his father for twenty roubles. He told me that his passengers came from Trebizond to Batoum, and hired him to land them somewhere near Sotcha, and that he was greatly afraid of coming upon any Russian vessel or port; and that they all knew the English vessel, and those aboard of her, that followed them; and that one evening, having his curiosity excited, he listened at the thin partition between the-hold and the main cabin, and he heard his passengers speaking in Russian, and Ivan Gortsare called one of the young maidens Princess Catherine."

"Ha! say you so," exclaimed Count Zouboski, with it start, his face flushed with excitement. "By St. Nicholas, I begin to gain a clue to this mystery. This Ivan Gortsare is a serf of the Princess Catherine Warhendorff, who it is now well known, is a captive to the Circassians —to Prince Sehamyl, I believe. As sure as you are there, one of these girls is the Princess's daughter. It must be so; and now the thing is to find out which is the Princess; but I think I could almost swear to her, if I saw her. As a child she had splendid large black eyes, and jet black hair."

"You are right, Count," interrupted Captain Kickemoff, "I saw them both, without being seen myself, at the hotel. One of the maidens is just as you describe her— a perfect Venus; the other is a splendid girl, more to my taste; I like blue eyes and light auburn hair; besides, she has a foot like an angel."

"Come, that's going a long way for a comparison, Kickemoff. Upon my soul, I don't think you ever saw or will see an angel's toot. However, who can this other girl be. Let me think. The Princess Warhendorff left St. Peterburg with this Ivan Gortsare, her daughter, and the daughter of an English merchant, who died at Odessa as rich as Croesus. I remember all the circumstances well; it's ten or eleven years ago, and they were never beard of after their departure. It was thought at St. Petersburg in the higher circles that she was overtaken, and imprisoned, by the Emperor's orders, in some distant fortress; so all about them was forgotten—indeed people were afraid to mention either the Princess's name or that of her husband, General Warhendorff. The Czar was so furious at the disgrace inflicted on the army by his defeat and slaughter by Prince Sehamyl. But, in these last few months or so, it has been discovered by the escape of some prisoners from one of the Caucasian fortresses, that the Princess Warhendorff is a captive to Prince Sehamyl; but they said nothing of her daughter being with her. Now if it should turnjout that one of these girls is the Princess's daughter, it would suit my views to make her my wife. The Emperor is sure to restore her mother's estates."

"Stiil," remarked Captain Kickemoff with some hesitation, as if he doubted the feasibility of the Count's project, "you must get the maiden's consent; for so highly connected as she is—even distantly allied to the Czarina, it would be dangerous to attempt to force her inclinations."

"My good friend," interrupted the Count, rather contemptuously, "do not trouble yourself about her inclinations. Who troubles themselves about the inclinations of a young girl of seventeen. When she is my spouse you need not feel alarmed about her inclinations; this is not the first time I have thought of this young princess for a wife. Now if you have a mind, Kickemoff, to become a Benedict, there's the other girl for you—a first-rate speculation; for if she turns out to be the English girl, she will no doubt have a noble fortune."

"You forget the war, Count Z(ou)boski; it's not very likely that her fortune would be paid to an enemy."

"War, indeed I" retorted Zouboski contemptuously.-" There will not be one of those boasting islanders left before next spring. They are only a handful of men. What with the bungling of their own blessed ministers, the cholera, and the severity of winter, they'll die like starved rats."

Captain Paul Kickemoff still looked very doubtful. He felt quite willing to enter into any project or scheme to better his fortunes, but to meddle with a young lady connected by family ties with the Czar, of whom he stood in awful dread, appeared astoundingly presumptuous.

"My first object will be to secure the person of this Ivan Gortsare," said the Count. "I suspect him; he is deceiving the Emperor, and is engaged in some schemes of his own. I will send a courier to Taganrog, to

D, the chief of the secret police; he is there now.

He has the superintendence of these spies. It strikes me as rather extraordinary that Gortsare should be ordered from England, where his presence is essentially necessary at this moment, to be sent into the Caucasus, where he can be of little or no service. I will have him arrested to-morrow; if I am wrong a few week's confinement »vill do him no harm, and during those few weekB I can make myself agreeable to the two maidens." CHAPTER XXIX.

Ivan Gortsaee felt it absolutely necessary that no time should be lost at Anapa—it was ticklish ground to loiter upon—for he was quite aware he had a dangerous eye regarding his movements; he, therefore, the third day of their residence, made enquiries through the town, and found a small party of Armenians, men and women, who had crossed from Caffa to Kouban, and were proceeding to Kasterth. The Armenians form the most numerous, and certainly the most influential bodies of Christians in Turkey, from whence they spread all over Russia, Circassia, and Georgia, to the shores of the Caspian Sea.

Their known wealth gives them importance, politically as well as civilly; their knowledge of both the Turkish and Russian languages, their great commercial dealings, and their Christian faith, are their passports even through the Russian provinces, whose jealousy and vigilance are relaxed in their favour.

Gortsare soon made arrangements with the chief Armenian, a merchant and banker, to travel in company, paying his alloted portion of expenses in the general fund; all the Armenians required was, that he should furnish himself with a pass from the Commandant of Anapa, as far as Walcheek, he would secure their safe passage through the Circassian outports. Gortsare was aware he could do that himself, but he did not think it necessary to say so.

MeetiDg Captain Kickemoff, he mentioned his intention of departing the next day, and his wish for a pass from Count Zouboski as far as their outposts of Walcheek.

"Certainly, certainly," said the Russian officer, "you need not trouble; I will get you the pass—let me see, for yourself, two daughters, and a Greek girl."

"Yes," replied Ivan, scarcely relishing the extreme? kindness of Captain Kickemoff, "that's the amount of our party."

"You shall have the pass this evening. I mil see Count Zouboski, and get it."

The Captain proceeded towards the Commandant's residence, and Gortsare walked towards his Hotel.

He was passing along the back of the church, Paul Petrovitch, when he felt his arm touched by some one whose footsteps he heard behind him. Turning round, he heheld a tall, powerful man, in the common dress of the Russian peasant, with his dirty beard, and hairy cap over his brow.

"What do you want with me, man?" asked Ivan Gortsare, eyeing him from head to foot, and meeting thedark, brilliant eyes of the man fixed upon him.

"Ha!" said the stranger in rude Russian, speaking like the hard working serf, "my disguise is good when Ivan Gortsare asks me what I want."

Ivan started back with a pale cheek, and looked hurriedly around him; they were alone, the church on one side, and a long blank wall, the back of a powder magazine, on the other.

"St. Ivan, Morowdilchi! it is possible?" he exclaimed, "this it madness."

"Not so," answered Lord Courtland, for he it was,, changing his voice and manner; "as you yourself have proved; but we may be observed together, so meet me to-night here when this church clock strikes six. Adieu, there are persons coming."

And without another word he walked on, so exactly imitating the slouching gait and slovenly manner of the Russian serf, that Gortsare remained rooted to the spot, in amazement and stupefaction.

Recovering, he repeatedly crossed himself, for he was a devout Catholic, and somewhat superstitious, notwithstanding all his reading and love of the sciences.

"By all the saints, he's a dead man if discovered," he muttered to himself. "How did he get ashore? how get through the gates? and so marvellously disguised."

The agitation of his manner and voice in speaking was so great when he entered the room where the young girls were sitting, and looking out upon the stormy waters of the Euxine, then breaking in angry inenances against the huge rocks supporting the outer fort, that they became alarmed; and Catherine Warhendorff immediately said—

"What has happened, Ivan? you look pale, and your manner is agitated."

He at first thought of concealing his meeting with Lord Courtland, but, on second thoughts, altered his mind, as he justly considered his lordship having in-

curred so terrible a risk would not be satisfied without an interview, which, if he refused to accede to, might compromise all their safety. He therefore replied to the young princess's question—

"In sooth, princess, I have had every reason to be agitated and uneasy. Mr. Fitzharding has contrived to gain an entrance into this strongly-garrisoned town."

"Merciful goodness!" exclaimed both girls, turning pale, and quite as agitated as Ivan Gortsare," how is that possible? How, and under what circumstances?"

"Ah, my God!" added Catherine Warhendorff, clasping her hands," if he is discovered, he will be shot to death as a spy by that horrid Count Zouboski."

"No, I do not think that, princess," said Ivan recovering himself. "You are getting more alarmed than necessary; his disguise is so perfect, and his assumption of the peasant's manner, tone, &c., so complete, that I was deceived."

He then related how and where he had met Lord Courtland, or, as they considered him, Henry Fitzharding.

Julia started to her feet, and clasping Gortsare's hand, while her cheeks flushed with excitement, exclaimed in an impassioned tone—

"I will for ever love and reverence your name, if you let me accompany you this evening, to meet my brother. Concealment is no longer necessary or possible; he knows who we are, and that we are here. If it were even possible for Harry to carry us off, he would still honourably.pay the required ransom.''

"Nay, Miss Fitzharding," interrupted Ivan Gortsare, "I never for a moment doubted that; but, as you say, there is no longer any utility in keeping you from the knowledge of each other. If I have broken my oaths, and forfeited my word to the chiefs, I could scarcely have avoided doing so, from unavoidable circumstances and most unforseen accidents; at all events, I am satislied neither Prince Schamyl's oath or the interest of the chiefs will be hurt by the betrayal. You shall accompany me, but we must be vigilant and cautious in the extreme."

A knock at the outward door interrupted the conversation, and.beforea word could be spoken, it was opened, and no less a personage than Count Zouboszi entered the saloon.

The ladies started to their feet, with a suppressed exclamation of fear and surprise, while Count Zouboszi stopped, looking at the two lovely and fascinating girls, so simply attired, and yet so strikingly elegant and graceful in manner and appearance, with unmistakeable admiration.

He was handsomely attired, in an undress military costume, evidently studied to set off his almost gigantic figure to advantage. Recovering from his surprise, he advanced in his usval easy manner, saying—

"I pray you, young ladies, to excuse my intrusion, and be seated; I was not aware I should see any one but Ivan (xortsare, to whom I wish to give a few instructions before his departure."

"Then, Sir, we will leave you," said Catherine "Warhendorff, with a slight and somewhat proud inclination of her beautiful head, her dark lustrous eyes meeting the enquiring glance of the commandant of Anapa.

"I am sorry you should think my presence an intrusion," said Count Zouboski, politely, " I pray you remain and I will retire."

A look from Ivan Gortsare showed Catherine Warheudorff, that she had better remain; so, with a slight inclination of her head, she and Julia sat down, the Count himself also taking a chair.

"There is your pass, Gortsare," said the Count handing him a printed document, signed by himself, "but I fear your daughters will suffer much, travelling across the great plain at this inclement season of the year, exposed on the backs of mules; if your young ladies will accept it, my drosky is quite at your service, till you reach Zidlinks, where your difficulties will end."

As the Count particularly addressed this speech to Catherine Warhendorff, her natural politeness caused her to reply. She thanked the Count, but said—

"They did not suffer from the weather, and after all, as the roads were so ex-tremely bad, as they were informed, a mule was perhaps the best mode of travelling."

Such is the contempt experienced for the lower classes in Russia; that the treatment they receive is little better than brutes.

Ivan Gortsare, a serf and a secret agent, dare not sit in the presence of a noble, or speak unless spoken to, therefore he remained standing, while Count Zouboski. in a manner, forced Catherine Warhendorff to listen to him, and of necessity reply. As to Julia Fitzharding, she regarded the Count with a feeling of detestation she took no pains to disguise; with a flushed cheek she rose from her chair, and approaching the window, gazed out upon the storm-tossed waters of the Black Sea; her thoughts all centered upon the brother she so dearly loved, though she had been separated from him from her earliest years.

At length Count Zouboski rose up, and taking a polite leave, repeated his proffers of service, which again as politely declined, retired.

"I mistrust that man," exclaimed Julia as soon as they were alone, "he had some object in this visit, why should he bring the passport, a most unusual proceeding for a Governor, when an attendaut, or that disagreeable Captain Kick-emoff could do it."

"All I feared," said Ivan thoughtfully, "was, that he might recollect or retain some remembrance of the Princess from her great resemblance to her mother, but he did not appear as if he did."

"If he did," returned Julia, "he would take good care not to show it—I wish we were a hundred miles from here."

It became a dark, stormy, cold evening as the sun sank beneath the crested billow of the Euxine. A courier from the Crimea had reached Anapa, crossing from Kaffa. It was only then intelligence of the battle of Inkermann reached tha fortress, and the news that the.Russians had been routed with great slaughter-created a sensation amongst the inhabitants. Not that they were at all afraid of a *coup de main* taking the forts; they were safe enough. Anapa was defended by a deep ditch, a very high escarpment in excellent order, with well kept parapets, ninety-four canon and four mortars, but still they were well aware the place could not hold out, for it posssesed only a few wells of very brackish water, and, once shut in, the garrison would be forced to surrender; it created the greatest surprise that they remained so long unmolested.

A little before six o'clock Ivan Gortsare, accompanied by Julia Pitzharding, left the hotel, the latter well wrapped in her mantle and hood, leaving Catherine with their Creek attendant. Ivan Gortsare led his fair companion through the town till they reached the church, and the blank wall at the back of the powder magazine—just then the clock struck six. There was not a soul to be seen, and the darkness increased till they came within the light of a small shrine, placed against the wall of the magazine, and in which blazed three or four candles, placed by devout Russians, who are quite as fond of paying their devotion to the Virgin and crossing themselves, as any Italian in the Pope's dominions.

A dark shadow passed the light, and the next moment the tall form of a Eussian serf appeared close to them.

"That is Mr. Pitzharding," whispered Ivan Gortsare.

Julia sprang forward.

No lover ever met his mistress with more joy in his heart, than did Julia when she threw herself into her brother's arms. She had thrown back her hood, and the light from the shrine fell upon her features.

"Brother, dear brother, we have met at last, and can acknowledge each other!" she exclaimed, as Lord Courtland caught her to his breast and kissed her fondly and joyfully.

"And Catherine r" he whispered.

"Oh! Henry, I can scarcely speak from joy," replied.Tulia. "Catherine is well, and her heart is all your own; but are you not running a fearful risk i"

And then she looked with amazement into his face, his long beard, great moustachios, and lank black hair, falling from under his great hideous hairy cap; the long grey coat, with its belt and coarse rusty buckle; his very hands were soiled. Altogether, he looked the Russian serf to perfection.

Cordially shaking Gortsare by the hand, Lord Courtland said—

"I thank you from my heart for this blessed meeting, and trust the time is not far distant when my gratitude will not be confined to mere words; but move this way a few yards, the gate leading into the churchyard is open, and the high wall will shut us out from observation should any chance stragglers pass, for it is yet very early."

Leaning on her brother's arm, and feeling an intensity of happiness such as she never before felt, Julia, with Ivan following, entered through the iron gate; which closing after them, they passed on till they came beneath a grove of yew trees, where Lord Courtland paused.

"I tell you what I can do," said Ivan Gortsare; "for this is a bitter cold night for Miss Fitzharding to remain exposed to—you can stay under the church porch,' it's not five minutes from this to the inn where the Armenians are located; I will bring you an Armenian dress, in which you may safely enter our hotel and pass a couple hours; your appearance will excite no suspicion, as it is known we depart to-morrow with a party of Armenians."

Lord Courtland was enraptured with the idea—he would thus see and converse with his beloved Catherine, who had won his heart as a child, and stole it again as an astrologer's daughter

Ivan therefore departed.

"Now tell me, dear Henry," said Julia, when they were alone, "how in the name of wonder, you came here, and how you contrive to remain in this stronghold of the enemy! I tremble when I think of the fearful risk you incur."

"Then do not tremble, my sweet sister, for I am quite at home—my only difficulty consists in swallowing the abominable compounds of my comrades, and in keeping my face, beard, and mustachios in a remarkably soiled state: for, you must be well aware, that anything like cleanliness would excite

suspicion. I shall have my story to tell "when I see dear Catherine; therefore you must have patience; but, in the meantime, tell me—for I have heard Ivan say you leave this to-morrow—tell me how, and for what place; for to take you away from here is totally out of the question."

Julia informed him they were to leave with a party of Armenians for Kasbeek; but where Kasbeek was she had no idea, but Ivan would give him all particulars: "But tell me, Henry," she continued, "where do you sleep and eat; for, though you are in love, and peril life to see your beloved, nevertheless, these are not the good old days when knights and ladies lived on love—never dreamed of creature comforts."

"Now, you do me and yourself an injustice, Julia, for, even were Catherine not here, I would peril life quite as freely for my own dear sister.",

"I know it, dear Henry, and I was wrong in saying what I did; then where do you live?"

"In the dirtiest and moat disorderly establishment, Anapa, or any other Russian town, could furnish. I sleep in a great stable, with about fiye and twenty-peasants, and a dozen or so of mules—these last animals being by far the most respectable and well-behaved; as to eating, except what I carry secretly about me, I do not attempt anything else, finding it impossible to overcome my repugnance to most villainous oil, rancid fat, and decayed vegetables steeped in atrocious vinegar.''

"Oh, horrid; what food, my poor Harry."

Lord Courtland laughed with a light heart.

Before he could reply, Ivan Gortsare joined them. He carried a bundle in his hand; it contained the long ample flowing robes of an Armenian, with their broadcrowned fur cap and sandals.

"Ha! I forgot," said Ivan, "your beard. "

"Do not trouble about that. Thank the stars it is not a fixture." And passing his hand round his head he removed it. "I had several of these prepared before I left England, though I thought I could

manage very well without such an appendage, as in many parts of Russia no beard, only the moustache is worn; but as I will explain by-and-bye, I altered my intention, and put on a beard as a more effectual disguise."

In a few minutes our hero was transformed iuto a tall and stately Armenian; his Russian great coat, coarse shoes, and cap, were deposited under a tomb, to be resumed on his return.

All three then left the place, carefully closing the gate, and proceeded towards the hotel, ceasing to converse on the way, as they passed many individuals going to and fro through the main street, in which the Hotel of the Duke Constantine was situated.

Lord Courtland passed through the great reception hall, where a considerable' number, of persons were assembled talking vehemently over some news lately received, with a grave quiet step; Julia going quickly on before to prepare Catherine. In a few minutes he reached the door of the saloon. His heart beat quicker as Ivan Gortsare whispered—"I will leave you to yourselves for an hour and keep watch below. On our way back we can make our future arrangements clear to each other."

Lord Courtland pressed his hand, and with an increased palpitation of the heart, opened the door.

Catherine Avarhendorff could not, nor indeed did she feel it necessary to conceal the joy and delight that filled her heart on seeing her lover; she sprang to her feet, her face flushed, her eyes sparkling with emotion. She held forth both her hands, but the young man threw his arm round her waist, and drew her to his heart, pressing the first kiss of love upon her burning cheek, as he whispered—

"My own Catherine, this meeting more than repays the sorrows of the past, you were my betrothed from childhood, and"

"Ah!" interrupted Catherine, with a sweet smile, while a tear ran down her cheek; "but you forgot poor Catherine, and gave your love to an astrologer's daughter. Can you deny that, Henry, and you now let the poor astrologer's daughter depart after winning her love, without one word."

"But my heart, Catherine, my own Catherine, acknowledged you from, the first, it was the same love from beginning to end.

"Then I suppose," said the happy girl, in her soft touching voice, " I must forgive you your wavering, and take it for granted it was love for Catherine after all."

Our hero again pressed the beautiful girl to his heart with an indescribable feeling; it was not till after his departure from the Medora, that he discovered how passionately he loved her; and the joy and rapture he experienced when he learned that Catherine and the astrologer's daughter were one and the same, exceeded belief.

After the first joy and delight of their re-union was abated, Julia, with a hand of her brother in hers, and Catherine on the other side, prayed him to relate minutely all that had occurred since their separation, and particularly how he had contrived to land and assume the disguise she first saw him in.

Lord Courtland did so, also acquainting them with his accession to the title of Courtland, and then his taking part in the Battle of Inkermann; there was a flush on Julia's cheek, and a tremor in her voice as she made some remark when he spoke of his friend, Lieut. Ervvin, and of Lis being wounded.

"I see, my fair sister," said Lord Courtland with a very pleased smile, " that you have not forgotten a certain young officer, and I assure you he has never forgotten you; but I am exceedingly sorry to say I have to accusehini of a very daring robbery."

Julia laughed.

"A robbery, Henry? of what?"

"Of your pretty face," replied our hero, "the miniature you left, and which he vows to retain till he obtains the original!" ," Oh! indeed," returned the lady, with a merry laugh, "he does not dream of that, surely; in these warlike times", I cannot think of accepting anybody of less rank than an Admiral or a Field-Marshal."

"Then I fear, my dear sister," said

Lord Courtland, laughing, "you must be content with a hero of sixty or seventy, as we cannot find you either a Field-Marshal or an Admiral under that experienced age."

"Very good,'' observed Julia, demurely, "the more years the more wisdom. Now go on with your story from the Battle of Inkermann." CHAPTER XXX.

Lord Coiirtland began his story, saying —" After leaving the coast of the Crimea, we encountered a heavy gale from the south-east—so heavy,, indeed, that I was forced to lay-to several hours. But the gales of the Euxine are generally short; though contrary, baffling winds retarded our progress, and kept us, as it fortunately turned out, well to the eastward: so that on the morning of the fifth day after leaving Balaclava, when we encountered the gun-brig off Soukum Kaleh, we were many miles out of our course.

"In passing near the Zetee you were in, I was forced to haul off to repair our wheel, which received a shot, wounding two of my men—but, thank goodness, not severely. Lieutenant Erwin, who had rapidly recovered after the piece of iron had been removed from the wound in his head, who was now on deck, looking at the vessel through his glass, observed female figures on the deck of the Zetee. To these he called my attention, declaring they were habited in European costume. With a wild indistinct hope, I snatched the telescope from his hand, and at one glance I recognised the figure of Ivan G-ortsare, and you, dear Catherine. I started, and exclaimed to my friend—

"' It is them! now, we must beat this brig; we have heavier metal, and will try and cripple him by aiming our fire at his masts and rigging.'

"Most fortunately, we succeeded in our endeavour— only three of our men receiving splinter wounds: for the enemy's fire was very badly directed; and I took good care not to expose my men to their fire more than was requisite.

"The Russian had troops on board; and, though she was disabled, I had no chance even if I had wished it, of taking

her. Just then, we perceived a steamer coming out in full speed from the land, and saw, also, that the Zetee had caught the wind, and was bowling away before it.

"I was, as you may suppose, exceedingly anxious to follow, but the steamer came up between the Zetee and the Medora. We saw that she was a small steamer with paddle-boxes; so we resolved to aim our guns at her clumsy-looking funnel and paddle-boxes.

"She had metal enough to sink us, had it been well managed, but somehow she appeared to be afraid of us—thinking us, probably, a corvette with more guns than. we showed.

"Strange to say, the first gun fired, and which I pointed myself, struck her huge funnel and knocked it clean overboard. Our crew gave a cheer that seemed to astonish the Russian. Nevertheless, they gave us a specimen of their heavy metal; which tore away some fifteen yards of the starboard bulwarks, and passing on, knocked the wheel to splinters; but, except striking one man and knocking down three others, who received bruises from splintered planks, we escaped. It showed us, however, that we had an awkward customer; so, giving a fierce broadside as we passed on the starboard tack, we left our opponent with the loss of funnel, and port paddle-box knocked to pieces.

"I now made sail after the Zetee, which was a long way ahead. I could not make out why she carried so much canvass to get away,.whilst to add to our vexation, the Medora's helm was damaged, and before we could repair this damage, a heavy mist spread over the water. We hove to, and in three hours got all to rights; we then made sail after the Zetee, wondering where she could be bound to. My friend and I consulted the chart; it it appeared then she was running for Anapa. This we knew to be a very strong place, but I could not imagine why Ivan Gortsare should seek a Russian port. In fact I was altogether astounded at your being on board the Zetee, for I thought you must have reached your destination long before.

"Next morning we came rapidly up

with the Zetee, and had there remained three miles further to run we had overtaken you; but she ran into Anapa and the Tower Fort opened fire upon us, knocking our main royal out of us. Exceedingly vexed and disappointed, I drew off the. land, but still determined, as I knew there were no vessels of war on the coast except the two I had encountered the day before, and also aware that two or three of our cruisers were intending a visit of inspection along the coast, to remain, and moreover, I had it then in my head to land and penetrate into Anapa.

"Erwin was most desperately anxious to accompany me, but I would not let him, as he does not speak a word of Russian, nor does he know anything of the manners of the people.

"Jmv sailing master also was miserable on hearing my resolution. However, to carry out my project, I stood in during the night close with the land, the wind blowing off the shore. I was about six or seven miles below Anapa to the southward, and about two miles below a strong fort—in fact, of a large and handsome mansion. It was a very dark night. "Erwin and I landed with a boat's crew, well armed, and after two hours' search, came upon a hut with two shepherds in it. These we carried on board with us without creating any alarm. The men were frightened out of their senses, but I assured them they should receive no hurt, but be well rewarded in the end. I soon pacified them, and by my questions soon learned from them all the information I required. One of the men was a tall, able-bodied fellow, and as greedy of gain as a Moldavian Jew. From him I discovered that the peasants in his vicinity were in the habit of visiting Anapa, with any sort of provisions they could procure, as the garrison required constant supplies, there being nearly nine thousand troops located in the town and forts, that they were never examined going in or out of the gates, and that they lodged in a kind of caravansary (tor it could scarcely be called an inn), as each man found his own food, all the owners of the establishment furnished being an immense out-

house, and as much quass as the, guests could afford to pay for.

"It fortunately turned out for my purpose that these men were twin brothers, and much attached to each other. I promised one of them fifty roubles if he would let me accompany him into Anapa, dressed the same as his brother. He was quite rejoiced at my offer. The thought of such a sum. as fifty roubles appeared to bewilder him. His brother was to remain on board my vessel till my return; and I impressed upon his memory that if he attempted to betray me I would assuredly blow his brains out and hang his brother from the yardarm. Of course this was merely said to intimidate him, or as a stimulant to his fidelity; but I need not have feared his betraying me, he would gladly have sold the town and the Czar Nicholas himself for another fifty roubles.

"I arranged that the yacht was either to keep near the coast, or anchor at Touaps, which is now abandoned by the Russians, and where there is excellent anchorage.

"Having. settled all my plans to my satisfaction, I attired myself in the serfs garments, over an inner dress. Fortunately I had on board all kinds of disguises, false beards, &c., which I had brought from England to use, if necessary to my plans of penetrating into the country. "When thus disguised I made a remarkably good Eussian peasant. We then landed during the night, and the next morning, with a rough basket filled with eggs and some half-starved fowls, we took our way to Anapa.

"We met numbers of persons, men and women peasants, going there also with provisions, some with mules and asses, and thus in company we passed through the gates, neither questioned or in fact noticed, by the soldiers. Michael Boris, the name of my guide, first showed me the house—or rather outhouse, a kind of stable—where he usually lodged, after which, giving him a dose of his favourite quass, I sent him to procure me a clean bundle of straw, and then to put it in a remote corner whilst I proceeded to have a look at the town and make cautious inquiries.

"Speaking the language as I do, I soon obtained a clue to where Ivan Gortsare and you were located, for your arrival and the approach of the English vessel off the port had created a stir in the place.

"The next thing was how to introduce myself, but whilst watching the door of the hotel I beheld Ivan come forth, and I followed him till he came into a quiet unfrequented place, and then accosted him; and thus, beloved Catherine, I gained what my heart panted for— this delightful interview.

"And now dearest, let me listen to your adventures," continued Lord Courtland, after a few observations from the Princess and his sister, " and then we will consult what can be done to facilitate your liberation from the Circassian Chiefs, for I am quite prepared to accede to all their conditions."

"In truth, Henry," replied Catherine who had listened with absorbed attention to her lover's brief narrative, "we have little to relate, for all we did was to sail from Constantinople to Sinope, and then from Trebizond and Batoum, and being afraid to pursue our journey by land, dreading to fall in the way of a Russian force, moving towards Kars from Tiflis, Ivan hired the Greek Zetee you pursued us in, which was to have landed us on the coast, but the padrone of the boat for reasons of his own, betrayed us, and ran into Anapa."

Turning to Ivan, Lord Courtland demanded how he intended proceeding on the morrow, "for I do not see," he continued, "why I should not accompany you in my present disguise."

"No, not in that disguise," said the Russian, "for each Armenian has his separate passport and all will be strictly examined and signed by the Governor; in fact, they are already for starting tomorrow morning. Still you may venture to accompany us in your peasant dress, without attracting observation, but with respect to getting on board your yacht again, I do not know how you will manage."

"Oh! I will show you how that is to be accomplished," returned Lord Courtland; "I have arranged that the Medora shall remain at Touaps for some days; we can, after we quit this town, get a messenger to go there. I am quite ready, as I have just explained to the Princess, to accede to Schamyl Bey's terms."

"Hush!" suddenly interrupted Julia, "there is a heavy footstep onthe stairs."

"Yes," said her brother, "so there is; I will retire; you Ivan can follow me to the church."

Catching Catherine Warhendorff's hand, which trembled in his, he pressed it to his lips, embraced his sister; and was just preparing for departure when the door opened, and Captain Kickemoff entered the room without any ceremony; he was evidently slightly intoxicated.

"Ha! who the deuce is this?" he exclaimed, his eyes resting with evident surprise upon the tall figure of Lord Courtland, who could see that both the maidens looked agitated, and that Julia almost made an advance toward him, as if for protection.

Looking calmly at the person of Captain Kickemoff, he replied—

"An Armenian fortune-teller, at your service." lie then moved towards the door, and with a good night to all present, and requesting Ivan Gortsare to le active in his movements on the morrow, he withdrew.

"What is that tall fellow's name?" demanded the Captain, turning to Gortsare, "he speaks the Kussian more like a native than an Armenian, and looks Utter for a soldier than a fortune-teller,"

"Hundreds," replied Gortsare in reply, "born in.Russia and never quitted it, speak the language equally as well as the native, but as to his name, I never aske 1 it, he is one of the Armenians travelling to Rasbeck, int» Georgia; they have changed their time of starting, and he came to warn me of the change."

The Captain appeared thoughtful for a minute, and then looking towards the two ladies, who were menially wishing him in Siberia, or anywhere else than in Anapa, he said, endeavouring to be very polite.

"You will please excuse my not delivering the message I am the bearer of somewhat sooner; his Excellency re-

quested me to say, that as he has to send hia drosky to JSauchink to-morrow for an invalid lady to return to Anapa, one of the officers' wifes at our out-posts, he insists upon your accepting its use as far as that place." ""We are much obliged to the Count," answered Gortsare quickly, before either of the maidens could, reply," " and will gladly accept of his offer as it does not put him to an inconvenience."

"Very good," observed the Captain, looking most intently at Julia, " I shall have the pleasure of accompanying the ladies, as I relieve Captain Borenkinski at Kunchink."

The Captain then got on his legs, which were not extremely steady under him, and saluting the two ladies,. retired, telling Ivan that the drosky should be at the Hotel door about sun rise, as the days were short, and the road none of the best.

"I trust that horrid man," exclaimed Catherine Warhendorff, as he quitted the apartment, " has no suspicion! he looked so inquiringly at Lord Courtland."

"He can have no suspicion," replied Ivan, " he was struck no doubt by his tall and noble figure, but I da not exactly admire the extreme politeness of Count Zouboski, yet how can we, situated as we are, avoid it; that rascally Greek padrone has placed us in this awkward position; yet in reality there can be nothing to fear, for if the Count Zouboski suspected anything, he would keep us here in his stronghold.."

"God send we may get clear," sighed Catherine.

"I feel no fear," cried Julia, cheeringly, "now that Henry is near us; his love for us and his courage and ingenuity will aid us depend upon it if we get into difficulties, but surely that horrid Captain Kickemoff does not intend to intrude himself into the drosky, if he does, we will mount the mules."

"Well, I must go and see Lord Courtland," observed Ivan, " before he seeks his quarters, and arrange how we shall proceed."

On reaching the church, the Russian found his lordship had resumed his

boor's attire.

"Who is that tipsy fellow, Gortsare?" he demanded, "who so awkwardly interrupted us 'i He looked very keenly at me, though apparently asking trivial questions."

"He's an infantry captain, a kind of spy of the Commandant's upon the other officers and the townsfolk of Anapa. Everywhere you go in Russia, in almost every mansiou, that hateful system is adopted; your very servants are paid agents of the secret police."

"It's an infernal speeies of despotism!" cried the young Englishman, "and reminds one of the Venetian republic before the French revolution swept away her institutions and her hateful policy, I trust for ever. At what hour do you commence your journey in the morning."

"As early as sunrise, my lord. You bad better not join us till we are a league out of the town. The Commandant of this place has insisted on the ladies accepting the use of his drosky as far as Nanchink; there was no possibility of refusing it without exciting surmises. When he offered it himself a day or two ago, it was declined, and it was to renew this offer that Captain Kickemoff came to the hotel; and to add to our discomfort, the said Captain goes with us as far as Nanchink. I own it makes me uneasy. "

"Who is the Commandant of Anapa?" demanded Lord Courtland in a vexed tone.

"The Count Zouboski."

"Zouboski," repeated Lord Courtland thoughtfully, "it's very strange! that name strikes familiarly on my ear."

"It's very possible, my Lord, that you may have some recollection of it, for the Count often visited at the Princess Warhendorff's mansion in St. Petersburgh when you were there; you were then about ten years of age, and may retain some remembrance of the name."

"I am certain I do," replied our horo. "Is the count a very tall, powerful man, eh?"

"Precisely; nearly six feet four; fully as tall as the Emperor Nicholas."

"Does our road lead near the sea

coast?" enquired Lord Courtland anxiously.

"For a couple of leagues it docs," answered Cortsare; "it passes within half-a-mile of the Governor's country mansion, near which they have erected a strong fort, as there is a safe inlet of the sea where vessels and boats can shelter. "

"I know the place you mean; we stood close in there the other day, and the fort tried the range of her guns upon us. We were out of the reach of lire, but with our glasses I could distinguish the mansion and gardens, and the inlet of the sea; it runs in about a mile, and forms a small basin or pond. I wish to God I had been aware of all this, and I might have carried you all off safely. I strongly suspect danger: that Count Zoubosld has often seen Catherine when a child, and her very striking likeness to her mother must have struck him."

"I fear so, indeed," observed Gortsare, "and now deeply regret not continuing our journey from Batoum by land. But we are now imagining evils."

"At all events," remarked Lord Courtland, "I will keep you in sight till you have passed the Russian outposts. Should anything unforseen happen, I shall then be able to plan a remedy. If the Count permits your passage out of Anapa, all's well; but should he detain you here, I should be perfectly powerless to aid or assist you."

A few more observations were made, and one or two arrangements completed, after which Lord Courtland bade Ivan Gortsare, good night, and both separating without the churchyard, his lordship proceeded towards the miserable inn, where he was to pass the night, taking with him a flask of wine and some biscuits in his pocket, all he ventured to take for that night.

Entering the great outhouse, he perceived a dozen or more peasants, who lived at a distance, lying on their straw, eating slices of raw turnip, and drinking quass out of dried gourds. Michael Boris, his comrade, was there, watching for his return. He came up to him, and pointing to a distant part of the out-house, some way from the mules and asses, told him he had got two bundles of quite fresh straw, and had swept the place clean.

Our hero was pleased to see he was separated from the rest, being quite aware that in Russia, amongst even the better classes,his rest would be likely to be much disturbed by the lively and hungry companions the Russian serf so liberally and unconcernedly feeds.

CHAPTER XXXI.

It was scarcely light when our hero jumped up, shook himself, and proceeded into the house itself, thinkinghe might ask for a cup of coffee without creating much curiosity.

Anapa is not exactly Russia, but its inhabitants are thoroughly so, though it happened that this traveller's inn was kept by a Jew—these people seeming to possess a prescriptive ri ght to be masters of almost all the inns throughout the whole of the empire, and who, though subject to great tyranny, are yet very numerous and greedy of gain.

Lord Courtland found the master of the establishment as miserable a specimen of his race as could well be seeu, and regarding our hero with great surprise when he requested to know if he could have some coffee. The man hesitated. His lordship showed him a silver rouble, and his wonder ceased; he thought only of the rouble, and led the petitioner into his own room, and in a very short time he got a basin of coffee, and also some tolerablebread and butter, for which he paid four times its value. The Jew asked no questions, and Lord Courtland, after his repast, went to seek Michael Boris, whom he found making his breakfast upon slices of raw turnip, and a cabbage not very fresh, chopped up in an earthen vessel, swimming in oil and vinegar, both of the worst description, and which he seemed to relish exceedingly. The other peasants were putting their panniers upon their donkeys, and getting ready to return to their homes.

They-proceeded in a body to the town gate. Lord Courtland perceived, as they reached the outlet, that there was a party of soldiers drawn up before the un-opened gate, and that a large party of Armenian merchants, with their mules, and several of their women—dressed in scarlet, with their heads and faces bound round with a most disfiguring wrapper of cloth—were all standing, as if waiting the arrival of some one.

While they paused, a drosky, drawn by three spirited horses abreast, yoked in the picturesque mode of Russia, turned the corner of the street, with Captain Kickemoff on horseback beside it. Seated inside were Catherine Warhendorff, Julia, the attendant, and Ivan Gortsare.

Captain Kickemoff rode up to the warder at the gate, saving—

"Open these gates now, and let these peasants out, but I must examine the passports of these Armenian merchants before they can pass." . Lord Courtland heard the words, and immediately surmised that, tipsy as the Captain had been the previous evening, he still had seen something that excited either his suspicion or curiosity; and then it was our hero recollected that when he removed his false beard, he had removed his moustache also, and all the Armenians wore very large ones.

However, hearing the guard order the peasants, and their mules and asses, to go on through the gate, he followed Michael Boris, and passed through, painfully anxious as to what might occur to Ivan Gortsare and his pretended daughters, but he dare not loiter and excite attention.

The Armenians, though surprised at this second examination of their passports, readily handed them to Captain Kickemoff, who scarcely bestowed a look upon the paper, but keenly examined the person of each traveller. He appeared exceedingly surprised and amazed as he came to the last, whom he addressed, saying— ,' Have you left any of your party in the town?"

"No, Captain, we have not, but there are many of our people still in Anapa."

Biding up to the door of the drosky, Captain Kickemoff said, addressing Ivan Gortsare, who looked quite careless and unconcerned—for the inmates of the carriage had at once recognised the tall figure of Lord Courtland, and with a feeling of joy saw him pass unmolested through the gate—

"How is this, Gortsare? that tall Armenian of last night, who pretended to be a fortune teller, is not amongst the party who have just passed out."

"How can I help that, Captain Kickemoff? I am not the director of the Armenians. He may still have business in the town for aught I know."

"Humph!" muttered the Russian officer, "we shall see. Go on slowly," he continued, addressing the driver, "keep with the Armenians till I rejoin you."

And turning his horse's head, he rode back into the town.

Ivan Gortsare made no remark before their Greek attendant; he saw the maidens look anxious, but the drosky proceeded, and soon came up with the travellers on their mules.

They could distinguish Lord Courtland amongst the peasants, but he made no attempt to advance near the drosky.

In this manner they proceeded for three miles. It was a still cold day, with a light grey mist hanging over the sea, and resting on the high coast.

When about five miles from Anapa, Captain Kickemoft' came riding back, followed by about half a dozen mounted Cossacks and immediately surrounded the drosky.

Lord Courtland at once perceived there was treachery intended, and which he could in no way prevent. He therefore said to Michael Boris—

"Now, mind me; be faithful, and before I leave you, you shall have a hundred roubles. Watch every movement of that drosky. will do the same; you see they are turning off by another road, leading down to the sea coast."

"They are going to the fort," replied the peasant; "it's not two miles, the road goes nowhere else: follow me, and I will take you a short way."

Slipping away from the surprised party of merchants and countrymen, the seeming peasant anil his guide climbed over a low fence, and running along under a rough stone wall, kept the carriage in sight. The mist and vapour from the sea increased each moment, still they kept the drosky and the Cossacks in sight, unseen themselves.

Captain Kickemoff rode in front; the road was steep and exceedingly rough, and they took more than half an hour to come within sight of the late Governor's country mansion, and the fort, a couple of hundred yards in advance of it, built upon a high range of rocks overlooking the creek,

Concealing themselves behind some huge masses of granite, the watchers could plainly perceive the drosky drive into the court before the house; but they could not perceive its inmates get out, as the out offices intervened; but presently the drosky and the Cossacks again came into view—the former being empty; and with the Cossacks it drove up the road, and soon disappeared.

Captain Kickemoff remained behind.

Itnowbecaine Lord Courtland's objectto regain his ship. He had above twenty-five leagues to travel through a somewhat dangerous country, inhabited here and there by fierce hordes of Circassian Tartars: who entertain the same kind affection for the Russians as the Chinese do for the English. It was through a country, also, covered with a great growth of timber, and the forests difficult to traverse; nevertheless, he must attempt it, for he had appointed Touaps as a rendezvous for the Medora—not exactly at the time heeding the extent of territory lying between Anapa and that port.

Michael Boris knew nothing of the district beyond his own village—the natives of which were a mixed race,, extremely fierce, and would shoot down a Russian as they would a mad dog. The few serfs never stirred beyond a mile or two away from the fortresses, and went into the forts when the Circassian Tartars came down from the hills. Still, the man—induced by the reward offered— was willing to try and find the way to Touaps.. /" Lord Courtland promising to land him and hia brother near their own village.

"How many men," demanded his lordship, "garrison yonder fort?"

The man thought about thirty or so;

he often went there when the house was inhabited by the late Commandant's family, who always lived there instead of at Anapa; he and his brother were serfs of Count Zouboski, who was a hard and tyrannical master. He allowed them to cultivate a piece of land near the fort, on paying a certain sum yearly."..

"If we were attired in Armenian garments," observed Lord Courtland, "we could pass through this country without risk or difficulty; but, as they cannot be procured, we must brave the risk."

That night Lord Courtland passed in the serf's cottage, and early the next morning prepared for the journey.

It was blowing a piercing cold east wind off the land, and recollecting that Lieutenant Erwin said, " Should the wind blow off the coast he would keep the yacht as close in as possible, so that if his enterprise failed, he might contrive, if he saw them, to make signals."

There was no road of any kind along the coast, therefore it was with great danger and difficulty they travelled along the shores of the Euxine.

Several villages could be distinguished on the heights above them, and to one-of these Lord Courtland determined to proceed and make enquiries, cost what it would. There was one thing that was very consoling—he was well armed, having two splendidly finished revolvers in his vest, and what is sometimes a most potent weapon— a well filled puree.

"Now I should think," said Lord Courtland to Michael Boris, "that the natives of these villages, if they are not Russian, would be friendly to the English."

The scenery, though it was winter, was wild and pic1 uresque; the remains of fortresses destroyed in former invasions, crowned the summit of the hills.

In the village there were but few inhabitants, chiefly-women and children of a mixed race, and who spoke a curious kind of language to the ears of Lord Courtland; but they willingly sold eggs and milk, and finally directed them how to reach the sea coast, near a large village, where vessels anchored, the inhabitants being half Tartars. With some difficulty they made their way to this village,-which was called Sabachuz, where they perceived a couple of coasting vessels, of small burden, lying at anchor for the night. One was a Greek mistico.

Their appearance created the greatest surprise at the little inn, but fortunately they encountered several xreek sailors standing before the door of the drinking house, to whom Lord Courtland spoke, and finding one was the captain of the mistico, he offered him a sum of money if he would get under weigh, and as the wind blew off land, and the water was smooth, there was no xisk. To the amazement of the Greek, he informed him be was an Englishman, and shewing him the money he iigreed to give him, the captain promised to put to sea with the day-light, but no persuasion could get him off during the night at that season of the year. He, however, used his influence most effectually to procure them comfortable sleeping accommodation in the village.

The next morning, with a strong breeze off shore, they got aboard the mistico, a half-decked boat, of about twenty tons, the crew consisting of the padrone, three men, and a boy.

"We can manage these fellows," observed Lord,Courtland to the Russian, "if they attempt treachery," shewing Michael Boris his weapons; for the man was very timid, and alarmed at the idea of trusting to the Greeks, who, he declared, would murder them if they thought he had much money.

The mistico was closely reefed, latine rigged, and sailed well. As the sun rose and dispersed the almost perpetual vapours hanging over the Euxine, Lord Courtland kept a sharp look-out. They would reach Touaps by sun set, but an hour before mid-day, the topsails of a sbip close in with the land were perceived standing towards them. In ten minutes more, to his intense joyT he recognised it to be the Medora.

Turning to the Greek skipper, who appeared remarkably sulky, and who kept forward, talking eagerly with the other Greek sailors—

"Do you see that vessel's topsails, her hull will be visible presently."

""Well," said the padrone, "what have I to do with that vessel?"

"Nothing whatever," returned Lord Courtland calmly, "but I have. Keep your vessel close to the wind, so that we may cross that ship, as I intend to board her."

"I shall do no such thing," said the Greek skipper sharply. "I engaged to take you to Touaps for a certain sum, and I shall lose the wind if I tack and cross that ship."

"But, my friend," returned our hero, still speaking quietly, "that is the vessel—there, you can see her hull now—that I expected to find at Touaps; that vessel is an armed yacht, and is mine."

"Yours!" exclaimed the skipper, with a start, and au expression of joy passing over his features; "by the blesled Panoda, you are a prince and can pay."

"Rascal," returned Lord Courtland, his face flushed with passion, all the anger in his naturally kind and noble heart excited when treated with ingratitude or deceit, and instantly grasping the skipper by the collar he swung him off his legs, holding him with a power that left him like a child in his grasp; the boy at the tilleri letting it go with fright, shouted for the men to come and help the padrone. There were two men forward who instantly seized their long knives, and the man below came armed with a musket whilst the Russian Michael Boris, who was stout hearted, seized a boat hook, and rushed to the rescue of the Englishman; but Lord Courtland pulled his Colt's revolver from his breast, and put it to the head of the horror struck skipper, saying—

"Miserable wretch, order your men to lay down their knives, or I'll first blow your brains out, and theirs afterwards."

Ever cowards at heart, the Greeks quailed before the stern look and commanding manner of Lord Courtland, who tossing the trembling padrone contemptuously from him, continued—

"Go, turn your sails, and stand in for the ship. You are seen already, beware how you attempt treachery again with an Englishman."

The skipper shook with passion, bit-ter disappointment,.and revenge; he was a stout broad shouldered man, but he felt he was nothing in the hands of the Englishman, whilst the sight of two six barreled revolvers were intimidating; besides, he saw the yacht, attracted by the mistico, was paying off and coming towards her.

The fact was, and it was well known to the British vessels in the Black Sea, that the Greeks were pirates on the water, and robbers on land; plundering where they could do so with impunity. Lord Courtland, the skipper knew well, was an Englishman, and he never intended to land him at Touaps till he had plundered him of everything he had about him; he intended to do so, during the night, when he and his crew were to seize him, and then put him ashore; he had seen his well filled purse, and he suspected he had more property about his person.

After a moment's consideration, the skipper threw himself on his knees, and in the name of the thrice blessed St. Anastasius begged for pardon. He said he only thought, finding he was so rich a Milor, to extort a larger sum.

Lord Courtland turned away with a look of supreme contempt, and, taking the helm, steered right in the course of the Medora, and then hove the mistico up in the wind. The Medora was now within two hundred yards, and, standing on the taffrail, he waved his cap. He was recognised instantly, and a cheer pealed over the Euxine from the rejoiced crew of the Medora, as her topsails were backed, and her boat lowered.

In a few minutes Lieutenant Erwin stood on the deck of the mistico, and embraced Lis friend, delighted to see him safe after the dangers he had encountered.

The Greek skipper and his crew had gone below, terrified at the consequences of their rascality and attempts at piracy. But Lord Courtland did not trouble himself about them; he merely observed to Lieutenaut Erwin, that the rascals belonging to the mistico had attempted extortion, after his having agreed with them for a liberal sum, and he had frightened them into submission.

Leaving the sum he had promised on the companion, and which was more than their conduct merited, he stepped into the gig with his friend and Michael Boris, and was pulled alongside the Medora, where he was received by Mr. Bernard with intense gratification.

Lord Courtland was as eager to relate his adventures on shore as his friends were to listen to them, being anxious to consult with them as to the best means of proceeding, though he had already hastily planned a project for the deliverance of Catherine "Warhendorff, his sister, and Ivan Gortsare.

CHAPTER XXXII.

In the meantime the Princess Catherine and Julia, with their attendant, after descending from the drosky, were conducted into a large saloon well furnished, in the mansion of the previous commandant of Anapa; they were growing distressed at being separated from their protector, who was conducted, by orders of Captain Kickemoff, into another part of the mansion.

It was quite useless for the indignant maidens to complain to Captain Kickemoff, at the cruel treatment they received, that gentleman declaring in the most polite manner, that he only obeyed orders; the Commandant of Anapa, had given him directions to conduct them to the place they were now in, and so at once, separate them from Gortsare, whom he designated a, traitor to, his country.

Catherine was shocked and alarmed. She felt great uneasiness about Ivan, being well aware he had not fulfilled his duties as a secret agent, a post he abhorred; he had also quitted England without permission; therefore, altogether, she considered his position one of great peril, if delivered over to the chief of the " Secret Police," a man of the most stern and unrelenting character; and more dreaded at St. Petersburg than the Emperor himself. The only consolation the two girls had was that when Grortsare was separated from them, he managed to whisper to the Princess Catherine—

"Be not alarmed, I have provided for an accident of this kind; declare at once

who you are, and you are safe from the schemes of Count Zouboski."

Now, it puzzled both Catherine and Julia why he was so anxious that the Count Zouboski should not recognize her, and now he desired her to declare herself as the daughter of the Princess Catherine; it appeared strange, but Julia supposed, that if they could have escaped without being recognised, so much the better, as then they would have rejoined the Princess, but declaring herself as Catherine Warhendorff, her mother connected with the Empress, would at all events, save her from the snares or projects of Count Zouboski.

It was early in the day when they became inmates of the late governor's house, and both simultaneously advanced to the windows, to inspect the outside of their prison, and both feeling immense relief, in the midst of their misfortune, when they considered that Lord Courtland had completely escaped suspicion, and would doubtless get safe to the Medorn.

Julia felt sure, and asst-. ting her belief, that he would never cease his exertions till he had effected their release..

"How is that possible, dear Julia?" exclaimed Catherine, pointing from the window to the strong fort erected in front of the mansion.

Julia gazed at the fort commanding the creek with a vexed look. It mounted several large guns on a parapet, and was defended on the land side by a very deep ditch, filled from the creek. The guns commanded not only the approach to the shore, but could also face the house and road.

Their Greek attendant, Irene, was at first greatly frightened at seeing the carriage surrounded by the fierce, wild-looking Cossacks, but finding that the place they were carried to was not a prison, but a very handsome well-furnished bouse, with several male and female attendants in it, she became quite reconciled to the change, especially as they did not confine them to their chambers. As they stood conversing and gazing from the windows, which certainly commanded a most varied and magnificent view of sea, and stupendous rocks,

with a great extent of forest towards the south, they perceived two officers and a lady leaning on the arm of one of them, leave the gate of the Fort, and, passing over the bridge, approach the house. As they came nearer, and then close under the windows, the lady looked up, and disclosed the features of a female about six or eight and twenty, not unhandsome features, but there was something about them, and the manner of the lady herself, who was wrapped in a fur mantle, more disagreeable than otherwise.

As her glance rested for a moment on the fair prisoners, she laughed and said something to the officer on whose arm she was leaning; he looked up, but both girls quickly drew back.

"I had at first rejoiced to see a female, and one apparently highly respectable," remarked Julia, "but I do not like the appearance of that lady nor the officer on whose arm she is leaning."

"Neither do I," replied Catherine; " there was a saucy curl of her lip as she looked up, that was extremely disagreeable."

She had scarcely spoken the words when the door of the saloon opened, and the lady, divested of her mantle, entered the room.

Both the occupants of the room rose with some surprise in their looks, but the lady advanced with a careless, easy air, and begged them to sit down, as she was come to have a little chat with them.

Divested of her mantle, the girls liked her appearence even less. She was showily if not gaudily dressed, wore a profusion of ornaments, and her manner and air not at all adapted to the higher circles. She appeared more like the Russian subaltern's wife, and those gentlemen they knew are generally anything but particular in their selection. She was handsome, certainly, but a disagreeable bold kind of beauty, agreeable only to a certain class of men.

"So," said the lady, seating herself with a very nonchalant air, "you are the daughters of the secret agent, Ivan Gortsare; but don't be alarmed about your father."

"Madam," replied Catherine Warhendorff, with a flushed cheek and a haughty bend of her beautiful head, "you are in error. My father was the late General Warhendorff, and my mother, before she married him, the Princess Maldovitchka."

The lady started to her feet with a look of intense astonishment.

"You say you are the daughter of the Princess Warhendorff!" at last burst from her lips, but she did not again sit down.

"Such is the case, Madame," said Catherine firmly and calmly, "and I protest against this outrage, which if known to the Emperor, would certainly bring punishment upon the heads of those who have committed it."

The visitor seemed stupified; she coloured to the very temples, and stammered out that she had been misled; it was not her fault if she had committed an indiscretion, as she was informed they were the daughters of Ivan Gortsare, a serf, and one of the secret agents of the police; and that the Governor of Anapa had ordered his arrest, for having betrayed his trust.

"May I ask, Madam," enquired Catherine, "whom I have the pleasure of addressing?"

The lady's face became scarlet, as she hesitated, and then said—

"My name is Golowin, Madame; but, pardon me, you must require some refreshment."

And with an humble salutation, she turned and left the room.

Catherine looked at Julia.

"This is very strange, dear Julia, I do not know what to think, I thought it better to declare at once who I was. I have followed herein Ivan Gortsare's directions, and we must wait the result."

Some short time afterwards, the Greek attendant brought up some fowl and other things on a tray, but the female did not make her appearance again.

"Did you hear who inhabited or inhabits this house, Irene?" questioned her mistress.

"The officers of tlie Fort and two ladies," said Irene with a little hesitation.

"And where have they put Ivan Gortsare," demanded Catherine.

"In the fort," returned the girl, "they say a Russian ship of war will be here in a day or two, with soldiers and workmen to strengthen this place."

Julia and Catherine looked serious and trembled, for both cherished the idea that Lord Courtland might contrive with the crew of the Medora, to release them; but they shuddered when they considered the strength of the place and how many lives might be sacrificed in the attempt.

During the remainder of the day no one intruded upon them: it blew hard and was very cold, but then the saloon and the adjoining bed room were well heated by stoves.

The following morning the wind had increased in violence and was accompanied by heavy snow squalls, which cleared off about mid-day, when they beheld Count Zouboski's drosky drive iuto the front court; they did not see who was in it, but they felt uneasy imagining the Commandant of Anapa was the inmate.

Count Alexander Zouboski entered the house and proceeded at once iuto another wing of the large mansion, . nnd, opening a door, entered a well furnished and well heated saloon, in which sat the lady who had given her name as Golowin to the two captives.

"Well, Mart ha," cried the Count, throwing himself into a chair, "how do you get on with the two pretty birds I sent you? Do you think you will be able to improve them?"

The lady called Martha laid aside the book she was reading, and, looking over at the Count, said seriously—

"Who are those two girls?"

"St. Nicholas! didn't I write you word they were Ivan Gortsare's daughters?" said the Count, with a slight change of colour.

"Ah, but did you believe so when you wrote?"

"Why, what the deuce are you pumping me for by these cross questions? What matter who they are if they call themselves Ivan Gortsare's daughters?

It's not my business to hunt out their pedigree, girl. Have you seen them?"

"Yes," returned Martha Golowin, "and if what I heard is true, you may get into a scrape, Alexander, with all your cleverness."

"Why, what the deuce did she tell you? Out with it," said the Count sharply. "I suppose you do not admire my taking one of them for a wife, eh P"

The woman laughed, saying—" As far as I am concerned, you may have the two. I was not aware you intended allying youraelf to the Emperor. It's a bold move, but will not succeed."

"What the deuce does the woman mean?" cried Alexander Zouboski angrily.

"Why," she replied, "the tallest of the two girls, said to me with a very haughty, disdainful look—' Madam, my father was General Warhendorff, and my mother was the Princess Maldovitchka before she married.'"

"Who? the deuce!" exclaimed the Count, springing to his feet; "she declared this herself!"

"She did, and, moreover, very pointedly hinted, or rather asserted, that those who committed this outrage upon her would be severely punished when it came to the ears of the Emperor."

The Count Zouboski sat down; he looked thoughtful, and then glancing up, said quickly—

"Go, send Zaroski to me, this affair puzzles and annoys me."

In a few minutes an officer with a very powerful bulky frame and a fierce dark expression of countenance, about thirty years of age, entered the room.

"What have you done with Ivan Gortsare?" demanded the Count.

"I lodged him as directed in the Fort, Count," returned Zaroski. "I have just this moment come from him; he asserts very strange things."

"Confound the rascal, what does he say," growled the Count, getting excited.

"He says, you have committed an outrage upon a lady highly connected, even allied to the Czarina, and that the Emperor is sure to hear of it, and severely punish the offenders. 'Why, what are you talking about,' I enquired. 'Are not the girls your daughters,' 'No,' he replied, 'one of the ladies is the young Princess Warhendorff.'"

"Well, suppose she is," retorted the Count almost savagely," how was I to know that; that traitor told me they were his daughters. I suspected, and arrested him and will send him by the first opportunity to Taganrog to the Chief of Police; let him deal with him. I have no proof that this girl is the young Princess Warhendorff; however, if she wishes it, she and her companion shall be sent to Taganrog also; let her claim be investigated by the Count Gregory Rugetschef, its nothing to me: they are well treated. When Kickemoff arrives send him to me." Lieut. Zaroski left the room.

The Count Zouboski was taking some refreshment, and drinking large glasses of wine to cool the excited temper he appeared to be in, when Captain Kickemofi' entered the chamber.

He easily perceived by his patron's countenance that something had,-gone wrong; he, however said nothing, but sat down by the Count's invitation, who pushed the wine towards him.

"Our matrimonial schemes, Kickemoff," began the Commandant, lighting a cigar, "are likely to be marred this time."

"I suspected so from the first," returned the Captain, "but what has happened, Count?" : Why, the girl has declared herself to be daughter of the Princess Warhendorff, which I never dreamed she would do; I thought there were some very cogent reasons for her concealing her name, and also that both she and Ivan Gortsare were most anxious to avoid falling into the hands of Russians, instead of which she not only declared who she is, but very haughtily threatens with punishment whoever detains her and her companion; who, by-and-bye, must be that English girl, Fitzbarding. Ivan Gortsare also threatens; now there is some under plot in all this; I sent them here thinking Martha Golowin would perhaps improve their morals, and so that after a time this proud young lady might listen to my proposals of espousing her, with a good

grace; now all this is knocked on the head."

"They were going, it appears, into Circassia," observed Captain Kickemoff, "where it is said the Princess herself is captive to Prince Schamyl, and that Armenian I saw last night was undoubtedly a lover in disguise."

"A lover," repeated Count Zouboski, with a start; "what makes you think that, for if a lover, depend upon it, he was an Englishman, and now I think of it— that English vessel—that yacht, that followed the Zetee almost into Anapa, was well known to them all—but let me hear what makes you think that the Armenian rascal or fortune teller, was a lover—"

"In the first place," answered Captain Kickemofl", " I remembered after he left the room last night, that he had neither beard nor moustachios, and that he was very fair for an Armenian. I confess to not being quite sober, or I should have been sharper. I also recollect that thf two girls looked remarkably uneasy till after the said Armenian left the room. I then determined to examine all the Armenians the next morning, before they left the town, but no such tall, handsome-looking fellow was amongst them, not one within six inches of his height. I thought he might still be in the town, so I hunted them all up—there were only half a dozen of them—but he was not one of them.

"So I became convinced he was either in the town or had gone out in some other disguise. I then recollected that as the Armenians were prevented going through the gate in the morning, a number of the peasants of the neighbourhood, with several Russian serfs, had gone out. They are never noticed, so I galloped after the lot, bur meeting the party of Cossacks coming into Anapa, and wns obliged to turn back with them, as it was your wish, to conduct the drosky and its inmates to this house. I selected half a dozen men, and did so"

"You are making a very long-winded story of tbi.", Kickemoff; you have not come to the point, yet who wa the Armenian you saw?"

"Ah! St. Nicholas! that I cannot tell

you, Count-. all I found out I will relate. On my return to the town, I went to the house of a Jew, who keeps a kind oi caravansary, where all kinds of travellers and market people put up.

"' Had you many strangers here, Hezekiah?' I demanded,'yesterday.'

"' No, Captain, only the usual run of people to the market. There was one of them a serf, I think, of our Governor's—one Michael Boris—who had a comrade with him, a fine, tall, strapping fellow, who did not seem to relish their usual fare; for hie came in the morning, and quite politely, as I thought, enquired if I could give him a bowl of coffee. I suppose I looked surprised, for he put his hand in his vest, and pulled out some silver roubles, and said he would pay for any decent food I could give him. Of course I gave him the beat I had, and, being a little curious, I charged him five times the amount of the coffee and bread and butter; but he threw me more than the sum I demanded, and went away without a word.'"

"Now we are on the right scent," said Count Zouboski, joyfully. "I forgive you, Kickemoff, 3'our prolixity. You have a nose like a blood-hound. Now, that Michael Boris and his brother are serfs of mine, I brought them here and gave them a few acres of land about three miles from this. Neither of them are tall men, and I'll swear neither of them possess a silver rouble. Send a couple of the men in the fort to the village, and have Michael Boris up here at once; I'll have the truth out of him, or his back will suffer. I thought there was an underplot with Master Ivan Gortsare, but I think we shall get to the bottom of it."

"May I ask you, Count, what you intend doing with the young Princess and her companion now she has declared herself?"

"Send them both to Kertch in the brig that we expect to-morrow, from thence they will go on in the Redditza war-steamer to Taganrog, where the Emperor will be nearly all next month; at the same time kindly beseech the Czar's pardon, and solicit the hand of the young Princess Warhendorff."

"And her companion?" demanded Captain Kickemoff, "who no doubt is Miss Fitzharding."

"I dare not detain her," said the Count, "the Emperor at one time was most anxious in his enquiries about her; her father was a prodigious favourite of his."

Captain Kickemoff looked disappointed, reflected a moment, and then left the room.

The Count Zouboski shortly after rose, and proceeded to seek an interview with his captives.

CHAPTER XXXIII.

We trust our readers retain a sufficient remembrance of the events that occurred to Mr. Shaw and his son George, in the town of Bantry, after the murder of Mr. Timothy Shaw, of Killgerran; a few words, however, will refresh their memories; George perfectly satisfied by questioning the servant girl at the time that it was Mr. Bullfinch, the attorney that had abstracted the papers from under the bolster, whilst he was conversing with his father and the policeman, left the Inn as we have already stated, and walked out into the street, his mind amazingly perplexed as to how he should act under the very singular circumstances of the case; reflecting in his own mind, he felt satisfied that Mr. Bullfinch must be aware that he, George Shaw, had abstracted those papers from the cheat, in Killgerran House. "Xow the ouly thing to be considered is," thought George Shaw, "whether Mr. Bullfinch took those papers for the sake of gain or to convict me of the robbery. "

George Shaw was very apt to judge most people by his own standard; he therefore set down Mr. Bullfinch as a man who would commit a bad act for a large bribe, provided there was no risk in the undertaking; besides, he argued with himself, he is an attorney.

Having brought his thoughts and mind to this conclusion, he set his hat straight on his head, and quickened his steps till he reached the front of the attorney's cottage. Without any further hesitation, he knocked at the door, requesting to see Mr. Bullfinch.

It was now about eight o'clock in the morning, and Mr. Bullfinch, notwithstanding the stirring events of the preceding evening, and his retarded hour of going to rest, was yet up, and in his study. Mr. Bullfinch had also made up his mind how to act; therefore, hearing Mr. George Shaw's voice in the hall, he opened his parlour door, saying—

"Pray walk this way, Mr. Shaw."

George Shaw walked in, and the attorney, pointing to a chair, begged him to be seated, at the same time carefully closing the door.

Now, George Shaw, once determined upon a course of action, was not a man to waste time beating about the bush, but jumped right into it, saying—

"You, of course, are aware, Mr. Bullfinch, what bringsme here. I have but one question to ask you, shall we pull together or not?"

"Do not speak so loud, my dear sir," said the attorney, blandly. "I understand you perfectly, and my reply is—pull together, of course, on certain conditions. "

"Without entering into particulars," said George Shaw, feeling relieved, "what are your conditions?"

The attorney took up his pen, and taking a sheet of paper with a legal stamp attached to it, wrote rapidly, and in less than five minutes finished, and then quietly handed it to his visitor.

George Shaw took the paper and read as follows:—

"We, the undersigned, agree to pay to Mr. Achilles Bullfinch, attorney, the sum of ten thousand pounds on our coming into possession of the Killgerran Estate and monied property, left by the late Timothy Shaw, Esq., of Killgerran, for services and money advanced. The said Mr. Achilles Bullfinch also agreeing to settle, for the sum of five thousand pounds, all the claims of Messrs. So-and-So against Mr. Eobert Shaw. Dated this 28th of November, 1852. "Witness"

"I am satisfied," said George Shaw, "provided there are funds to meet this demand."

"Funds!" repeated Mr. Bullfinch; "I know there is over forty thousand pounds in securities, without the estate, and whatever money there may be in the chest. Why two large legacies fell to the late Steadman Shaw, and some old leases expiring, the Killgerran Estate nearly doubled itself; and neither of the late proprietors spent five hundred pounds a year—the last not fifty.

"Oa the fulfilment of tbis agreement," said George Shaw, looking steadily into the attorney's face, "you will place in my hands the documents you are possessed of."

"I will destroy them before your own eyes, or you shall do so, which will be far better for all parties. Papers;ire dangerous articles to keep, if their evidence was ever wanted against you."

"Very true," said George Shaw, taking up his hat; then, pausing, he said, "You will require a witness to our sigaing that document. Can you trust any one?"

"Bless me," returned the attorney, "it's a straightforward document—money advanced, services, &e. But do not be uneasy. I have a elerk, who has served me these five-and-twenty years, who neither sees, hears, or reads, when not wanted. Will you and your worthy lather dine with me to-day after our proceedings in court are terminated."

"No," said George Shaw, "we shall require an outfit first. We left," he added, with a sneering smile, "our wardrobe in Australia."

"Well, as we must meet and talk on business matters, we will drink a bottle of wine together; you will see no cue here—say six o'clock."

To this George Shaw assented, and took his leave, the attorney accompanying him to the door, and cordially shaking him by the hand at parting. There was a strange feeling creeping over George Shaw; he felt as if he could have spurned the hand he shook. He felt the hot blood rush to his cheek and temples, and quitting the cottage, he muttered to himself—

"Now am I an accomplished villain! I have robbed an orphan girl of her rights, and become the accomplice of a murderer."

There was a strange working in that

man's breast. The pale but beautiful face of the young girl Nelly, as she knelt beside him, holding the head of the dying raiser, haunted him. What had his career of vice and dissipation brought him? Could he probe his heart, and say to himself, that his past life was one of happiness or enjoyment; tar, far from it. George Shaw was not an utterly reckless man that never thought; he plunged frequently from one vice into another, to drown thought, to keep up a feverish excitement; for, in the midst of all, there was a struggle between the one good spirit and the demon of evil.

As he proceeded, with a gloomy, disturbed look down the street, a young girl came running up to him, and, looking up into his face, said—

"Please, sir; bain't you Mr. George Shaw?"

"Yes, girl, I am." -'Here is a note for you, sir. I went to the hotel with it, but they told me you were gone out."

"And how did you know, girl, that I was Mr. Shaw?"

': I seed you last night at my mother's, sir, I'm Mrs. Sullivan's, as keeps the turnpike, daughter."

George Shaw took the note, put his band in his pocket, and gave the child a sixpence, and then walked on, opening the note, without perceiving that the child still followed him. He read the note, which contained these words—

"Mrs. Steadman Shaw will feel deeply grateful to Mr. George Shaw if he will favour her with ten minute's conversation before ten o'clock. The bearer will show him the Mrs. Shaw's cottage."

George Shaw turned round, and beheld the little girl at his side.

"Please, sir, I will show you the way to the cottage."

"Do so, child, I will follow you. Is it far?"

"Not so far as Killgerran, sir. Can walk there in ten minutes." .In something about that time the little girl stopped before the door of a small but very neat cottage—a humble cottage it was—with its two windows, but the small garden in front, though in winter, was neat, and the whole front was cov-ered with an evergreen parasite plant. As he reached the door, a female threw it open, aud he beheld Mrs. Steadman Shaw. She was very plainly but neatly attired and there was no mistaking, even at glance, that the female before him was entitled to the rank of a lady.

There was still much beauty in her pale but finely formed features; there was a grace and elegance in ber manner unmistakeable, as she said—

"I am sorry, Mr. Shaw, to have given you this walk, probably before you have breakfasted; if so pray come in and partake of ours. We are, you know, doubly connected in relationship."

George Shaw bowed, coloured, but answered, as he followed Mrs. Steadman Shaw—

"You are very kind, madam, and I am happy to have obeyed your wish."

As they entered the little, but very neat and wellfurnished room, a young girl started up from the breakfast table, and, with a flushed cheek and most expressive eyes, held out her hand, saying, in her gentle soft voice—

"I am so glad you are come. You must have thought it strange, after saving my life at the risk of your own, that neither my mother or myself expressed gratitude for the service."

George Shaw held the small fair hand a moment in his. He looked into the pale, but exquisitely interesting face of the young girl. He felt his own cheek was pale, and his voice faltered, as he pressed his lips on her hand, saying—

"You owe me little thanks, cousin; I did only what any other man would have done."

"No," replied Nelly Shaw, with a sweet smile, "not every man. But pray sit down, and let me help you to some coffee; you cannot have breakfasted yet. "

George Shaw sat down, his heart smote to the very core, while Mrs. Shaw poured out a cup of coffee, and placed it before him; while Nelly Shaw got him an egsf, and paid him all those little attentions, coming from fair hands and bright eyes, so endearing and so loreable.

"I wished to see you, Mr. Shaw," said his hostess, sitting down, "before the meeting of magistrates, for several reasons. In the first place, the wretch who committed the crime of taking that poor unhappy miserable being's life, when a few short weeks would assuredly have seen his end, is taken, and the body of the other found early this morning."

George Shaw could scarcely control his emotion, but making an effort, he said—

"They have secured a man whom they suspect, but from a circumstance that occurred to me, I am inclined to imagine he is not the man."

"Oh yes," said Elinor Shaw, "there is no manner of doubt about it. The man who committed the crime is James Hillas. I have seen him several times, and when he broke into the room last night, I instantly recognised him, and, as I shrieked, he caught me by the throat, and threw me back against the bed, saying words too dreadful for me to mention—ending with, 'As you know me, and can hang me, you must die.' He would then have killed me, but your step in the corridor startled him, and I then broke away; before he could grasp me again, you rushed in; therefore I cannot be mistaken. I wish to God that I could, for bad, wicked, and horrible as that man's crime is, I shudder at having his death to answer for, for my evidence must prove his guilt."

George Shaw was confounded—this was startling. After Elinor Shaw's evidence, how would his swearing that James Hillas was the man, he encountered two minutes before he heard the shriek, be received in Court.

Mrs. Shaw looked at George Shaw's troubled expression of features, not with surprise but with commiseration; other thoughts were struggling in her breast, but finding he remained thoughtful and silent she said,—

"Another thing, Mr. Shaw, presses upon my mind, and which I wished to speak to you about; excuse me, if I hurt your feelings, but believe me, I mean far differently, you saved my beloved child's life; she is all that is left to me of the past; I had a son but I lost him; he perished in a most melancholy way, but another time you shall have a history of the past. At present, I will return to my object in requesting this interview. Front what I heard your father say last night, I am led to believe tha t you both have returned from abroad, almost pennyless, and that on the death of Timothy Shaw, your father expected to succeed to the Killgerran estates. My claims, and the papers that will be found in the great chest in Killgerran house will deprive you of all. Now, Mr. Shaw, 'you will believe me, when I solemnly declare, neither my daughter or myself covet one shilling of the Killgerran property; my whole heart is bent on getting the papers in that chest, because those papers clear me from all shame of the past, and establishes my child's right to the name of Shaw; all this appears mysterious to you, but it will be explained hereafter. What I wish to say now is this, that the moment our rights are established we will divide the Killgerran estates with you and your father; this is not my wish alone, but the ardent desire of my Elinor's also."

If ever George Shaw felt remorse, he felt it then, with the sweet speaking eyes of Nelly Shaw fixed upon his face, with a look of such kindness and anxiety. Oh! if man about to commit crime were to pause and think for one short hour, and tax and probe his heart and ask himself one question, would there be the same amount of crime as now and ever has been r"

Thus it was with George Shaw: the look of Elinor, the impression of her deeply interesting countenance— her ardent wish to serve him—changed the whole tenor of his destiny and his designs—his good genius triumphed. A feeling entered his heart for that young girl, all powerful and engrossing; it was one of those strange promptings from a higher power given us at times opening to us an opportunity to retrieve the errors of the past. Like a flash of light it passes through our brains; if we follow its dictates we are saved—if we spurn it, we are lost.

George Shaw was saved from that hour from further crime. He rose up from his chair pale and agitated. We

have said he was remarkably handsome when his features were not disturbed by passion or evil thoughts; Elinor gazed into his serious features, wondering at their troubled expression, and letting young love steal into her own pure, innocent heart, for the preserver of her life, and the intended destroyer of herself and mother's fame. Turning to Mrs. ' Shaw, he said—

"Madam, I shall leave you now, highly impressed by yours and your daughter's grateful feelings and intentions towards my lather and myself. I do not attempt to deny but that he will feel his hopes disappointed, but, at the same time, he will be far from destitute. The legacy left myself and sister by my uncle Pitzharding is amply sufficient for whatever he may require. Before I leave you, will you favour me with pens, ink, and paper, and, singular as the request may be, permit me to occupy this room alone for a quarter of an hour."

Struck by the serious tone, and the calm, self-possessed manner of George Shaw, Mrs. Steadman Shaw instantly said—

"Certainly. Nelly, put my desk before Mr. Shaw, and come with me into the next room."

Elinor looked startled, was paler, and became agitated as she mechanically obeyed her mother, casting a timid look at George Shaw, as she placed the desk before him, and took out paper—her mother had retired. Acting from an involuntary impulse, he took her hand, and looking into her sad, but sweet face, he said in a low and impassioned voice—

"May Q-od bless and protect you, my cousin. You have saved me; and, though we may never meet again, pray remember one who will never cease to remember you."

He pressed the hand of the confounded and agitated girl to his lips almost passionately, and then added—

"Leave me, I pray you, and forgive me."

Elinor Shaw felt her limbs tremble under her. She wished to say something, but her lips refused to utter a word. Tbe strangeness of George Shaw's manner,

bis looks, his agitation, confounded and bewildered her. Trembling with an unknown dread, she passed out of the *r* room, and joined her thoughtful mother in the other chamber.

George Shaw took up the pen; for an instant he hesitated, and then bending down, wrote rapidly for some moments, folded the paper, put a gum wafer on it, and directed it to " Mr. Bullfinch, Attorney, Ban try."

He then commenced another; this was short, and was directed to Mr. Shaw, Mariners Hotel; he took another sheet, and continued rapidly to write for nearly ten minutes; this he folded, wafered, and directed it to Mrs. Steadman Shaw, and then underneath the direction he wrote "Mr. George Shaw earnestly requests Mrs. Steadman Shaw not to open this till she receives a note from Mr. Bullfinch." Having finished writing, he rose up from the table looking infinitely more composed, and with a more buoyant expression of countenance than for many a day had illumined his features.

Hearing no noise in the next room, or the sound of voices, he conjectured that Mrs. Shaw and her daughter were at the back of the cottage, lor he knocked at the door—he thought for a moment, and then said half-aloud, "It is better;" and placing the three letters on the desk, he wrote on a slip of paper, " be so kind as to send the letters according to their direction." Taking up his hat, he moved out from the house, and walked rapidly on over the same road he and his father had traversed two days previously—two days so eventful, and having such powerful influence over his after life.

Mrs. Shaw and her daughter were in the little kitchen which formed one of the two back rooms of the cottage when George Shaw passed out. They did not hear hira, for mother and daughter were earnestly conversing, and of him, in a low tone; time passing over, and a knock at the front door roused them from their conversation.

Mrs. Shaw proceeded to the parlour, but seeing a policeman standing at the door, she went to him, while her daughter entered the parlour, uttering an exclamation of surprise and sorrow when she perceived that George Shaw was gone.

"Please ma'am," said the policeman, very civilly, "Mr. Daunt's compliments, and hopes you and your daughter will be punctual; you will have a private room at the Eose and Grown till you are required. Twelve o'clock is the hour ma'am."

', Very well, thank you," said Mrs. Shaw; "we shall be punctual."

The policeman touched his hat, and was retiring, but Elinor Shaw, who had looked with intense surprise at the letters on the desk, took up the one directed to Mr. Bullfinch, and the one to Mr. Shaw, and came out saying, "the policeman had better take these two letters to the parties addressed."

The policeman paused; Mrs. Shaw looked surprised, but seeing the direction of the letters, she requested the policeman to deliver them, which he promised to do, and departed.

"This is very strange," said Mrs. Shaw," he went away-without saying a word; his manner and conduct was altogether most unaccountable."

"Very probably this letter to you, mamma, will explain all," said Elinor, in a sad and serious tone.

Mrs. Shaw took the letter, and read the request underneath the direction. She remained very thoughtful for some moments, and then said, "I dislike mystery; however, we must have patience;" and then locking the letter up in her desk, and she and Nelly proceeded to get themselves ready for the very unpleasant proceedings that were to take place that day.

But Elinor Shaw's thoughts were more fully occupied with the mysterious conduct and the strange departure of her cousin, George Shaw; and wondering if she should see him at the examination of the man taken, for aamehow she imagined, why she could not exactly say, indeed she felt almost certain, that George Shaw would not appear.

In the meantime Mr. Bullfinch was very busy tying up some papers and getting ready for the business of the day,

his thoughts at the same time fixed upon the handsome sum of ten thousand pounds he had, as he imagined, so cleverly secured to himself; he did not bestow a thought upon the widow and her daughter he was so contentedly robbing of their fair name and inheritance.

A knock at the door and the voice of the policeman desiring the girl to give the note to her master, roused him from the train of pleasing reflections he was indulging in.

The girl handed him the note and retired; finishing tying up his papers, he took up the note carelessly and opening it, began reading; scarcely had he perused the three or four first lines before he staggered back, dropping into a chair—his face pale as death, though the perspiration fell from his forehead, while he exclaimed in a voice of agony, "ruined, destroyed; villain! villain! what can be the meaning of this?" He trembled in every limb, but again seizing the note, he read on. "Ha," he exclaimed, as he read on, drawing his breath, and wiping the moisture from his forehead, and smiling somewhat ghastly; "lam safe after all, but the fool, idiot, and worse than madman—coward, has tumbled to the ground all my dreams of aggrandisement and wealth." Again he slowly read over the letter. We use our privilege, and looking over his shoulder, read as follows:— "Sib,

"On the brink of a precipice I pause, and thus I save you and myself from crime and bitter remorse. I have disclosed to Mrs. Steadman Shaw, the fact of my having robbed the chest in Killgerran house of most important papers, relative to the rights and succession to the Killgerran property.

Having no desire to ruin or involve you, I leave the door open by which you may escape all consequences of the foul, unmanly, and treacherous act we intended to commit. When you have perused this, write at once to Mrs. Steadman Shaw, and to this effect:— "' Madam,

'I have this moment received from Mr. George Shaw a bundle of most important papers and documents, apparently belonging to you, as the widow of

Steadman Shaw, Esq.

How these papers came into the hands of Mr. George Shaw I am not able to say, neither is it important to know. However, madam, your papers are perfectly safe with me; and, from what I can judge from a rapid glance over them, they fully substantiate your claims to the estate and funded property of the late Steadman Shaw, Esq.'

Yon may now add what you please, and of this be perfectly satisfied, your part in this miserable transaction will ncver be betrayed by

Geobge Shaw."

For a few moments the worthy Mr. Bullfinch was utterly confounded. Mentally he cursed the writer, as a weak, conscience-stricken coward; but after some moments of earnest reflection, he saw the absolute necessity of action, not thought.

It then suddenly struck him that some very pretty pickiugs might still be had, by managing affairs for the widow Kavanagh—now Mrs. Steadman Shaw. He therefore sat down to his desk, and wrote nearly verbatim what George Shaw had dictated, and then added— that he (Mr. Bullfinch) would feel very proud and happy if he could, in his law capacity, and knowing so much of the Shaws' (of Killgerran) family matters, in fact being an agent at one time for Mr. Shaw, render Mrs. Shaw any assistance in his power. This note he folded, sealed, and sent off immediately. Taking two or three glasses of wine to strengthen his nerves, a little shaken by the recent untoward event, as he styled it, the attorney collected his papers, and prepared for the business of the day, certainly most amazingly crest-fallen, but still curious to see how George Shaw would bear himself through the trial of the day.

CHAPTER XXXIV.

Me. Bullfinch, in a very thoughtful mood, with his papers under his arm, proceeded to the inn. He reckoned upon a very unpleasant examination, though he relied upon his usual good fortune to come out of the scrape with his character unimpaired.

He found Mr. Daunt and three other

magistrates assembled, awaiting his arrival, but neither Mr. Shaw or his son had yet made their appearance.

After aorne unimportant remarks and observations upon the recent event, the magistrates and the attorney proceeded to the Town Hall, and a policeman was despatched to the Mariner's Inn, to request the immediate attendance of Mr. Shaw, senior and junior; the presence of the prisoner was also commanded. The coroner was there also, and a very great crowd were assembled before the court house; for, although no one felt any very great regret at the death of the unfortunate miser, Timothy Shaw, still a murder under auy circumstances, has always a wonderful effect upon the lower classes in Ireland, and indeed fully as great in England, where infinitely more murders take place, and for, alas! very trivial causes.

It chanced also to be a market day, and numbers of carts and cars came in from the vicinity, but on this occasion buying and selling were neglected—all the interest, all the curiosity of each person being concentrated in the examination of the prisoner, a notoriously bad character, and well known to hundreds.

Whilst the magistrates were conversing in the Town Hall, the policeman sent to summon the Shaws returned, raying that Mr. Shaw himself was coming, though he felt exceedingly ill, but that his son was no where to be found.

Mr. Shaw stated that he had not seen him that morning, but the girl of the inn related that she had spoken to Mr. George Shaw that morning, after which she saw him leave the house, before seven o'clock, and he had not returned since.

"Ha," muttered Mr. Bullfinch to himself, "absconded for a thousand; thought he would scarcely face the magistrates; glad he's gone, however." Then turning to the magistrates, he said aloud, "Mr. George Shaw called upon me this morning at eight o'clock, to consult me upon some law matters; he remained with me half an hour. I wonder what keeps him away."

"Oh, he will be here," remarked Mr. Daunt, "no doubt, in time. He is not a very likely-looking man to be spirited away; he is a very powerful, determined young fellow."

Mr. Daunt had scarcely ceased speaking when a violent uproar was heard without, and looking through the window, a scene of confusion and commotion was seen taking place in the great crowd round the place. There was a dreadful noise of exclamations, cries, and shouts, and a few short stout sticks appeared now and then above the heads of the crowd.

"What is the matter? Brady, why is this tumult permitted?" exclaimed Mr. Daunt angrily, to a police sergeant. "Ha," he added, as he continued to look down upon the crowd, " there is some one hurt; they are bringing in the body of a man on a stretcher." Great confusion and trampling of feet was heard on the stairs; the door opened, and the sergeant of police entered, looking uneasy and rather agitated.

"What's the matter, Sergeant Brady?" demanded the magistrates in a breath, getting excited themselves.

"Why, sir," returned the sergeant, "a sad affair has occurred. James Hillas, the man arrested on suspicion, has been killed."

"Killed!" exclaimed all present, looking at each other in amazement.

"How has this most unexpected event happened?" enquired Mr. Daunt, whilst the coroner became more interested and listened attentively.

"Why, sir," replied the police sergeant, "the men went to the look-up house for the prisoner, who seemed to be perfectly unconcerned, and came cracking his jokes with the people who followed them, till, as they were crossing the street, not two hundred yards from here, two carts, with the horses in a furious gallop, and without drivers, turned out from the market-place. A rush of the frightened people upon the four policemen guarding the prisoner threw them down, and one of the carts came with such violence against James Hillas, that the shaft brained him on the spot, and the wheel at the same time broke the arm of one of the men who was holding the prisoner. Several females in the crowd were also severely injured."

"Let the rascals who owned these carts be instantly arrested," said Mr. Daunt; "they shall pay for their abominable negligence. This is a most untoward event, especially if this same James Hillas was innocent."

"He as surely committed the murder, sir," said the sergeant, "as I did not." The dead body found this morning is an old crony of James Hillas', one Con Maher; and besides, sir, Miss Shaw, as she is now called, has declared she recognised him at once when he entered the miser's, or rather Mr. Timothy Shaw's chamber in Killgerran. He also recognised Miss Shaw, and then it was he wanted to murder her, and would certainly have done so but for Mr. George Shaw's unexpected appearance. The body found this morning was Maher's, who owed his death to the blow of a crowbar."

""Well," remarked one of the magistrates, " God has judged him, and as he was guilty, he has met a better fate than he deserved. What is to be done now?"

We will spare our readers the dull details of law, magistrates' and coroner's speeches, comments, &c., upon the case.

The coroner pronounced this verdict, after a very sagacious jury had returned their opinion, that James Hillas was killed by a blow from the shaft of a cart, &c.

The magistrates examined Miss Elinor Shaw, and felt quite satisfied. Her details of the transaction leaving no doubts on their minds but that James Hillas and Con, or Cornelius Maher, were the real culprits.

The disappearance of George Shaw was certainly mysterious, and caused much surprise; but the following day it was ascertained that he had sailed from Killmore Bay, in the Lord of the Isles, having sent a note to his father to say that that ship, having repaired to a certain degree' her damages, had put to sea, and continued her voyage to Liverpool.

As George Shaw was not required, it was of little consequence his departure, however strange it appeared; still he escaped all suspicion of any wrong having been committed by him; on the contrary his courage and presence of mind was much spoken of, and it was generally supposed, that a feeling of disappointment, at finding the Killgerran Estates would pass away from him and his father, caused his sudden departure, and perhaps an objection to appear as the principal witness against the murderer. But the most melancholy part of the whole affair was, the serious illness that attacked Mr. Shaw, senior, the day after his departure. Whether the privations and hardships he had suffered in Australia had broken up a naturally strong constitution, or the shock and disappointment he had received, when feeling secure of the Killgerran Estates, affected his mind, we cannot say, but he took to his bed: his son's letter, though a kind and dutiful one, also preyed on his mind. George Shaw stated how he intended to act, viz., that he would settle the whole of the Pitzharding Legacy upon him, he himself intending to enlist in any regiment proceeding to the Crimea.

It was very evident to all around him that Mr. Shaw was seized with a mortal illness, and which in fact carried him off in a fortnight.

Every attention that the dearest relation could bestow was lavished upon him, during his illness, by Mrs. Steadman Shaw and her daughter; gentle Nelly scarcely left his bedside, whilst life remained; he died repentant and consoled, blessing his sweet and affectionate nurse, and praying that his son might yet become a good and honest man, worthy of the love of so pure and good a heart as Nelly's, for to soothe the old man in last moments, Nelly confessed she could love George Shaw if his future conduct became consistent with his promises, as she felt sure it would.

"He has performed a noble action," exclaimed Nelly, "he has conquered himself, and the Almighty will, I trust, bless his efforts, to turn from the path of evil."

Thus died Robert Shaw; he was laid beside many of his race and name in the romantic churchyard of.

If there were few mourners followed his remains to their last resting place, there was at all events one true and affectionate heart that shed tears over his grave, repeating to herself, "There is more joy over one sinner that repenteth," &c.—

The papers, documents, and will of the late Steadman Shaw, completely established the claims of mother and daughter, (the son being supposed dead) to the Killgerran Estates, and whatever property was left, in whatever shape it might be. Nearly six thousand pounds was found in gold and notes and securities in the chest, and it appeared by the will and other documents, that Timothy Shaw had at no time, any right to the property, as he was left an annuity of three hundred pounds a-year in his brother Steadman Shaw's will.

It will be now necessary to lay before our readers a brief narrative of Mrs. Steadman Shaw's previous life, from the period of her mysterious disappearance, 'and also to account for the manner in which Mr. Timothy Shaw came into possession of the property. Those matters remained unexplained to'the public, therefore the good folks in Bantry and its vicinity were permitted to put their own constructions upon this certainly mysterious affair, which to this moment perhaps is puzzling their brains.

As to the worthy Mr. Bullfinch he profited but little, in any way, for all Mr. Shaw's affairs, legal or otherwise, were managed by a Dublin solicitor, who, arriving at Bantry, kindly relieved Mr. Bullfinch, not only from further trouble and anxiety, but also from any future reneration, in the way of bills of costs, a prejudice arising from some cause, and an unpleasant feeling in Mrs/Shaw'a mind, with respect to Mr. Bullffoch, in the transaction of the documents in his possession, added to which'Nelly plainly stated, that she felt satisfied that the attorney must be fully as guilty as poor George Shaw. She did not like his manner or his look during his examination, before the magistrates, therefore our worthy and respected attorney had the mortification of finding that projects of

evil, let them be ever so well conceived, and projected, do not always prosper—though they may appear so to do for a time.

Killgerran was ordered to be fully and handsomely repaired and put in order, the grounds to be agaiu laid out and restored. In the meantime Mrs. Sbaw and her daughter proceeded to Dublin, and after a short residence sailed for England. To make our readers acquainted with Mrs. Shaw's history, we must go back to the period of her disappearance from her sister's house in Dublin.

With many good qualities of heart and mind, Elinor Fitzharding had imbibed, from a very early period of her girlhood, strange and unnatural prejudices against matrimony, regaring it as the grave of love. Unfortunately left without a mother, and under the care of a sister, careless and indifferent as herself about forma or ceremony, and who gay, light headed, frivolous and vain, was a bad example to a beautiful, high spirited, and eccentric girl.

The constant reading of French authors, who gloried in endeavouring to spread their pernicious thoughts, reflections, and ideas upon marriage, and the happiness of the human race, unshackled by ties, operated powerfully upon her mind; and this added to an intimate friendship she formed with a young lady, a disciple of Owen's infamous doctrines, destroyed the few remaining doubts that still struggled in her perverted mind; and thus she became a firm believer in freedom of will, and liberty of all kind to be accorded to both sexes. Unfortunately also, her sister's example as a married woman was not calculated to shake her opinions or feelings.

About this time she met, at an evening party, Mr. Robert Steadman Shaw, who was then known in many circles in Dublin as one of the most eccentric young men in Ireland, or anywhere else probably.

He was imbued with exactly the same principles as Miss Fitzharding, only carried out to a much more exaggerated extent.

Mr. Steadman Shaw was a remarkably dangerous person to fall in the way of a beautiful, misguided, romantic girl like Miss Elinor Fitzharding.

We have not space to dwell upon this portion of our narrative, or we might paint the struggles of reason against the false glare, sophistry, and delusion of a newcreed.

These two disciples of freedom of thought and action fell in love with each other, and finally Elinor Fitzharding agreed to elope and live with Mr. Steadman Shaw, provided she could save her name and relations from the shame that would fall upon her and them by the act she was about to commit.

This very resolution proving, though she would not then acknowledge it, perhaps it did not strike her, her belief in the creed she professed was after all very weak, since it did not enable her to brave the world's scorn.

Miss Elinor Fitzharding disappeared, while Mr. Steadman Shaw stood his ground, frequenting his usual society, and wondering like others, where the beautiful Miss Fitzharding had gone, and with whom.

After a time the death of Mr. Steadman Shaw's brother made him master of the Killgerran estate, and he left Dublm.

Elinor Fitzharding and Steadman Shaw, under the name of Kavanagh, lived in a romantic cottage in the vicinity of Glengariff Lakes, he at times visiting ELillgerran, which he left to the care of his deformed but powerfully-minded brother Timothy, who somehow con trived to acquire a powerful influence over his brother. It was mind over matter; for, after all, Steadman Shaw was weak, enthusiastic, and marvellously easy led. He had no regard whatever for money, though neither extravagant or penurious.

For eighteen months this connection continued without change or regret entering Miss Fitzharding'a mind, but Steadman Shaw, wavering and unsettled, often left her weeks alone, and then came thought and reflection.

She perceived she would soon become a mother, and an accident changed the whole tenor of her destiny. Steadman Shaw was absent, when a fall from a favourite horse brought on a premature confinement, the child died, and the mother was laid upon the bed of sickness for weeks and months. Now it was that the holy and sacred tie of a husband, that fond and beautiful reciprocity of feeling only to be experienced between man and wife; that blessed unity of thought and feeling, that renders the two but one—one-soul, one heart—was keenly made perceptible.

Steadman Shaw failed in the hour of trial, for his affection was not founded upon a solid basis—the tie he had formed had not been entered into with the solemn pledge before God, to be a stay to each other in sickness and sorrow—the connection proved, as it always has done, and will do, a false and glaring breaking of-the commandments of God, and never ends otherwise than in shame, sorrow, and remorse.

Tired of the monotony of their cottage, when his victim was no longer able to join him in rambles about the lovely scenery of the lake, shut out from society, having no pleasure in quiet pursuits, he left the cottage, and proceeded to Dublin to enjoy himself.

Thus abandoned and alone, on a sick couch, without a friend, relative, or acquaintance, at times suffering severely, Elinor Ktzharding did what she hitherto had not done—she looked back upon the past, and then, with a deep sigh, thought of the future.

In this, her hour of trial, Providence sent a kind and sweet consoler to her weary couch, and this conlsoler was the young pastor of GlengarifFs wife.

Pity and compassion at Elinor Fitzharding's lonely state and sufferings triumphed over prejudice and the world's sneers.

Mary Keatly was what a clergyman's wife ought to hepious, cheerful, benevolent, and unassuming. Well born and beautiful, she had married for love, and love had made her home—humble and unpretending as it was— all the world to her. We shall not detail minutely the progress of Mrs. Keatley's and then her husband's influence over Elinor Eitzbarding's mind, actions, and thoughts. It will be sufficient to say that they triumphed in their work of love, for they both became exceedingly attached to their beautiful, but erring pupil. Elinor's false reasonings and delusions fell to the ground before truth and example, and to the last hour of her life she blessed the name of Keatly.

CHAPTER XXXV.

"when Mr. Steadman Shaw returned to the cottage, Elinor, then very much recovered, resolved to carry out her purpose. She fir.st calmly and quietly stated her wishes. Steadman Shaw appeared shocked at such a fickleness of purpose, and commenced reasoning; but Elinor, no longer to be led astray by false reasoning, was determined to conquer. She threw herself on her knees before him, weeping passionately, and implored him to make her his wife. If he refused, she vowed to leave him for ever.

Shaw struggled to maintain his false position, and when at last he did relent, it was on one sole condition— That during his life she should never publicly claim to be his wife, or declare their marriage to human being.

Elinor was about a second time to become a mother, and finding it impossible to move him further, finally consented to the weak minded man's stern resolution. She obtained, however, permission to rear her child, if she and it survived, under the name of Shaw.

They went to England to be married, and Steadman Shaw so managed it, that he alone knew the name of the place, and the clergyman who married them. He deceived his wife, and left it out of her power to prove her marriage, should she feel inclined to break her oath.

But Mrs. Sbaw had no such intention; she became an altered woman in every sense, but her esteem for her husband was gone; whilst to gratify a false pride in adhering to principles he knew in his heart to be a delusion and a snare, he sacrificed his own happiness and the' love of a woman, who, chastened and enlightened, would have rendered the remainder of his life blessed.

They returned to Ireland, but to Mrs. Shaw's grief and disappointment, her beloved friend, Mrs. Keatley, and her husband, had left the place, her husband being presented with the living of.

Mr. Steadman Shaw purchased a cottage in the vicinity of Castletown, to the westward of Bear Haven, where Elinor gave birth to a son, and five years after to a daughter. She saw her husband only at intervals; he had strangely altered, and lived, after the birth of his daughter, entirely at Killgerran, and gave himself up to, the dominion of his strange, incomprehensible brother.

Mrs. Shaw never communicated with her family, or claimed the fortune left her, bound as she was by a vow, and besides quite incapable of proving her marriage, it was useless. She passed her whole life in seclusion, devoting herself to her children.

When her son had attained his fourth year, a serious illness attacked her husband, and he wrote to her to visit him, but still come under the name of Kavanagh. She went to Killgerran, and then, for the first time, beheld her extraordinary brother-in-law. On the bed of death, as she feared, she surely thought Steadman Shaw would relent; but no, the ruling passion prevailed, he declared before his mother, that her rights and the rights of her children should be secured, now this was an admission; he made his will, which was witnessed by two respectable farmers on the estate, but, in the end he recovered.

"When Mrs. Shaw returned to her cottage, she was horror struck at being told that a boy, of the name of Mullaghan had taken her son out in a small boat, late in the evening. They were not missed till night, when the woman who had the care of the children became distracted. Mrs. Shaw was paralyzed, for no trace of the boat, which belonged to Castleton, could be discovered, though several fishing parties put to sea that night, but a thick mist prevailed and no signs of them could be seen, and a3 it blue a gale the next day, they were considered to have perished. Mrs. Shaw's distraction brought on a fever of long duration; before she was recovered sufficiently to leave her bed, she received a note from Mr. Timothy Shaw, in which he stated, that his brother was attacked with the same disease as before, that he

had destroyed his will when he heard of his son's loss and probable death, with the intention of making another, and begged her to leave again for Killgerran.

When she reached Killgerran, which she could not do for more than a week after receiving the letter, to her grief and amazement, she found her husband was not only dead but buried, and that Timothy Shaw considered himself the heir; as no will or document remained to prove Mrs. Shaw's assertion, that she was his wife, and not, as Timothy Shaw boldly asserted, his mistress.

Disgusted and deeply grieved in mind at the falseness and treachery of the miserably deformed wretch her brother-in-law, Mrs. Shaw proceeded to England to endeavour to discover the place, and the clergyman who married her; but, baffled in every way, dispirited and broken-hearted, she returned to Killgerran, to try and soften the strange being who held her fair name, and her daughter's, in his hands.

All her efforts proved unavailing. She even feared to irritate him too far, lest should he possess the documents she so earnestly desired, he might in his frantic passion destroy them.

Too proud and too sensitive to seek her relatives, without some proofs of her child's legitimacy, she for several years lived in England in total obscurity, educating her daughter. She fortunately possessed jewels to the amount of nearly a thousand pounds, and a large sum of money deposited in a banking-house in Dublin by her husband, in ner name, and for her use, two years previous to his death; and on this, and the sale'of her jewels, she and her daughter lived; and a sweet, innocent, well-informed beautiful girl did Nelly Shaw become, till at length Mrs. Shaw received a letter from Mr. Timothy Shaw, as strange in its contents as that strange and wayward being himself.

In this letter Mr. Timothy Shaw stated that he was ill, and he earnestly requested her to come to Killgerran; that he would clear her fame in the eyes of the world, and reinstate her in all her rights, but he required her to faithfully

promise that, whilst he lived, things should remain as they were.

Mrs. Shaw at once made up her mind to go over to Ireland, leaving her daughter under the protection of & kind acquaintance, who kept a school. On reaching Killgerran, which she had not seen for years, she stood bewildered and confounded, for she beheld it in the same dilapidated, ruined state, George Shaw first saw it. She found Timothy Shaw shut up in one room, and that room in a most miserable and disorderly state; she saw at a glance he was not long for this world; he had ordered a cottage to be prepared for her reception, and which he intended her to take possession of under the name of the Widow Kavanagh.

Thinking it better for her own and daughter's welfare to comply with his strange wishes, she took up her abode at the cottage, writing for her daughter to join her in Dublin, where she went to receive her. "When Elinor, arrived at Killgerran, ber mother proposed to Timothy Shaw to let Nelly attend on him, for the mother knew how winniug and gentle her daughter's manners were.

But the miser shrunk from seeing anyone, a stranger to bim; but one day, when very poorly, Nelly determined to see and assist bim, and that one day established her influence for ever over the stony heart of the miseraable misanthrope.

Nelly completely changed the appearance of the room, which became as neat as it was possible to be. She procured him good and nourishing food, and made him eat it, too, when perfectly satisfied that it cost him nothing. Strange delusion of the human brain! Knowing that the lamp of life was flickering in its socket, the miserable man yet strove to retain that for which he had not only bartered life, but perilled his own seul.

One day, as he lay sleeping, half dreaming and waking at intervals, he made a sign to Nelly to come to his bedside.

"Nelly, dear," he said in a low voice, " when I die you will be as rich as the queen."

He then closed his eyes, and lay for some moments still, then with a start he tried to sit up, and fix his weak gaze upon the great chest.

"Nelly, do you see that chest? Take care," he added sternly, though his voice trembled with the effort, "do not dare to think of looking into that chest; if I ever thought you wished to do so I would burn it—destroy every paper in it!"

"Dear uncle," replied Nelly soothingly, "do not distress yourself. I do not bestow a thought upon what is in it. Alas!" said the poor girl mentally, "this is not truth, God 'forgive me, for my beloved mother's whole heart and soul is there, and mine too, but we care not for the gold it contains."

The miser lay for some time looking earnestly at Nelly. No doubt he could see the tears stealing down her cheeks. Perhaps his heart did soften, for he said—

"Nelly, your father's will is in that chest; your mother's certificate of marriage."

Elinor's heart beat.

"Ah!" continued the old man, "I have been a monster all my life.. I killed your father."

Nelly shuddered.

"Yes," he continued, more wildly, "my avarice killed him!"

"Oh! uncle;. do see a doctor?" entreated the poor girl earnestly.

"Doctor!" repeated the miser with a groan, " it was my not getting a doctor killed your father. What pay a doctor! No, no, no. That would be ruinous. If you dare to send for a doctor, I will burn the room and all in it."

Nelly soothed and calmed him by her own gentle, persuasive voice, and then he slept.

Similar scenes frequently occurred, till the night of the murder. Nelly had arranged everything for the night, and was leaving the room, previous to the coming of the old woman who usually kept watch in the outer room, when the door was pushed open, and James Hillas and his comrade entered. But for George Shaw, Nelly's days had surely been numbered that night, for James

Hillas knew her well by sight and Nelly him.

In bringing Mrs. Steadman Shaw's early history to a close, we have from necessity been as brief as possible.

After mother and daughter reached England, Mrs. Shaw's first thought was to make every necessary enquiry about her relatives. She was well aware that her brother and his wife had died at Odessa, leaving immense wealth to his son. She also was aware that her niece Julia was not to be traced. The only relative, therefore, that she knew of in England was Sir Edgar Manners, who she found lived at "Wild Drake Lodge, Babbicombe.

As Torquay was a beautiful and charming residence, Mrs. Shaw proceeded there, and took a furnished horse for the winter, and when settled, she wrote a note to the old Commodore, stating who she was, and requesting an interview.

The astonishment of Sir Edgar Manners was indeed great when he perused Mrs. Shaw's note.

"Well, by Jove! here's a hurricane of news! Hallo!-where are you, Tom?" shouted the Commodore to his coxswain, who was busy in the next room.

"Aye, aye, sir! what's the matter?" sung out the coxwaiD, stumping into his master's presence. The baronet had not yet screwed on his leg, and was sitting in an easy chair before the fire. "Faith, I, thought the Russians had"

"Choke the Russians and you, too, you villain! you know deuced well that no Russian bear dare growl on England's soil. No, but here's a hurricane of news. Do you know who's turned up?"

"No, faith, your honor, I do not. Old Mother Mangle yesterday tripped over the stair-carpet, and stood on her head for five minutes, on the windey place, but I capsized her right on end." -' Hold your tongue. If your wife knocked your figure-head against that noisy, old fool's, it would do you both good," said the Baronet. "But give me my cork leg, I have a visit to pay; Mrs. Shaw, of—there, 1 forget the name."

"Mrs. Shaw," repeated the Coxwain, rubbing his chin; "faix, I thought, sir,

she was dead. Sure, that's the name of the proprietor of the great Sunbeam Company; be gor, I remember."

"You're an old fool, you know nothing about this Mrs. Shaw," cried Sir Edgar. "This lady is the Miss E.tzbarding that disappeared from Dublin, some twoacd-twenty or more years since. She married a Mr. Shaw, of Kill something or other. Always some outlandish names to places in Ireland."

"Be gor s;r, 1 don't see that, this here place is called Baby Comb, that's an outlandish name, if you like; but the place you mean is Killgerrau."

"Ah, that's it—give me my leg—Mr. Shaw, of Killgiant."

"Killgerrau," put in the coxwain.

"Well, Killgerran, it's always Kill something. Now screw on my leg, and go get the carriage rigged."

"You don't get along half as well with this new fangled thing, with as many springs in it as an old watch, as the old timber one," said the coxwain, as he strapped down the baronet's trousers over a very smart cork leg.

"Ha! ha!" laughed the Baronet, "you're saying that because your wife wouldn't let you mount the same. She said it wasn't ship-shape to see the Commodore and his coxswain in the same rig, so stump off and get the carriage brought round."

Wild Drake Lodge, since the marriage of Tom Delany, had undergone a very remarkable change; he had quite remodelled the establishment, there being no less than four female inmates of the mansion; a very smart damsel, indeed, attending to the Baronet's comforts, at dinner; he was even heard to say, if ever he had to go to sea again, he should certainly be of opinion that two or three females to keep the cabin tidy would be a great acquisition.

Aout one o'clock in the day, Sir Edgar Manners' carriage stopped before the residence of Mrs. Steadman Shaw, and out stepped the old sailor, looking as hearty and fresh as when last he trod on the deck of the old Trincomalee; he was remarrkarkably sprucely dressed, and his fine portly figure and good humoured features struck the beholders with a feeling of pleasure. It was not without a palpitation of the heart and a cheek a little paler than usual, that Mrs. Steadman Shaw stepped forward to meet the warm-hearted Sir Edgar Manners; mother and daughter were both in deep mourning, but, having recovered their peace of mind looked remarkably well. Nelly positively beautiful and interesting.

The Commodore, with unaffected emotion, kissed the cheek of Mrs. Shaw, and welcomed her return to the world and her kindred with so much of kindness and affection in his manner, that Mrs. Shaw could not help being deply moved. He also embraced Nelly with the manner and affection of a father; kissed her blushing cheek, and told her she was the prettiest girl in all Devon and would create a feeling of admiration amongst the beaux of Torquay.

Verily, verily, Tom Delany had worked wonders with the stout old Commodore. There was no longer to be seen at Wild Drake Lodge "petticoats scouring across the lawn at gun fire." Indeed, Tom hinted that his commander would not have much objection to get spliced if any good-looking dame knew how to work to windward of him.

For some moments after the first ceremony of meeting had passed over, there was a slight hesitation in all three; but at length Mrs. Shaw said—

"My dear sir, can you make it convenient to spend the day with us; for really I have so much to say, and indeed so many questions to ask, that I fear I shall weary you."

"Not at all, my dear madam," replied Sir Edgar; "nothing could give me greater pleasure than a long conversation with you and your charming daughter. I came with the intention of requesting the pleasure of your company at Wild Drake Lodge, but since you have got the weather-gage of me, I yield, on the promise that you favour me with your company to-morrow."

To this arrangement both ladies most willingly agreed.

CHAPTER XXXVI.

The day passed away pleasantly, for Sir Edgar Manners was, when free from his redoubtable enemy the gout, a most agreeable companion.

In the evening Mrs. Shaw, as the baronet was exceedingly anxious to hear all the particulars from the period of her mysterious disappearance in Dublin, commenced a narrative of her life, neither attempting to conceal the errors of a false education, or to extenuate her faults of character. But when she reached that part of her narrative which related to the loss of her httle boy Edgar, the baronet could not control his excitement; he staried from his chair with such precipitation, forgetting his cork leg was not near so substantial as its humble rival, the timber one, that, but for Miss Shaw, he would have measured his length on the floor.

"God bless my soul I" he exclaimed, recovering himself. "I very nearly capsized you, my dear Miss Elinor; that confounded rascal of mine, having a spite against this cork leg, has left a screw loose, and but for your timely aid, my dear, I should have come down like the mainmast of the Trincomalee in a typhoon."

"I have still to beg your pardon, Mrs. Shaw," continued Sir Edgar, re-seating himself after settling his deranged supporter with Nelly's assistance, "for my singular excitement at that part of your narrative concerning the loss of your little boy Edgar. You are looking agitated, I pray you be calm; I am an old excitable fool at times. Now, do not be too sanguine, but, by Jove! I think we can find your lost son."

"Oh, Heaven!" exclaimed Mrs. Shaw, trembling with intense agitation, and pale with excitement, whilst Nelly sat gazing with clasped hands at the Commodore, burning with impatience, and feeling such a fever of hope at her heart with the thoughts of having a brother to love and cherish.

"I must not keep you both in suspense," said the baronet, looking at Nelly's bright eyes fixed upon his, "and yet I do not wish to raise hopes that may be fallacious. You shall hear-all I know. I have only heard it a week ago from my gallant nephew, now Lord Courtland, who was present at the fight of Inker-

mann, and met with a strange adventure there; but I will not be working across hawse in this manner, but go straight to the fact. You are aware, my dear madam, from our previous conversation, that Lord Courtland proceeded as I considered it, on a mad cruise after his lost sister! I thought it a wild project because of this war; however he set sail, in his yacht, the Medora, one of the handl somest crafts afloat, and, after a variety of strange ad ventures, by Jove! he not only found his sister, but a young Russian Princess, to whom he was in a kind of a way betrothed when a boy, and for whom he always retained a romantic attachment, and with whom he is now desperately in love; by Jove! that love must be a very curious thing," continued the Commodore, with a very serious face looking at Nelly, who involuntarily blushed. Perhaps she thought so too; but seeing Mrs. Shaw looking anxious, the baronet continued—" I am a bad story-teller, madam, I yaw about in my tale just like my old ship when scudding under more canvass than she liked. However, about a week ago I received a packet of letters from my nephew; he was then in the Medora, lying with the fleet before Balaclava; he had gone into action aboard the frigate, Captain P.

Aboard this vessel he had a very dear friend indeed—a companion of early days—and his comrade in many a bold exploit. This friend's name is Edgar Erwin."

Mrs. Shaw's heart beat quicker at the name of Edgar.

"Lieut. Erwin," continued the baronet, "received a slight wound, and he had permission to remove him aboard the Medora. Now it appears according to his letter—I wish I had it here, but you shall see it tomorrow—it would save me, working and! backing and filling in this way. But the short and long of it is, his friend Lieut. Erwin told him that he had no real right to the name of Erwin, that he was picked up at sea when between four and five years of age, in a small boat, by a ship called the Ocean Queen, but off where he had no kind of remembrance, but he knows he was called Edgar."

"Oh, my God!" exclaimed Mrs. Shaw, as the tears stole down her cheek, and her hands clasped together. "he must be my son, my own boy over whose loss I have wept at times for many a long year."

Nelly passed her arms round her mother's neck kissing her fondly, and whispering, "Oh, mother, Providence ia ever good and watchful; there, is great happiness in store for us yet."

The old Commodore looked at mother and daughter, wiped his eyes, and thought Nelly the prettiest maiden he had ever seen. Called himself an old fool to have let life slip by. "If. I had got spliced when I was young, I might now have just such another sweet loving child to soothe my passage out of this world. But it's too late," aaid the Commodore, involuntarily, speaking out loud,-' at least, I think so."

"What's too late, my dear sir," said Mrs. Shaw, recovering herself and looking np.

The Baronet smiled, saying, "It's never too late, my dear madam, to make an old fool of oneself. But I must go ahead, and not keep you so long in suspense. It seems aboard this Ocean Queen, that picked up the boat with the child in it, was an Irish seaman, of whom the child became extremely fond, and he of the boy. But the Ocean Queen was boarded by pirates in the Chinese seas, I believe, and every soul murdered except the poor boy; at least the boy thought so. But strange to say, at the battle of Inkermann, Lord Courtland fell in with a wounded soldier who belonged to the Connaught Rangers. Now this man told my nephew, that his brother, who was once a seaman on board the Ocean Queen, was still alive, and actually serving in one of our ships of war at anchor before-Balaclava.

"Edgar Erwin became extremely eager, of course, to see this man, and my nephew obtained permission to have him for a few hours on board the Medora. It will be sufficient to tell you, my dear madam, that he at once, from some token or other, remembered Lieut. Erwin to be the little boy picked up by the Ocean Queen, and he said the child

called himself, when taken aboard, Eddy Shaw, and he cried bitterly after his mother."

"Thank God! there can be no doubt now," said Mrs. Shaw fervently.

"I do not think there can, my dear madam," said Sir Edgar; "there are other means mentioned by my nephew, which you shall see in his letter, but the most important one is the sailor's name; he is called—bless me, I forget it!—Howl—something, I know, but he says he is a native of Bantry, and he knew there was a family of Shaws living at a place called Killgiant—"

"Killgerran!" interrupted Nelly, with a smile.

"Ah! that's it, Miss Elinor; my old sea-bear, Delany, whom you shall see to-morrow, has been driving that name into my head all the morning, and, by Jove, he has drove it out instead of in. But Lord Courtland requested me to consult my solicitor, and to send an intelligent person to Bantry to make enquiries about the Shaws of Killgerran, and to try and discover if a child was lost in a boat some five and twenty years ago, and there he is now I suppose, for I have not heard since. And now I think I may congratulate you both, for if Lieut. Erwin turns out to be your son, he is as fine a young man as any in the service, and, by Jove, strange to say, he has fallen in love with my niece, Julia Fitzharding, and that before he knew who she was, having met her in England; but one of these days you will hear all their adventures from themselves; it would take me a week to relate half."

"Most wonderful are the ways of Providence," said Mrs. Shaw, earnestly, "when we least expect it, we receive consolation and happiness. Though perpetually haunted with the image of my lost boy, I never expected again to gain the least trace of his fate, for all at Castletown felt so confident that the boat must have foundered in the gale that followed its drifting away."

After some further conversation on this, to all parties, interesting subject, Mrs. Shaw, by Sir Edgar's request, resumed her narrative, which she fin-

ished. In speaking of George Shaw, she strictly refrained from mentioning the act he had committed, but expressed her gratitude in warm and affectionate terms for the preservation of her daughter's life.

"I am sorry to think," remarked Sir Edgar, "that Mr. Robert Shaw should have suffered so much and died so suddenly, but it is a great satisfaction to know that his son has acted so well. You have, my dear madam, a niece still alive, either in Australia or Xew Zealand; George Shaw alone can give us any information about her. But, with respect to the young man himself, his conduct has greatly surprised me. My solicitor wrote to me to say that Mr. George Shaw applied to him for his share of the legacy left by Mr. Fitzharding, and expressed a wish to settle the whole on his father, and in such a manner that his creditors might not be able to deprive him of this, his only support, in his old age. My solicitor wrote to know my wishes on that subject, and I *at* once wrote back to say—certainly to comply with his desire. At the same time I felt surprise at the young man's leaving himself without the means of support; 1 have not heard since from my solicitor. "

"I wish I could have an interview," said Mrs. Shaw, seriously, "with him; I really wish to share the Killgerran Estate, and let him have a sufficiency to live as a gentleman."

"But, my dear madam," said the Baronet, " the father and son were far from destitute; the legacy amounts now to £8,000, and it was Lord Courtland's wish and express desire—nay, command—that if Mr. Shaw's creditors' claims were *bona.fide,* honest, and straightforward, to pay them their demands, and also help Mr. Shaw and his son in any way desirable and for their benefit. Now Mr. Cartwright, Lord Courtland's solicitor, after a strict and careful investigation, clearly made out that the firm of So-and-So were actually participators and partakers in the fraud committed on the public by the notorious Sunbeam Company, and that the £10,000 they claimed as their money, was, in fact, the money lodged in their hand by the 1,000 poor dupes, led into the snare by their false representations. How Mr. Shaw contrived to get this large sum out of their hands, he could not find out; but I know myself that Lord Courtland ordered Mr. Cartwright to pay several thousand pounds to the real sufferers of that company."

""What a kind, noble-hearted being his lordship must be," cried Elinor with energy.

"Tes, my dear young lady, so he is," returned the Commodore, with a pleased smile. "Fortune has this time not only favoured the brave, but the good and generous. To-morrow I will shew you his full length portrait in his lieutenant's uniform; it was painted by Sir, and is a remarkably fine and striking likeness."

Elinor Shaw was delighted with the promised visit to Wild Drake Lodge. She already felt an affection for the kind-hearted, cheerful, old Commodore, and she also wished to see his favourite coxswain, whom he told such droll stories about, and to whom it was very evident that Sir Edgar was greatly attached.

At a late hour the pleased old sailor entered his carriage to return to his residence, vowing that Elinor Shaw should be his heiress, as Lord Courtland had more riches than he knew what to do with; and now that belly's brother was in the land of the living, and would inherit Killgerran, Elinor would be without the fortune she would otherwise have inherited."

"Well, your honour," enquired Tom Delany, as he unscrewed the cork leg, preparatory to the Commodore's retiring for the night, "what are the ladies of Killgerran like? nice people?"

"The young girl is an angel,'' answered the baronet, "and her mother as fine a woman as ever I saw. They will be here to spend the day to-morrow, so you must brush up thejwomen, get the flags out, and everything in ship-shape. "

"Oh, be the powers, let me alone for that; I'll stir the petticoats about."

"Yes, you old villain, I dare say you will; you could not exist if you hadn't th'em flirting about you like so much bunting on a Queen's birth-day; but do you know who Lieutenant Erwin turns out to be?"

"Faix, I don't know; a Russian, perhaps."

"Pooh! you're always dreaming of Russian s. By the bye, you rascal, you purposely left a screw loose iu my leg. Ah, you are grinning, are you? take that," and away went the pillow.

"Upon my conscience I did not," exclaimed Tom,' clucking as the missile flew over his hesd; "but I alwavs warned you that it is a poor substitute for a stout stiff' timber supporter. Here's a piece of stuff continued the coxswain, turning up his prop; "a ty phoonwouldn't bend it, if you stuck it up for a skysail yard. But your honour, did not tell me who the Lieutenant was. "

"Why, Mrs. Shaw's son, of Killgibbet."

"Killgerran, I told you a hundred times this morning. It's easy to remember a name like that; 1 had an aunt that lived at Ballygruddy."

"Devil take you and your aunt. Hold your tongue and put out the candle, and take yourself off to your wife; I hope she will take your old leg, and give you a dozen with it. I might have smashed a whole table of ornaments by your leaving the upper screw of my leg loose."

"Be gor, that's too bad," said Tom indignantly, "when you know I'd rather break my own neck than raze the skin of your little finger."

"Well, well, I believe you, Tom," returned the Commodore kindly, "but to-morrow you will see one of the prettiest girls you ever saw. Ah, if I was a young man—"

"Oh, faix, it's well you ain't, you were bad enough, —do you remember the two pretty Creoles at?"

"Put out the light, you villain," roared the Commodore, raising his head from his pillow, "you want to deprive me of my natural rest, I want to be fresh to-morrow."

"Aye, aye, sir, I'm off; though, be gor, I can't make out how Lieutenant Erwin can be a Shaw. Never mind, I'll find it out to-morrow; he's a true blue, whoever he is." And off stumped Tom to his better half, who gave him a curtain lecture for stopping spinning yarns with his master at that late hour.

"Oh, bother," said Tom, turning in, "if we were two old women, we wouldn't be done till morning."

The following dav, at an early hour, all were on the alert in Wild Drake Lodge; the carriage was sent for Mrs. and Miss Shaw; the battery was dressed with flags of all nations—the Queen's standard above all; the women as smart as possible, and Mrs. Delany herself, as Tom declared, like a full-rigged ship.

As soon as the carriage made its appearance at the lodge gates, bang goes the battery of four guns, one after the other, to the delight of Nelly. Her mother thought the horses would be off, but they were quite accustomed to Tom's mode of reception, and, indeed, seemed rather to like it.

The Commodore was at the door, hat in hand, to band them out, and Mrs. Delany behind, with her handmaidens: whilst Tom himself, the beau ideal of an old man-of-war's man, still erect and full of vigour, came stumping up to see the angel; and, as Tom told his wife in confidence. "that be the powers, if angels were only half as beautiful as pretty Nelly Shaw, he didn't care how soon he was amongst them."

The day spent at Wild Drake Lodge was an extremely pleasant and happy one to all parties. Nelly was in raptures with the really splendid view, even in winter, over the rich woods and sloping heights of Babbicombe, and over the waters of the beautiful bay. The Commodore was delighted with his fair young guest's praises: he walked by her side all over his well laid-out grounds, Tom Delany following with a telescope and folding chair for the ladies to rest upon, and have a view through the glass at the shipping in the far off waters. Mrs. Shaw praised all the baronet's improvements; Nelly even, to Tom Delany's delight, inspected the battery, and actually stood by without winking, he declared, when he fired the evening gun. She also expressed great admiration of the magnificently executed portrait of Lord Courtland; she thought him the handsomest man she ever beheld.

Mrs. Shaw was completely happy. She saw her daughter with the bloom of health and contentment on her cheek; she was restored to her relations and the world; and she looked forward with hope to a re-union with her long-lost son, to whom she had commenced a long letter that very morning'.

But, in the midst of all her happiness, Nelly never forgot the unfortunate George Shaw. She could not but remember that he had saved her from a cruel and early death. She forgave him in her heart the error he had intended to commit; her gentle nature found excuses for his crime. She imputed his conduct to the impulse of the moment, at finding himself deprived of an inheritance he considered his father's, and not the premeditated act of a bad and wicked nature.

A day or two after Mrs. and Miss Shaw's visit to Wild Drake Lodge, Sir Edgar paid them a visit. He showed Mrs. Shaw a letter from his solicitor, the principal purport of which was, that he had positively ascertained that Mr. George Shaw had enlisted in the gallant —th Regiment of Eoot, then recruiting its ranks after its terrible losses at Alma, and had already sailed for the Crimea.

Nelly sighed, and hoped that fortune might smile upon him yet, and that Providence would shield him in the hours of strife and battle.

CHAPTER XXXVII.

"we must now, kind and considerate reader, quit our happy island, and again visit the dark and turbulent waters of the Euxine.

Once more then we step on board the graceful Medora, at a time when, under easy sail, she was standing in for the bold coast of Circassia, between the Russian fortress of Anapa and the handsome and picturesque town of Norva Rassiska.

Lord Courtland had stood in close to this town which seemed to have been recently abandoned by the Russians. It had the appearance of being a remarkably pretty place with hospitals, barracks, and a church of considerable size and elegance.

The fortress and the town were built upon a steep hill, and by the look of the whole place it was evidently a town of recent construction.

The coast from thence to Anapa was a succession of richly wooded mountains and hills, but beyond Anapa, the desolate steppes of the Crimea commenced.

Lord Courtland and Edgar Erwin, with Mr. Bernard, held many anxious and protracted consultations on the best means of prosecuting their voyage, under the then existing state of affairs.

It was now the first week in December, and already heavy gales swept the turbulent waters of the Black Sea.

So far to the eastward as they were, and on the Circassian coast, where the water is profoundly deep to the very shore, the extreme severity of the approaching winter was not yet felt. But already they had experienced what the Buxine could do, when putting on its wintry aspect. Fortunately the wind kept well to the eastward, leaving the water within many miles of the Circassian coast quite calm and smooth.

After several consultations with Lieutenant Erwin and Mr. Bernard, Lord Courtland came to the resolution of landing in the night, at the same place as before, some three miles below Fort Alexandrine, and the late governor's mansion. He felt satisfied he could implicitly trust Michael Boris, both he and his brother having earnestly implored permission to enter his service, and make themselves useful in any way, as the life of servitude, slavery, and degradation they endured under Count Zouboski rendered life hateful. Our hero, therefore, intended taking Michael Boris ashore with him, proceed to his village, and procure eggs, fowls, or vegetables, and then visit Fort Alexandrine, and thus be able to judge whether he could, with the force he possessed on board the Medora, carry it by a *coup de mam.*

Michael Boris declared that he never saw more soldiers in the fort than thirty, with two officers; but he at the same time intimated that the guns of the fort could be directed upon all the approaches to the mansion.

To ascertain this accurately was Lord Courtland's principal motive in landing.

"If," said our hero, addressing Edgar Erwin, " by any unforseen accident I should be detected in my disguise, which I do not think probable, and thus fall into the hands of the enemy, your best plan of proceeding, my dear Edgar, will be to go in the yacht to Ghelendjek, or anchor in the Bay of Semes, where you know there is safe anchorage in all weathers; there you will find two British cruisers. You can thus return and rejoin your ship, while Mr. Bernard can make arrangements for either lying there or at Touaps, both places being abandoned by the Russians. Mr. Bernard can remain there for a month or two, or till I can manage to send him a messenger; for even should I be discovered," added Lord Courtland, "Michael Boris will be able to communicate with you."

Lieutenant Erwin was most anxious to join our hero in, his adventure, but Lord Courtland would not listen to his proposal; his ignorance of the manners and language of the Russians would betray him; besides, his Lordship considered his character would be injured by remaining longer than his health required from his ship.

"I have nothing to detain me ashore more than fourand-twenty or thirty hours; and though I have arranged everything as well as I can for a mishap, I really do not seethe slightest chance of any *contretemps* occurring."

Notwithstanding all Lord Courtland's reasoning, and the security he expressed concerning the safety of his adventure, Mr. Bernard was much depressed, and felt very anxious at his determination of a second time venturing himself within the grasp of the enemy.

He had become sincerely attached to his Lordship, whose uniform kindness and sweetness of disposition had greatly endeared him to all on board the Medora; but it was useless to remonstrate.

It was nearly dark when the yacht stood in for the wild and desolate spot

Lord Courtland had selected for his first landing. Bold precipitous rocks, their summits covered with noble trees, deep inlets, and at times shingly beach of small extent, formed this part of the Circassian coast.

The Medora was hove to within a mile of the shore, the boat lowered, and our hero and Michael Boris seated in the stern sheets. It pulled away from the side of the yacht, the former bidding his anxious friends farewell, and requesting they would have no apprehensions about him, as he should not be long held captive, even if discovered; and, at all events, was sure of good treatment.

In less than half an hour the boat reached the place where they intended to land, and Lord Courtland and Michael Boris leaped ashore; his lordship, telling his men to be of good heart and keep a sharp look out, followed his trusty guide, and soon disappeared amid the dark woods that bordered the shore. His faithful and attached crew lost sight of him with extreme regret that they could not share whatever perils he might be likely to be exposed to; not one amongst them would have hesitated cheerfully to peril his own lifts at all times to serve their commander.

During the night the Medora stood off to sea, and remained lying-to during the greater of the following day.

About mid-day the crew beheld two large ships, and a steamer, standing away towards Soukem Lvaleh.

The steamer at once altered her course and came rapidly towards them; Lieutenant Erwin, who was on deck, recognized the ship, and cried out, " It's the Braganza, Mr. Bernard, hoist the yacht's colour, and also the distinguishing flag of Lord Courtland."

As soon as these were observed by the steamer, she hoisted her own colours, fired a gun, and altered her course. A gun was returned from the Medora and the colours hauled down.

"Captain Beard is a great friend of Lord Courtland's," said Edgar Erwin; "those ships no doubt are bound for the bay of Semes."

"I wish," observed Mr. Bernard thoughtfully, "that we had his lordship

back safe and sound. I cannot but consider his adventure very perilous and a very wild one."

"It certainly would be a rash act in any other Englishman," returned the lieutenant; "but remember, Lord Courtland is perfectly master of the language and manners of the people, besides which, he feels a confidence it is more than possible another would not; besides which his energy, courage, and presence of mind, can carry him through any difficulty."

The weather during the day continued fine and moderate, and as the sun went down the yards of the Medora were braced round, and her graceful bow turned towards the shore.

As soon as the night was sufficiently dark the boat was lowered, and Lieutenant Erwin took the tiller, while the six sturdy oarsmen pulled in for the appointed spot.

On reaching the rocks, they were hailed by a low voice —it was that of Michael Boris, apparently greatly exhausted, and bleeding from two musket shot wounds. Erwin was shocked to see him, but could only understand by signs that Michael Boris made, and the single word— prison, that his beloved friend had been in some way or other captured.

The crew entreated Lieuteuant Erwin to let them proceed on shore, but the Russian, by signs, made them to understand that there were more than a hundred men in the woods above them.

The peasant had scarcely ceased speaking when a bright flash was seen in the wood above, and the rattle of musket balls dashed the water up beyond the boat.

"Hush, not a word," said the Lieutenant, "they cannot see us, and only fired at random, but put your jackets in the rullocks, and pull steadily out; we could do nothing but sacrifice life uselessly."

The men were savage, and Lieutenant Erwin greatly distressed, but as he could understand very little or anything from Michael Boris's signs and unintelligible language, delay was useless, so repeating his injunctions, they pulled rapidly to the yacht. There was a ground swell rising, which betokened a change of

wind, and luckily it was intensely dark, which doubtless saved them from a second volley of musket balls.

On reaching the side of the Medora, Mr. Bernard anxiously looked for Lord Courtland, and was shocked when Lieutenant Erwin declared he was a captive to the Bussians.

As soon as Michael Boris's wounds were dressed, themaster, who understood a little of the language, and which he had improved by study and Lord Courtland's instruction, managed, though with difficulty, to make out Michael Boris's account of the mishap. The poor fellow's wounds were fortunately not dangerous, and as soon as he gained strength, for he was evidently greatly exhausted by some violent exertion, he gave the following account of Lord Courtland's capture.

On landing, his lordship and Michael made their way through the woods, and reached the village where the hut of the latter was situated. They found the door closed as he had left it. It was standing a few hundred yards from the little village, which Boris said did not contain one hundred and sixty inhabitants altogether.

At that late hour not a soul was to be seen, and, entering, Lord Courtland threw himself down upon some dry fern and rushes, and Boris, lighting a very primitive lamp, a wick swimming in oil, held in an earthern bowl, his lordship commenced eating his supper, having brought some from the ship in a basket.

As soon as it was daylight Boris proceeded into the village to collect eggs, fowl, and other articles, so that they might fill their baskets, and then proceededto the Port to dispose of them.

He stated that just as he was entering the village, he perceived a party of soldiers with their muskets shouldered, marching in from the Anapa-road; fortunately for him, two or three of the men, perhaps from pity, gave a loud shout, crying out, " there he is."

Michael at once turned and fled, knowing that if he was caught he should suffer the knout, till he died under it. Several of the soldiers pursued by order of their officer; he had to run past his own hut, and as he did so, Lord Courtland came to the door.

"We are discovered," shouted Boris, "fly for your life," but his Lordship stood his ground.

Several of the soldiers then fired their muskets at him, and he felt himself wounded, but being a strong man and swift of foot, he held on and plunged into the thick wood and thus baffled bis pursuers. He concealed himself in a spot he knew, and tearing up his garments strove to staunch his bleeding wounds. When it became dusk, he stole up to the hut of a comrade he knew would not betray him, and there learned that the soldiers of the Fort had been hunting for him and his brother for two days, by order of the Commandant of Anapa. He also learned that Lord Courtland was made prisoner, and taken under an escort to the Fort, and there were fifty or more men added to the garrison of the Fort, and every precaution taken to prevent a surprise, as it was reported that an English corvette was cruizing off the coast. His comrade advisen him to fly, as he would be shot if taken; he was so faint and weak from his wounds, that it waa with difficulty he could move, but he made the effort, as a party of the soldiers were still in the village. He therefore summoned all his energies, and made lor the landing place, and was nearly discovered twice by a party of soldiers in the wood in ambush.

Such was the substance of Michael Boris's narrative, understood with considerable difficulty by the vexed and distressed Lieutenant Erwin, and Mr. Bernard.

The entire crew of the Medora came in a body to them, and anxiously requested that an attempt might be made to surprise the garrison at the Fort, and release Lord Courtland at the risk of their lives, protesting they were ready to sacrifice them at any time in his service.

Edgar Erwin thanked them warmly, but declared, ready as he was himself to risk life for his friend, it weremadness to think of it. The Fort, by Michael Boris's account, was now strongly garrisoned, the enemy on the alert, and evidently in force along the shore, watch-

ing - aDy attempt at landing; and, though he felt deeply grieved, he said he felt sure Lord Courtland would be well treated when his rank became known. The men were forced to appear satisfied, but they felt exceedingly excited and anxious.

During the night it came on to blow hard, sending a heavy surf in on the rocky coast, under their lee. It was not a season of the year to loiter upon so wild a shore, so, after an hour's anxious conference with Lieutenant Erwin, Mr. Bernard bore up for Ghelendjek.

The next morning the Medora was plunging her graceful bows into a heavy cross sea, under single reefed topsails and housed topgallant masts. Amazingly chagrined at the result of Lord Courtland's projects, Mr. Bernard worked the yacht skilfully and well till he ran into the Bay of Semes, where they beheld a screw sloop of war, and the Braganza steamer lying at anchor, the latter with her steam up, preparing for sea.

The Medora anchored close to the steamer. Lieutenant Erwin was perfectly aware, it was his duty to return as quickly as possible to his own ship, therefore, though sadly vexed and disturbed in mind about the fate of his friend, he requested Mr. Bernard to lower the boat and put him on board the Braganza, which, perhaps, was returning immediately to the Crimea, or it was possible they might be engaged in reconnoitering the coast, previous to an attack upon Anapa, which had been talked of before he left the fleet.

On gettiug on board the Braganza, he learnt from Captain Beard, that they had been reconnoitering Soukem Kaleh, and were now returning to Eupatoria, off which the fleet lay. Captain Beard was extremely sorry to hear of Lord Courtland's capture. Lieutenant Erwin briefly explained the reasons that caused his Lordship to run such a risk. He then anxiously enquired how the fleet and the army got on, in their endeavours to reduce Sebastopol.

"Badly, badly," returned Captain Beard, "there will be but the shadow of an army there next spring. I cannot say where the blame his, but it's heartrend-

ing to behold the sufferings of the army. "

"And has there been no fresh attack made by the fleet upon Sebastopol?" enquired Lieutenant Erwin.

"No, we have been lying there inactive, and risking the ships in the terribly sudden gales that sweep over this sea. It is a wild anchorage, and I fear that some of these nights we shall And that out."

CHAPTER XXXVIII.

As Michael Boris had stated, he left Lord Courtland sleeping, while he proceeded into the village to procure some egg3, fowls, or vegetables, but very shortly after his departure his lordship awoke, and getting up from his extremely humble couch advanced to the door of the cottage, and was no little startled and astounded at seeing Michael Boris, running for his life followed by a dozen or so soldiers who were pursuing him. As he passed near the hut, Michael Boris shouted "fly and save yourself." Just then the soldiers levelled and fired at the fugitive. With a feeliDg of relief he saw the unfortunate serf still pursue his flight with the soldiers after him, while another party of eight or ten, with an officer at their head, came running up to the hut. To fly he had not the slightest intention, and to resist was equally futile: to take life uselessly, or lose his own by a mad resistance, never entered his head, but at a glance he saw that death would be his fate if he remained in his serf's garments, so, casting off the belt, he rapidly threw aside his disguise, pulled off his false beard, 'fcc., and just as the Russian officer came up, whom he at once recognised as Captain Kickemoff, he was standing quite calmly at the door of the hut, vested in the neat but simple garments of a British sailor, which he wore beneath his disguise.

Captain Kickemoff paused, amazingly surprised, but he ordered his men who were rushing eagerly upon Lord Courtland with their hayonets to fall back, whilst the worthy Captain looked at the tall, noble figure of his prisoner, and then up to his features, upon which there was a smile; Captain Kickemotf started and exclaimed,—

"By St. Nicholas, the Armenian fortune teller," and then added, "you are my prisoner, whoever you may be in real earnest."

"Such I suppose would be the case, Captain Kickemoff," returned Lord Courtland, calmly; nevertheless. I demand, as a British subject, honourable treatment."

"By St. Ivan, you may be a British subject," replied Captain Kickemoff cavalierly, "but as to the treatment you may receive that depends on the will of my commander, Count Zouboski; you seem to forget that you are found on this coast in disguise, for there it lies at your feet," kicking the false beard and coat in the road. "You have also tampered with the loyalty of a Russian serf, and made a traitor of him, and even introduced yourself into one of our fortresses—therefore, by the rules of war, you are a spy, and incur the doom of a spy"

"Have a care, Captain Kickemoff," said our hero sternly, "what you say: at all events, conduct me to your commanding officer, and recollect—for I may have to remind you some of these days—that you have dared to apply to me a term that may cost you dear yet."

The Russian officer grew red in the face with rage, but stepping back, he ordered his men to take charge of the prisoner.

"He may learn yet," he said bitterly, "how Russia treats British subjects, aye, and British peers when caught in disguise on her coast."

"Ha!" thought Lord Courtland, "they do know something about me."

The soldiers now formed round him, their captain telling them to move on. The distance between the village of Varsa and Fort Alexandrina might be five or six miles, through a thickly wooded country and over a. wild rocky, and mountainous region. Twenty men formed the escort, ten marching before, Captain: Kick emoff proceeding alongside the prisoner, and the rest following.

Though Lord Courtland felt very little anxiety respecting his life or being condemned as a spy, he still was deeply distressed at the discovery of his project, for it appeared to him very evident that they had someway or other gained intelligence of himself and his plans. His mind also dwelt upon the Princess and his sister, exposed to the schemes of Count Zouboski. However, naturally not easily daunted or his energies depressed, he walked on, devising many schemes to free himself from his present difficulties.

The road—if indeed it could be called a road—wound between masses of red rocks crowned by magnificent pines, of a size sufficient to form the masts of a line of battle ship. For the space of a mile, Captain Kickemoff kept eyeing his prisoner keenly. At length he said, in a more moderate and placable tone, for the worthy Captain bad some projects of his own to bring to perfection—

"Yeu cannot blame me for doing my duty."

"I do not blame you for doing your duty," returned Lord Courtland, "only for being insolent; an officer can perform his duty even upon a criminal without being brutal."

The Russian bit his lips, but he restrained his temper.

"You might find it better, my Lord," the title he pronounced with emphasis, "to make me your friend instead of an enemy."

"I must consider every Russian an enemy whilst this war continues; pray how did you discover who I am."

"Oh! that was very easily surmised," returned the Captain, "our prisoners—I mean the female—in the Count Zouboski's charge, made no secret of who you were." j

"Now tjtat is false, Captain Kickemoff," returned our hero indiahantly. "You cannot impose on me; you have Bomjf project in view in thus conversing with me; go straight to the p&nt and I will answer you."

The Captain wan about to reply when his men formed into a file two abreast, for they were then entering a very singular and wild defile, the rocks on one side rose to the height of more than a hundred feet, and through an immense cleft gushed one of those violent streams, that form the tributaries to the Kouban.

This stream crossing the road, rushed with prodigious violence over the rocky impediments in its course. It was too deep and violent to ford, and the rocks too slippery and steep. So across the torrent was erected a rude bridge, constructed of trunks of gigantic pines, thrown across. Only two persons could pass abreast.

The advanced soldiers had passed and Lord Courtland and Captain Kickemoff were proceeding across, side by side, when a volly of rifle balls from the rocks above, and another from a thicket below into the soldiers in the rear, stretched nearly half the number dead or wounded on the ground.

With an exclamation of fierce rage, Captain Kickemoff drew his revolver, and grasped the prisoner, swearing with an oath he should not escape, but the next moment the pistol was wrested from his hand, and Lord Courtland exerting all his strength tore the Russian officer from the bridge, and pitched him headlong into the deep foaming pool beneath.

Whilst this short struggle was taking place the few Eussian soldiers surviving the two discharges, fled and sought shelter in the wood, that stretched for miles to the westward. A body of armed men now showed their heads above the rocks. His lordship who stood his ground, guessed at once that they were Circassians; he perceived Captain Kickemoff without his hat crawling out of the pool and dodging amongst the rocks to avoid the dropping shots from the Circassian rifles. Not knowing how he would be received, our hero moved off the bridge towards his deliverers, who were now descending the rocks. As he stepped off the bridge, a very young and fine looking man with the picturesque cap of the Circassian tribes on his head, and his breast protected by a shirt of mail, and carrying in his hand a very richly mounted rifle, approached, and in a very kind tone said some words in a language our hero did not understand.

"Ah," added the Circassian, immediately, "you do not understand me, do you speak the Russian language?"

"Yes," returned Lord Courtland, "in

that tongue allow me to thank you for my restoration to liberty. I am an Englishman."

"Good," returned the Circassian, "I am aware of that, and it was to release you we planned this ambush, but follow me, for we must not loiter here."

"Whilst our hero and the Circassian chief were conversing, his men were very busy stripping the dead Russians of their arms, and ammunition, and accoutrements, but the sound of a Russian bugle disturbed them from their pleasing occupation.

Speaking to his men, in an energetic tone, they all sprang up and commenced ascending the same rocky mount from which they had fired upon the Russian soldiers.

Lord Courtland and their leader followed; they had scarcely cleared the steep ascent, when a volly of musketry pealed through the air; the balls rattling against the face of the rock, scattering pieces of them over the fugitives; before another volley reached them the Circassians threw themselves on their faces, and creeping to the edge of the cliff with their rifles, prepared to pick off any of the Russians that became exposed to their fire.

Lord Courtland was quietly looking over the cliff, when he felt himself pulled down by the Circassian chief. He had barely sunk down when another volley rattled against the rocks, but injuring no one. Our hero counted about thirty Circassians besides their leader, who, addressing him, told him that there were above one hundred Russian soldiers concealed in the wood, not that they were quite ignorant of what force he had, for further back, about two leagues, he had nearly two hundred men.

The young chief now desired his men to commence their retreat, and not to fire any more.

"You-will come with us, Bey; you have no other chance of safety. You cannot regain your ship, a3 the Kussians have dispersed a number of men along the coast.".

The English nobleman was exceedingly surprised to find his deliverer so well acquainted with himself and his movements, and although exceedingly uneasy about the fate of the unfortunate Michael Boris, and distressed at being thus cut off from his friends and his yacht, he was too thankful for his preservation and escape from captivity not to appreciate the service rendered him.

The Russians made no attempt at following the Circassians in their retreat; they therefore proceeded leisurely on their way through the wild hills, during-which Lord Courtland had time to examine his deliverer and his gallant little band. The young chief himself could-notbe more than one or two-and-twenty, his features were remarkably handsome, and his figure tall and graceful. Over his tunic he wore the highly-polished steel shirt of mail, and in his embroidered belt was placed the double-edged Circassian dirk; and slung over his shoulders his handsome rifle. Added to his equipment was a Damascus blade; excepting his rifle he presented a perfect picture of the warrior of olden times.

His followers without one exception were young men. They called themselves "Dell Khans," or wild bloods. Their dress differed from their chief's. They wore the sheep-skin bonnet, collarless fr6ck, with loose hanging sleeves. Their frock or tunic fastened in front with loops, and on each side of the breast a row often cartridges. Their trowsers were wide above the knee, but at the knee and calf they were tightly gathered in. Their parti-coloured, and gaily-gartered overalls completed their costume. Their boots, however, were remarkably neat, being made of red morocco, trimmed with silver lace.

They were all armed alike, with rifle and dirk, and a single pistol, mounted in silver, and stuck in the belt.

There was a peculiarity in their swords, having no guard whatever, the sheath being of wood, covered with morocco leather, and ornamented with silver lace.

Altogether their appearance, manner and arms, added to their erect and manly figure, gave them an extremely martial look.

Their road lay through a singularly wild and rocky district, extremely difficult of ascent and descent, and utterly impossible that any one unacquainted with the features of the country could attempt to traverse.

So occupied were all the party in the difficulties of the road that no attempt at conversation was thought of. In truth Lord Courtland was sufficiently employed with his own thoughts and reflections.

Having at length surmounted the chief difficulties of the road,.they commenced descending from the heights into a more open tract of country, though still shut in by high rocky hills.

Getting on tolerably level ground, the young Circassian chief came to the side of the Englishman, and said—

"I hope, Bey, you do not feel fatigued. We shall come to the farm where we left our horses in a verst or 80. "

"Oh, no," returned Lord Courtland, "I should be sorry to feel fatigued from such slight exertion; but may I request to know to whom I owe my release from captivity, and how I came to be known to you."

"My father is Schamyl Bey," replied the young man, with an air of conscious pride; "you have heard hia name, I am sure."

"That most certainly I have," exclaimed our hero, greatly surprised; "and a gallant noble chieftain he is considered by all Europe; but I understood Prince Schamyl's son was a prisoner to Russia. Doubtless, you have a brother?"

"Yes," answered the young Bey, "I was a prisoner to our hated enemy, but was exchanged some months back for several prisoners of importance. My father offered to restore the Princess Warhendorff, and her daughter, and attendants for my release, but the Emperor's answer was, they deserved their imprisonment, and in their stead accepted others. General W, wife, and attendants, were therefore Teleased intead of the Princess "Warhendorff, who still remains in my father's fortress."

Lord Courtland was greatly surprised, but before he could make any remark, the young Bey said—

"When we get to our 'konaz,' (resting place), tonight, I will be more explicit, and explain matters. You will, I fear, find your present costume ill-adapted for the severity of the weather you will experience. Our winter sets in very rapidly; but if you will adopt our costume for a time, I can supply you."

Lord Courtland expressed his thanks, but said he hoped to be able to rejoin his vessel. He had left directions, in case of a mishap, that she should put into Ghelendjek, and remain there for some time.

"Ah! that is fortunate, for many reasons," remarked Schamyl Bey, "we may now do something; but yonder is the place where we left our horses."

A few minutes afterwards they halted at the principal farm house of a small village, consisting of about two dozen houses; there was a large wall-inclosed yard, and most of the inhabitants were collected round the place, seeing the party coming up in the distance. The principal personages assembled round the young Bey, no doubt anxiously seeking for news. The intelligence they received did not, however, seem to please them; for the word " "Wai, wai, wai," was uttered several times.

Schamyl Bey requested his companion to follow hint into the house, and take some refieshment before resuming their road, which led, he observed, towards his destination—the Bay of Semes.

Within the large room were assembled many of the inhabitants, among them some young females, led by curiosity to see the "Inglis Beyzade." Our hero saw one or two extremely pretty maidens amongst them; the room had little or no furniture in it, which he afterwards perceived was invariably the case in all the houses he visited. He was received by the owner, a "lion eater," and a bush ranger, who boasted of having slain half-a-dozen Russians for exercise before breakfast.

The low table was covered with many sorts of refreshments—simple of their kind; but tbe wild goats' flesh formed a considerable portion of these. For drink they had "boza," and "bocksima,"—the latter is a very potent kind of mead, and a much more palatable drink than the other, though more intoxicating.

None but Schamyl Bey spoke the Russian language; but Lord Courtland, through the interpretation of the young Chief, expressed his thanks for the attention he received, '-and trusted now that France and England had attacked their detested enemy, they would be able to draw the Russians from the Circassian territory; that their just cause was highly popular in England; and that all lovers of freedom wished them success."

This short speech gave great satisfaction, and numerors exclamations followed; but Hadji Gruz Bey, the owner of the village, and the son of the once famous Guz-Bey, the " Old Lion," declared that the Ingles Bey was fit to be a Circassian Chief; and that he should ride his favorite white horse as long as he remained amongst them.

This, Schamyl Bey assured Lord Courtland was an immense favor— Hadji Guz Bey being a chieftain of considerable importance, possessing other large villages and land.

Having finished their repast, Lord Courtland followed the iyoung Bey into the yard, where stood the white steed ready accoutred.

On preparing to mount the remarkably handsome and powerful horse, held for him by one of the Bey's grooms, Lord Courtland was particularly struck with the fashion of the Circassian saddle, so very different from all European accoutrements.

It was a mere frame of wood very light, covered with red morocco leather, surmounted by a small flat and oblong cushion, stuffed with wool and covered with eather, and trimmed with silver lace; but what puzzled our hero at first sight was a piece of wood, polished, about four inches high, and which rose right up from the saddle bow, and another, exactly similar, from the back.

To one unaccustomed to mount this saddle, there was a considerable risk of impaling one's self. Our hero however mounted, and being a splendid horseman, and the animal being one of great spirit and action, the young Bey looked with a smile of great satisfaction at the ease and grace with which Lord Courtland checked the somewhat affrighted beast; and as the troop filed through the gate, the horee, either knowing he was mounted by a stranger, or from a naturally wild temper, became so desperately unruly that Lord Courtland, partly to show the natives that England could boast of good horsemen as well as the mountains of the Caucasus, pushed with spur and voice at the stone fence encircliug the farm yard, and which was full five feet high, and, to the amazement of the assembled Circassians—who, though splendid horsemen, never take a fence—the noble white steed of the Old Lion cleared the wall without touching; reining in the almost equally astounded steed, beside the young Bey, panting with so unusual an exploit, who exclaimed with delighted admiration—

"Wain, wahi; well done, by my soul;" whilst the troop raised a shout of applause, and then their chiefs exclaiming "Duz Dogbru" (right away), they all gave the spur to their steeds, and dashed over the short plain of three miles like the wind, and then checked their horses so suddenly that they came upon their haunches, firing every one their pistol at the same time, without being remarkably particular as to the direction of the balls.

Though our hero was surprised he evinced none, knowing the custom of Asiatics is never to show surprise, although his feat of leaping the wall did for on.ce take them unawares. He therefore checked his steed quite calmly beside the Bey, remarking—

"You reverse our custom, Bey; for when we start in England for a ride, we breathe our horses before we test their power of speed."

"Mere custom, mere custom!" replied the Circassian; "the horses are accustomed to everything: they will go full speed down the side of the mountain at starting, when a man can scarcely keep his feet; there is no doubt but that you English surpass us in taking walls and fences—for you train your horses I suppose to it—I see you are a perfect horseman; but now I will show you a little feat common with us Circassians, and perhaps quite new to you."

Calling to one of his followers, he spoke to him, giving him some directions in the Circassian language.

The man spurred on his horse—while all the rest halted: and when at some hundred of yards distant, he threw his pistol on the ground.

Young Schamyl Bey then put his steed into a wild gallop, and just as he came up with the pistol, he flung himself as it were from his horse, holding on with one hand by the upright piece of wood rising from the saddle bow, picked up the pistol, was in his saddle the next moment, and turning round levelled his weapon at the trunk of a tree, lodging the ball in it while in full speed.

Lord Courtland had heard and read a great deal concerning the Circassian horsemen, and their rifle shooting; therefore, when he returned to his side, he paid him some graceful compliments upon his skill, good-humouredly challenging him to a shot with the rifle, being himself rather a remarkable marksman with either rifle or pistol; and, he well knew, if a stranger wished to gain the esteem and good will of a wild chivalric race like the Circassians, to show skill in arms or in any warlike exercise was the true way to do so.

"Most willingly," answered the young Prince, with a gay smile; "but I must warn you that I am accounted the best shot in our tribe, after Man sour, my father's henchman; and no man has ever excelled him yet."

"Then there will be no disgrace in being vanquished," observed Lord Courtland gaily.

"There, take my rifle," said the young chief, "we shall soon come up with some wild goats, on yonder hill," and, calling one of his men up, he took his rifle.

The young Prince's weapon was a remarkably handsome one. They now rode on. All the troop already were, by the fine figure and manner of Lord Courtland, and his skill in horsemanship, anticipating a good contest, but never imagining their young chief could

be equalled. They soon came up to the hill, where over a dozen wild goats flew up the steep rocks with the swiftness of a deer.

"I will take that milk white goat in the haunch," said the young Bey, and lifting his rifle, he fired. It was a very long shot; the animal rolled over, but jumped up again, and bounded higher up the rocks; but just as it reached a rock, nearly perpendicular over the road, Lord Courtland raised his weapon and fired; the animal sprung into the air, falling dead into the plain beneath.

As the troop of Dell Khans raised a shout of approbation and surprise, all were startled by a cry that rung through the air, instantly followed by the hollow sound of the trampling of many horses.

"Fall back, fall back," shouted Schamyl Bey, "the Cossacks!"

As he said the words, Lord Courtland perceived, turning the abrupt angle of the rocky mountain, a large body of Cossack horsemen. With a wild yell, they bent their heads to their horses' necks, their long lances in rest, and their small but wild vigorous horses, with their nostrils distended and their long manes waving in the strong wind, came over the space between them and the Circassians like thunder. There were more than fifty of them, and Lord Courtland, with no other than an unloaded rifle, began to think his situation rather critical, when the young chief turned to him, saying—

"Trust to your horse, Bey, and you will see what it has been bred to; "and turning themselves, the whole troop spurred furiously up the side of the rocky hill, opening their ranks, and dividing into twos and threes, they completely avoided the shock of the Cossack lances; at the same time turning in the saddles, they discharged the rifles with unerring aim, emptying the saddles of four or five riders.

Lord Courtland followed the young Bey closely, sur prised to a degree at the almost miraculous power and endurance of the Circassian horses, who kept their footing in places apparently only for the mountain goat. The Cossacks did not appear to relish this mode of

proceeding, for they did not check the speed of their horses till out of range of the Circassian rifles, they then leisurely halted, and appeared to deliberate upon what was next to be done. The Circassians threw themselves from their horses, slacked their girth, and sat down amongst the rocks, calmly reloading their rifles, and laughing merrily at the discomfiture of the Cossacks, who, if they fail in their onset, rarely attempt to dislodge the Circassians from the heights.

Lord Courtland had dismounted, and was patting and soothing the high-spirited beast that had carried him up the steep bank with such power and endurance, when Schamyl Bey came and sat down by his side.

"I did not expect to meet that troop," said the young chief, "they are quartered in the fortress of Aloon; there must be a Russian infantry force not far off."

"It was very fortunate," observed Lord Courtland, "that we were close to this hill, for I don't see how, armed as you are, you could abide the charge of the Cossack lances."

"They are dangerous enemies on a plain, I confess,", said the young Bey; "for their horses are fleet, and as wild as their riders; but a stone wall, or any kind of fence will stop them; they will not stand a second discharge of our rifles, if they can any way get out of shot. "

"Then what do you propose to do now?" enquired our hero; "they are hovering on the edge of the plain watching us."

"Oh, you will see our mode of warfare now, Bey. I regret it, however, for your sake, but here we must entrench ourselves, let our horses loose, and send a few scouts out to examine the country, and bring up my men, who are within a few versts of us. Those fellows will keep hovering about the plain till we drive them off."

Lord Courtland would rather, if the choice had been left to him, have encountered them at once; with a welldirected volley of their rifles they could check their charge, when prepared for it, and with their sabres and pistols meet the rest.

On proposing 'this to the young Bey, he appeared to think for a moment, and then went and joined his men. to whom he spoke very energetically for several moments, when they all started up, saying they were quite willing to face the enemy if the English Bey considered they had a fair chance of success.

Immediately two of the men descended into the plain with the intention of plundering the dead Cossacks of their arms and ammunition. In a very few minutes they returned with several brace of pistols, two lances, and the short firelock of the Cossack.

Schamyl Bey then presented Lord Courtland-with a brace of pistols and a gun, but our hero requested one of the lances, preferring it to the short musket.

Leading their horses down the steep hill, the sagacity of the animals was wonderful, carefully letting themselves down on their haunches.

As they commenced descending the hill, they perceived the Cossacks moving gradually nearer, and divided into two bodies.

In a moment the Circassians were mounted, each man with his rifle ready. The young Bey's plan was to move on on their intended road, and as the Cossacks came up, as they generally did, at full speed, to give them a volley, and then suddenly open their ranks, let them pass, anil reload, giving them a shower of balls from their pistols at the same time.

Keeping a wary eye upon the movements of thr enemy, the Circassians moved on. Lord Courtland rode by the side of Schamyl Bey, but the Cossacks contrived to keep the same distance, evidently not liking, though superior in numbers, to attack them. Now they were prepared, their mode of warfare consisting chiefly in sudden surprises, or wild charges upon infantry.

Skirting the side of the mountain, they continued through a wild and desolate track, the Cossacks still following, though out of reach of shot, till they were forced to leave the side of the hills, and cross a plain of some four miles in extent.

"Now," said Schamyl Bey, halting for a moment, " be prepared; they will charge us as we cross this plain to yonder hill. Do you see Bey," he added turning to Lord Courtland, "that stone pyramid on yonder bill? We cross that low range. If they charge us, give them a volley coming up, and then each make for yonder pyramid; up that hill they will not follow."

The English nobleman felt a strange excitement in the affair; the picturesque costume of the troops, the wild spirit of their horses, their own animation and ardour, united with the savage picturesqueness of the surrounding scenery, all conspired to raise a feeling of a chivalric' description; and as he grasped the lance he held, he almost fancied he had plunged back into the warfare of the middle ages.

They had scarcely moved half a mile out from the side of the hill, before the Cossacks evidently increased their pace'; the Circassians seemed to fly without striking a blow, and when at last the wild, fierce yell of the Cossacks pealed over the plain, the whole troop wheeled round, and unstrung their rifles.

On came the Cossacks like the tempest, bending beneath the necks of their steeds—so much so as to offer but small mark to the rifles of the Circassians. When within less than five hundred yards, Schamyl Bey gave the word to fire, and a simultaneous discharge from thirty rifles aimed with deadly accuracy, sent near a dozen horses and men rolling over on the plain; still on the survivors came yelling, and their long lances prctruding far before their horses; while, at the same time, the Circassians perceived, coming out from the range of wood on their left, a large body of Russian infantry; who opened tire upon the Circassians at three hundred yards, but without emptying a single saddle.

"Now, Bey, for the hill!" shouted Schamyl, "there is no dishonour in flying from such odds."

Like magic every man wheeled his horse; and, just as the Cossack lance was within a dozen yards ofthem, they

dispersed.

Mounted on a magnificent horse, Lord Courtland could not bear to fly till he had crossed lances with a Cossack, if it was only for once in his life; and remarking one of the enemy riding somewhat apart from the rest, and on a very fleet steed, he singled him out and rode full speed at him; but the Cossack, thoroughly accustomed to his steed and his lance, swerved on one side, discharging his pistol when within a few yards, knocking Lord Courtland's hat off, and slightly grazing the skin; nevertheless, our hero, though quite unaccustomed to encounters of the sort, was rapid of action, and snatching his pistol from his belt, he levelled at the rider; both horse and man came to the ground—the ball unfortunately striking the horse on the head, the rider's head and part of his body being protected by the neck of the horse.

Lord Courtland perceived the Cossack regain his feet, as he spurred after tbe flying Circassians; and his delay subjected him to a cross fire from a party of Russians, who (had run'out from the main body; but from the hurry of the moment and the rapid pace of his horse, they missed him; with all their speed and quickness of motion, the Cossacks had overtaken and unhorsed one of the Circassians—two of the Russian infantry were running up to secure him, when Lord Courtland rode at them full speed. Aiming his lance at the Russian soldier who held the Circassian, the fellow let go his hold, and threw himself back; while the Circassian, in an instant caught a grasp of the short stick rising from the back of Lord Courtland's saddle, and was on the horse, behind our hero, the next minute.

Then it was he recognised Schamyl Bey; who, with the same chivalric spirit as Lord Courtland, had tried to unhorse a Cossack, but a Russian bullet brought down his horse.

While this scene took place, tkc Cossacks were scouring the plain after the dispersed Circassians—the Russian soldiers making great efforts to reach the hill and cut off their retreat.

"Turn your horse to the right," said

the young chief; "do not fear, he will carry us both well, for I know him. You are as gallant a fellow as ever breathed, and I owe you my life. Push the horse for yonder steep hill; we cannot rejoin our troop without running the gauntlet through the Cossacks. I will guide you to a path they cannot follow."

A dozen of the Cossacks saw their purpose, and wheeling their horses, pursued, but the white steed of the "Old Lion," was not to be overtaken though doubly laden, by a Cossack horse. The foot of the steep hill was "reached, and then Schamyl Bey threw himself off, and ran up the hill with singular speed and endurance; up the steep galloped the noble steed, over rock and bramble, with distended nostrils he urged his way. The Cossacks completely at fault, discharging their muskets after the fugitives, shattering the pieces of rock close by them, but leaving them unhurt.

CHAPTER XXXIX.

In a chamber of Fort Alexandrina, or rather in the mansion belonging to the fort, some eight or ten days after the events recorded in our last chapter, sat Count Zouboski, Captain Kickemoff, and Lieutenant Jaroski.

It was late in the evening, and the Russian officers were regaling themselves with wine, of which they had all partaken rather freely—a very common practice with all Russians, from the noble to the serf.

"You certainly made a very pretty mess of this affair. Kickemoff," observed Count Zouboski, lighting a cigar; "letting a few of the natives rob you of your most important captive, to say nothing of the disgrace and loss of upwards of nine men, their arms and accoutrements. and though Jaroski came to your rescue, you both of you let them escape."

"St. Nicholas! Count," returned Kickemoff, almost savagely, "how could I help it? It was an ambuscade; there were more than fifty or sixty of well-armed Circassians on a height, and another party concealed by the rocks. They fired upon us crossing the Tarsee Torrent; and that cursed Englishman, who has the strength of a dozen, seized me be-

fore I could possibly draw a pistol, and hurled me into a hole; I escaped, by a miracle, having my brains knocked out against the rocks."

"To judge by that day's work," said the Commandant with a sneer, "you had deuced little brains to knock out."

Captain Kickemoff by no means relished his commander's sarcasms, but he imitated the example of his comrade, Jaroski, and remained silent.

"I have sent a man I can depend upon," continued the Count, after a moment's silence," to the outpost of Aloon, with instructions to Captain Sobeskoff to track these Circassians; he has a party of mounted Cossacks with him. There is a report abroad that young Schamyl is in these parts, with a strong party of Dell Khans, but I do not believe it; for our last news from Tiflis was, that he and his father were raising forces all through Georgia. I expect further intelligence every moment, some news ought to have arrived yesterday."

"I can't imagine," said Lieutenant Jaroski, "how those Circassians came to know about this English lord. They were evidently watching for Captain Kickemoff's party in order to release him; it was a regularly concocted plan; besides, those traitors, the two Boris, have managed to escape on board this Englishman's ship. We tracked one of them to the sea-coast, and thought we had him at one time, and even fired into their boat, but it was too dark to distinguish objects, and the next morning we could see the ship standing out to sea."

"Then this Lord Courtland," said Count Zouboski, "still remains with the Circassians; he may be captured yet."

""What is your intention," demanded Captain Kickemoff, "with respect to the young Princess Waxhendorff and the English girl?"

"Why, I have forwarded despatches to Taganrog, stating how the Princess and her companion, Ivan Gortsare, have come under my protection. I also mentioned the daringattempt of this Englishman, whose name, I did not mention: for I understand from this Ivan Gortsare that his father was a prodigious favourite of the Empress; but, as I was

saying) I stated that this Englisman entered Anapa for the purpose of inspecting the fortifications, that he commanded a corvette, and intended, if possible, to carry off the young Princess "Warhendorff. I humbly beseeched the Emperor for permission to marry her, boldly asserting the lady was willing; and ended by offering all the serfs on the Zouboski Estate, amounting to four hundred, as recruits for the army in the Crimea; I now await the return of the courier; and I have a very strong idea that the Emperor will grant my request, for I have secret information that he is inclined to pardon the error I committed, and give me the command of Taganrog, instead of this out-of-the-world place."

Just then there was a knock at the room door.

"Come in," cried Count Zouboski; and then added, 'c doubtless this is my messenger."

The door opened, and a courier, booted and spurred, entered the saloon.

"Ha, Pestal, so you are come at last."

"I should have been here sooner, my Lord," said the courier, " but I went first to Anapa, as I did not know you were here."

"Well, what news do you bring?" demanded the Commandant.

"Not very good, my Lord. I got to the outpost, and delivered your letter to Captain Sobeskoff. Luckily, the Cossacks were mounted and prepared for a foraging expedition, and the Captain started thei% at once by a short cut, while a party of infantry got ready to follow. The Captain knew the Circassians were out, with young Schamyl Bey, but he did not know what force he had— he thought they were in the vicinity of Hyderberg, and that they were making a reconnaisance towards Ghelendjek—intending, probably, to strengthen their Portress of Nicolai. I remained four days waiting the return of either the infantry or the Cossacks; and towards night the Cossacks returned, with a loss of nine men killed and nine wounded—three very severely."

"Curse the rebels!" growled the Count, savagely, "there never will be an end of their audacity till they are exterminated root and branch—well, what next?"

"The Inglis Bey, as they style him, is with them, and actually unhorsed Metchiff, the Cossack Chief, after he had captured young Schamyl Bey, and released him; and finally they retreated and crossed the hills towards the Province of Semes: where it is said the whole country is in arms, and greatly elated, as two British frigates and a large war steamer were at anchor for two days off Ghelendjek. This is all I have heard, my lord, so I hastened back. "

"These cursed Islanders will assuredly attack our forts on this coast, said Captain Kickemoff.

"Tut," muttered the Count, "they are all abandoned, except Soukum Kaleh and Anapa—the winter is setting in, and no ships could possibly keep the sea till the spring. There will be no attempt made for four months, and I doubt not but that, what between their own cursed bungling and the severity of the winter, and disease, we shall hear no more of them; but I wish I could capture this Croesus of an Englishman: he should pay dearly for his liberty. However, we must remove our fair guests to-morrow to Anapa—it's no longer safe to leave them here—a *coup de main* might take the mansion, notwithstanding the fort: in fact, I intend dismantling the fort, stanc and abandoning this station, now quite useless: as this creek will not be visited by vessels of any sort during the winter—What kind of night is it, Pestal?"

"A very wild one, my Lord; blows hard off shore, with cold, and threatening snow."

As the man uttered the words, the loud boom of a cannon from the fort broke upon the night wind, startling all present, and shaking every casement in the room —all sprang to their feet, while Lieutenant Jaroski rushed from the room, exclaiming, " Some ship in sight of the fort, depend on it;" the next moment a volley of musketry pealed from the court yard of the mansion, and then a scene of confusion that baffles

description ensued; all the females in the mansion, excepting Catherine Warhendorff and Julia Fitzharding, rushed, half-dressed, into the room, followed by a sergeant of infantry with a discharged musket in his hand.

"There is a numerous force," exclaimed this man, "landed below the fort, from a large ship, which has run in out of shot before she was seen."

"Make all the speed you can, Pestal," exclaimed Count Zouboski, greatly excited, "to Anapa, and order Captain Aleavitch to bring up his company without a moment's delay; curse them, they are keeping up a fierce fire. Now, Golowin, get you and all the women into the fort as fast as possible; treat the Princess gently, but oblige her and the other maiden to go with you; we can hold it for a week against any force without cannon."

While speaking, and the women were running from the room, the Count and Captain Kickemoff were putting their pistols in their belts, and arming themselves; they knew Jaroski had fifty men without; if he could keep the assailants off till they all got into the fort, all would be well, but this they were not destined to do, for Jaroski and his men, just as they gained the court yard, were driven back in desperate confusion. Just then a blue light was burned on the summit of the fort, throwing a bright steady flame upon the surrounding scene, and a wild and startling scene it was.

We have stated that Fort Alexandria commanded the entrance to a fine, though narrow, inlet of the sea, but after passing the entrance, a high cliff shut out the fort. The vessels passed this cliff and anchored in the pool within. The fort also commanded the approach to the house. At the back of the mansion rose the high woodcreated hills of the coast, broken here and there by immense masses of rock.

The picture disclosed by the brilliant flame of the light on the fort was one of confusion and dismay on the part of the Russians, and triumph on the side of the assailants; a strong party of Circassians, led by Schamyl Bey and Lord Courtland, were driving before them, sword

in hand, the Russian soldiers, while a party of British tars were scaling the rocks to take the mansion in the rear, evidently to cut aft" escape by the back.

As soon as ths soldiers on the fort made out the Circassians, they began wheeling their guns round, to bear upon them as they came up from the creek, when suddenly the loud boom of cannon from seaward startled them, and the moment was lost when their fire would have committed serious havoc amongst the Circassians, who, with a loud shout, leaped over the low walls, and mingled in a furious hand to hand encounter with Lieutenant Jaroski's men.

Count Zouboski was a man of unquestionable courage, and so was Captain Kickemoff. They made desperate efibrts to rally their men, and drive the assailants from the'yard, so that the guns might play on them, but the fort was undergoing a furious cannonade from the twelve pounders of the Medora, the men full ef courage and enthusiasm, and encouraged by the gallantry of Lieutenant Erwia and Mr. Bernard; the fort was plainly visible to them from the lights they burned, while the intense darkness that lay over the face of the waters/hid the Medora, except when the flash of her guns shewed her position. The Medora was simply firing to distract the attention of the fort from Lord Courtland and his party.

Sword in hand, our hero and Schamyl Bey drove the mortified Russians before them. They were aware they must be quick, as the sound of the cannonade would reach. Anapa, and bring down assistance. At length the Russians gave way, and fled for the fort, just as Lord Courtland had struck down captain Kickemoff, and stood face to face with Count Zouboski, who, furious with rage and disappointment, fought like a madman, slaying two of the Circassians who strove to seize him.

"Surrender, and your life will be spared," cried Lord Courtland.

"Never, curse you! never," fiercely roared the Count, attempting to fire with his left hand, his pistol in our hero's face.

By one of those chance circum-

stances that happen at times, in his violent hurry the Count's pistol had no
cap, and Lord Courtland thus escaped
its discharge. Attacking the Count with
his sword, he drove him back despite
his fierce resistance, when, stumbling
over a dead body behind him, he fell,
and was instantly secured.

But his vanquisher did not wait. He
rushed within the mansion just as one of
the guns from the fort opened fire upon it, the ball crashing through the front
wall, raising a cloud of dust and broken
pieces of stone and brick.

A wild shriek escaped the females
within, while Lord Courtland, trembling
with anxiety, seized a torch lighted by
some of the Circassians, and rushed up
the stairs, calling upon the name of the
Princess Warhendorff, and his sister Julia, with all his might.

"Here, here," with frantic joy exclaimed;Julia Fitzharding, who stood
supporting Catherine at the end of the
corridor. With a bound he reached their
side, and without a word he caught the
half fainting form of Catherine in his
arms, and recovering his breath, exclaimed—

"Follow me, dear Julia, and for God's
sake take courage."

"I feel no fear now," said Julia, with
a firm voice. "I knew not who were the
assailants till I heard your voice."

As she spoke, again the thunder of
the cannon shook the house, the ball
smashing the front door and part of the
staircase to atoms; but the crew of the
Medora had broken in through the back
of the house, whilst Schamyl Bey and
his followers rushed through the front,
and all emerged into the gardens at the
back, where they were safe from the
guns the Russians had the barbarity to
level against the house—though knowing it contained many of their own females, besides the assailants.

"Extinguish your torches," cried
Schamyl Bey to his men. "where"is
Count Zouboski?"

"He got off to the fort during the confusion caused by the first shot from their
guns," replied one of the Circassians.

"We must regain the creek," observed
the young Bey to Lord Courtland, who

was whispering some words of encour-
agement to Catherine, though she declared she no longer felt any fear.

"We must be very quick, Bey," continued Schamyl, "and keep a keen look
out, and avoid crossing and exposing
ourselves to the fire from the fort. The
men will not face us again, but keep
within."

"I trust you have not lost many men,"
said Lord Courtland, assisting Catherine
over the obstacles in their path.

"Three or four, Bey, have fallen, but
they are gloriously avenged, for more
than twenty Russians lie stark and stiff
in the front of this mansion."

The firing had ceased from the fort,
and from the Medora. The latter had
again run into the creek, concealed by
the intense darkness, but emerging from
the cover, of the trees, again became for
a moment exposed to the fire from the
fort, but they were past the spot before
the gun blazed out its deadly contents.

"My God, I trust no one has fallen!"
exclaimed Catherine in a low voice, as
the ball tore up the ground not three
paces from them, scattering the sand
and stones over their persons.

"Not one, fortunately," replied her
supporter, press ing the small arm that
rested on his. "Dear Catherine, this is
the proudest moment of my life."

"Ah," observed Julia, who was close
by his side, "if we had known it was you
and your brave friends that were fighting for our restoration to liberty, we had
not suffered so much as we did, when
we heard the firing at first."

They reached the side of the creek,
where three boats lay alongside the
beach, when an officer in a British naval
uniform sprang ashore, and reaching the
side of Lord Courtland, exclaimed—

"Thank God! I see you have succeeded and are safe."

Julia Fitzharding littered an exclamation of surprise, and the next moment
Lieutenant Erwin was by her side.

She had recognised his voice, and he
felt an emotion of exquisite pleasure as
he offered to assist her into the boat.

"I little expected, Lieutenant Erwin,"
observed Julia, in reply to some words
addressed to her by him, "that the next

place in which we should meet, would
be on the wild shores of Circassia
amidst strife and warfare."

The main body of the Circassians
kept back, some distance, to guard
against an attack from the men in the
fort should they think of renewing the
strife; but both the count Zouboski and
captain Kickemoff were badly wounded, and lieutenant Jaroski, with the few
men he had, feared to leave the fort; the
whole party feeling keenly the wild gust
of the east wind, as it roared down the
defile, sweeping across the creek, raising the water in foam, round the boats.

In a few minutes the two rescued
ladies, wrapped in mantles, were placed
in the boat, the rest of the party,
amounting to nearly sixty men, getting
into the others from which they had
landed. As they did so, borne on the
strong wind, came the sound of the
Russian bugle from the direction of the
Anapa road.

"The troops are coming up from Anapa, attracted by the firing," said
Schamyl Bey, who was in the same boat
with Lord Courtland and the two ladies,
with their terrified Greek attendant, who
clung to them most pertinaciously.

-' How unfortunate," remarked Catherine, "Ivan was immured in the fort.
Would we could have rescued him!"

Strange, but at that moment a loud
voice hailed them from the shore.

"Good heavens! that is his voice,"
continued the young Princess. "Oh, how
rejoiced I am."

One of the boats pulled in shore by
Lord Courtland's orders. The next moment they were alongside the Medora,
at anchor close under the cliff that sheltered her from the fort.

Her commander saw at a glance that
she had been hit by the guns; her jib-
boom was carried away, and several
yards of her starboard bow.

"No one hurt, I trust?" he anxiously
demanded, as he helped the girls up the
side.

"Two or three; but very slightly," said
the voice of Mr. Bernard, who then
added, catching Lord Courtland's hand,
"Thank God, my Lord, you are unhurt
and have succeeded. Are any of your

party killed? for there was some heavy firing, and I feared you did not take them so much by surprise as you expected."

"1 fear our gallant friends have lost six or seven; one or two of ours are hurt; but we have, thank God, succeeded. You had better get at once under weigh, for there is undoubtedly a force marching here from Anapa, and they may do mischief from the shore."

His Lordship then took the maidens into the cabin, and pressing Catherine to his heart, and impressing a kiss upon her pale cheek, and fondly embracing his delighted sister, and telling them not to be alarmed if they again heard the cannon from the fort, hurried upon deck.

The other two boats were alongside, and Lord Courtland, while speaking to Schamyl Bey, saw Ivan Gortsare ascend the side.

"1 rejoice to see you, Ivan," said our hero, pressing his hand; "the only drawback to the success of our expedition is removed by your presence; we could not attempt the fort with our force, and yet it grieved me to leave you in captivity."

"I thank you, my Lord," returned Ivan, " but thanks to the confusion and the ball from one of your guns, which, singular enough, went in through an embrasure, shattered the wall of my chamber, and left me at liberty to scramble out—the wreck and the terrible confusion that ensued, when Count Zouboski was brought in wounded, gave me an opportunity to steal out and make for the beach."

It was blowing hard—extremely cold, and at times showers of sleet falling. Just as the yacht swung round, and her topsails filled, a bright blaze burst from the shore, followed by a shower of balls that whizzed and tore through the rigging of the Medora like hail, but luckily injuring no ore, being fired from the beach. They only lodged in the spars and cut some of the rigging.

"I'll pepper the rascals now," said Lieutenant Erwin, as the yacht's broadside faced the spot where the fire came from; and one of the crew running up

with a match, it was applied to the touch-hole of a gun. The report was echoed from fifty places, and bad scarcely died away, before another volley was fired from the muskets of the enraged enemy. But the Medora tore through the water under her double reefed topsail, amid a thick aud soaking shower of sleet, which alone would have hid her from the enemy's sight, even if the darkness had been less. intense.

CHAPTER XL.

Bepobe we follow the Medora in her course, after leaving: the Fort Alexandrina, we will briefly record the events, that preceded the rescue of Catherine Warhendorff and Julia Fitzharding by Lord Courtland and young SchamylBey.

We left the two young men, after their flight from the Cossacks and Russian infantry, on the side of the steep hill that bordered the western border of the plain on which they had been attacked by the Cossacks.

The rest of the Circassians made good their retreat to the hill of the Pyramid, which was separated from the hill they were on about a league. The Cossacks arrived at the foot of the hill, but did not attempt to urge their horses up the rugged and steep ascent, and after discharging their pistols at the fugitives, turned their horses' heads towards the Russian soldiers, who were rapidly crossing the plain.

"We must push across this range of hills," said Schamyl Bey, "till we rejoin my followers, about two leagues from here; they know where to join me, and also know that once amid those fastnesses I am quite safe. "We shall have to pass through a very wild district, but I know every inch of the road, and the Russians with their small force will not attempt to enter the district through which the Hyderbeg flows, as we can muster more than, four hundred men along its banks."

"Very good," replied Lord Courtland, "you lead and I will follow; this ascent for a horse is no joke, and would puzzle the best hunter in England."

"I have no doubt of that," observed

the young chief. "Our horses are trained from two years old to this work, and pass through a very rough apprenticeship, but we shall not go near the summit; past yonder monster rock, there is a cleft in the hill, a wild gorge it is true, but Guz Bey's good steed will carry us both to our konaz before dark, some half-way down the gorge."

Having toiled up the ascent, the horse, left to himself, followed with the docility of a lamb, and the activity of a goat; keeping its legs in an incredible manner in places that required all Lord Courtland's vigour and strength to surmount.

"You would make a famous mountaineer, Bey," said the young Chief, witnessing a spring our hero made across a chasm, by way of a short cut. "I see you Englishmen, can leap as well as your horses."

"It 13 an amusement," returned Lord Courtland, "we practise in our youth, and are extremely partial to; for almost all our sports require activity and skill."

By this time they had reached the gorge, and a piercing East wind blew violently through the extreme summit of the range of hills, which were covered with snow; and beyond them, rising in all the grandeur and magnificence of their vast altitude, was the higher range of the mighty Caucasus.

"Wild and strange as the scene was, with the last raya of a wintry sun struggling through a mass of fast-drifting clouds, casting a transient brightness upon some giant rock, a contrast to the deep gloom and sombreness of the defiles, it was not without a sublime beauty.

They had scarcely emerged from the gorge, and come out upon a heath scattered over with low brushwood, when the young Bey's troop of horsemen came galloping up, with a loud shout of congratulation. Schamyl Bey's horse was with them; for after his master was unhorsed by a Cossack riding right across his course, the horse regained his legs, and followed his comrades.

The Englishman received no end of congratulations and encomiums for his gallantry, and the preservation of their chief from captivity, in the Circassian language, which Schamyl Bey interpreted; and then all set forward in high spirits, not having one of their number wounded. According to the chiefs account, the Cossacks had a great dread of encounters with the Dell Khans; their wild horsemanship and better horses, at times sweeping in amongst them like a whirlwind, cutting their way almost with impunity through them, when not supported by infantry, of which they stand somewhat in awe. It was quite dusk when the troop rode into the large intrenched village, where Schamyl Bey's horse, amounting to near two hundred, were located. They halted before the kenaz, or guest house, for there are no houses of public entertainment throughout Circassia.

The young chief and his companion entered the principal apartment of a rather extensive building. The owner himself was absent, but his wife and daughter were seated on a small divan at one end of the room; they rose up at once to receive the young Bey and our hero; then, for the first time, Lord Courtland beheld one of the beauties so celebrated and so dearly purchased by the Turks. The daughter was scarcely sixteen; she was extremely demure, and could not be prevailed upon to resume her seat, she and her mother remaining standing, while Schamyl Bey became seated, the young chief whipering our hero that it was the custom of the country for the women to remain standing while men were present.

Fizahe—the daughter's name—was singularly lovely, beautifully soft melting blue eyes, and an extremely fair brilliant complexion; her hair being a light auburn, hanging in a profusion of banded tresses over her shoulders from beneath a bonnet of scarlet cloth, trimmed and decorated with broad silver lace.

She was tall, and though still slender, exceedingly gracefully and beautifully formed, and, like all Circassians held herself erect. This fair maiden, as Lord Courtland afterwards understood, was Schamyl Bey's intended bride—her father being a Hadgi, and very wealthy.

She was very tastefully attired in a bodice of blue silk, with rows of silver studs in front, and fastened by large silver clasps, shaped like shells; loose Turkish trowsers or shalwer, and from beneath these peeped a pair of white delicate feet, always uncovered in the house.

The attire of the mother was very different indeed, having nothing either costly or graceful in it; the worthy dame being muffled to the nose in the Turkish style. The room was totally unfurnished, unless several clumsy boxes, containing their beds, might be styled furniture, and a few spindles.

A table was soon laid and then Schamyl Bey's followers assembled, and the usual fare being laid down, and trenchers for each guest, the business of the evening began, under sundry ejaculations of Bishmilla, and other Turkish expressions of satisfaction; then the conversation turned on the war; the blade bones of the shoulder of mutton, picked perfectly clean, were handed round, held up to the light, and the oldest of those assembled gravely gave their opinion of the signs they saw developed in the mutton-bone.

Schamyl Bey and Lord Courtland sat apart, and in the course of the evening the Circassian Chief explained to our hero the manner in which he became acquainted with his project, and why he had come forward so gallantly to assist him.

The young Bey's narrative we will give ourselves, in as few words as possible.

Ivan Gortsare was aware of the danger of falling into the hands of his countrymen, which would not only place his life in jeopardy, but for many a long day separate the young Princess from her mother, and deprive the Princess Warhendorff of all chance of being ransomed. "When, therefore, he was forced into Anapa by the treachery of the Greek padrone, he wished to counteract, as far as he possibly could the evil of being discovered. With the Armenian character he was thoroughly acquainted, the people acting at times as spies for the Russians upon the Circassians, and

spies for the Circassians upon the movements and projects of the Russians.

Fearing something might happen to betray them to Count Zouboski, a man he feared and hated, Ivan Gortsare proceeded, after his meeting with Lord Courtland in Anapa, to the lodging of a certain Armenian he knew to be in the pay of Prince Schamyl, and whose interest it was to be faithful. To this man he confided his situation, and the risk he incurred if discovered; also, that there was an English lord concerned in the affair, who would pay him like a prince if he served him well. The Armenian had a monstrous reverence for an English milor, and his ears opened immediately,

"We leave this to-morrow," said Ivan, " all together. So, if you see that any of us are stopped going through the gate, get this letter (giving the Armenjan one) conveyed to Prince Schamyl Bey."

"Tou are not aware, then," enquired the Armenian, "that his son, the young Bey, is within six leagues of this; and that the whole district of Hyderhez is in arms, and the Russians have abandoned Ghelendjek."

"No," returned Ivan Gortsare, with exceeding delight in this manner, "then since that is the case, you that pass the fortress of St. Nicholai will see the youug Bey; if we are stopped give him the letter and explain to him about this English Lord, whose ship is off this coast at this moment, perhaps actually at Ghelendjek."

Thus Ivan Gortsare provided as far as lay in his power for any mishap, and when he and Catherine Warhendorff and Julia were carried off by orders of Count Zouboski to Fort Alexandrina, the Armenians continued their journey till the man entrusted with the letter encountered young Schamyl Bey and his Dell-Khans.

The young Chief quite aware that his father held the Princess Warhendorff and her attendants captives in his fortress, understood the letter at once, and immediately selecting some thirty of his Dell Khans, set out for the vicinity of Port Alexandrina, to see if it would be possible to surprise the fort, but the scout brought him word of the seizure of the Englishman at the village, and of Captain Kickemoff holding him a prisoner, proceeding to Anapa with him.

Schamyl Bey at once dismounted his force, crossed the hills and formed an ambuscade over the torrent of the Tarsee.

The rest is already known to our readers.

"Now, Bey," continued the young chief," I owe you my life, perhaps; at all events, what is dearer to me—my liberty; for I might have lingered years in Russian slavery. Do you think we could surprise Port Alexandrina? if so, I offer you my services, and the services of my followers."

Lord Courtland grasped the chiefs hand, and pressed it warmly, saying at the same time how grateful he was, and then added—

"I think with about sixty of your followers, and my own crew, for my ship is now lying at Ghelendjek, we might carry the mansion, where the females are confined, by a *coup de main.* The nights are intensely dark. We will embark aboard the ship, run in for the coast, and land and take it by surprise."

This was immediately agreed to by the young Bey, and instantly proposed to his Dell Khans, who gave a shout of intense satisfaction at the proposal,— the only difficulty was to restrain their enthusiasm, and permit him to select sixty.

The next morning the party started on horseback for Ghelendjek. It was a toil-some passage to the coast, sometimes up a precipitous path, then diving into a romantic glen, beneath the double gloom of overhanging hills and dense woods, to some rapid stream at the bottom, the Circassians relieving the tedium of the way by a song, and the chorus dying away in the words, "Ay, A-ri ra." The effect, our hero thought, was beautiful.

The scenery, however, began to open as they descended into the main valley of Hyderbez. The mountains then rose on their left as perpendicular as a wall. The shades of evening were coming on as they came in sight of the abandoned fortress of Ghelendjek, but, to the immense relief of Lord Courtland, he gained a glimpse of the Medora lying at anchor in the bay.

They all raised a shout when the ship was discovered, for then they knew that there was no fear of the enterprise not being followed up, for the Circassians dearly love what the Turks call a "chap-pore."

Having left the horses in a village on the heights, the whole party descended to the beach, and the Medora hailed. In a few moments a boat put off, and, to the extreme astonishment and delight of Lord Courtland, he beheld Lieutenant Erwin in the stern sheets.

The two. friends embraced each other with unmistakeable delight.

"In the name of wonder, Edgar, how is this?" said our hero, "that I find you here; I expected ere this you were storming Sebastopol."

"Sebastopol is very much obliged to you, Harry," said the Lieutenant, "but the said Sebastopol is laughing at our puny efforts. The green old fortress defies us. But, you see, when I found the Braganza steamer here, commanded by Captain Beard—you remember him—I went aboard, and said I would accompany him back to my old ship, but he gave me a letter from Captain P, in which he said, 'we are doing nothing, and likely to remain so, certainly for this winter, so take your time and get well,' &c. But when you come on board, Harry, I will read you his letter. I was so dreadfully anxious about you that I could not rest; and as to poor Mr. Bernard, he was fit to hang himself, but, thank God! here you are. But who are all these fine-looking fellows? By Jove! their leader looks like one of the knights of the olden time."

Lord Courtland explained, introduced the Lieutenant to Schamyl Bey, and then all were taken on board the yacht, whose size and beauty, and arrangement kept them in a perfect state of bewilderment. Two hours afterwards they were under weigh, as not a moment was to be lost.

Having now briefly accounted for the attack on Fort Alexandria, we return to the Medora, as she bore out of the inlet, amidst a perfect whirlwind of sleet and snow.

CHAPTER XLI.

Me. Bernard had been extremely careful in taking the bearings of the two rocky points forming the entrance to Alexandria Creek, for owing to the dense darkness and the thick squall of sleet, it was impossible to see a yard a-head. Under her double-reefed topsails the Medora flew before the gale, and though various lights were burnt on the ramparts of the fort, for the purpose, no doubt, of making her out, yet so thick was the filling sleet and snow mingled, that she passed without being perceptible to the anxious and enraged gunners on the walls.

To clear the land the yacht was permitted to run for nearly an hour dead before the wind, and just as our hero was consulting Mr. Bernard upon the expediency of heaving her to, a man on the look-out forehead called out in a voice of intense alarm, "We are right into a large ship;" the very same instant the Medora ran with tremendous violence alongside a large vessel, and before either Lord Courtland or the master could reach the wheel, or call to the man at it, the shock threw every one off his legs; the two ships then became locked together, a scene of terrible confusion ensuing, for the Circassians, totally unaccustomed to sea affairs, thought it was all over with them, ran here and there tumbling about in everybody's way.

Neither of the ships carried a light, the Medora for the best possible reason; the other had also her reasons, for she was the Radamez corvette, of 22 guns, and 150 men, commanded by a Captain Borksow.

The moment the two ships struck, a loud voice from the Russian corvette called out, " What ship is this?"

"By Jove," said Lord Courtland to Mr. Bernard and Lieutenant Erwin, who came running up, "this is a Russian vessel of war. We must carry her by surprise."

Lieutenant Erwin had the men together in a moment, whilst our hero explained to Schamyl Bey; "if we hesitate we are lost;" therefore, the words, "what ship is this," had scarcely escaped the lips of the Russian captain, when Lord Courtland, cutlass and pistol in hand, threw himself over the bulwarks, followed by his eager crew; whilst Edgar Erwin and the Circassian chief, were roused into energy, dashed after, fully alive to their situation, and all their fierce hatred revived when they understood that they had their detested enemies before them.

With wild cries, the Circassians, unacquainted with the technicalities of naval warfare, swarmed over the sides as best they could, and attacked the amazed and astounded Russians.

There was only the watch on deck, but the alarm had spread, and the crew were tumbling up, half dressed and half armed. At first they offered but a feeble resistance, but as their officers recovered their surprise, and battle lanterns gleamed along the decks, the fight became a fiercely contested one. But the hardy crew of the Medora, led by their young commander, drove all before them. He knew that his liberty, and the liberty of those dearer to him than life, depended on his efforts.

There was not a heavy sea, for the furious gale blew from the shore, but the squalls were of such terrible force that they threatened the masts of both ships, and still so fierce was the contest, made visible by the partial and flickering blaze of blue lights and battl &lanterns that the hurricane was scarcely attended to. The vessels were still fast, when Mr. Bernard with the remainder of the crew of the Medora sprang aboard and joined in the desperate contest, not a single cannon and but a few pistol shots were fired. A furious *melee* interrupted only by the heavy plunges and shocks of the two vessels, as they ground against each other and reeled under the effects of the squalls. The decks of the Russian corvette were strewed with the dead and wounded, and slippery from the snow and sleet, mixed with the blood of the victims that fell. The Russian captain was slain by Edgar Erwin, and Prince Schamyl lay stunned upon the deck, by a blow from the butt of a musket.

In the midst of this terrible night's contest, a sudden change of wind and a squall fiercer than any yet, struck the corvette, and her topsails taken aback, the foremast went by the board, falling with all its top hamper across the deck. Just at that moment Lord Courtland had pinned the officer commanding against the mainmast, when he called out he surrendered the ship. The Russian crew then threw down their cutlasses and ran below.

The commander of the Medora wiped the blood from his face, which ran down from a cut across the forehead; he had two other wounds, but not serious ones, and turned to Mr. Bernard, who came limping up.

""We had better, my lord," said the master, "separate the two vessels; this ship is grinding our bulwarks to pieces, and our spars will go; thank God you have escaped! it's heen a terrible contest, though short."

"Yes; I fear it has," returned our hero; "where are Lieutenant Erwin and Prince Schamyl?"

"Lieutenant Erwin is unhurt, if you except a gash from a cutlass; he has just had the Circassian chief carried on board the Medora—he is only stunned."

"We must be quick in our movements, Mr. Bernard, for when day light comes—and it is close at hand—and when they see our size and numbers, they will be too formidable for us."

""We will spike the guns," said the master," and bringoff all the arms we can."

"Very good," said Lord Courtland; "now, my lads," he continued to some of his gallant crew, "get your wounded on board the Medora; I trust in God we have not many dead."

"Five, my Lord," said the mate and several of the Circassians, "but the deck is strewed with Russian dead."

"Well, by Jove, dear friend," exclaimed Lieutenant Erwin, coming up to Lord Courtland, who was speaking to the Russian officer who surrendered the ship, "here is an adventure, a Russian corvette taken by a yacht. Are you hurt, you are bleeding?"; Dr the light of a lantern fell upon our hero's face.

"It's nothing, Edgar; I see you have got a mark to keep you in remembrance of this night's work, but be quick and clear the ships. I will go and see how our fair guests have borne this terrible trial."

With some difficulty he crossed to the Medora. The men were actively engaged clearing the ships, and the squalls came at longer intervals and with less violence; the showers of sleet and snow ceased to fall, but the cold was intense.

On gaining the cabin of the Medora, he found Catherine Warhendorff and Julia wrapped in their fur mantles, seated with their arms round eacn other's necks, looking pale and terribly agitated. Both sprung from their seats, and both gave bim their hands, Julia joyfully, Catherine trembling with the emotion that was overpowering her. Pressing a kiss of fond affection upon Catherine's cheek, he made her seat herself on the sofa, while he soothed their apprehensions, both with respect to the contest between the two ships.

"My gallant friend, Edgar, and good Mr. Bernard have both escaped with light remembrances of Russian cutlasses, but I deeply deplore the loss of some gallant fellows—luckily they are all single men. I was at considerable pains in selecting them, knowing the perilous 'nature of the voyage I was undertaking."

"You have received a horrid gash yourself, dear Henry," said Julia, whilst Catherine shuddered.

"Had you not better have it dressed," asked the Princess anxiously. "Our fears are now relieved, but the horrible noise of the combat, and the fury of the storm through the rigging of the vessel was terrible to hear, besides the frightful shocks from the two ships striking. Is the Medora injured?"

"No dearest," said Lord Courtland. "Her bulwarks smashed, and her light spars cracked and broken, is all our injury. I will now beg of you to retire, and endeavour to get some rest. In a few hours we shall be all in order again."

Bidding the two fair girls good night andpressing'Catherine's hand fondly, his lordship proceeded on deck. Lieutenant Erwin and part of the crew were still on board the Radamez. The vessels were separated, and the Medora with the corvette in tow was standing out to sea, under the close reefed top-sails, the squalls moderate, the wounded had been carried below and left to the care of the surgeon.

Lord Courtland had a boat lowered and then proceeded to join his friend on board the Bussian vessel.

As he gained the deck he perceived that some of his own men and some of the Russian crew were busy clear' away the wreck of the foremast. Numbers of the Russians were, however, loitering about, sulky and savage in their looks. Numbers of lanterns were swung here and there to give light. As the Englishman was walking aft to speak to Edgar Erwin, a Russian officer, a tall, fine looking man, with fierce dark eyes, but exceedingly pale and with large whiskers and moustachios, approached our hero, at whom he looked with exceeding surprise for he was not in uniform, having simply a sword by his side and brace of pistols in his belt.

"I am informed," said the Russian, haughtily, "that you are the commanding officer to whom Willminoff so cowardly surrendered this ship."

"Such is the case," replied Lord Courtland, with equal hauteur, "but why should you accuse your superior officer of cowardice?"

"He was only my superior officer nominally and for a time," returned the Russian; "I am the real commander of this ship; I was in bed ill of a fever; and now I can scarcely stand. Had I been well the reverse of this scandalous affair would have taken place."

"That's as may be," observed Lord Courtland calmly. "I allow you were surprised."

"Sir, there could have been no surprise if the discipline of this ship had been carried on as it used to be; there was gross negligence and cowardice too. Pray what is the name of your vessel?"

"The Medora," answered our hero.

"Medora," repeated the Russian, "I know of no vessel in your fleet of that name."

"The Medora is a yacht," observed Lord Courtland.

"Ha!" uttered the Russian, with a terrible oath, and convulsed with passion, "we were sent here to capture a yacht, which had the extreme insolence to fire into one of our gun brigs, and by a rascally chance shot, disabled her. By St. Nicholas—"

"For a prisoner, sir," interrupted Lord Courtland, haughtily, "you are speaking rudely and unthinkingly. You will please to accompany me on board my vessel, for, after your intemperate language, I shall not leave you at liberty."

"You will not—do you threaten me?" burst from the lips of the furious and intemperate Russian. "This will cool your pride." And drawing a poignard from his vest, he aimed a sudden and violent blow at Lord Courtland.

"Shame, shame, Demetrius; would you turn assassin in a moment of passion and vexation?" and a slight figure in a fur mantle threw itself on the Russian's arm. But before that, he was in the strong grasp of Lord Courtland, and the poignard wrested from his hand and cast into the sea; while our hero indignantly said—

"Sir, you accused your brother officer of being a coward. You have just proved yourself both a coward and, what is worse, an intended assassin."

"Great God! I am a madman," almost frantically exclaimed the Russian, striking his forehead passionately. "Sir," turning to Lord Courtland, "put your pistol to my head. Let me die the death of a man, though I do not deserve it."

"Excuse him, my lord," said a gentle voice, coming from the figure in the mantle, which, partly thrown back by the wind, displayed the figure of a female, while the light of the lantern fell upon a pale but very beautiful countenance. "He is a gallant gentleman, but passion at times deprives him of his reason. Had he committed the deed he attempted, he would have slain himself when his passion cooled."

Lord Courtland was amazingly surprised, first at being termed "my Lord" by a total stranger, and then at the singular scene he had been witness of. He, however, instantly replied—

"Madam, I can make every allowance for irritation of feeling. I think no more of the circumstance."

"Allow me," said the Eussian officer in a subdued tone, "to introduce my wife—the Countess Warhendorff."

"Heavens! Did you say Warhendorff?" interrupted Lord Courtland, greatly surprised.

"I can imagine you are astonished, my Lord," said the Countess, "but this is neither time or place for explanation. Will you permit us to retire to our cabin? My husband is scarcely able to stand, but I will answer for him and all on board. We have surrendered, your conquest is safe; there shall be no disturbance.""

"Certainly, Madam, certainly," replied Lord Courtland. "No one shall intrude upon your privacy; as the ship is disabled, I shall keep her in tow till morning. Pray have you a surgeon here that you can spare."

"We have two; one is at your service," said Count Warhendorff, who seemed deeply humiliated, and with a bow he retired; leaning on his wife's arm.

Lord Courtland now began to feel that his own wounds, though trifling, required attending to, and retiring to the Medora with the Russian surgeon, who was a remarkably civil obliging young man, had them dressed.

"I fear you have many wounded on board your ship," said our hero, as the surgeon sewed up one of the gashes somewhat deeper than the rest.

"There is scarcely one that was engaged," returned the surgeon, "who is not wounded, some desperately, and our temporary captain is dead."

"How do you mean temporary captain," questioned Lord Courtland.

"Why, my Lord, Captain Warhendorff is the real commander, though some slight disobedience of the Emperor's orders caused him to take from captain Warhendorff the command, making him serve for a time as second lieutenant—it is only for a few months; but this unfortunate affair will greatly engage the Emperor. The Radamez is a very favourite corvette with our Czar, he sailed in her from Kertch to Sebastopol, a short time before the breaking out of the present war; in fact, she was a kind of yacht, The Countess's father is governor of Kertch."

"Well, I will not detain you," said Lord Courtland, "I am sorry to say there are several others require your attention. I can only say, you shall receive your liberty as soon as I find an opportunity of restoring you to your country.

"Thank you, my Lord, liberty is precious, and I love it dearer rhan life."

"And yet," observed Lord Courtland, with a smile as the surgeon was leaving his cabin, "you live in a country, and under a rule, where liberty never flourished."

"Yet such as it is, we love it," returned the surgeon, "and reverence our ruler," and with a low bow he retired, conducted by our hero's personal attendant to the other parts of the ship, where every possible attention was paid to the wounded.

Lord Courtland in the morning went into the principal saloon, where, as he expected, he found the young Princess and his sister Julia, for they could rest but little.

Though pale and still somewhat agitated, Catherine Warhendorff looked exquisitely lovely. He dark eyes beamed with such affection on her lover as her lover sat down by her side. Kissing the fair hand held out to him, though it trembled with the feelings of the Princess's heart, there was a whole world of meaning in the eyes of each; they knew each possessed the other's heart, and there was confidence and pride in the thoughts of both.

"What a terrible night this has been, dear Henry," said Julia, Seating herself by the side of her brother, and looking up into his handsome, thoughtful features; "you look pale, have you had your wounds attended to?"

"Oh! yes, fair sister; my wounds are mere scratches, in fact, we have been very fortunate. Erwin escaped with only a cut, Prince Schamyl with a smart contusion on the head, and worthy Mr. Bernard with a bruised leg, but I have lost five of my brave fellows, and several wounded; and sorry am I to add several of these gallant Circassians have fallen."

"Ah?" said Catherine, with a sigh and a shudder, "victory, with all its false gWy, leaves always a sad tale to be told; victor or vanquished, mourning always follows."

"True, dear Catherine, such is and always must be the case, constituted as the world now is. War, even with the savage, is terrible, but with civilized nations horrible. But do you know who commands this Russian vessel, or rather who did? for he has been displaced, by order of the Czar, for a time."

"Who, Henry," exclaimed both the girls.

"As far as name goes," returned Lord Courtland, "a relation or connection of yours, Catherine, a Count Warhendorff. His Countess, who appears both an amiable and beautiful woman, is with him on board."

"Count Warhendorff!" said Catherine greatly surprised. "I remember hearing my mother sjpeak of my father's brother; he was a Count, and held a Colonel's commission in some cavalry regiment; not unlikely but the Captain of this Russian vessel may be his son."

"Most likely, indeed. But I came to see you," continued Lord Courtland, "before you take some refreshment, after the terrible night of alarm and disturbance you have experienced, I intend, please God! to run, before to-morrow night, into Ghelendjek with our prize. From thence you can reach, with perfect safety, the fortress of Prince Schamyl."

"Oh!" exclaimed Catherine, the tears flowing from her eyes with pleasure and anticipated joy. "My beloved mother; oh! the rapture of again embracing her, and restoring her to liberty. Dear Henry, but for your noble generosity and courage—"

"Nay, not a word of that, dear Catherine. Who would not sacrifice a Croesus, for such a prize as this?"

And drawing the blushing girl towards him, he pressed a kiss upon her forehead, and then rising and whispering some words in Julia's ear that banished the paleness on her cheek, he hastened upon deck.

Edgar Erwin had returned ou board the Medora; he had been indefatigable, and so had Mr. Bernard and the Medora's crew. Ivan Gortsare was below, attending to, « and acting aa an interpreter for the young surgeon, who was most kind and gentle in his manner to the wounded.

"Deuced good sort of a fellow, Harry, that surgeon— handles our wounds as delicately as a lady's fingers would," observed Erwin. "How do you feel?"

"Famous," 'replied Lord Courtland. "Where is Schamyl Bey?"

"Snug—rolled up in my berth. Gave him a stiff tumbler of brandy punch. He's snoring loud enough to split one of the planks over bis head."

"Deuced curious remedy of yours, Edgar, for a blow on the head," said our hero; "did the young Bey seem to like it. "

"Like it, by Jove! he would not go to rest till I mixed him a second, Depend upon it, if the brain is all right, it's a capital remedy. You see we have got our prize in tow. What a cheer the little Medora would have if we had to pass through the fleet. A two-andtwenty gun ship taken by a yacht in seven-and-twenty minutes. Do you know, these Circassians are splendid fellows! I saw a dozen of them, just live minutes before we went bang into the Russian, with their heads over the side, 'shooting the cat,' and by the Lord Harry, the moment we went to work with the Russian bears they pitched over the bulwarks, and ran at the enemy as if lighting on their native rocks."

"It was a fortunate surprise, Edgar. Had it been daylight, we should have had either to surrender or shew him our stern. They were lying-to, it appears, waiting for daylight. They could not have heard our guns; we are full ten miles off Fort Alexandrina, and they might have been seven or eight more, and did not heave-to till a few minutes before we ran into them."

"By Jove! your men and the Circassians fought like Britons; that young Bey cut away like a lion. What a fortunate circumstance that her foremast went by the board in that precious squall—her rigging must have been either very slack, or the shock carried away her chain plates—she would be sure to give us the slip and pepper us tomorrow morning only for that."

"I suspect she would, and for that reason I spiked her guns," said our hero; "which leaves her at our mercy, if the crew turn out rebellious. By-the-bye, the whole affair is curious." And he then related his encounter and conversation with the Count Warhendorff, and the singularity,of thus stumbling upon most probably a relation of the young Catherine Warhendorff.

"How extraordinary!" remarked Edgar Erwin, but he was prevented from saying more for just then Mr. Bernard came up from below, accompanied by Ivan Gortaare and the Russian surgeon.

Lord Courtland had ordered wine and refreshments to be placed upon the table in the saloon, he now invited those present to descend and partake of it. "How are the wounded, Mr. Bernard," demanded our hero, walking apart with his sailing master. "I trust no more will be added our list of dead."

"No, thank God!" returned the master, cheerfully, "there are some severe injuries, chiefly cutlass wourids, for strange to say, very few pistol shots were fired by the Russians."

"They were utterly confounded and bewildered by our running foul of them," said Lord Courtland. "Still there was want of method and a bad commander. I hear there were above one hundred and sixty men on board, besides twenty or thirty marines; where they were I can't say; we were nearly a hundred and thirty men ourselves, fully armed, and heated and excited by previous contest, everything was in our favour."

"What is your intention, my Lord, with respect to the vessel; there is a tremendous strain on now; luckily the sea is smooth, though the squalls are at times violent and freezing cold."

"I wish," answered Lord Courtland, "to get him into the Bay of Semes; we

can there land most of her crew, keeping eighteen or twenty to work her; we can spare some twenty of our men, and Lieutenant Erwin—aft we rig up a jury foremast—can make a run of it for either Balaclava or Varna, as the case may require; but I wish to restore the Countess and her husband, and the young surgeon, to their liberty, if I knew how to manage it; we cannot remain much longer on this coast, and I require eight or ten days, after we reach Ghelendjek, to finish my business on this coast. Thank God for a train of fortuitous circumstances! everything has turned out most happily; if this 'wind drops at all as the day opens, I will board the corvette, and see and get a jury-foremast up, something to help us into Semes. I shall go below now and visit my gallant fellows, and our brave allies, the Circassians; pity such a fine and chivalrous race should be left to the tender mercies of the Turks, which they assuredly will if the war terminates in our favour." CHAPTEB XLII.

The changes of temperature in the Black Sea are singular and extremely rapid—the storms of short duration, and shifting their direction almost as suddenly as they commence.

As the sun increased in strength, the storm of the previous night calmed down, and the wind shifting into the westward, the sky became broken, and then the clouds slowly drifted to the eastward, the sea gradually fell, and the promise of one or two quiet days appeared in the look of the weather, though Mr. Bernard said it was not to be depended on.

Lord Courtland and his friend, Edgar Erwin, were on deck, Mr. Bernard having just turned in. Several of the Circassians, who could not bear the between decks, were huddled together, smoking their pipes, and at intervals conversing.

The Itussian corvette, with her mainsail and topsail set, was still in tow; the wind was light, and the two vessels moved but slowly through the water.

Lord Courtland stated to Lieutenant Erwin his future intentions with respect to his prize, and his own purpose immediately on reaching Ghelendjek, which

was to proceed with the two ladies to Schamyl's fortress, to which the young Bey proposed to conduct him in less than three days. He would then finally conclude a negociation with the Circassian chiefs for the ransom of the Princess "Warhendorff and her attendants.

The young Circassian chief joining them on deck, prevented any further conversation on private matters.

Our hero congratulated the Bey on his recovery from the stunning blow he had received, all the token remaining being a piece of plaster, and the loss of hair over the spot.
-Enquiring after his wounded, the young chief assured him they were doing very well, and though be lamented the loss of his followers, he gloried in the achievement they had assisted to perform.

"Do you think," questioned the Circassian, " that you will reach Ghelendjek to-night?"

"Not unless the wind freshens," replied Lord Courtland. "We make little way with the corvette in tow, but as the wind is so light, I will go on board and see if I can get a jury-foremast up; that would help us much."

Accordingly, the Medora's two boats were lowered and with Lieutenant Erwin and a dozen men, pulled alongside the Radamez.

Our hero was received politely enough by the officer who had surrendered the ship to him, though groups of Russian sailors, with sullen and dogged looks, were assembled upon the deck, which, with all the washing, still shewed traces of the last night's fierce contest.

Lord Courtland requested to know how Count Warhendorff felt himself, as he had suffered the day before from fever.

"He is much worse to-day," said the officer. "It's a kind of ague, but the Countess requested me to say she wishes to see you, my Lord, in the cabin. She saw your boats pulling alongside."

"I shall be most happy to attend to her wishes," said our bero. "I have brought my carpenters to assist," he added, "in getting up a mast or large spar, if any of your men will aid them. It is not my wish to detain any of them prisoners, and if I can find the means and procure a small craft, I will permit them to proceed to ADapa."

The officer looked astonished, but immediately said:

"The men, my lord, will appreciate your generosity, and I will mention your intention to them. When they hear it I am sure they will gladly assist."

"By-the-bye," interrupted Lord Courtland, "I think in two hours, with this wind, I could land you all at Fort Alexandrina—provided the garrison there will respect a flag of truce."

"Unquestionably, my lord, it will be respected. We are not barbarians."

"No," observed his lordship, "I did not mean to insinuate such to be the case, but the affair of the Vixen some years ago on this coast, and one or two late instances, whether from mistake or what I cannot say, makes me cautious in risking my men's lives."

The Eussian coloured, but merely said, " Permit me to show you the way to the state cabin."

On entering the saloon, which was remarkably elegantly decorated with a half length portrait of the Czar Nicholas, in a superb frame, Lord Courtland perceived the Countess Warhendorff, and seated by her side a very fair and lovely girl, scarcely fifteen, evidently her daughter, from the likeness.

The countess rose and held out her hand, introducing her daughter Catherine, saying at the same time, "You must notice, my lord, that Catherine is a favourite name with the Warhendorff family."

"And also, madam," returned Lord Courtland, saluting the fair girl, who blushed like a rose, "that with the name, they inherit also the beauty of the Warhendorff race."

The countess herself, a very beautiful woman, smiled with a pleased manner as she replied, " At all events, my lord, you perilled your life if not your liberty, for the beauty of one of our family."

"Before I seek to gratify my curiosity, countess," said our hero seating himself,

"may I enquire how the count ia F"

"He has had a very severe attack of tertian ague today," returned the countess, with a flush upon her cheek, "but distress of mind, I may say agony, at the loss of this favourite ship, and his," she hesitated, and then added, "subsequent conduet."

"I pray you, madam," interposed Lord Courtland energetically, "assure him that not one thought of what you allude to remains in my mind, and also I beg you will state to him that it is not my intention to retain as prisoners one single individual in this ship."

"You have all the nobleness and generosity, my lord, of your father," said the countess with much emotion.

"The ship, countess, was taken by a surprise. You did not attack me, but I attacked you for self preservation; not being a vessel of war, I can act, I think, on my own responsibility. The ship being the property of the Czar, and of consequence to my country, I must surrender to our admiral."

"You overpower us by your kindness, my lord; for me, I shall always remember the event as long as I live. But let me explain how it is that I am apparently so well acquainted with your name and intentions, and reasons for being on the coast of Circassia, for shortly after your yacht ran foul of our ship, I guessed it was you. In the first place, my husband is nephew to the late General Warhendorff, and of course we are all acquainted with the unfortunate fate of the Princess Warhendorff, only a few years younger than my aunt, and consequently a grown girl at the time. I remember all the circumstances attending the loss of her husband, and her disappearance from St. Petersburg, and also the death of the wealthy and generous hearted Mr. Fitzharding, for my father, Count Orloff, then resided at Odessa. I remember your father well, and as a boy I have seen you many times.

"My father, some years after the melancholy events at Odessa, was made Governor of Kertch, hut a: short time before this I married Count Warhendorff, at that time a lieutenant in the navy; he had not then succeeded to his

father's title. Shortly after the declaration of war, my husband was made a commander, and as a special favour he was appointed captain of the Czar's favourite corvette, the Radamez. I will not touch upon the subject that has reference to the Emperor's displeasure. Sufficient to say, the Count, after his father's death, which occurred about two years ago, offended the Czar, who nominated another to the command of the Radamez, ordering my husband to remain as second lieutenant. In his passion, he would have thrown up his commission, and then most probably have been sent to Siberia, but my tears prevailed, for when not irritated, no kinder man breathes than Michael Warhendorff, but he is, alas! a slave to impulse.

"Whilst lying at Kertch, intelligence reached the governor that an English yacht, belonging to a British nobleman, called Courtland, but previously Fitzharding, was on the Circassian coast, for what purpose was not known. Shortly after the man-of-war brig, and the steamer Czarina, both came into Kertch, the brig disabled and the steamer injured, by an encounter with the English yacht.

"This created the greatest surprise and astonishment, but every one conjectured that this supposed yacht was a corvette, designed for some secret purpose. Intelligence of this event was sent to Taganrog, where the emperor then was, looking over its defences. At the same time it became known at Kertch, that the Commandant of Anapa had secured the person of a traitor—one Ivan Gortsare—formerly a secret agent of the government, and that the Governor of Anapa had also in his power the persons of two females, under the protection of this Ivan Gortsare—one turned out to be the daughter of the Princess Warhendorff, the other the daughter of the wealthy Odessa merchant, the late Mr. Fitzharding.

"This intelligence was brought to Kertch by some Armenian merchants, who crossed to Caffa from Anapa in a small sailing vessel, and then came on to Kertch.

"You may be sure I became greatly

interested, and when, shortly afterwards, a gun-boat from Taganrog brought letters to my father, orders came from the Emperor for the ltadamez to put to sea, with strict directions to capture the yacht, and also to call at Anapa, and take on board the young Princess Warhendorff and her companion, and carry them to Kertch, to place them under the protection of my father. My husband was promised a re-instalment in his former command on the capture of the yacht. He had also strict orders to treat Lord Courtland with every civility, and to send him forward under an escort to Taganrog. This was by order of the Emperor himself. My husband was at this time attacked *by* the fever and ague.

"Principally on that account, and also indeed hoping to be of some comfort to my young relative in her misfortune, I and my daughter accompanied him in this voyage. For though the unfortunate officer who nominally commanded this ship held the title of commander, yet all knew the Count would in a very short time be reinstated in his command.

"It was a very dark, stormy night, as you know, as we approached Anapa, and the count understanding you were with your yacht at Ghelendjek, which intelligence he picked up in a small coasting vessel, he resolved to surprise you; the corvette was hove to till morning, and, thus strange to say, the. 'ltadamez was captured by the very yacht we intended to take."

"Well, in truth, madam," said Lord Courtland, "though I cannot regret our not being captured, yet knowing who you are, and other circumstances attending this adventure, I regret capturing your ship, as her loss may exasperate the Czar, and be prejudicial to the count, your husband; but as this cannot now be remedied, we must do our best to mitigate the evil. I.intend standing in for Fort Alexandrina, from which place I last night managed, by a surprise and great good fortune, to carryoff my sister and the young Princess Warhendorff."

"Heavens!" exclaimed the countess, "is it possible you have the young Catherine Warhendorff and your sister on board your yacht. What incredible daring; and so you took them off in despite of the garrison at the fort. I am bewildered."

"' Nothing venture, nothing have,' dear madam," returned Lord Courtland with a smile. "In early boyhood Madam Warhendorff promised me the hand of her daughter. I have never forgotten the words she uttered."

His lordship then briefly related how he had sailed from Gibraltar with his sister and the young princess, without knowing her—indeed, believing the latter to be the daughter of Ivan Gortsare—and then he related the sequel of his adventures on the Circassian coast.

"Well, you are one of fortune's favourites, my lord," remarked the Countess, "and I am sure, my daughter here, who is quite absorbed in your narrative, must look upon you as the last remnant of chivalry for gallantry and devotion; you have fairly won your beautiful betrothed. Now, I have one favour to ask, and that is to accompany you on board your yacht, that my daughter and myself may embrace, for once, my unfortunate aunt's daughter, for I suppose we shall never enjoy that opportunity again, owing to this odious and fearful war."

"My dear Countess," said Lord Courtland, much pleased; "ypur wish is easily gratified, and I feel satisfied will afford the greatest delight to Catherine Warhendorff and also my sister."

"Then I will just speak a few words to my husband, and will then be ready to accompany you."

"In the meantime," returned Lord Courtland, "I will proceed on deck and await you there."

On reaching the deck, he perceived a number of the men very busily employed under Erwin's directions in getting up a jury foremast; all seemed to work cheerfully, Erwin making immense efforts to keep up a conversation with one of the Russian officers, mixing English, French, Turkish, and Russian words together in a curious manner. However, they seemed mutually pleased, for the Eussian was lighting his cigar from the lieutenant's most amicably.

"Your promise of landing them at Anapa, Henry," said Erwin to Lord Courtland, as he joined them, "has done wonders: we shall have a respectable foremast up now before night. "We can make out Anapa tbis last half hour."

His companion looked in the direction, and readily made out the very high land behind Fort Alexandrina.

"We must keep a sharp look out, Edgar; it would be rather awkward to meet with another antagonist."

The countess and her daughter coming on deck, completely muffled in rich fur mantles, caused Lord Courtland to quit his friend and attend them to the boats.

"What a singular change in the weather from yesterday," observed the countess, "but we are a great deal colder at Kertch than on this coast."

"What magnificent mountains!" exclaimed the daughter; "the Caucasus, I suppose; I bore the strong bitter wind for an hour yesterday, hoping to get a sight of them."

There was a something in the young girl's tone and manner strikingly like his beloved Catherine. Lord Courtland directing the young girl's attention to a very lofty mount, told her that under that hill was Fort Alexandrina, but the boat ran up along side the Medora, and both mother and daughter exclaimed as they gained the deck, "what a beautiful vessel," for every rope was coiled away so critically neat, the planks of her deck so beautifully white and clean, her lofty tapering spars, in fact, the whole of her fitting out so simple, and yet so perfect and elegant, that their admiration was greatly excited.

They entered the principal saloon of the yacht, which surpassed the saloon of the Eadamez in length, and beauty of arrangement. But the countess only saw the sweet youthful figure and exquisitely lovely features ot" the young princess, as she rose from the sofa, and advanced to meet her, for Lord Courtland had sent her word that the countess and her daughter intended paying them a visit.

"The living image of your mother,"

exclaimed the countess, with considerable emotion, as she warmly embraced Catherine, and kissed her repeatedly. The countess's daughter looked upon the lovely girls introduced to her with delighted astonishment. They were both most simply attired, having no time to do more than hastily dress themselves the night they were rescued from the custody of Count Zouboski. But neither Catherine nor Julia Fitzharding required the advantageous addition of dress—" unadorned, adorned the most." Lord Courtland left them to themselves, and returned to the deck, to have some conversation with Mr. Bernard.

CHAPTER XLIII.

Whilst walking the deck with the master and conversing upon the circumstances of the late fortunate capture of the Radamez, they were suddenly startled by the loud boom of a gun, and the shot rushing through the rigging of the Medora, cutting away a backstay and some heavy rigging.

In an instant the crew of the Medora rushed upon deck, whilst her commander and the master, seeing that the shot came from one of the bow guns of the Russian corvette, were hesitating what to do. When they perceived a boat leaving the side of the corvette, and in it Lieutenant Erwin. At the same time all appeared tranquil on deck.

In a few minutes Lieutenant Erwia was alongside, whilst the Countess Warhendorff was perceived coming from the cabin, no doubt alarmed.

"Faith, I suppose you thought we were going to attack you," said Edgar Erwin, springing upon deck, "any harm done?"

"No, luckily," said Lord Courtland. "What on earth caused you to fire a shotted gun?"

"Well, thauk God there is no harm done," said the lieutenant; "it was accident,"

This slight *contretems* was then explained to the countess, who looked alarmed, but smiling, she returned to reassure the two friends below.

Lord Courtland, his friend, and the master, retired to a private cabin to take some refreshments; and then all ascended upon deck, and shortly after Lieutenant Erwin returned to Radamez.

"The sky looks very extraordinary," observed Lord Courtland to the master.

Mr. Bernard looked up, saying, after a moment's attention, "Faith, it's a very strange wild sky; it's no harm to be prepared."

The firmament appeared as if divided in furrows, long lines of densely black streaks stretched across the expanse, and from these streaks long feathery lines floated away to the eastward, at the same time a low moaning sound was heard in the air.

"I do not like it, indeed, my lord," observed Mr. Bernard; "it's a bad sky in these seas, and at this time of year; especially. Look! the Russians are sending down their main-topgallant mast, and therefore we will.do the same; there's nothing like being caught prepared." "You are quite right; my good friend," said our hero, walking towards the cabin.

Just as he was preparing to descend, a seaman in the foretop called out, "either breakers astern, sir, or a whirlwind—the sea is all white with foam!"

This was the commencement of the ever-memorable storm that swept the Black Sea and destroyed so many of our transports and ships; the splendid steamer, the Prince, amongst the rest, at Balaclava; and created so much misery in our camp before Sebastopol, and destroying so many lives.

Scarcely had the words left the sailor's mouth, before a whirlwind of extraordinary violence struck the water within twenty yards of the Medora, and swept her into its vortex, tearing her top-gallant masts and sails to ribbons, and whirling them into the air, bending the vessel till the water poured over the bulwarks; snap went the tow ropes, aud then the Radamez felt its influence, but having started their top-gallant mast, the sails only suffered, but she heeled over, and then spun round as if some mighty monster had hoisted her like a top. Those on board the yacht were thrown from their feet against the bulwarks; the Circassians were terrified, and called upon Ali and Mahomet loudly.

A shriek of alarm from the saloon caused Lord Courtland, as soon as he regained his legs, to rush down below, where he found the females all thrown on the floor of the saloon, the tables torn from their fastenings, and hurled against the sides; and a crash in the steward's room announced that he also had been caught unprepared.

As Lord Courtland entered the saloon, the Medora regained a partly upright position, but there was a roar like thunder above their heads, and our hero knew that the tempest had burst on them, for the vessel again heeled over fearfully.

"Good God, what has occurred!" exclaimed the Countess Warhendorff, fearfully pale, while all regained a position on the sofa—Lord Courtland assisting them.

"A violent squall or tempest," replied our hero, "has suddenly burst on us, but I pray you be under no apprehension, we have plenty of sea room."

"Heavens!" said the countess, "how shall I regain our ship. Oh! how wrong I was to leave my husband. Oh! God! listen to that!"

As she spoke, the yacht reeled under the shock, and the roar of the tempest, as it sported in its might over the stricken sea, was like the thunder of Heaven.

The females were forced to retire to the inner cabins and lie down, and Lord Courtland having said all he could to re-assure them, hastened upon deck, but stood amazed at the scene he beheld. The sky had become one dense, unbroken mass of low pall-like clouds; the sea a boiling cauldron; the light waves, for there was no time for heavy seas, were torn from the surface, and driven over the ship in one uneasy shower; every sail set and exposed had blown clean off the ropes; the vessel was going dead before the furious tempest, under bare poles. There were two able seamen at the wheel; Mr. Bernard standing near, looking amazed, but self-possessed. The Circassians had been hurried below, Schamyl Bey alone remaining, with a rope in his hand to support himself, as the ship reeled under the shifting shocks of the tempest.

Lord Courtland looked round. The Radamez was close to them, also, without an inch of canvass standing.

"This will not do," he cried, joining Mr. Bernard; "we shall be on the coast in an hour; we must heave to."

"So I wish to do, my Lord," answered Mr. Bernard, "I thought to let the first fury of this extrordinary tempest pass, but Lsee it increases; the men are bending on our two new storm-staysails. Now, if they stand, well and good, but I fear the Russian corvette will go ashore, unless, indeed; they can contrive to get canvas on her jury foremast. If the wind would let us make the Bay of Semes, we could run in and anchor, but it will not; it blows us direct upon the ironbound shore, some twenty miles below Fort Alexandrina."

The storm continued to rage with extraordinary fury, and the sea also began to rise rapidly. Lord Courtland was extremely anxious. Lieutenant Erwin, with fifteen of his crew, were in the Radamez. He was not exactly uneasy about their being ill treated by the enemy, for having the Countess Warhendorff and her daughter on board the Medora, secured their liberty, should the crew of the corvette think of running the ship ashore under Fort Alexandrina, but he perceived they could not do that the way the wind blew. The Countess Warhendorff became so terribly distracted that she made her way to the deck, wrapped in her fur mantle. She did not venture out from the stairs, but holding on there, gazed out with amazement upon the storm-tossed sea. Lord Courtland showed her the Eadamez, within three hundred yards of them, at times enveloped as if with a snow-drift. The peals of thunder were awful, and the lightning blinding.

"Now then, my lord, we are ready," said Mr. Bernard, coming aft; " two more men at the wheel, and if the sails stand I'll answer for the Medora's lying as tranquil on the water as a duck in a mill pond. When the Russians see us, perhaps they will imitate us, for we are not more than six miles off the coast, though it is hidden in clouds of foam and mist."

"I have never felt so tremendous a gale," said Lord Courtland, grasping the spokes of the wheel. "Now, my men, be steady," he added, aiding the seaman on the other side of the wheel.

. "Aye, aye, sir," returned the man, preparing himself for the trial, for it was a serious and trying moment. If the sails held and filled, they had no fear; upwards of twenty hands had hold of the sheets and tackles, ready tohoist and sheet home. Gradually the Medora was allowed to come round to the wind, but so terriffic was the storm, so deafening the peals of thunder, that even the hardy seamen were bewildered.

As the ship came up to the wind, the roar of the gale through her rigging was appalling, while sheets of water dashed over her bulwarks with such violence as to tumble over many of the men, but skilfully handled, and the sails not allowed for an instant to shake, they filled, and fearful as was the strain upon them, they held well, and gradually the Medora was brought to face the whole brunt of the furious tempest.

"All right, my lord," said Mr. Bernard cheerfully, running aft. "The Radamez is doing the same thing. God send she succeeds, for if she fails, she goes ashore."

"Now, God forbid," exclaimed our hero, giving the spokes into the hands of the first mate—a strong, powerful man—while he watched the manoeuvres of the Bussian corvette. The sailors had got the rigging of the jurymast up, and the mainstay, and when not concealed by the spray and the driving seas, they could see them getting ready their staysail and trysail. As the Medora rounded up into the wind, the Radamez shot past like a meteor, and the next instant she attempted the same manoeuvre as the yacht; but to the horror of all, the sails blew into ribbons, and again the corvette payed off. The trysail and another storm-sail were then set; for au instant they fluttered in the wind, and then disappeared.

"My God! they will be ashore," exclaimed Lord Courtland. "I can see the land not three miles under our lee, but not very distinctly."

"They have let go their anchors, my lord," said the second mate, who was looking through a glass; "and she appears to be holding."

"Edge us away, Mr. Bernard. Though the sea is rising fast, the extraordinary violence of lhe tempest, I think, abates. "

"It is settling, my lord, into a steady gale, of singular violence. But as long as it is steady, and does not veer two or three points at a time, the Medora is quite manageable, and I think it possible to make the Bay of Semes."

Gradually they edged down on the Radamez. It was now past three o'clock; in less than two hours it would be dark. Their position was, in truth, critical: with a long night, a furious gale, and an iron-bound coast only three miles distant, under their lee.

The Radamez was riding with two anchors a-head, with immense scope; but she plunged tremendously in the broken sea. So beautifully was the Medora handled, and so extraordinary were her qualities as a sea-boat, that before four o'clock, though the gale was as heavy a one as ever Mr. Bernard or our hero witnessed, yet she was able to carry a close-reefed trysail, a storm jib, and two storm staysails, under which she was perfectly manageable.

Lord Courtland had several times descended, and spoken to the anxious party below, who were now able to keep on the sofas in the saloon, where they awaited iu deep anxiety for intelligence.

Schamyl Bey, though totally unaccustomed to the sea, gazed upon the, to him, extraordinary and frightful scene with calm demeanour.

The Medora was hove to within a hundred yards of the Radamez. Her decks were covered with men, all seemingly at work to get a foretopmast up. She rode very heavy, and Lord Courtland felt exceedingly anxious about her; for the sea increased rapidly, and should her anchors drag, or her cables snap, nothing could save her from running ashore.

At this time it was growing very rapidly dark, and very little appearance of the gale slacking; the thunder had ceased, but the lightning was still extremely vivid. The wind came from the south west, which always sends in the heaviest sea upon the Circassian coast.

A gun from the Russian corvette called all their attention. "Ha," said Lord Courtland, in a tone of deep regret, "her cables have parted." They could just see that eail was made upon the corvette, and whatever sail she set appeared to Stand, and also that she steered a course for Alexandrina; she kept steady in one direction, and that favoured her. She hoisted lights and so did the Medora, steering close after her and keeping her in view.

But it was all up with the unfortunate Kadamez; ten minutes had hardly elapsed, ere a tremendous sea struck her, when her mainmast and mizen went over the side, the stays having previously snapped, the corvette instantly payed off, going before the wind, firing two guns in succession.

The intense anxiety of the Countess Warhendorff was distressing to behold. She wept hysterically, bitterly lamenting her folly in leaving her husband. In vain Lord Courtland and Catherine and Julia strove to reassure the distressed countess and her daughter. Our hero assured her even if she ran on shore she would not break up before assistance could be rendered them.

It was a night of intense darkness and storm, and the sea tremendous; they could still, at times, see the lights the Badamez burned, for the Medora followed her closely, terrible as it was, till at the last the conscious watchers saw her take the ground, as well as they could judge, upon a reef of rocks, within a long projecting mount of land, which they could just distinguish.

Though close in shore, the Medora had twenty fathoms of water; she was instantly put with her head offshore, and notwithstanding all Mr. Bernard could say, Lord Courtland had ordered his life-boat, a very beautiful craft he had built at Cowes, to be put over the side.

Volunteers were not wanted, for all were ready where their Commander led, the rudder was shipped, eight stout oarsmen seated, and then wringing Mr.

Bernard's hand, Lord Courtland jumped in, leaving the Princess Catherine and his sister in an agony of apprehension and tears, at what they considered an act of madness.

But the night brightened a good deal, though the storm still raged, with scarcely any mitigation of its violence.

The life-boat swam like a cork and soon left the Medora, standing off to sea steadily enough, carrying her canvas wonderfully.

The life-boat flew before wind and sea, topping the huge waves like a wild sea bird, and with scarcely a sprinkle of water over her gunnel. Those on board could see the lights of the Radamez, and a blue light at times, and the report of the guns had a dismal effect in the howling of the wintry storm. In less than a quarter of an hour Lord Courtland was within one hundred yards of the stranded corvette, and then he ignited the blue light in the life-boat.

The moment its glare was seen over the storm-tossed sea, a loud cheer arose from the Radamez, which was heard even amid the wild howling of the storm.

CHAPTER XLIV.

To Lord Courtland's great surprise, he perceived that the Russian corvette was driven ashore upon a reef of rocks, some five hundred yards from the main land; the force with which she came upon the reef sent her jury foremast over the side, and to add to their misfortunes; she heeled over considerably to seaward, so that her decks were repeatedly washed by the seas that broke violently over the reef. It was seen at once she was a lost craft, and all hope of getting her off was instantly abandoned, and perceiving that the water was comparatively smooth, he ordered his crew to pull carefully and steadily round the reef, and come up uDder her bows.

During this proceeding it continued to blow with exceeding fury—the broken seas going over the boat in all directions. Battle lanterns were hanging in all directions on the corvette, and just as the life-boat rounded the reef, Lord Courtland was hailed by Lieutenant Erwin, who said, as the crew of the boat

caught the ropes thrown them, and made fast, "Why in the name of the fates, Harry, did you leave the yacht? We are in a nice fix, but there's no danger of life."

"I do not know that, Edgar," returned Lord Courtland, laying hold of a rope, and gaining the deck of the corvette, "Where is Count Warhendorff?"

"He's safe enough; we got him up out of the cabin, which is half full of water; you see we do not lift with the seas—we are wedged fast somehow. I left him in the round house on deck—he is fearfully anxious about his wife, but I told him she was as safe on board the little Medora as the Czar in his palace in St. Petersburgh. Luckily he speaks French. Now if these confounded Russians had as much pluck as a calf we should not be here now."

""Well, let us now see, Edgar," said our hero, his crew having got on deck, "what can be done to get you all ashore. "

The deck of the Russian corvette, Radamez, was, at this time, a scene of indescribable confusion and dismay, a heavy sea had now just righted her— this was decidedly an advantage—but the deck was encumbered not only with the wreck of spars, masts, rigging, &c. , but the Eussian sailors were crowding up, each man anxious to save his own kit, and totally disregarding the orders and directions of their own officers. To add to tbe confusion— rendered but indifferently clear by the waving light of the battle-lanterns blown furiously about by the wind—oaths and vociferations, shouts, imprecations, and even blows, uttered one party against another, in their selfish eagerness, rendered the scene one of horrible confusion.

The commander of the Medora, his friend, and the armed crew of the boat, pushed their way amidst the crowd, our hero calling upon the men in a voice of conimand to fall back and recover their presence of mind, and listen to the orders of their officers, but many of them were already drunk and riotous, and they seemed, excited by the liquor, much inclined to turn upon the English sailors, who were, however, all well armed, and kept together, and ranged themselves under Lord Courtland; the Russian officers were also well armed, and joined the ranks beside our hero and Lieutenant Erwin.

Numbers of the Eussian sailors were making vigorous efforts to get the corvette's boats free from the spars and wreck that covered them, but their efforts not being systematically directed, were fruitless.

Just as Lord Courtland was endeavouring to reach the spot where Count Warhendorff lay, one of the Russian mates, followed by a crowd of men loaded with plunder, some carrying lanterns, pushing their way on to the bows of the corvette, he heard the man say, "Come, my hearties, we'll sheath our knives in those English, and take their boat."

"Without a moment's hesitation, Lord Courtland pulled a pistol from his belt, and caught the mate by the throat, saying, in his commanding tone and manner—

"Rascal, if you do not want to get hanged the first thing to-morrow, return to your duty; you are within a lew miles of a fort where there are above six thousand men."

"With a savage execration, the man, who was a strong, powerful fellow, drew his knife, and strove to stab our hero, but the next instant he was cast sprawling over the / bulwarks, and then tbe English sailors rallied round their commander, thinking there would be a fight with the mutineers, but several of the Russian officers, with Count "Warhendorff, who, though extremely weak, and shaking under a terrible attack of ague, hurried to their side, and in a stern determined manner ordered the rioters to fall back.

Awed by the firm determined conduct of Lord Courtland, and the bold front of the British tars, armed with pistol and cutlass, and the presence of their commander, the men wavered, but the next moment dropped their plunder and fell back.

"My lord," said Count "Warhendorff, holding on by a rope, "you are very generous to thus risk your life to save ours.

As these men seem willing to return to their duty, we may be able, with the assistance of your gallant fellows, to launch the boats; you see we are a good deal sheltered by the high rocks to our right, but it's a tremendous night. God send that your vessel may be able to keep off shore."

"I think, Count," returned our hero, "I may make your mind easy on that subject, the gale has settled steadily into the south-south-west; thus, my ship can lie well off the coast on one tack, and though the storm is still severe, yet my little craft is able to carry her canvass well."

Lieutenant Erwin, in the mean time, finding the mutineers were awed, and willing to obey commands, commenced getting out the boats. The corvette freed from her masts appeared to be steady, notwithstanding the shocks of the seas, which, however, were subsiding a little from the shift of wind; the sky also appeared to open, and, like all storms in the Euxine, there was evident symptoms of a lull.

Still there was no prospect of getting the ship off the rocks, and after an hour or more of hard work, the boats were launched, and just as a faint light appeared in the sky, betokening dawn, the gale rapidly fell, and the sea also. Finding all danger of remaining aboard passed, it was resolved to delay an hour or two more till strong daylight enabled them to reconnoitre clearly their situation. Lord Courtland and his friend carefully examined the ship, and found that her cabins and lower decks were full of water, and that there was some danger of her capsizing over the ledge into deep water.

"The fact is," said Edgar Erwin, to his companion, "the Count and all his officers would rather she should perish in this manner, than remain a trophy in our hands."

"That is natural," returned our hero; as he spoke an alarm spread through the ship that she was on lire, and suddenly a dense volume of smoke burst up through the fore hatch.

"This is the work of some of our traitorous villains," said Count Warhen-

dorff, as he joined the two friends, "and it will be fruitless attempting to extinguish it," and then he added in a low voice, "there is a large quantity of powder in the magazine; we had better get the wounded and the rest ashore as soon as possible."

All again became a scene of indescribable confusion; those who ran to look for the cause of the smoke, and to ascertain the extent of the fire, exclaimed that it was all over with the ship, as the flames were already spreading into the main decks.

In vain the English and the Russian officers strove to stay the panic; some of the mutineers attempted to seize the boats, but the Russian officers and the English sailors kept them off, and got the boats clear of the wreck, many of the men still remaining true to their duty. The wounded were brought up in their bedding, and placed in the launch. Lord Courtland pointed out to them the means of reaching the shore by placing the spars from the ship to the rocks; the water being so deep that she lay almost as if alongside a quay. Numbers availed themselves of this mode of getting on land; others dropped from the bowsprit, and some swam, for the fire had burst up in a vast volume from the fore hatchway, and some minutes afterwards from the main deck. So great now became the panic, that several lost their lives, notwithstanding the strenuous exertions of Lord Courtland, his crew, and the Russian officers. The scene was truly appalling, for the flames raged furiously, with the gale blowing, but fortunately blowing from the sea, and her stern being to the sea, they did not advance aft with the rapidity they otherwise would.

"You must not wait here, Henry," said Lieutenant Erwin; "you have done all you can; the wounded are in the launch, and the other boats the rascals have carried off, in despite of us; for, of course, though I threatened them, it would not do to cut them down, as they deserved. Get the Count and his officers into your lifeboat, and pull off; she will blow up shortly.''

The Russian officers seemed of the

same opinion, for several of the guns, though spiked, were loaded, and they went oft from the intense heat of the flames.

So brilliant was the light from the burning vessel, that the whole shore to some distance was illuminated.

Every one had now quitted the ship, the facility for doing so being so great by means of the spars on to the rocks; but they were still eight hundred yards from the main land, those in the boats having pulled in for the shore, with heartless indifference about their comrades' fate; for so limited was the space afforded by the reef, that the chances were, when she blew up, that many might be killed by the falling timbers.

The Russian officers were exceedingly disgusted and ashamed of the conduct of the men. The gale, as day broke gloomy and lowery, and piercing cold, abated, and most considerably shifting into the N'.N.W. Taking the officers into the life-boat, and towing the launch, full of wounded and marines, and some canvass and sails to form tents, also some valuables and papers belonging to Count Warhendorff, Lord Courtland pulled away from the burning ship towards the side of the little cove, for such it was, as offering the smoothest water for landing.

They had not yet reached the beach, when the corvette blew up, with a terrible explosion, scattering her timbers and spars, and all her materials, to the air, and causing so violent a commotion in the water, that the launch, being heavily loaded, was nearly swamped.

Numbers of the men, after getting out of the boats, were about to proceed up into the country, when a numerous body of Circassians, all armed with their rifles, appeared on the heights, and some shots being fired at them, they retreated in dismay to the boats, irresolute what to do, for they were caught in a trap.

"This is a dismal affair," observed CountWarhendorff. "The natives will collect, and massacre the men."

Our hero felt that their situation was in truth critical, for so terrible was the animosity of the Circassians to their cruel oppressors, that there was very little doubt but they would evince small respect for their misfortunes, but shoot them down like dogs.

By this time it was broad daylight, the gale had degenerated into a stiff breeze, and the sky opening over them, and a ray of sunlight strugged through the masses of cloud. Before the boats touched the beach, there was a cry from the English sailors rowing the life-boat of "Here's the Medora."

All started and turned round with a feeling of relief and joy, and beheld, not two miles off, the yacht, under doubled reefed topsails, standing in, and looking as if she had encountered nothing very unusual the preceding night. She was standing in for the cove, the wind being a side one, and permitting her to run in and out.

"Ah! thank God!" exclaimed the Count, who was shaking terribly in a fresh attack of his ague, which appeared amazingly severe.

Lord Courtland himself felt a load taken of his mind.

"Lie on your oars, lads," he exclaimed; "she will no doubt anchor in the mouth of this cove, the sea is falling rapidly; the best place for the Count will be in the Medora; at the sametime she will keep the Circassians on the heightsin check,till SchamylBeylandsand controls them."

Casting the launch off, the men in her attending to the landing of the wounded, Lord Courtland ordered his crew to pull towards the yacht. But the Medora was now within musket shot, and running into the bight, furled her topsails and anchored

In ten minutes the life-boat was alongside, and a loud cheer testified the satisfaction of the crew. Lord Courtland saw that all the females were on deck, wrapped in their fur mantles, and also Schamyl Bey and bis Circassians. The joy of the Countess was great, indeed, when she beheld her husband. There were other hearts equally glad, equally anxious, and which beat more rapidly, perhaps, when Lord Courtland sprang upon deck.

The young Princess Warhendorff had suffered many hours of deep anxiety, and so had Julia Fitzbarding, but all was forgotten when they beheld our hero and his friends safe and well. A pressure of the hand, and a look, which said more than a thousand words, told the mutual joy and rapture of their hearts. Our hero's first care was to get the suffering Count Warhendorff into his own cabin, and the surgeon and the Countess to attend to him. He then, after shaking the worthy Mr. Bernard by the hand, proceeded to confer with Schamyl Bey, who instantly became eager to land with his followers, promising to protect the Russians from injury, and also to permit them to make their way to Anapa.

Tt was also arranged that after landing the Count and Countess Warhendorff at Fort Alexandrina, Lord Courtland should proceed to Ghelendjek, where Schamyl Bey agreed to meet him, and conduct him to the fortress of his father. At the same time he demanded of Lord Courtland permission to raise from the wreck of the Radamez as many guns as he could, or arms, to which our hero most willingly assented.

After some rest and refreshment, Lord Courtland and lieutenant Erwin, and the Russian officers returned to the wreck, and with the aid of the Medora's boats, removed all the men from the reef—all escaping with a few bruises, the rocks and holes on the reef protecting them from the falling spars and timbers of the Radames when she blew up.

Not a vestige of her was to be seen above water. Several of her deck guns were blown out and were lyiug on the rocks.

Before evening the men were on march, under their petty officers, for Anapa, carrying their wounded on hastily constructed litters; Schamyl Bey having prevented, any molestation. Indeed, so elate were the Circassians at the prospect of getting at the wreck of the corvette, that they troubled themselves about nothing else, and sent messengers along the coast for boats and implements to work at her.

A calm and not unpleasant evening followed the storm of the night, the sea gradually resuming tranquillity, and every appearance of frost setting in—

the wind getting well into the north. The Medora's anchor was got up, and under easy swell, she ran out from the little cove that had witnessed the destruction of the Czar's favourite corvette, the Radamez.

Only the Count and Countess Warhendorff and the young surgeon, Alexis Rostoff, remained in the Medora, which, with a steady leading breeze, two hours before sunset the following day was lying-to, some two miles off Fort Alexandrina.

Lord Courtland had a quantity of quinine aboard, which afforded immense relief to Count Warhendorff, whose gratitude and admiration of Lord Courtland's gallantry and noble generosity were great. The Countess wept unrestrainedly as she embraced the young Princess and Julia, and kissed them repeatedly; whilst her daughter seemed to feel her separation from the two beautiful and charming girls, who had shown her so much attention and affection, most acutely. In truth, both Catherine and Julia deeply regretted their separation.

"Oh! that this odious, hateful war was over," sobbed the Countess; "that makes enemies of those who are so inclined to love and admire each other. Farewell, my lord," she added, visibly much effected: "the memory of your daring courage and noble generosity will never leave my heart as long as life lasts, and I trust in God the day may come when Englishmen and Russians will cease to destroy each other for a nation that has ever been the bitter persecuting enemy of Christianity.

Lord Courtland kissed her cheek and said—

"I hope the day may come, dear Madam; for peace is the only true blessing to civilized nations and to ail the world."

They had approached the creek in the Medora's boat, with a flag of truce flying in her stern.

The English commander had purposely)'delayed arriving at Fort Alexandrina, that the crew of the Radamez proceeding over land might get there first, feeling not at all certain that Count Zouboski would respect a flag of truce knowing it came from the Medora, and thus some injury might occur to the party in the boat before it was knownthatthe Count and Countess Warhendorffwere in it.

As the boat's keel touched the strand, those in her could perceive that the walls of the fort were crowded with armed soldiers. The party stepped from the boat out on the beach, and as they approached, our hero perceived Lieutenant Jaroski coming towards them with a strong party of soldiers fully armed.

""What can that man mean," said the Count, sternly, "surely he intends to respect a flag of truce." The men drew up within a few yards of the party, and then lieutenant Jaroski himself approached; he had a deep gash acoss his forehead, and along his cheek was a narrow plaster, which proved that the intended husband of GhIowin had not improved his beauty during the attack on the fort. Saluting the Count and Countess Warhendorff, he said with a look of savage ferocity at our hero, "I regret my Lord Count, that you should have so severely suffered from the attack of this piratical crew of Englishmen."

"Take care, lieutenant, how you allow your tongue to take such liberties with my nation and myself," observed Lord Courtland, advancing close to the Russian, bis cheek flushing with resentment.

"Cursed Englishman," returned the lieutenant, boiling with rage at his recent mishap, and the wounds he had received. Before he could finish his sentence he measured his length on the sands, receiving a blow from the clenched hand of the incensed young noble; the soldiers lowered their pieces whilst the unarmed crew in the boat leaped on shore, but the Count "Warhendorff broke from the hold of his agitated spouse and advanced close to the furious Jaroski as he rose from the ground humiliated and crest fallen, for he saw by the Count's stern features, and felt that he would not be supported by him in his rash and brutal conduct, the servility to rank in Russia being great indeed, and Jaroski was of low birth.

"Ground your arms men," exclaimed the Count fiercely, "do you dare to disgrace your Emperor in thus breaking a flag of truce. la this the way to' receive a nobleman who has acted with the greatest generosity, restoring the the Emperor's subjects to liberty when he might have retained them as prisoners. As to you, sir," turning to Jaroski, who was livid with rage, "I shall report your conduct to the Emperor you may depend." Jaroski, though trembling with rage and vexation, dared not show his passion further. After a moment of hesitation he said, humiliated and crest fallen——

"My lord, over zeal has caused me to forget myself."

"Nevertheless, sir," interrupted the Count, "the less you say the better. March your men to the fort. I can. take care of myself so far." Then turning to Lord Courtland he said, "farewell my lord, you have my heartfelt thanks for your generosity and kindness; the full and true account of this affair shall be forwarded to the Emperor, who, I am quite satisfied, vexed as he may be at the unfortunate loss of the lladamez, will fully appreciate your gallant conduct throughout the affair. We are only, thank God! political enemies; our hearts are free to love and respect those we are forced from circumstances to call foes."

"Believe me, Count," returned Lord Courtland, grasping the extended hand of the Russian with a real friendly feeling, "your feelings are those of thousands of my countrymen, who have been driven into this war without any feelings of hostility in their breasts." Pressing the Countess's hand to his lips, and receiving many kind expressions for his welfare and happiness, and her fervent hope that Catherine Warhendorff would enjoy her future existence as her amiability and beauty merited, and as she was sure she would, the Countess and her daughter bade bim farewell.

Lord Courtland then re-entered his boat and pulled off for his ship.

The boat was 'soon alongside the

Medora, and springing on board, Lord Courtland joined the princess and his sister, who had anxiously remained watching them with the glass.

"I see you have been anxious, Catherine dear," said Lord Courtland, looking into her sweet expressive features.

"I confess I have," replied Catherine, "for I dreaded that Count Zouboski; and now confess there was something unpleasant ashore, for we watched you closely, and good Mr. Bernard was quite as uneasy as we were; he did not like to let me see he was, but I saw he considered you ran some risk."

"None whatever with the Count and Countess "Warhendorff; but, I confess, without their presence, a flag of truce from the little Medora would have received small respect."

The Medora was now turned with her head for Ghelendjek, and crowding all the canvass she could carry, aa the breeze was light and favourable, she soon left Tort Alexandrina far behind her.

CHAPTER XLV.

Winteb, grim, stern, unflinching winter, with all its concomitants of frost, sleet, snow, and storm, had set in throughout all the region of the Caucasus. The entire summits of the mountains were covered with snow, the rivers were frozen, and the valleys were cheerless, and deserted by shepherd and wayfarer, for the flocks were driven into the enclosed farms, and the natives themselves kept, for the most part, in their homesteads. Notwithstanding the drawbacks of snow, frost, and their attendant hardships, a very gay and pleasant party were assembled in the strange rambling, but comfortable old fortress of Aleucho—Prince Schamyl's favourite winter retreat.

The Prince himself was, however, far away, watching the Russian forces, and advancing his own troops upon Tiflis.

The fortress of the renowned Circassian chief at this time, contained nearly all the chief dramatis persona? of our story.

Nearly a fortnight had elapsed since the events recorded in our last chapter had taken place. The Medora had reached the bay of Semes, but Ghelendjek affording the best and safest anchorage on the Circassian coast, she cast anchor there, having for a companion in its lonely and then deserted harbour, a British vessel of war.

The place and town was then in the possession of the Circassians, Turks, and Armenians.

But Lord Courtland, Edgar Erwin, with his fancharges, and Ivan Gortsare, set out immediately under the guidance of Schamyl Bey for his father's fortress of Aleucho.

Handsome mules gaily caparisoned, mantles and hoods lined with fur, and a gallant escort of Dell Khans, were all provided by the young Bey with prodigal liberality.

When they commenced their journey, the weather was bright and clear, from an exceeding hard frost; though cold, the air was bracing and exhilirating. All were in high spirits, for the Princess and Julia considered their troubles ended. Julia was with her brother, and apparently with her lover also, for the high spirited, merry hearted lieutenant was making fair progress in the affections of his mistress.

It was a remarkably pleasant journey of three days to the fortress of Aleucho, and though not a time of year for enjoying scenery to perfection, in such a country as Cireassia, yet in her wild glens and-lofty mountains, traversing her majestic forests, there was much to allure and captivate the imagination.

Added to which, the escort of Dell Khans, by the direction of Schamyl Bey, and their own secret wishes of shewing off before the two beautiful maidens they escorted, performed various feats of horsemanship and rifle practise,.in all which Lord Couutland and Edgar Erwin eagerly joined, and secured their position for daring and skill amongst the wild riders of the Caucasus.

At night care was taken that they should, reach the most influential konaz or guest-house, where they were received with a sincere welcome and unbounded hospitality.

Catherine "Warhendorff and Julia confessed they had never enjoyed a more delightful journey, for certainly with their lovers on horseback beside them, attending' to the most trifling want, and watching over their safety with most devoted attention, they thus passed without restraint or peril through a track of country the wildest and most sublime in all Asia, and at length arrived at the fortress of Prince Schamyl.

That Catherine's mother might not be surprised, and that all might be ready for their reception, Schamyl Bey sent a couple of horsemen on before.

We need not describe the meeting of the long captive Princess with her beautiful and accomplished daughter. The moment she held her in her arms repaid her for years of anxiety and apprehension, whilst Julia was embraced as a second daughter, and in truth was loved as such; and as the elder Princess gazed upon the fine features and noble form of Lord Courtland, she thanked God that had prompted her to betroth her little Catherine to her favourite, for he had never forgotten her words, and now he had rescued her beloved child from many perils and came to restore her, and to release herself from a long captivity; for though perfectly at liberty to enjoy with her attendants the beautiful scenery of the valley in summer, and every attention paid to her wishes and wauts, still it was captivity.'

Toung Schamyl Bey, after a few days rest, set out for his father's camp. His followers had fished up from 'the wreck of the Russian corvette several guns, arms, and balls, and other articles highly prized by them.

Ivan Grortsare was received by the Princess Warhendorff with distinguished favour; and shortly after his return, in the presence of Lord Courtland, Schamyl Bey, and two other Circassian chiefs, she formally renounced her rights over Ivan Gortsare as a serf. This freed Ivan from the chain that bound him, the weight of which he had never felt except in the recesses of his own heart. Lord Courtland, who felt great obligation to Ivan Grortsare, declared, if he would return to England with him, he would settle a handsome independence on him for life. To this proposition the Russian returned many grateful expressions, but stated that it was his wish to remain with the tribe of Prince Schamyl the remainder of his life.

After this, Schamyl Bey and Ivan Grortsare proceeded to the camp of Prince Schamyl, finally to arrange the terms of the ransom.

Nearly three weeks elapsed before young Schamyl Bey and Ivan Gortsare returned, the difficulty of traversing the mountainous region of the Caucasus, and the Prince having advanced towards Tiflis with his forces, retarded their journey.

The young Bey declared that his father and some of the other chiefs intended visiting the Portress of Aleucho. He was then at Dargo, and they might expect him in four or five days, as he was extremely anxious to see Lord Courtland himself.

The fifth day a long procession of mounted cavaliers was seen from the fortress, descending the steep side of the mountain—the only passage into the singular valley, in the middle of which was situated the Fortress of Aleucho.

The fortress was not, in itself, a remarkable place of strength; though, apparently, from its ditches and walls, and other defences, to a casual observer it might look capable of standing a siege from an enemy without cannon; and so it would, but being commanded from the neighbouring heights, a few pieces of artillery would crush it to pieces. But the Circassian tribes, in their own internal feuds, have no cannon to use; indeed, the bow is still in use with many of the tribes.

"It was a bright, clear day, with a hard frost, which rendered the snow—that covered every part of the valley of Aleucho with its white mantle—hard and firm to the tread. When the approach of the renowned Prince and Prophet was announced, Lord Courtland, Schamyl Bey, and Lieutenant Erwin mounted their horses, to go and meet, as courtesy required, the gallant Chief of the-Caucasus. The ladies, wrapped in their fur mantles, assembled on the long rampart wall, to behold his

entrance. The gates were thrown open, and our hero and the rest, with some twenty followers, all handsomely armed and mounted, rode forth from the fortress, descended the mount on which stood the building, surrounded by walls, ditches, and various defences.

"Positively, Harry," remarked the Lieutenant to Lord Courtland, "if it was not for our ungraceful modern costume, we might readily imagine we had gone to sleep and awoke in the middle ages, what a picturesque and warlike array these careering cavaliers present, with their chain mail, long spears, and richly caparisoned horses."

"They are certainly," returned our hero, "a noble looking race, and their costume most becoming, and no doubt adapted to their peculiar warfare. That foremost warrior on that superb black horse in the chain armour is Prince Schamyl, I am sure."

"That is my father," cried the young Bey, with natural pride in his manner, " and that black barb is the very horse he rode when he had to face a Russian square, after defeating one army under General Dolgoroucki; he threw the square into disorder, and with only a few followers, cut his way through the second army sent to oppose him; that horse has a charmed life, he has borne him through fifty hard-fought fields unscathed."

They were now close to the cavalcade of the Prince, when the young Bey said, "I pray you, Beyzade, ride forward with me till I introduce you to my father." Lord Courtland rode the famous white charger of Guz Bey, which that worthy chieftain had sent down to Ghelendjek for his use, whilst he remained in the country. Our hero had adopted part of the Circassian costume, so much better adapted to the severity of the climate than his own.

He wore the ICircassian bonnet, and tunic lined with fur, the broad belt with the lance and scimitar, a present from the young Bey, and a splendid pair of pistols and a handsome rifle slung at his back; knowing how fond and partial all the Circassian chiefs are to all kind of arms, and how much they admire a mar-

tial appearance, induced Lord Courtland to adopt their customs; his tall, powerful, and noble figure became his attire, simple as it was, and the high spirit of Guz Bey's horse showed his perfect horsemanship to great advantage. As the young Bey and our hero came up, Prince Schamyl checked his horse, looking at Lord Courtland with much surprise and evidently much pleased. On being introduced, the Prince said to our hero, speaking in the Russian language—

"You are welcome, Beyzard, to our mountain home; I am happy to meet you, for I have heard a great deal of you lately, and I assure you your name is already spoken of with profound admiration by my countrymen." He then stretched out his hand, and shook that of Lord Courtland heartily, in the European manner, while our hero replied, "I assure you Prince, I shall always remember this meeting with pride and pleasure; the name and heroic deeds of the Circassian chief, who has defied, with his gallant followers, for more than twenty years, the power and might of the Russian Autocrat, rings throughout Europe at this moment, and prayers for hie success and the cause of freedom are in every man's mouth."

"Bishmilla, God is great." We may now hope for victory over the Russian bear," said the prince, requesting Lord Courtland to ride by his side. They kept conversing earnestly upon some recent news the prince had heard from Sebastopol.

The procession entered through the gates of the fortress, and then the Prince and his followers alighted, and, for a time retired, to the different chambers of the fortress, preparatory to seeing and conducting the Princess and our hero to the repast prepared for them.

Our limits will not permit us to dwell upon minute details. The first two days passed without any referenceto business; the third, a meeting of the Chiefs took place, Lord Courtland, Lieutenant Erwin, and Ivan Grortsare being present.

We will not detain our readers with a full account of what passed at the meeting, nor give the entire speech of Schamyl Bey the elder. Suffice it to say, he declined all ransom for the Princess Warhendorff and her daughter. It was the unanimous decree of himself and the other Circassian Chiefs. He considered himself absolved from his vow by the circumstances of the case. The Princess had been deprived of her estates by the Czar, therefore shepossessed no property.

The noble conduct of Lord Courtland in conducting back the young Princesss and his own sister as captives till ransomed, had created great admiration in the minds of all the Circassian chiefs, who were now unanimous in restoring them all to liberty.

Lord Courtland was considerably moved by the generous expressions and intentions of the Prince and the assembled chiefs. His manner and expressions, and his great desire to see prosperity attend their cause, pleased the chiefs greatly; to which his noble figure and the feats he bad performed—in taking the corvette, saving young Schamyl's life, and attacking the fort and releasing the maidens—greatly contributed. A feast followed the meeting, and two days afterwards Prince Scbamyl took a most friendly and even affectionate leave of the Princess Warhendorff, her daughter, Julia, and Lord Courtland, but leaving his son and fifty followers to conduct them in safety to Ghelendjek.

At length a day was pronounced favourable for departure. The females, well protected in their fur mantles and hoods, and mounted on careful mules, left the Fortress of Aleucho, to proceed to Ghelendjek.

This difficult journey was performed without much fatigue even by the females. Suitable guest-houses had been selected, and the travellers everywhere were received with a grace and kindness of manner and attention highly gratifying.

In summer time the journey would, the Princess "Warhendorff informed Lord Courtland, be one of extreme enjoyment, the woods being full of aromatic plants, and swarming with nightingales.

The last night of their journey they reposed in the habitation of a very renowned chieftain, Slited Mehemet Indor Oglu.

At length they beheld the bay and harbour of Ghelendjek, and, riding at her anchors, the Medora, and a screw corvette, with the British ensign and pennant floating in the breeze.

No sooner was the party descried by those on the deck of the Medora than, like magic, her masts were covered with gay flags, and a salute from her guns announced the pleasure "their safe arrival caused.

The boats were soon on the beach ready to receive them. The chiefs of the Circassians accompanied them onboard, and the rest of the day was passed in mutual and friendly intercourse, and they sat down in the Medora's handsome saloon to partake of the last meal they were ever to enjoy'together, towards the close of which a degree of sadness came over all. At last young Scbamyl Bey, Ivan Gortsare, and the young chief they had met on their way, rose to take their leave.

Scbamyl Bey was not parted from without deep regret by Lord Courtland. They had gone through scenes of peril together; each had rendered the other important services, and they separated with all the regret brothers could experience.

The Medora lay that night at anchor in the bay, and the next morning, with a favourable breeze and a bright sky, her disasters repaired, and her spars replaced, under a cloud of canvass, she glided out from the harbour of Ghelendjek.

CHAPTER XLVI.

Eobttjnately, though the winter had fully set in, and the waters of the Euxine were at times lashed into foam, the Medora safely held on her course, through storm and sunshine, over that boisterous sea, till at length, after a moderately quick passage, she came in sight of Sebastopol, upon a bright, clear, but intensely cold day. Wishing to put his friend, Erwin, on board his ship, which he knew was with the fleet from the commander of the screw ship he had left in Ghelendjek, induced our hero to pursue his course towards Sebastopol. Even his fair guests wished to have a view of this renowned fortress. There was a fresh but not a powerful breeze blowing, as the Medora, under her topsails only, stood in for the allied fleet.

Many a hearty cheer was permitted to the crews of those ships to whom Lord Courtland was known, as his yacht glided gracefully by, and came to an anchor near the frigate of his old friend, Captain P—, who manned his yards, and gave our hero one true British cheer, which was returned by the surprised Medora's crew.

Edgar Erwin's first duty was to proceed to his own ship. The Medora was to sail the following morning, as Lord Courtland well knew it was no time of the year to be loitering on the waters of the Black Sea.

Our hero accompanied his friend on board the frigate, where he was most warmly greeted by her commander and his officers.

"By jove! my Lord," said Captain P, " you put us in the back ground, with this redoubtable yacht of yours, there is scarcely anything else talked of at our tables but the exploits of the Medora; whilst here we are, loosing topsails and furling them, only I am sorry to say today—"

"All things will change in the spring," said Lord Courtland, "we have had a long peace, old England will prove her right, and maintain her glory yet."

Lieutenant Erwin at this moment joined them, and Lord Courtland knew he had received important intelligence by his countenance, which was flushed and his manner excited.

Begging Captain P 's pardon for intruding on them,

Lieutenant Edgar said, addressing his friend, " My dear Henry, I have just received a long, long letter from my mother; thank God I have found a relative, and a dear one at last.!"

"Mother!" repeated Lord Courtland, surprised, "I rejoice with you, Edgar; that is a dear tie to discover."

"Yes," returned Edgar, with a delightful smile, "and that mother is your aunt, Julia Fitzharding that was, now Mrs. Steadman Shaw."

"Well, in truth, Edgar, you bewilder me," observed Lord Courtland, after a moment's silence. "However, I always imagined there was some strong sympathy attracted us to each other from the very first hour of our acquaintance, and now I find we are cousins."

As it was just then impossible to acquaint Captain

P with family matters, the two friends took their leave to return to the Medora, Lord Courtland having received his packet of letters, which had come out from England in the government steamer.

It will be unnecessary for us to explain to our readers the contents of the letters received, as the events they recorded are well known to them; sufficient to say that Lord Courtland and Julia were rejoiced to find in Edgar Erwin, not only a lover and a friend, but a near relation.

It was impossible to leave the fleet, without accepting a farewell dinner on board the frigate. At the hospitable table of Captain P were assembled several of the principal commanders of the ships then at anchor before Sebastopol. But the following morning the Medora was again under weigh.

After a very rapid and pleasing voyage, they reached Naples where they resolved to pass the winter, Lord Courtland having a handsome villa on the shores of its magnificent bay, and there his lordship, in the presence of the British ambassador and many distinguished English residents, received the hand of the beautiful Catherine Warhendorif, whose exquisite grace and loveliness elicited universal admiration.

In the month of March the Medora once more spread her canvass to the breeze, and leaving the beautiful shores of Naples, bore away for Gibraltar. After a stay of a few days for repose, the broad Atlantic was crossed, and without any mishap or much delay from adverse weather, the noble little yacht swung to her anchors in the waters of Torbay, the whole party landing at Torquay, to the

infinite delight of Commodore Manners, and the bewildered joy of Tom Delany.

Wild Drake Lodge, where the whole party took up their abode, became the scene of most uncommon rejoicing. Tom and the Commodore were in their glory; such an incessant firing of cannon, letting off rockets, hogsheads of ale tapped, and tents erected for the tenants to enjoy the scene, that the people in the interior began to fancy that the Russians had effected a landing.

Lord Courtland embraced his aunt and charming cousin with sincere affection and pleasure. The former perused the long letters' written by herston, and brought by our hero, with tears of grateful affection, returning earnest and heartfelt thanks to Providence for restoring to her such a son.

-After a residence of a fortnight with the kind and jovial old Commodore, who seemed since the return of his nephew to have taken out a' new lease of life, so youthful and active did he become, that Tom began to fancy he would make a start for Sebastopol in order to lend a hand in the downfall. Lord Courtland and his bride and the Princess, set out for Courtland Tower, which place had undergone by his lordship's directions, considerable repair and alterations, and might then be looked upon as one of the handsomest residences in England.

Before soliciting employment from the government, Lord Courtland exerted his interest in procuring a commission for George Shaw, who without knowing through whose interest it was obtained, was promoted to an ensigncy. Lord Courtland solicited and immediately was appointed to the command of one of the finest screw frigates in the service. The Medora, accompanied him with the same crew and commander as a tender, for though little glory was to be won by the flag of old England, in the late strange and mysterious war, yet his lordship had his share of such glory aa was to be won. Lieutenant Erwin shortly after his cousin's arrival in the Black Sea, was appointed his first lieutenant, and through his lordship's interest he obtained the command of one of the fast

gun boats destined for the Sea of Azoff, in order to have a share in the bloodless victories our gallant little crafts obtained in those seas. Just before the fall of Sebastopol, for a very brilliant exploit, he was made a commander.

In the meantime G-eorge Shaw, resolving to redeem the past, by future good conduct, and having his heart and mind fully occupied with the image of his fair cousin, Nelly, and ardently desiring to distinguish himself, took, every opportunity to do so, with the rest of the officers of our brave army, who had abundant opportunities of showing their moral as well as their personal courage, in which George Shaw was second to none.

Several gallant acts obtained him his lieutenancy, and the attack upon the Redan, where he most conspicuously distinguished himself, procured him a captain's commission.

At last Sabastopol, the mighty, almost invincible, fell before the glorious efforts of the allies.

Courtland Tower and Wild Drake Lodge again became the scene of rejoicings and heart-felt joy. Lady Courtland had become the mother of a noble boy; and fondly and ardently the beautiful Catherine looked forward to the return of the husband she so truly and fondly loved.

Julia Fitzbarding had heard of her lovers's exploits in the Sea of Azoff, and his promotion to a commandership —with an agreeable palpitation of the heart; and gentle Nelly, the adopted daughter of the old Commodore, listened with pride and a joy in her innocent and affectionate heart to a recital of George Shaw's gallant conduct.

Peace, so ardently wished for, by all who felt no glory was to be won or false renown gained by the wholesale slaughter of the human race, was proclaimed, but before it was fully ratified, by the contracting parties, Lord Courtland had returned to England in the Medora.

The rapture of Lady Courtland when she placed her boy, the future heir of a noble race in his arms, repaid her for all the sufferings she had endured during his absence.

The Medora, by the author of 'The two midshipmen'. by capt. Armstrong • F Claudius Armstrong • 125

Commander Shaw, as we may now style Edgar Erwin, for on his return with Lord Courtland, he had fully proved his right to the name and estates of the Sbaws, of Killgerran, received the hand of his beautiful and amiable Julia.

Captain Shaw had not then returned but was expected, and there was every reason to suppose that Nelly, though she retained her maiden name, would change her single state for happy wedded life.

CPSIA information can be obtained at www.ICGtesting.com
Printed in the USA
BVOW08s2023011214

377429BV00015B/296/P